STO

# Memorandum for the President

Can any President now effectively govern and manage the domestic side of the federal government? This subtle and comprehensive book tries to answer that question for one person, the President himself.

Written by two Carter administration assistant secretaries with responsibility for social policy in HEW, Ben W. Heineman, Jr., and economic policy in Treasury, Curtis A. Hessler, *Memorandum for the President* takes a hard-eyed insiders' approach to problems of governing in the 1980s. Unlike others who write about the presidency, the two men do not dwell on the constraints limiting White House action, but present an extended brief specifying how to run domestic affairs at a time when the nation's politics are fragmented and choices in economic and social policy uncertain.

Heineman and Hessler assert that any chief executive must conduct a strategic presidency on the domestic side. He must, that is, forge an explicit four-year plan of battle that encompasses the competing and often contradictory claims that arise from the four dimensions of executive government: substantive policy and practical politics, the structure of the executive branch and the processes of decision and implementation that drive events and get things done.

Comprehending the four pieces of the strategic puzzle, and their relationship to one another, can create coherence for the President and his administration. Such coherence is essential if the President is not to be overwhelmed by the incessant pressure to make decisions of all shapes and sizes and if he is to work with, or best, the competing forces in and out of the political system. The strategic approach is, in short, the best available method for combating presidential weakness and reviving presidential power.

A set of interrelated questions must be answered in a strategic context. Among them: How many important initiatives can an administration advance during a single term? How does setting economic policy limit other objectives on the domestic agenda? How can the intricate interest group and subcommittee-specific politics of governing be meshed with the often contradictory and ever-present politics of renomination and reelection? What is the proper way to use Cabinet officers? Should the President appoint a Deputy President for Domestic Affairs? Can the war between the White House staff and the departments be stopped?

Heineman and Hessler call the strategic presidency a "practical ideal, neither liberal nor conservative, neither optimistic nor pessimistic, neither active or passive. A strategic approach is simply necessary. It does not guarantee success, but without a strategic approach, presidential failure is virtually certain."

The memorandum addresses "you," the President, in the second person, which helps draw the reader into the world of domestic affairs as the President would see it. The book will become indispensable for those who want to make intelligent judgments about presidential performance and similarly invaluable for those at the center of executive government who must plan and manage the presidency itself. Possessing a fundamental urgency, *Memorandum for the President* presents a vivid and sustained analysis of the contemporary presidency that must be understood. The book will both define the terms of the public debate about a troubled institution and improve the quality and sophistication of that debate.

# MEMORANDUM FOR THE PRESIDENT:

## A Strategic Approach to Domestic Affairs in the 1980s

# Ben W. Heineman, Jr., and

# Curtis A. Hessler

Random House · New York

Copyright © 1980 by Ben W. Heineman, Jr., and Curtis A. Hessler

All rights reserved under International and Pan-American Copyright Conventions. Published in the United States by Random House, Inc., New York, and simultaneously in Canada by Random House of Canada Limited, Toronto.

*Grateful acknowledgment is made to the following for permission to reprint previously published material:*

Harcourt Brace Jovanovich: Excerpt from *Roosevelt: The Lion and the Fox* by James M. Burns. Reprinted by permission of the publisher, Harcourt Brace Jovanovich.

Library of Congress Cataloging in Publication Data
Heineman, Benjamin W., Jr.
Memorandum for the President.
1. Presidents—United States. 2. Executive power—
United States. 3. United States—Politics and
government—1945–     I. Hessler, Curtis A.,
joint author.     II. Title.
JK516.H366     353.03′2     80-5308
ISBN 0-394-51365-7

Manufactured in the United States of America
9  8  7  6  5  4  3  2
First Edition

*For our parents—and for Cris and Chris*

# CONTENTS

# ACKNOWLEDGMENTS

We are deeply grateful to those who have read and criticized all or parts of the various drafts: Bob Barnett, Mike Barone, Mike Barth, Dick Beattie, Fred Bohen, Rick Cotton, Karen Davis, Paul Gewirtz, Joel Havemann, Jim Mongan, Joe Onek and Stan Ross. Many helpful insights were provided in conversations with Sam Hughes, Stephen Hess, Arnie Packer, John Palmer, Donna Shalala, Bo Cutter, Bert Carp and Bob Zoellick. Ben Heineman, Sr., has thought deeply about and discussed incisively with us many of the concepts included here, especially the differences between political and corporate executives.

Senior Faculty at Harvard's Kennedy School of Government, including Graham Allison, Mark Moore and Don Price, were kind enough to host a seminar that tested many of the book's ideas. We are especially indebted to three men at the school: Dick Darman, who unselfishly spent substantial time providing perspective from the Nixon-Ford years; Dick Neustadt, whose pioneering work is as fresh today as it was twenty years ago and whose comments were penetrating; and Hale Champion, whose intelligence, humor and common sense are models for government work.

John Todd and Dick Michel represent the best of the civil service tradition and brought high technical skills to the task of developing many of the numbers and checking most of the facts in the book. Dick Warden's professionalism, knowledge and guidance are reflected in those sections of the book relating to the Congress. Dick was especially generous with his time and challenging with his comments.

Joe Califano has spent more than half of the last two decades in government service. By his experience, his example and his continual preoccupation with things governmental, he has provided counsel, insight and vision beyond measure.

Grant Ujifusa could not have been a better editor. He has been thoughtful and supportive, always trying to pull the best out of the material and ever willing to take risks with a somewhat unusual book. We would like to thank Nancy Inglis for her patience and skill in copy-editing the manuscript and Arlene Modica for her fine work in presenting the book to the public. Lois Dulin, with help from Joyce Bentley and Anne Spinks, was swift and sure in typing, and retyping, the manuscript.

Cris Russell Heineman and Chris Hessler have been nothing short of marvelous; while meeting the demands of their own professional lives they have tolerated our intolerable jobs, discussions about government without end—and now this.

# PREFACE

$\mathbf{F}$OR most Americans, the presidency today is symbolized by the North Portico of the White House. That historic facade serves as the backdrop for the network newscasters and their daily reports on the doings and undoings of the powerful. Whether framed by the manicured greenery of its grounds or set in flood-lit brilliance against an evening sky, the old building conveys a reassuring sense of order—of tradition, stateliness and serenity.

But the symbol is misleading. The modern presidency is an institution in trouble.

The man who lives and works in the White House after his inauguration on January 20, 1981, will look out on a society suffering from an unaccustomed disorder in its economy and an unsettling distemper in its political system. Yet his ability to impart order to the troubled world of domestic affairs is far more limited than he thought before taking office.

The President and his top personal staff are presumed to direct the operations of the executive branch from the White House's West Wing offices. But, with nearly three million civilian employees and $600 billion plus in annual expenditures, executive government and its thirteen departments sprawl across the city of Washington, send their dollars and their dictates to every corner of the nation, and, in significant ways, touch the life of every American—often without the President's direction, or even his knowledge.

The President will try to lead a cohesive team of top executive appointees. Yet he can draw on very few enduring traditions to order his administration's internal power relationships. And, if not properly structured by him, those relationships will constantly threaten to tear the administration apart.

The President will initially imagine that four years is a long time, but in fact his moment in history will be very brief. Because national policies and institutions, let alone underlying economic and social conditions, change only slowly and with the assist of herculean efforts, he can press for but a handful of major initiatives in the time that is his.

And, though the President sits at the apex of national government, his lines to the other forces in society—his own departments and agencies, the Congress, state and local governments, the interest groups, the media and the public at large—are less reins of command and more a skein of tangled threads that he must somehow weave into a coherent pattern which gives political definition to his substantive ideals.

Indeed, although the institutional facade of the presidency gives him a measure of support (the cracks and fissures of the past fifteen years notwithstanding), the man who resides behind the North Portico may find his weakness, and his branch's troubles, to be a rude surprise. We expect the President to govern the nation. In fact, he must struggle mightily even to influence the course of events within his administration. And for all his moments there, he will be preoccupied with one human and pressing fact of life at the top: the inevitability of making decisions, often among difficult, technical, unpleasant and uncertain alternatives. If to campaign is to make vague promises and blur issues in order to broaden appeal, then to govern, once the electoral prize is won, is to make precise, detailed choices in order to get things done.

- He must choose from among the vast range of national problems and issues—inflation, energy, productivity, unemployment, education, transportation, state and municipal finance, health care, racial discrimination, or income security —those few matters, all deemed crises in our hyperbolic era, which he will make the themes, and thus the test, of his presidency. He must then develop hard-edged positions on those transcendent issues. But he must understand how these decisions then inevitably limit his freedom to act on other pressing problems. If he chooses to balance the budget, he cannot at the same time have immediate implementation of a national health insurance plan. If he chooses big tax cuts for business to spur productivity, he cannot then reduce the rising tax burden for the average American. He cannot, in short, do all that he might wish—a very discomfiting realization for someone who will be president but once.*

• He must choose political coalitions that will provide unwavering support on the key issues. But in selecting political friends to help him govern—to influence the Congress, goad the bureaucracy or neutralize rival interest groups—he may anger, alienate or irrevocably estrange those who helped him win nomination or election, and who might do the same again, either for him or for his chosen successor. The elderly, to take one example, may have voted for him in record numbers, but can he gain a measure of control over federal spending in the coming decade without incurring their active opposition? With organized groups and interests vying avidly for an increasingly restricted share of uncommitted federal dollars, he cannot please everyone. As he makes choices that have real bite, he is likely to find his adversaries growing in number. And he will discover that there are few cross-issue coalitions remaining in American politics—no fixed constellation of interest groups that will vote with him on a wide range of important issues. Patching together different coalitions for each major issue is hazardous duty when his allies on some key matters become his adversaries on others.

• He must choose how to structure executive government so that it handles with a maximum of competence and a minimum of infighting not only the preeminent issues but also the hundreds of other major questions the administration must address. He must, that is, impose a system of delegated authority and orderly decision-making on the most complicated in-

---

*Said Franklin Roosevelt, in an oft-quoted bit of presidential lore: Lincoln "was a sad man because he couldn't get it all at once. And nobody can."

stitution in the United States and perhaps in the world—an institution that has no firmly established rules or accepted procedures for resolving its most important internal questions. The rules of the game that he ordains for the administration's structure and for its basic process—among them, policy development, budget-making, congressional relations —must domesticate the inevitable conflict within his own personal staff and between that staff and his top appointees in the departments and agencies, conflict that is often debilitating and occasionally destructive. To ignore or to fumble the elementary questions about how his own appointees share power and conduct his and their own business is to risk defeat before he begins to joust in the larger, harder contests with the other forces in the political system.

• He must choose quickly and make few mistakes because time has him in a vise. He is caught between the limits on his own time and the contradictory and often confounding pressures of historical time. He is unable to apprehend in depth and to deal personally with more than a few major matters in domestic affairs because there are simply not enough hours in the days and months ahead. And as he takes the oath of office, historical trends present him with deeply flowing economic and social processes that are inordinately complex and extraordinarily hard to change. He can, for example, seek dramatic redemption in our nation's energy policy, striding back and forth in the bully pulpit hoping to convince contentious forces in Congress, the press, the interest groups and the public to put aside their differences, however deeply felt, and to join with him in that national endeavor. But he cannot replicate that kind of heightened effort very many times during a single term. He lacks the political resources, and his parishioners lack the attention span. His place in history, and his success as president, will depend critically on how he links his personal schedule, concentration and efforts to the deeper forces operating on the country's domestic destiny.

The essay that follows deals with these and other basic choices in domestic affairs confronting the President who will serve the

first full term of the 1980s. As he turns away from the frenzy of
running to the trials of governing, he must, by his decisions, set
the direction of executive government for the next four years.
Although he can change that direction in midcourse, the basic,
initial decisions on the conduct of his presidency will have
unquestioned importance: for him, for his administration, and
for the nation. It would have been helpful, both to the citizenry
and to the President, if these basic choices had been hotly
debated in the election campaign. But they were not. In our
time, electoral politics and national governance rarely converge,
and then, it seems, only by coincidence.

The essay is styled as a "Memorandum for the President" and
is written *as if* it would serve as a central background or organizing paper on domestic affairs for the man who will be sworn in
on January 20, 1981. We have adopted this quintessential governmental form—and its Morse code oddities, an abundance of
dots and dashes—to help give the reader a chief executive's view
of the domestic presidency.* By domestic presidency, we mean
those aspects of executive government that directly shape domestic programs and economic policy.

The book has two broad goals.

*First,* the "memorandum" seeks to provide an overview of the
domestic-affairs world that the newly inaugurated President
will see from the Oval Office. The terrain of domestic affairs
must be mapped in broad outline before the chief executive can
know where in particular he wants to go—and how to avoid the
fens and bogs, the wild boars, stubborn donkeys and rogue
elephants that may block his path.

*Second,* the book is prescriptive as well as descriptive, outlining an approach to the domestic presidency and offering concrete recommendations wherever possible. It seeks to present
basic issues that the President will face in domestic affairs; to
suggest ways to think about those issues; and in places to argue
for a detailed course of action that any president should follow.
This essay attempts to set forth a related set of ideas on important aspects of how to be president in domestic affairs. But this

---

*The "memorandum" itself is also styled as coming from several authors since such a
document is likely to be written by a small group of advisors. Also: the pronoun "he"
is intended to refer to persons of either sex.

forbidding task is undertaken with only a modest hope: that the essay be useful.


As will be developed in more detail below, the basic argument is the need to manage a *strategic presidency*. The ability to act strategically proceeds from a president's "personal influence on governmental action."* But it recognizes that the President's continual efforts must be substantive, political *and* organizational; that he must not just exercise but *share* influence and responsibility with other key actors in his administration, especially in the executive departments; that he must thus depersonalize his office and ensure that all important decisions do not flow directly to him; and that he must pursue his highest priorities as part of a battle plan that relates these and other major issues in clear chronological sequence over the whole term. The strategic approach is the essence of advancing presidential power today, or the essence of combating presidential weakness —and it is possible only within a web of delegation and priority-setting that the seminal concept of presidential "personal influence" alone may not illuminate.

Most succinctly stated: *to be strategic a president must see clearly the basic dimensions of executive government—substantive policy and practical politics, administrative structures and action-forcing processes —and then relate each to the other in a four-year time frame.* The President cannot simply decide what is the best policy for a particular problem without determining whether that policy can survive in a highly political world. To be "right," but impotent, is not a prescription for success in office. Nor can the President simply let political forces outside his administration dictate the course he should follow. He cannot, that is, maneuver without that clear purpose which is the wellspring of effective and significant political action. Nor can he be successful in either policy or politics without executive decision-making structures and processes that leverage his limited time and influence into an effective governing administration. In fact, the nuts-and-bolts concerns about sound structures and sensible

*Richard E. Neustadt, *Presidential Power: The Politics of Leadership from FDR to Carter*, xi (1980).

processes are crucial in presenting decisions to him clearly and concisely and in maximizing his administration's effectiveness through a workable system of delegation.

Indeed, if the President is to shape and not just rail against or ride with events in the 1980s, he must be strategic, molding the four fundamental dimensions of his domestic presidency into a subtle and sophisticated plan of battle for the next four years. There is no other way. *His must be the central organizing intelligence of his administration:* and that requires a vision, a mental strength and a procedural discipline—a political, substantive and managerial sense—that has been all too rare in our chief executives.

A president's perspective must, to the greatest extent possible, approximate the reality of the world in which he operates. The distinguishing features of that world are complexity and breadth. The degree to which he is able to integrate the decisions, issues, trends, pressures, problems and crises that bear down upon him will determine his success on each individual issue, especially those core matters that will define his domestic presidency. The President's great opportunity—and his great difficulty—is that his vision and his responsibilities are so broad. He can be overwhelmed, stumbling from incident to incident. But by the same token, only he can masterfully relate seemingly disparate events and policies and structures to help work his will.

We do not underestimate the surpassing difficulty of this task —of seeing domestic affairs whole and forging a four-year battle plan that has subtlety and strength. The strategic presidency is an ideal—but a practical ideal. Crises, mistakes, personality problems (either with the President or key actors), the inherent contradictions of economic and social policy in a time of constrained resources or the sheer orneriness of today's politics—these are just some of the forces that can derail or defeat it. But a strategic approach has to be tried, even if it is only to be partially successful—even if it only takes the President 50 (or 20) percent of the way to his goals. *The strategic presidency does not guarantee success, but absent sheer dumb luck, failure is assured without it.*

A disciplined, coherent and incisive strategy that failed was not, however, the story of the Carter administration in domestic affairs. For example:

- The President sent a flotilla of major proposals to the Congress in the first eighteen months of his administration—cuts in water projects, social security finance, a comprehensive energy program, a tax rebate scheme, hospital cost containment legislation, comprehensive tax reform, welfare reform. Many of these proposals went to the tax-writing committees of the Congress: Senate Finance and House Ways and Means. And because the President had overloaded the Congress and those committees with reforms that would not command ready assent, because he was not able to marshal the administration's resources and develop political support for all the major battles that were required, and because many of his top political lieutenants were untutored in the ways of the Congress (and at the outset didn't seem to care), most of these proposals were either sunk or badly damaged. President Carter's reputation as less than skillful in domestic affairs and with the Congress was thus firmly established.

- This fundamental mistake—which President Carter himself ultimately recognized as a major error*—resulted not only from his own misjudgment of the Congress but also from another fundamental error of strategy that bedeviled the administration throughout the first term: an inability to join policy and politics systematically in a realistic time frame. The political and the policy advisors talked to the President, but they all too rarely talked to each other. Moreover, many of his top political advisors had little understanding of the detailed interest-group-and-subcommittee-specific politics of governing, as opposed to the broadly thematic media and party politics of the nomination and general election. And this meant that there could be no overall strategy for the four years that would have guided the resolution of controversial

*The following is from a transcript of a question-and-answer session on May 13, 1980, between the President and editors and broadcasters:

Q: Mr. President, what are two or three of the most serious errors you've made since you've been in the White House? . . .

The President: . . . I think the lack of close coordination with the Congress at the beginning to lay down a clear agenda and my over-optimism about the speed with which Congress could act on controversial matters was the biggest misjudgment I made.

policy choices (what *kind* of energy program, tax reform package or national health plan?) and tried to energize the coalitions and alliances necessary to give those choices political life. Indeed, the split between the policy and the political advisors—their ability to talk separately to the President, moving him back and forth to their positions, and their inability to talk systematically to each other—was a major source of the wobbles and inconstancy on many major issues.

To be sure, some of President Carter's difficulties were beyond his control. During his term, major problems that had been building for a decade or more broke down with great force on the presidency: energy limitations, increasing international economic dependence, lagging productivity at home, a Congress simultaneously more independent and more fragmented than at other times in the recent past, and general skepticism about the ability of government to perform basic functions—to name but a few. Added to these problems was the extremely ticklish task for a Democratic president of bringing the Democratic Party into a new era of economic constraints when many of its most active members were initially hoping for a return to something approaching the expansionist glory days of the mid-sixties in domestic affairs. And President Carter did make a number of difficult, if ultimately ineffective, decisions. As Joseph Pechman, an acute observer sympathetic with the administration's broad thrusts, wrote in 1978:

> President Carter has proposed significant changes in a wide variety of federal programs: energy, social security, food stamps and welfare, employment and training, education, hospital cost control, urban policy, defense and taxation. Judged solely on the basis of whether the administration has identified major issues and made difficult choices, its performance must be regarded as courageous. But . . . the performance is disappointing.*

Indeed, on his way to a disappointing domestic performance, far too many of President Carter's wounds were self-inflicted. In an age when the powers of the presidency are sharply cur-

*Setting National Priorities: The 1979 Budget (Joseph A. Pechman, ed., 1978), p. 19.

tailed, much more sharply constrained, for example, than during the flood tide of the domestic presidency under Lyndon Johnson, it is all the more important that the President operate with skill, wit, shrewdness and, most important, *a strategy of governing*. The President's margin of error today is unfortunately small. Far too often, the administration seemed to lack the will, the skill and, ultimately, the decisiveness to give the domestic presidency strategic coherence—to identify what was essential, stick with it, develop political muscle, drive to get it done and delegate other important matters. This central failing continually undermined sound decisions in discrete areas of concern.

In the end, many who served during the Carter term felt a sense of sadness that a striking opportunity—and an enormous amount of effort—was somehow being wasted by the administration, despite the President's unquestioned personal strengths, especially his intelligence and his integrity. The last years of the seventies and the opening years of the eighties are likely to be viewed as a watershed in domestic affairs: the economy is beset by many problems and uncertainties which, in turn, impose sharp limits on social policy. During his term, Jimmy Carter could have begun to take the nation sensibly across that watershed, giving domestic affairs direction for the next decade and defining clearly the issues that should be the focus of national debate and decision. Instead, the domestic legacy of his term was confusion—and a general perception of inconsistency and ineffectiveness.

This sense of the Carter administration's lack of strategic direction and inability to get things done was not just confined to the Washington press corps and to other knowledgeable observers. It was a constant subject of conversation within the administration itself—and at the highest levels of the White House among those most devoted to the President. While serving in positions of responsibility in the federal government,* we

---

*Heineman served as executive assistant (1977–78) to HEW Secretary Joseph A. Califano, Jr., and then as HEW assistant secretary for planning and evaluation (1978–79). Hessler served as executive assistant to Treasury Secretary W. Michael Blumenthal (1977–1979); associate director for natural resources, energy and science, Office of Management and Budget (1979–80); and Treasury assistant secretary for economic policy (1980).

As personal staff to Cabinet secretaries and then as sub-Cabinet officials, we incurred

were consistently struck, as were many of our colleagues, by the extraordinary—and disheartening—difficulties the Carter administration and, more important, the executive had in being effective.

This essay is an attempt to reflect systematically on that experience. In simplest terms, we have tried to answer the question that so preoccupied those inside the administration: how could the presidency and executive government be handled better? It is based on insights gained by observing—and to an extent participating in—domestic-affairs decision-making, and domestic-affairs mistakes, in the upper reaches of the Carter administration. And it is especially informed by our experience in two of the major departments of executive government.

The essay is not a memoir, much less a history, of the Carter administration's first term, however. Nor is it intended to render a judgment on the Carter administration, a task for the pundits and the historians. We must draw from our own experience, but in so doing, we wish only to suggest how any President might better do his job in the early 1980s and not to dwell on the past performance of a particular president in the late 1970s. The Carter administration had its own peculiar failings and virtues, but the structural problems of domestic government and the domestic presidency are more enduring than the experience of a single administration, and their solutions will require more than avoiding the particular errors of the past four years.

In addition to the problems of writing about the future while drawing upon an experience immediately past, two other difficulties became apparent as we drafted:

- Could the book inform the general reader not intimately familiar with the strange mores and folkways of the capital city, but also speak to government professionals, those who report on government and students of government? For some

obligations of confidentiality and trust. As to confidentiality, we do not reveal details of off-the-record, high-level meetings we attended, nor do we quote from internal documents to which we had access. As to trust, we believe it is appropriate to publish these reflections after the 1980 election. If the administration is defeated, the "memorandum" will have had no effect. If the administration is victorious, we would hope that the "memorandum" would be a part, however great or small, of the inevitable reassessment of what went wrong during the first term and how to do better during the second.

readers, there may be too much descriptive material, for others not enough. Certainly the "memorandum" is longer and
more discursive than any actual memo a president, or a president-elect, would receive—or read.

• Could the book be useful to either a Republican or Democratic administration—could it offer generally relevant obser-
vations about the presidency and executive government? The
solution was to be most prescriptive on matters of structure
and process, and general approach to the office. Appropriate
arrangements of executive government—and some general
ideas about its conduct—should not turn entirely on presidential personality, partisan preference or the painfully learned
experience of a first term's mistakes. These prescriptions and
ideas are applicable, in our judgment, whether an incumbent
wishes to be active or restrained in the conduct of the presidency.

As to questions of policy, the book seeks to describe major
issues, explore their connections and highlight the implications of making particular decisions. The basic policy problem facing the President in the next four years will be choice
among conflicting goals, especially with a reduced rate of
growth in national wealth. And it is important to understand
the increasing tightness of the economic and budgetary box
in which any president will find himself and to appreciate
what he will give up by choosing among alternatives. Moreover, many of the policy problems facing the chief executive
after November 4, 1980, whatever the policy preferences of
his campaign, are likely to be perceived as much from an
institutional as from a partisan perspective: what can an executive government really do?

As to precise questions about how to build particular political coalitions for particular issues, these will turn upon the
man and his party, and so, while underscoring their importance, the book seeks to indicate the kinds of political considerations that ought to be taken into account without attempting much detail.

What is prescribed can be at the service of a president's
purpose. But there should be no mistake: it cannot substitute
for that purpose. The "memo"—which was written before the

1980 election—is meant to be helpful to any president. But a president cannot succeed, and no memo can help him much, unless he has convictions about where the nation and the government should be headed and fairly sophisticated notions about how the nation and the government work. We presume, in short, that the reader has, or will soon develop, an almost visceral sense of what he wants to do with the presidency. Purpose provides coherence, countering an unfortunate trend of the times: citizens and presidents are told more but may know less because there is not an adequate framework for understanding the significance, or insignificance, of the endless stream of facts and information about the national government that flows past us daily.

One last preliminary comment. This essay was of course framed at a particular point in history. The presidency is an evolving entity that seeks to confront the problems of the future but is a product of the past. Yet political rhetoric in this nation tends to be ahistorical. Politicians are always promising simple and sharp discontinuities with the past to meet the exigencies of the present. But the reality of governing is that the continuities are usually dominant (unless there is a great historic shift like the Depression of the thirties or the civil rights movement of the sixties), and the technical complexities of policy are so pervasive that politicians, the press and the public cannot follow them with care. The nation may be traversing a watershed, but the journey is more likely to be tortuous and slow than straight and swift. The same is true for the institution of the presidency. We have sought to be systematic but practical, and do not recommend that the President spend much time pursuing dramatic reforms (like revitalizing the party system or restructuring the federal government through constitutional amendment to make it more parliamentary) that might help him do his job better but don't appear likely (to say the least), however great his effort.

If the "memorandum" succeeds in providing government professionals, concerned citizens and the working press with a view of the domestic presidency, from the inside, as the President himself might see it, then there may be a more complicated set of standards for playing the national game: how well is the

President doing? This view may also provide a broader context for making sense of the daily press accounts that provide us all with most of our information about public affairs. It might even help in developing a more life-sized view of what the President can and cannot do, since the President is often viewed in extreme terms—as a "magnificent lion who can roam widely"* or, more recently, as a trussed-up Gulliver. The truth, obviously, lies somewhere in between.

The media, especially, mirror the rhetoric of the politician, even as they seek to get behind that rhetoric. Professional proclivities mean that the media emphasize the discontinuous (read "conflict") and the simplified (primarily because there are severe limits on what can be written, and read, in 18 column inches or 36 or even 136, and even sharper limits imposed by 90 seconds of broadcast time). The media are often concerned with the drama of politics and not with the details of governing—partly because that may be what their readers, viewers or listeners want. Yet just as one of the most difficult tasks for a president is to make the transition from running to governing, so one of the most difficult tasks for the media is not to treat the sitting president as an eternal campaigner (is he winning or losing?) and to recognize that the policies, politics, structures and processes of governing must be seen together in terms of what can realistically be accomplished in the four years of the coming term.

Washington, D.C.
November 1980†

*Clinton Rossiter, *The American Presidency* (2d ed., 1960), pp. 68–69.
†The book was completed prior to the 1980 election. Most of the economic and budgetary statistics were developed in the spring and summer of that year. Some of these numbers are already in need of revision—but the broad and sobering lessons which emerge from the numbers are unlikely to change much over the next several years. Throughout the book, we used statistics primarily to indicate general magnitudes and relationships.

# Memorandum for the President

# I·
# THE LION
# AND THE FOX
# REVISITED

**A**s you prepare for the inauguration and the four years ahead, you must make an extremely difficult transition—from running for office to running the government.

As you do, you must craft an approach to arrest the decade-long decline in the power of your office. The domestic presidency today is beset on many sides: by an assertive but fragmented Congress; by an aggressive press; by resurgent but atomized interest groups; by an interventionist judiciary; by an often unresponsive bureaucracy; by a skeptical, if not cynical, citizenry; by a faltering economy; by sharp limits in social policy due in part to that economy; and by pervasive doubts whether government in general and the presidency in particular can make a difference.

To be sure, the domestic presidency in the early 1980s is not as strong as it was in the mid-1960s. But it is not as weak as the downfall of Nixon, the inertia of Ford and the uncertainty of the Carter term have led observers to believe.

Indeed, after malfeasance, inaction and ineffectiveness in the domestic presidency during the 1970s, your great challenge is to demonstrate skill as the 1980s begin. You will have to take on major no-win issues like the economy. But you must also define other important but manageable tasks for executive government and then have your administration carry out a high percentage of those tasks successfully.

Your political strength now comes not from elections past but from successes future. To become powerful as President, you must win. In executive government, unlike electoral politics, that means getting things done. But over the next four years, it will often involve fairly allocating pain rather than distributing the bounty of a productive economy. This is an era of severe budgetary constraints and corrosive doubts about the efficacy of executive government, and you must therefore marshal your resources with great care and shrewdness.

In meeting that challenge, you will draw upon the thirteen departments, the hundreds of laws, the thousand plus political appointees, the millions of people in the ranks of the civil service, and the hundreds of billions of dollars in annual expenditures which, in sum, constitute executive government. We stress the phrase "executive government" because one of your central tasks will be to reinstitutionalize an overpersonalized presidency. You must spread publicly to others in your official family some of the responsibility for executive government. You cannot—and should not—escape personal identification with the most important domestic issues and major policy themes of your administration. But as you manage the executive branch, you must also acknowledge that executive government is much too vast for the personal attention of one man—and that many other critically important questions will be handled directly by key subordinates without your intimate involvement. As Dwight Eisenhower observed at the end of this nation's last two-term presidency:

> The government of the United States has become too big, too complex, and too pervasive in its influence in all our lives for one individual to pretend to direct the details of its important and critical programming. Competent assistants are mandatory; without them the Executive Branch would bog down. To command the loyalties and dedication and best efforts of capable and outstanding individuals requires patience, understanding, a readiness to delegate, and an acceptance of responsibility for any honest errors—real or apparent —those subordinates might make.[1]

Recognition of this home truth is not weakness on your part, but wisdom and a way of developing and maintaining strength.

## A. The Dimensions of Executive Government

The question of when and how to delegate is only one of the basic choices you must make to give an unmistakable direction and thrust to your administration for the next four years.

*Our basic purpose in this memorandum is to describe the first-order decisions you must make—substantive and political, structural and procedural—in order to provide leadership and give strength to your administration's handling of domestic affairs during the first half of the 1980s.* We seek to define the key issues in these four fundamental dimensions of executive government; to identify important factors that should guide their resolution; and, where possible, to make firm recommendations about the appropriate course of action. We hardly claim to have all the answers, but we do maintain that this memorandum lays out fundamental first-priority problems you must confront if you are to succeed. And we further assert that these issues are tightly interwoven— and must be seen and addressed together as part of a coherent, strategic approach to the whole that we term the domestic presidency.

As the chief of executive government, you will face decisions in three broad and overlapping areas: foreign policy, economic policy and domestic programs. The domestic presidency is concerned with the latter two—that is, with

- domestic economic issues—primarily fiscal and monetary policy, inflation and unemployment, energy and productivity— that relate to improving the aggregate measures of national economic health.
- domestic programs—the range of laws that involve the federal government in such matters as health, income security, education, housing, racial equality, transportation and community development and that entail the allocation and distribution of the federal share of our national wealth.

The amount of gross national product devoted to domestic programs directly affects the health of the economy, while the health of the economy in turn directly affects whether additional resources can be—or should be—devoted to completion of an unfinished programmatic agenda. This is just the most obvious connection between economic policy and federal domestic programs—connections now so multiple and intricate that the line between the two policy areas is very fuzzy. Our focus is not only on how to structure your handling of both economic policy and the domestic program agenda, but also on the relationship between these two broad areas of presidential responsibility and concern.*

*Our basic thesis is that you should conduct a strategic presidency in domestic affairs.* To make the best use of your limited resources and to increase the chances of overcoming the significant constraints on your powers, you must, that is, develop, and consistently test against a changing reality, a sophisticated strategy of governing that systematically incorporates and vigorously integrates the four fundamental dimensions of the domestic presidency—substantive policy and practical politics, administrative structures and action-forcing processes—over at least the four years of the coming term.

These four dimensions of a strategic presidency—policy, politics, structure and process—can be broadly and colloquially defined as follows:

—*Policy is where you want to go.* You must delineate first-order national problems and issues; see the connections between them; determine what, at least by your lights, is the *right* solution or response; and establish priorities. Your administration must also develop substantive positions on the vast array of other issues—legislative, budgetary, regulatory—that the administration must confront, while at the same time making sure that these positions are consistent with your major policy themes and priorities. You must, that is, set clear goals, while understanding that with limited resources, the

*Although this memorandum will not deal with diplomatic relations at all, nor with the organization of your foreign policy apparatus except in passing, it will refer to international economics because the state of the domestic economy is, increasingly, shaped by decisions made outside the United States. Much of what we say here may nonetheless have relevance to your conduct of foreign affairs. More importantly, we must stress—although then leave—the fundamental point that *domestic and international affairs, from your perspective, are deeply intertwined and that decisions in each sphere do not, and cannot, take place in hermetically sealed boxes but must be made with an understanding of their mutually reinforcing or their inherently contradictory consequences.*

goals you prefer may be in ineluctable conflict with one another.

—*Politics is how you get there.* It is the medium for realizing or frustrating your substantive objectives, involving a constant tug of war between what you believe is right and what you believe is possible, between what is desirable and what is feasible. From the organized forces in society—many of them with competing claims and interests—you must fashion coalitions for governing: strong allies who will provide you with the political muscle and influence for overcoming the manifold obstacles in your path and for reaching your goals. But in practicing the politics of governing, you must balance the sometimes contradictory claims of the politics of nomination (or renomination) and the politics of the general election.

—*Structure is how you distribute power within executive government.* You must organize the staffs of the White House and the Executive Office of the President (EOP) so that they serve you rather than bicker and fight among themselves. And you must define their powers in relation to the departments and agencies.

—*Process is how you run executive government to make policy, to play politics and, generally, to get things done.* It involves the basic ways in which issues are identified and analyzed, choices are made and decisions followed within the administration. You need, in effect, an elaborate set of rules, some written, some unwritten, for carrying out the business of the most complicated institution in the world and for untangling the oft-confused roles of decision-making, advice-giving and process-managing that are fundamental to executive government—especially when subpresidential decisions are made, as they must be, without your ongoing, in-depth attention.

—*Time is of the essence.* You must weave the threads of policy, politics, structure and process on a four- or five-year time frame. Your inauguration is a fleeting moment of history, and the next four years will be divided and then subdivided into tiny segments of time which must somehow accommodate big decisions. You may have sixty days to select key personnel; ninety days to forge a draft of your first strategy of governing; twenty days to decide on your term's first budget; and so on, until the next campaign. But controlling your ability to move are institutions and practices, attitudes and resources shaped by a long sweep of years. Before rushing into battle, you must plot out very carefully what you and your administration can conceivably hope to accomplish in the coming term, and then update that systematic plan periodically as events warrant.

The four dimensions of policy and politics, structure and process—organizing themes to which we will return repeatedly —may seem obvious. But to view your administration systematically from all four perspectives, and with a proper and heightened sense of time, is extremely difficult. Indeed, what we urge—a strategic approach to the domestic presidency—may have eluded nearly every president of the modern era. Making sense of the four dimensions of executive government involves decisions that are confounding in and of themselves, let alone when you seek, as you must, to deal with them together.

To give a strategic coherence to your administration will require an extraordinary act of political and governmental will on your part: an unceasing, even ruthless insistence on seeing executive government whole—that is, from four different perspectives—and understanding how the large pieces fit together and to what purpose. It will be easy, seductively easy, to stay busy: decisions of all shapes and sizes will rush at you with frightening speed. While extremely difficult, it is not, we think, impossible to set *and then continually reassess* a general strategic direction, even as you are drawn to decision-making on the most important, discrete issues of your term.

Your first-order decisions in domestic affairs are important for another reason. If history is any guide, your attention to foreign affairs will increase over the course of your term at the expense of domestic concerns. There are many reasons why foreign affairs make such significant claims on presidential time: an international crisis may be more pressing than the intractable and long-standing problems on the domestic side; the President has more (though not absolute) autonomy and more direct personal responsibility on the foreign side; and presidents tend to become frustrated with the difficulties—some have doubtless felt the impossibility—of working real change in domestic affairs.

The probable drift of your attention to foreign affairs is not, however, due to the political insignificance of domestic affairs. In fact, absent a war or a prolonged international crisis, the public will likely judge you on a combination of your character and your success in dealing with domestic issues.[2]

Mistakes in foreign affairs may literally involve life and death. But mistakes on the domestic side often open serious political wounds that can lead to a political death—yours.* The strategy you will develop now in domestic affairs—and the people, processes and structures that you put in place to deal with the problems you define and with the inevitable adversity just over the horizon—is thus a matter of the utmost urgency and gravity.

## B. The Memorandum Summarized

This memorandum has six chapters.

• In the rest of *Chapter 1,* we discuss in greater detail the nature of and the need for the strategic approach to the domestic presidency.

• *Chapter 2* lays out the basic constraints on your scope of action. Presidents often find out how limited their powers are by trying to exercise them. Other than the behavior of your own political appointees in the executive branch, there are very few areas in which you can issue a command and compel a result. Executive government is government by request, not by fiat. To move, you must secure acquiescence from competing centers of power in an increasingly fragmented political system.

Less than a month before he was assassinated, John Kennedy remarked: "the powers of the presidency are often described. Its limitations should occasionally be remembered." A first step in managing a strategic presidency, therefore, is understanding the forces that hedge you in—limited resources and balky institutions, divisive practices and inhibiting attitudes. The dominant features of the political and governmental landscape are too often obscured by the smoke from the immediate battle—smoke that obscures not only a single feature but the cumulative impact of all the dominant features, which can be quite profound.

*There is the other side of this point: strength in domestic affairs is one of the prerequisites to a president's strength in foreign affairs.

Everyone knows that the world has changed. But we will try to outline how and why by comparing the mid-sixties to the early eighties with respect to the forces that curtail your personal influence and the powers of your office—a malfunctioning economy, the growth of an uncontrollable federal budget, a hard-to-manage federal enterprise, a fragmented Congress, intensified group politics, an adversary press, a weakened party system, public doubts and imperfect understanding of the processes that work social and economic change.

Although you promised the electorate a dramatic break with the past, in reality you have much less room to maneuver than you might think, or would like to think, absent a historic tide sweeping all before it. Identifying constraints does not lead us to counsel despair. They may cause difficulties, but they are not immutable. It does lead us inexorably back to our fundamental theme, however. You cannot avoid all the slings and arrows of outrageous fortune, but with foresight and shrewdness, you should be able to avoid at least some of them.

• *Chapter 3* makes the case that the Cabinet officers are the crux of executive government. There will always be a dominant role for Cabinet officers in the modern executive branch because you do not have enough time to deal with all important questions personally; because your personal staff cannot make many of these decisions from the White House; and because you can only attract talented Cabinet secretaries if you are willing to give them significant responsibility and discretion. To make executive government work requires a system of delegation that keeps the President and his top aides close to the first-order issues of the administration but allows the Cabinet secretaries significant discretion in other major matters.

The key to the tricky relationships between the White House and the departments—one that turns upon the administration's ability to think and act strategically—is a simultaneous process of centralization and decentralization. This comes from a division of the major issues facing the administration into three types: presidential, presidential/secretarial and secretarial. The presidential issues (five to ten in number) will be your major test during the next four years. On these you should be deeply involved in strategy and tactics; there should be strong central control; and the Cabinet officer should be only one of several direct, personal advisors. On the mixed presidential/secretarial issues (twenty-five to thirty-five in number), you should be involved in setting the general policy direction but cede secondary decisions to the Cabinet officer within the framework you have established. At the other end of the spectrum you and the White House staff should have relatively little involvement on the secretarial issues (a hundred to a hundred and twenty-five in number), a domain in which the Cabinet secretary should have significant autonomy.* The three-part scheme should, in other words, convey descending order of importance to the administration, decreasing presidential and White House staff involvement, and increasing secretarial discretion. It should also be flexible, with issues moving up and down the scale of priority as events require.

• *Chapter 4,* a companion piece to Chapter 3, recommends the appropriate arrangements for the personal White House staff and for the larger, more institutional staffs in the Executive Office of the President. These staffs should provide coherence to the strategic concerns of the administration and should guide the development and implementation of presidential-level issues. On the other hand, these central staffs must allow decision-making authority to be delegated away from your desk for the many issues that can be handled by the departments and agencies. And they must be structured to deal with the central problem that our proposal in Chapter 3 does not address—how to make subpresidential decisions on important administration matters that you should not resolve but that cannot be delegated to a Cabinet officer because too many departments and agencies have a substantial stake in the outcome.

The EOP has suffered for a decade from serious weaknesses. It has become too big, containing too many staffs and advisors peripheral to its central functions. It has also been structured in a confusing manner, inviting internal conflicts over decision-making, advice-giving and coordinating authority. Its operating procedures have been haphazard, unfair and easily "gamed." Its inability to make decisions short of the President has led to

*The issues at these three levels will be the basic policies on which the administration seeks to build its record. Beyond these are hundreds of more routine issues that must be handled properly by your appointees and their subordinates.

delay, uncertainty and presidential overload. And it has lacked a strategic center able to marshal the forces of executive government so that the President can get done what he wants done.

To avoid these problems, we suggest, among other things:

—A rigorous consolidation of EOP offices into four main channels of activity that lead to you: economic policy (headed by the treasury secretary but with an independent, EOP coordinating office); domestic affairs (headed by a presidential assistant but restricted to the presidential and presidential/secretarial issues); budget and management (headed by the OMB director); and political affairs (headed by a new assistant for politics who oversees deputies responsible for the Congress, the interest groups, state and local governments and media strategy). The Vice President, legal counsel and press secretary will have direct access to you and special roles outside these four main channels.

—A consequent realignment of the roles of the Office of Management and Budget and the Domestic Affairs Staff to avoid, or at least minimize, the rivalry that has grown up between them over the past ten years.

—An enhancement of the chief of staff, who should sit above all other EOP aides (except the Vice President) and who should in essence relate to you as an effective deputy secretary in a major department relates to the secretary. This person—whose major qualification should be experience and judgment and not a dominant role in your campaign—must have your absolute trust because he or she will have critical tasks: developing and updating the strategy of governing; reconciling the often competing demands of policy and politics; and keeping second- and third-level decisions off your desk by actually resolving conflicts between other key actors in the administration if his efforts at conciliation fail. In many respects, this person, who has power only in your name, replaces the OMB director or the treasury secretary as the most important appointment you will make in domestic affairs. The Reagan forces at the 1980 convention in Detroit were right that a role like this should exist in modern executive government. They were wrong in thinking that a vice president could fill it.

• *Chapter 5* offers cautionary tales drawn from the Carter administration's experience which elaborate our basic theme that a four-year strategy of governing is absolutely necessary for any chance of success in the domestic presidency. In economic policy, the Carter administration encountered enormous problems in settling upon a realistic long-term plan for improving the economy's performance and for explaining to the American people why this performance, even with the best of luck, would inevitably be disappointing. Instead, the administration overpromised at the beginning, both to the people and to itself, and spent much of the next four years engaging in tactical retreats and half-explained efforts to evade perils and crises which it had not foreseen. The moral for economic policy is to plan carefully for the worst, to educate the American people on the limits you face in making things better—and to keep in mind at all times that mistakes or surprises on the economic front can swiftly undermine every other promise of your domestic presidency.

By contrast, an examination of two major social policy initiatives—welfare reform and national health insurance—shows major mistakes of political strategy. Both were highly controversial proposals and either would have required an all-out legislative campaign on the part of the administration, and only two or three such campaigns are possible in domestic policy during the four years of the first term. But neither initiative was handled that way, and despite a significant amount of attention, neither had much chance of enactment because of fundamental confusion about the administration's priorities and timing. The moral is to keep the very top of your domestic program agenda lean, to effect a powerful fusion between policy and politics, and to be sensitive to the details of timing.

• *Chapter 6* sets out the major problems and choices you will face in the domestic presidency. We argue that you should consider economic policy, budgetary policy and domestic program policy in a four- to five-year time frame. And we set out a relatively simple example of the way to think about such problems—an example that can be made much more sophisticated by your experts. In essence, the budget will be a key battleground for both economic and domestic program policy because you cannot simultaneously—or over the four-year period of the coming term—achieve the goals of tax reduction, reduced budget deficits and increased defense or domestic spending.

In economic policy, you will find, as we recover slowly from the recession, that you face the same dismal problems that boxed in the Carter administration: a high underlying rate of inflation, low productivity growth, a fragile dollar, budget chronically in deficit even at high tax rates, and a dangerous dependence on highly uncertain sources of overseas oil. To confront those problems in a meaningful way may well take you into perilous political waters. Controlling inflation may require a degree of fiscal and monetary restraint, amidst high unemployment, which will rapidly erode your popularity. Raising the rate of productivity growth may require highly regressive tax cuts; offsetting cuts in government spending trends will strike large segments of the population as highly inequitable; and the exercise may yield few if any tangible benefits in the next four years. Cutting back on foreign oil dependence (and bolstering the dollar) will continue to require sharp increases in energy prices, which will upset virtually everyone.

In social policy, you will face a constant tension between the expansionist agenda that emerged with great force in the 1960s and the managerial agenda that was its powerful counterpoint in the 1970s. The impetus for both will continue in the 1980s, although the more conservative temper of the times will obviously create difficulties for those who advocate dramatic innovation in domestic programs.

The expansionist agenda primarily involves establishing rights and expanding benefits for the poor, minorities, aged, infirm and dispossessed of America. These social policy functions have grown from just over 30 percent to more than 50 percent of the federal budget during the past fifteen years. And because many of the programs are entitlements that are automatically required by law, are *not* subject to the annual appropriations process, and are often indexed to inflation, just the existing domestic programs alone will continue to exert dramatic claims on the federal budget.* But there are still a host of problems that require attention: among them, expanded health-

---

*In fiscal 1980, $247 billion of the $299 billion in federal social policy expenditures were automatic entitlements. And of that $247 billion, approximately $154 billion—or roughly one quarter of the total federal budget—was indexed to the rate of inflation.

care coverage, long-term care programs, additional financing for the social security system, establishing greater equity for women in the social security program, and providing training and finding jobs for the hard-to-employ young. You will also face severe budget pressures for increased spending on the public infrastructure—highways, ports, railroads, urban sewer systems, mass transit and the like. As we will show, the net "new" cost to the federal budget associated with a basic but not exhaustive list of initiatives can total as much as $125 billion per year by fiscal 1985.

In an attempt to prevent the undisciplined growth of domestic program initiatives, to make some of the existing programs more orderly and to increase program effectiveness, government officials in the 1970s began to give far more attention to items on the managerial agenda than their counterparts in the 1960s did. These initiatives fall into three broad categories: expenditure reductions, improved efficiency and reorganization. Of the three, the Carter administration placed the most public emphasis on the least fruitful: reorganization. Reorganizing structure engenders enormous political opposition; requires significant political capital to realize; often fails; and even if approved, often has little to do with improved government performance because the inevitable political compromises create new organizational anomalies. The other two issues will dominate the future: the need to discipline selectively existing federal programs through the budget process and the need to make existing programs work better.

You may wish to emphasize one of the two social policy agendas and ignore the other. But you do so at your peril. Richard Nixon sought to repeal the Great Society programs, with the result that the Congress took much of the initiative in domestic programs away from him. Jimmy Carter sought comprehensive reforms on the expansionist agenda and was by and large rebuffed by the Congress, stimulating a debate about his governing abilities.

Indeed, if you wish to push for expansionist reforms, you must build a strong managerial record to avoid the opprobrium of being merely a big spender and to demonstrate that you can control existing programs so that the new initiatives will not grow out of control. Similarly (and more likely), if you wish to

be a more competent manager, you should also seek to control
—and that means set priorities for and selectively endorse items
on—the expansionist agenda to avoid being under siege from
special interests, opinion makers and authorizing committees of
the Congress as insensitive and uncaring.

Finding the proper balance between the expansionist and
managerial agendas in domestic programs is essential to your
successful tenure as domestic president, whatever your party or
politics.

## C. The Strategic Approach

In schematic, abstract terms, there is no mystery about the
strategic approach to executive government. It involves laying
out the host of possible objectives; understanding the connections among them; choosing priorities among them; defining the
roles and responsibilities for your top officials; assessing the
impact of outside forces, both those which can aid you and those
which will oppose you; assessing the limits on your resources;
establishing discrete steps that should be taken within a specific
time frame to achieve the priority objectives; and leaving
enough play in the joints to take into account the unexpected.
Reduced to a single sentence, our catch-phrase formulation is
that a strategic approach to executive government involves joining (and understanding the tensions between) policy and politics, structure and process in a coherent plan for four or five
years that can change (not too often) with events and that takes
into account constraints (see Chapter 2) and available resources
(see Chapter 6).

For military and business organizations (and for good campaign organizations), strategic thinking is a commonplace. But
the domestic presidency bears only the vaguest resemblance to
either the armed forces or a corporation (or a political campaign)
—and indeed, analogies with any of them are probably more
misleading than helpful. The reason, simply put, is that the
domestic presidency has a vast number of possible objectives,
any one of which may be more complicated than turning a profit
or winning a battle—objectives that are often broad, vague and
in ineluctable conflict with one another. Moreover, unlike a
corporate chief executive or a line commander, you operate in

a world awash in politics where power is fragmented and shared.

Nonetheless, the strategic imperative—even if it means something markedly different with respect to executive government —must be followed. We believe that *the nature and degree of presidential power you will be able to exercise turns on your ability to act strategically.*

**1. The Reasons.** A strategic approach to the domestic presidency is necessary because it is the best method for helping you think about and resolve the painful tensions at the core of your stewardship—trade-offs and dilemmas within and between the four dimensions of executive government. The tensions, for example,

—between the real constraints on your power and the persistent expectation that you can direct sweeping change.
—between the inconsistent or contradictory demands that will be made on the federal government in the coming decade, for example, between increased military spending and enhanced domestic programs.
—between an economic policy whose purpose is to dampen inflation and stimulate productivity and one designed to further social equity, full employment and income redistribution.
—between the expansionist agenda, with its dramatic claims on the federal budget and the national conscience, and the managerial agenda, with its uncontroversial goal of making government work better and its controversial goal of disciplining government programs that don't work well.
—between the need to attack some major national problems that pose unavoidably high risks for you and the need to define an agenda that includes a number of issues with a higher probability of success.
—between the demands of policy and the imperatives of politics.
—between the politics of governing and the sometimes contradictory politics of nomination and of the general election.
—between the need for a four-year perspective and the pressure to deal, at whatever the cost to that perspective, with the highly publicized, politically volatile crisis of the moment.

—between the need to plan carefully and stick with a consistent approach and the need to be flexible and to account for changing events.

—between the need to provide central leadership to executive government and the need to decentralize responsibility through delegation.

A strategic approach to the domestic presidency will not remove the sting from choices that seek to resolve these tensions and dilemmas and trade-offs. But it will help you understand how these choices, and others like them, relate to one another; it will bring into more complex but also sharper relief what you are gaining and what you are losing by those choices; and, we hope, the approach will improve the odds of reaching your goals.

Three additional reasons for adopting a strategic approach deserve special attention here as elementary points upon which the rest of our argument builds.

*First, adopting a strategy that encompasses and blends policy and politics, structure and process, allows you to give your clear, personal direction to domestic affairs without having to make every important decision.*

The key people, both in the White House and in the departments, must understand your sense of direction, your goals, your timing—in other words, your strategy of governing—if they are to serve your interests and not their own. If you do not make clear in a broad outline where you stand and where you want to go, your administration will fumble its tasks and trip over itself. *Not only will a strategy of governing allow you to concentrate your personal resources in a timely fashion on the most important issues, but it will also provide a framework for resolving the inevitable disputes that will constantly arise within the administration.* It provides needed guidance for reconciling the hundreds of subsidiary questions that executive government must answer. Among them:

—If you are serious about balancing the budget, then you preclude certain initiatives in the near term. If, on the other hand, you are willing to operate at a certain level of deficit, that will sharply pose choices about how to spend any new funds (tax cuts? defense spending? long-term care for the elderly?).

—If you want to push only a few major initiatives in the coming Congress, that will preclude others—or at least preclude giving them first-order presidential treatment.

—If you make clear, to the greatest extent possible, what the key roles for your Cabinet and your top personal staff in the Executive Office of the President are, and how the people in those roles interlock with each other, you will not be endlessly making ad hoc organizational decisions to dampen the conflict that is sure to erupt.

*Second, a strategic approach helps you to find the most appropriate ways of winning in domestic governance.* In essence, these "ways of winning" stem from the four types of functions that executive government performs.

• *Innovation in Policy.* The standard measure of a president's domestic success is whether he can work with the Congress to enact major pieces of legislation. But innovative policy can take many forms: new authorizing legislation, new legislative approaches to the federal budget, new regulations on controversial issues, developing new types of regulations or gaining the assent of private parties to voluntary action (as in the case of wage and price guidelines). Policy innovation can deal with big issues— such as comprehensive tax reform or a national energy plan— or small ones, such as setting up a regulatory review council that merely establishes a calendar of all regulations published by the federal government in a given year.*

In simplest terms, policy innovation involves changing the basic norms or rules—statutory, regulatory, managerial or voluntary—that govern governmental or private behavior. *Success in policy innovation is securing the agreement of important parties to all or most of the rules or norms you propose.* These actors include the Congress, state and local officials, interest groups, the press, the federal bureaucracy and the public generally, depending upon the type of innovation you are proposing.

There are two basic aspects of policy innovation. You must first develop positions *within* the administration on the changes

---

*You have, of course, numerous routine methods for trying to effect policy innovation: an annual budget, an annual legislative program, executive orders, regulations, executive positions on questions of law, and speeches or messages.

in law, regulation, rules or norms that you wish to advocate. But generally you must then organize an effort outside the administration to secure as much agreement as possible from the relevant actors. Both aspects—developing the internal position and securing the external acquiescence from the relevant parties—must be seen as one, but too often they are not.* It is critical that internal development always keep the need for external assent in clear and constant view. But as it becomes harder and harder for the President to work with the Congress, it may be increasingly important to explore systematically the extent to which you can innovate in policy with existing authority.†

- *Implementation of Policy.* Policy innovation deals with the world of ideas, and an agreement between the relevant actors merely translates those ideas into law or regulation or directive. But implementation must follow an agreement on an innovative policy.

*Success in policy implementation is showing results in the real world* —to make the new law or rule or norm change behavior or alter economic or social conditions. To the extent that policy implementation involves actually changing the behavior of federal employees (after you agree on a policy change), a command structure does exist. You can give an order and, in theory at least, your subordinates should carry it out. You can, for example, decide that federal paperwork should be reduced by a certain percentage in a given year (policy innovation) and then ensure that the required reductions indeed take place (policy implementation).

But most policy implementation involves processes much more complex than making the federal bureaucracy respond to

---

*Some observers of the presidency distinguish between internal policy development and coalition-building. As we argue throughout this memorandum, that distinction drives a wedge between policy and politics. Developing policies internally and gaining external assent are better seen as part of a more unified policy innovation task.

†Policy innovation may also mean taking defensive action. The Congress may push issues that are at odds with your agenda, and you must clearly counter such thrusts. During the Carter term, for example, an elaborate plan was devised to defeat pressures within the Congress for a tuition tax credit in both higher and elementary and secondary education. By mounting a negative campaign (the credit was bad educational, budgetary and organizational policy) and offering an alternative (the Middle Income Student Assistance Act of 1978), the administration was able to work with strong allies in and outside the Congress to defeat a tax credit bill deemed a sure winner before defensive efforts were undertaken.

your commands and the commands of your top political appointees (even though that, on closer examination, is tough enough).
Most federal programs or policies involve the cooperation of
either private centers of power or state and local officials. For
example, will state and local officials use federal compensatory
education funds for their *intended purpose* (and discerning that
purpose is often very difficult). And even if federal programs or
policies are carried out according to their intended purpose by
either private or governmental officials, it is by no means certain
that they will achieve their *intended result.* Changing social and
economic conditions is much more complicated than changing
the behavior of public or private officials. For example, even if
the compensatory education funds are used for their intended
purpose by the states and localities, will they achieve the intended result of improving the basic educational skills of poor
children?

As in policy innovation, your constant problem here is executive government's dependence on the actions of others. Although you can establish innovative economic policies (usually
with the aid of the Congress), the effective implementation of
those policies turns on the behavior of the private sector. Similarly, in domestic programs, most of the basic services are delivered by state and local governments or by private contractors
and consultants, and the actions of leaders in nonfederal institutions determine whether federal moneys are used for intended
purposes and achieve intended results. Indeed, although it is
popular to rail against the federal bureaucracy, federal employees don't deliver many services or directly manage many
programs; they watch private or public middlemen do that and
try to devise ways to hold them accountable to congressional
purposes.

Nonetheless, despite the significant difficulties that we will
discuss in greater detail below, policy implementation is a
sphere of action with important potential for the domestic presidency. The public has developed striking skepticism about
whether government works and whether its tax dollars are
spent effectively. With as much as 70 percent of the federal
budget—$400 billion dollars in fiscal 1980—devoted to the func-
tions of the domestic presidency (that is to say, to the nondefense, noninternational, nonspace functions), there is a broad

range of issues from which you can choose should you wish to make policy implementation a test of your success.

• *Crisis Management.* Natural disasters, civil disturbances, strikes, energy shortages, newly emerging and unanticipated political forces, problems in your own inner circle or scandals in the executive branch are just some of the crises that may be thrust upon you on the domestic side of the government. Some crises—such as scandals in your administration or other problems in your official family—may break upon you unexpectedly. But you or your top officials should be able to anticipate many of these crises and have well-thought-out contingency plans at the ready—strikes or cold weather that causes energy distress are two obvious examples. Developing early warning systems and having contingency plans for some obvious potential crises are elements in strategic thinking. Your key people must constantly be anticipating what the general public sees as unexpected.

To a large extent, crisis management simply means confronting problems of policy innovation or policy implementation in an accelerated fashion and at a time not of your own choosing. But your ability, or the ability of your administration, to handle these crises with common sense, resolution and dispatch will play an important part in the perception of you as a successful domestic president. Indeed, crisis management on presidential issues usually affords you an opportunity to rally the nation and to do more readily what in more normal times is quite difficult: actually exert strong leadership. You must leave enough flexibility in your administration's structure—primarily by understanding that crisis management will require an inordinate amount of time—to absorb the shocks of the unexpected.

• *Moral Leadership.* There are two strands here. Not every national problem has, or requires, a solution. And there is no reason that you must have a federal answer and a national solution for everything. You can instead win credit by structuring a debate on important innovative issues for the future—by introducing new ideas into national life without firmly committing yourself to them. As Franklin Roosevelt said in 1932: "The presidency . . . is preeminently a place of moral leadership. All our great presidents were leaders of thought at times when certain historic ideas in the life of the nation had to be clarified." This technique is not only the responsible course at times— when there has not been enough thought on the problem to yield intelligent proposals—but also a good expedient for deflecting political pressure.* Proposing legislation that you know has little chance of success, however, is usually not a good expedient for such purposes. Unless you are enjoying a period of enhanced reputation, both in Washington and in the nation, you cannot afford repeated legislative defeats on major issues, even if you fully expect them. But you do have an almost unparalleled opportunity, because of your position and the vast resources in the executive branch, to give a few major speeches each year to a prestigious audience describing a problem that will assume (or has assumed) national import and laying out alternative approaches rather than proposing solutions. A thoughtful speech on alternatives for regulatory reform or long-term care for the elderly could win you plaudits and stimulate a useful debate.

There is also a conservative element to moral leadership: articulating and reaffirming the historic values that form the core of shared beliefs uniting the nation. If your efforts here are merely platitudinous or jingoistic, the nation will tune out. But if you have a sense of history and a sense of language, and if you do not overuse the role, you have an opportunity, as the preeminent spokesman for the nation, to underscore what binds us together, especially when the divisions that now separate us are all too evident. FDR's speeches in the depths of the Depression, Lyndon Johnson's speeches during the Selma civil rights disturbances in 1965 or Gerald Ford's address immediately after Nixon's resignation are good examples of the technique at its best.

A *third* important reason for adopting a strategic approach to the domestic presidency is that you must systematically untangle the often inconsistent requirements of the different levels of

---

*It is, however, well understood by students of presidential commissions and other formal outside advisory groups that they present a danger as well as an opportunity to the President. If the issue you are studying is a hot one—and likely to demand some sort of decision on your part during your stay in office—make sure that your study group is not a loose cannon that careens out of the control of your top aides. It can then present you with a series of recommendations that are sharply divergent from your overall sense of direction.

politics at which you must operate: the politics of governing, the politics of nomination and the politics of the general election. These now diverge more sharply than in Lyndon Johnson's time, to say nothing of Franklin Roosevelt's, which perhaps is why recent presidents have had such trouble coping with the differences among them.

When you want to do things as the chief of executive government—whether in policy innovation, policy implementation, crisis management or moral leadership—you will need to be a master practitioner of the politics of governing. You will have to build coalitions around your programs and politics; map out a systematic method of relating to those who will be important to you throughout the term (not just on the issue of the moment); and devise ways of disarming or blunting the thrusts of those who would oppose you. Under the broad rubric of the politics of governing are a series of separate but intertwined political relationships: with your appointees in the departments and agencies; with the political and permanent (civil service) officials who manage domestic programs; with members of Congress and their increasingly numerous and powerful staffs; with state and local officials; with the interest groups and other organized sectors of American society who exert political influence or shape public opinion; and with the various appendages of the media.

But your success as President will also be measured by your ability to perpetuate electoral power. Of course, your broad political power will be enhanced if you successfully practice the arts of governing in policy innovation, policy implementation, crisis management and moral leadership. But you must constantly seek ways of increasing your party's power or the power of those who would help you politically: by winning state and local offices, by securing more seats in the Congress and, of course, by controlling your party's nominating process and then continuing to hold the presidency.

But the imperatives of the politics of governing are often at odds with political demands in the two other spheres.

—*The politics of nomination* (either for you or for a person of your choosing who will carry on the themes and work of your presidency) involves making peace with the groups or interests or types of voters who are likely to be energetic and influential in the *next* presidential selection process of your party. These people are customarily activists in the party or those most likely to vote in primaries or participate in conventions. Building coalitions for the politics of governing primarily means dealing with the special interest groups and with the specialized concerns of the congressional committee and subcommittee system on particular matters that often require detailed compromises and not platform purity. In this period, these shifting governing coalitions may be strikingly different from a coalition of those within your party who have been, and will be, influential in the nominating process. In schematic terms, the political center of gravity of the parties—of the nomination process—is often significantly to the left or right of the political center of gravity of the country as a whole, the center that must be occupied when you are governing. But the process of knitting together governing coalitions can cause your nominating coalition to fracture, and even fly apart.

—In the *politics of the general election* just past, you were concerned about striking broad centrist themes, projecting a presidential image, and attracting a broad coalition of voters. This general approach is likely to be followed for the next general election, which will rush at you, or your chosen successor, with surprising speed. But as you know, the politics of the general election—and your attempts to connect firmly with the center of the voting public—are often at odds with the *themes* of the politics of nomination, even though the *style* of the politics may be similar (broad, telegenic, impressionistic appeals). Indeed, nomination politics can often lead to problems in general election politics. If you placate the outer wing of your party, you may have trouble explaining those positions to the general electorate; but if you hold the center ground during the nomination, you may alienate the more liberal/conservative wing of your party, leading to defections.

Moreover, the politics of the general election are obviously different in both style and substance from the detailed, technical processes of bargaining and compromise that are likely to characterize the politics of governing. To be sure, you will continue to seek the support of the broad middle of the electorate. But your governing objectives may be ahead of the nation, especially if you are thinking strategically about the nation's substantive problems. And in this sense the politics of the general election may inhibit your ability to govern as you would wish. Moreover, as we have noted, you must make choices when governing that you tried to finesse when running. And the untidy compromises needed to get things done with a fractious Congress and various interest groups are likely to bring you down from the Olympus of national leadership and inject disturbing static into your attempt to articulate clear, understandable national themes. Yet if you cannot get things done by working with the Congress and the powerful organized forces in the society, then your primacy of place in the national political system may be merely a hollow, mocking honorific.

The process of making the budget in 1980 (for fiscal 1981) provides an example of the tension between the three political spheres in which you must operate as President.

—In January 1980, President Carter first proposed a politics-of-nomination budget. It was essentially a current-services budget that did not permit much new growth in programs, but did not seek to cut any politically popular programs significantly. This budget, with a $16 billion deficit, was developed before the primary season began and at a time when the threat from Senator Kennedy dictated that activist, liberal groups in the Democratic Party should not be offended. Although these groups were not happy with the Carter administration's budgetary restraint, they were not, generally speaking, profoundly angry. They would have become so had there been deep slashes in domestic programs.

—After the consumer price index shot up in late January, the bond markets panicked, and a national clamor for a balanced budget erupted, the administration reversed course. In a virtually unprecedented action, it abandoned its January budget within weeks of its transmittal to the Congress and resubmitted a politics-of-general-election budget that proposed a $16 billion surplus, primarily by seeking to increase revenues rather than cutting painfully into popular programs (which by and large were still kept at current services). With the quest for a balanced budget suddenly elevated to the top of the national agenda, the Carter administration could not go to the general electorate in the fall with a proposed budget that had a discernible deficit.

—Yet during the politics-of-governing phase, when the administration had to press its revised proposal before the Congress, it basically lost leadership of the process. The loss was symbolized by the Congress' overwhelming repudiation of the President's proposed tax on imported oil and an equally overwhelming vote to override his veto. The tentative budget approved in the first congressional budget resolution was much closer to proposals that emerged from the Congress than the administration's resubmitted budget, in part because the Carterites were still worried about the nomination challenge.

—And, to add insult to injury, the Republicans, playing the politics of the general election, were able to compose their differences over the shape of a tax cut and to propose, in June 1980, a major tax reduction (that would have thrown the budget into even larger deficit). Tax-cut fever led some Senate Democrats to break from the administration and prompted the administration, once again, to shift course under the press of events and to announce that it too had been considering a post-election tax cut that would end, with finality, pursuit of the balanced budget will-o'-the-wisp for fiscal 1981.*

The administration's shifting course—which was based in part on its difficulties in successfully negotiating the treacherous passage between the three political worlds—contributed, in an election year, to the perception of an administration with limited influence over a major item on the national agenda.

You are well aware of the three levels of politics. But their divergence today means that you must start now in a systematic fashion to think about how these three overlapping but distinct

*Of course, the recession made the budget balancing exercise meaningless. As this is being written in the fall of 1980, estimates of the fiscal 1981 deficit range from $30 billion to $50 billion, *without* a tax cut.

spheres of politics relate to each other in the coming four years, and which type of politics should have precedence when. The contradictions between the levels of politics may force you to live with inconsistencies, but to the extent possible, they should be planned and carefully modulated, not forced upon you.

**2. Some Implications.** There are numerous implications of the strategic approach. In light of the past four years, some of the most salient follow:

• *Use your peripheral vision.* As we have emphasized, you must constantly ask whether the direction of the administration as a whole, and the strategy for your major, presidential issues, has adequately fused the four dimensions of policy, politics, structure and process. Put another way, you must develop and then heed your own peripheral vision—to be sensitive, and to urge your top aides to be sensitive, to the subtle, occasionally obscure connections between the disparate spheres of your domain. Your breadth of vision and responsibility is a source of strength. Of all public officials in the nation, you alone have it and you alone can use your influence over diverse areas of national life to create a genuine form of synergy which can translate into political power. But your breadth of responsibility, and the potential importance of matters on the apparent periphery of your priority objectives, is also a source of danger. These peripheral matters can suddenly catch fire and consume or injure the priorities. And you may be held responsible for the unexpected even if the fault lies elsewhere.

If looking around corners from the side of your eyes is not something you do easily and consistently—many previous presidents have not—then you owe it to yourself to supplement your natural style of looking at problems (one by one perhaps, as many of your predecessors have) with some key members of your staff whose peripheral vision is particularly good.

• *Decide what you want done.* The strategic approach has little value if you cannot decide what is essential to your presidency —if you do not know what are the core accomplishments that you would like memorialized in the reception hall of your presidential library. Despite the inevitable unforeseen crises and the undesirable limits on your power in the contemporary political system, you can, especially at the beginning of your term, choose those issues on which you will try to get things done. To an important degree, you can set the national agenda, focus the national debate. This is a precious presidential asset which must not be wasted. If you fail to choose clearly and if you fail to communicate those choices dramatically, you will squander your capacity to lead and hopelessly confuse your followers.

• *Stick with it.* The importance of your initial set of priorities is underscored by the necessity of not shifting course every time you meet with a minor setback. Stick with those basic choices —not in bullheaded fashion but with persistence. Just as a failure to choose priorities will sow confusion, so also will a hasty retreat from them. Your message must be clear, and your persistence credible. If you ultimately decide that you have chosen badly, expend as much time and energy in making an orderly withdrawal as in substituting your alternatives. A major change of direction should not take place more than once (or at the most twice) during the coming term, but you must candidly confront the dilemma that your most important strategic, priority-setting decisions will come when you are least prepared (that is to say, 90 to 120 days after the election).

• *Think comprehensively but act incrementally.* Our time is not hospitable to grand visions and comprehensive solutions that yield few results. At least early in your term, setting more realistic goals for your domestic presidency—with broad and bold thrusts held in reserve until the timing is opportune—is far more desirable for you, for the presidency as an institution and for the nation. Your vision of what the nation should become is necessary, and explaining how your near-term proposal fits into a broader view of the future is important. But limited progress toward your goals is preferable to overwhelming defeat. Curb your understandable ambition for dramatic and sweeping solutions. If you make an important change consistent with your more comprehensive views, you will be doing well.

• *Always remember: time is short and change is slow (unless you get lucky).* Time is your constant enemy. Choice in policies also means choice in timing. Most major pieces of innovative legislation take at least two years to enact, and if they are especially innovative, they can occupy almost the whole of your coming term. Most major changes in implementation take an equally long time: first in determining what you want, then in effectively establishing new systems and structures, and finally in seeing results. Time will surely defeat you if you try too much —unless you are lucky and a clear tide of events begins to run with you. Think constantly about how short the four-year period is. However short you may now think it is, it will be shorter still, partly because our nation's bizarre presidential selection process can begin as early as eighteen months before the next election (at least it did for both Gerald Ford and Jimmy Carter). And once the campaign begins, the problems of getting things done while governing increase exponentially.

• *Protect the presidency's—and the president's—reputation for competence.* Competence in the discrete tasks of executive government—relating to Congress, making the budget, being consistent on major pieces of legislation—is the bedrock on which rests the power you have when you assume office. And it is vital if you are to execute the more complex strategic maneuvers which can augment your power, building the momentum that can help you drive toward your major goals. You must pay more than routine attention to the minimal requirements of doing business in Washington. The press will, for a time, be looking for elementary errors—the most damning being clearly inconsistent and contradictory positions and a failure to keep the administration's house in order.

**3. The lion and the fox.** In his Roosevelt biography, written nearly twenty-five years ago, James McGregor Burns drew upon the metaphor used by Machiavelli in *The Prince*—the lion and the fox—to illustrate some essential qualities of the president. At times the president can be leonine, acting with great boldness, swiftness and force; supreme as the most powerful among unequals, and able to work his will because of that extraordinary power. But at other times, when bedeviled by forces that he cannot control but only influence (and even then perhaps only influence slightly), the president needs to emulate the fox by using craft and cunning; by temporizing and avoiding battles; by seeking marginal advantage; and by using indirection and wit to achieve what the lion could win by dint of strength alone.*

This era is likely to treat a leonine domestic presidency

---

*Machiavelli used the image of the fox in a second sense: the need for conscious deceit by the leader. We do not intend that use here.

harshly. The world is too complex, the other forces arrayed against any president too powerful. The qualities that characterize the fox—shrewdness, an intuitive sense of timing, a sharp awareness of existing limits and the skill to maneuver around them—must be dominant. This sense of timing, of waiting for events, was one of Roosevelt's most finely honed political skills. If a president in the 1980s is to survive politically, to act as a lion if events allow, he must first practice the political arts as a fox.

But perhaps a more appropriate image for these less dramatic, more technocratic, yet no less troubling times, is to see the presidency in general and the domestic presidency in particular as the ultimate chess game. Your scope of action is limited. Other players have pieces of equal power, and you can prevail only by your wits. Before you can make dramatic moves that will lead to decisive victories, you must systematically develop the smaller pieces at your command; the premature frontal assault will lead rapidly to defeat. Even as you move forward according to your strategy, you must have a defensive structure that can handle strong counterthrusts, the inevitable crises that will arise through no fault of your own. All your pieces relate to one another, and can create across-the-board strength or lead to numerous crisis points. Stalemate is always a possibility, but may be preferable to a bold sweep that ends in a crushing defeat.

Just as chess is the most complex of games, the presidency is the most complex political and governmental enterprise imaginable. It is elementary that you must think ahead in chess. For the presidency, the board is vastly bigger, the pieces and players far more numerous, the rules and boundaries of the game much vaguer, the time frame of the exercise much longer and the stakes much higher. A strategic approach is clearly necessary here as well. And yet something about the office—the kind of men who reach it, the time pressures from the inevitable crises, the institutional fragmentation and rivalry, even within executive government itself—resists a strategic approach. Overcoming these problems and doing the obvious will not be easy.

## D. Politics and Policy

Of the four dimensions of executive government, two are constantly at war. In fact, no tension that you face will be more

difficult to resolve cleanly, or more important to resolve successfully, than the perpetual conflict between policy and politics.
Reconciling policy and politics is at the heart of a strategic
approach to the domestic presidency. It is thus worthy of special
note.

The presidency is not merely a political office, but if it is not
political it is nothing. You are chief executive, commander in
chief, chief economic policymaker, chief proposer of legislation,
chief of state, and many other "chiefs" of this or that. But as you
actively practice the politics of governing, you must constantly
exercise the traditional politician's skills in order to be effective
in your various "chiefdoms." These old-fashioned political talents may have withered under the hot, telegenic pressures of
media campaigns, but they are vital if you are to govern: both
the genial talents—the personal contact, use of persuasion, patience, ability to compromise, development of personal trust
and goodwill (even when disagreements are deeply felt and
hotly contested); and on occasion the hardfisted talents—the use
of threats, pressure, favors and perks in ways that reward
friends and punish adversaries.

When you hear the strains of "Hail to the Chief," you may be
tempted to forget you are first and foremost a politician. But
that would be a mistake for a number of reasons.

    —Chief among them is the consuming need to untangle the
potential conflict we have described above between the politics of governing, nomination and general election.
    —Your electoral mandate means far less than you might
think. After all, not that many of your fellow citizens actually
voted for you.* And you cannot assume that your support was
issue-specific, that the voters who propelled you to office endorsed every position advanced by your issues staff. All presidents pretend that, because they were selected in a national
election, they somehow speak for the whole nation. This is a
thin fiction. You may have a more national perspective than
other actors on the political stage, but you must still forge

*In 1976 less than 30 percent of the eligible voters cast their ballot for the victor in the
presidential campaign. (Only about 65 percent of the eligible voters were registered,
and, of registered voters, only 83 percent actually cast their ballots and of those voting
only 50 percent marked their ballots for Carter.)

coalitions and alliances with particularistic interests if you are to succeed. Waving the wand of the electoral mandate is likely to be a futile gesture.*

—The traditional alliances of American politics that were forged in the early thirties have been eroding and changing since the mid-sixties.[3] Many of President Carter's major legislative initiatives were sent to Capitol Hill without strongly based political support from the nation's organized political interests, and this in part accounted for their demise. An issue like energy creates all sorts of new cleavages in the political system—not the least being a heightened regional rivalry between the energy-poor Northeast and the energy-rich Southwest. And the traditional Democratic coalition of yore—liberals, labor unions, minorities—has clearly lost its cohesiveness on a number of legislative issues. Organized labor, to take one example, did not work with much enthusiasm for President Carter's initial welfare reform plan. In sum, as we discuss below, we have entered a period not just of single-issue groups but *single-issue coalitions:* you can get supporters for one major controversial issue, but the coalition may fracture into many pieces when you pursue another goal of equal prominence and controversy. It will, in other words, be hard, if not impossible, to create a multi-issue coalition of governing that will stay with you on a range of matters.

—Perhaps most important for you directly, two presidents —Richard Nixon and Jimmy Carter—paid a high price for being uncomfortable with the personal aspects of the politics of governing. They tried to insulate themselves from the routine give-and-take of the Washington political game—from bargaining, persuasion and compromise. Had Nixon not been so isolated, perhaps he would not have been as prone to cross the line from acceptable to unacceptable behavior. Had the first-term Jimmy Carter been less isolated at the beginning of the administration and more cognizant that he needed the support of others to achieve controversial objectives—support that had to be won, not just demanded—his record in the

*If you win in a landslide and run ahead of members of the Congress, you may benefit from the goodwill created by the coattail effect—so long as you stay popular. But in the last decade the general rule has been that representatives and, to a lesser extent, senators have been more popular in their districts or states than the sitting president.

domestic presidency might have been different during 1976–80.

As president, you must, of course, be a politician with a purpose—a purpose that finds expression in policy. It is fine to promise the American people that your presidency will bring about economic well-being, social justice and a decent life for all. But now you have to do something about it. And just as you face conflicts and contradictions at the three levels of politics, so you will face equally difficult problems in trying to make sense out of policy. As we discuss in more detail below, this is due in part to the ineluctable conflict between policy objectives today—you can't have it all. But there are more subtle problems. Time pressures, mind-bending detail, lack of knowledge, disagreement among your policy advisors and more widespread disagreement among policy experts in the society at large make your policy world an uncertain, confusing and contentious place.

But the complications of these confusions and contradictions within the respective spheres of policy and politics are compounded when you try, as you must, to bring the two worlds together. And the tension between them cuts across all facets of executive government.

—The rhetoric of politics (simple, evocative) is often hard to reconcile with the language of policy (dense, technical). You will be perpetually tempted by the big (but often misleading) simplification that has short-term political impact but longer-term dangers (since messy reality will catch up with and mock it). But the alternative to the dangerous simplifications of politics may be the unintelligible and politically unappealing complexity of "policy-speak" (even if it gives a better account of that same messy reality).*

—Your political advisors—even those most concerned about the politics of governing and not of renomination and election—often have very different concerns and approach

---

*For instance, a case can be made for long-term fiscal restraint in response to the present high rate of inflation. But in the world of politics, the case almost inevitably gets boiled down to the symbolic and simplistic—and misleading—call for a balanced budget.

problems through a different set of questions than do your
policy advisors. Your political advisors ask whether it will sell
on Capitol Hill or placate a powerful committee chairman or
satisfy an interest group that is important on another bill.
Your policy advisors ask: What is the nature of the substantive
problem? What are the causes? What are the probabilities that
the preferred solution will achieve its objectives? How much
do the solutions cost? What are the competing uses of the
funds? Which levels of government, if any, should be given
what kinds of responsibilities?

—*The increasing professionalism of both the political advisors and
the policy advisors has served to widen, not narrow, the gap in language and approach.* Both the political and policy types have
become experts in their own fields, armed with their own
technical paraphernalia—from elaborate polls and election-
law memoranda for your political gurus to computer models
and research studies for your policy wizards. Rarely do the
pollsters ask the really subtle questions that could provide
concrete guidance to the formulation of major but necessarily
detailed policy. Indeed, a discussion between your political
and policy advisors can be akin to a cocktail-party discussion
between a doctor and a lawyer about malpractice. The divisive impact of increasing professionalism in *both* the political
and policy spheres has not been adequately appreciated by the
press, by the policy and political types themselves, and by
those, like you, who must fuse and make sense out of their
respective arcana.

—You must, of course, constantly struggle with the tension
between what is possible (which is what your political advisors are paid to tell you) and what is preferable (the province
of your policy advisors). An energy plan may be a thing of
beauty, but only the historians will admire it if it is launched
with fanfare in the East Room and immediately sinks to the
bottom of the Potomac. Yet an energy plan that is merely the
result of endless congressional haggling may be no plan at all.
In short, you may be able to craft a coherent approach to
policy but find that, even with extraordinary leadership, it is
not as yet (and may never be) politically viable.

—And if all this, even in its barest outlines, is not daunting
enough, there is the more subtle but ever-present tension

between the lack of information that bedevils you in the political world and the lack of information that besets you in the policy world. For example, the policy types may in all honesty be able to tell you that there is only a 40 percent probability that their cost estimates (on a synfuels program, for example) or their predictions about behavior (the effect of a politically painful gas tax on consumption, for example) will be accurate. And even if the political types consult with great care before you announce an innovative policy, they may not be able to predict with much accuracy what will happen to the proposal politically because the relevant actors outside the administration will not really examine it in a detailed, critical way until *after* you have become publicly committed to it. Very often the tension between policy and politics is a conflict not between facts or well-developed positions but between guesses. In reconciling policy and politics, you will find that in important respects you are ignorant about both.

But however great the tension between policy and politics, they cannot be separated. A fundamental mistake—and one that was made continually during the Carter administration's term —is to isolate politics from policy. The President's chief political advisors cannot be uninformed or uninterested in the substance of policy. That substance is politically charged, with important implications for the politics of governing, renomination and reelection. Without an understanding of policy details and the relationship between major policies, it is impossible to gauge the political impact of and devise appropriate strategies for specific issues—let alone to devise and then revise the overall strategy of governing.

Similarly, the policy people must constantly have a double vision. They must do a superior job of analyzing problems and designing the most feasible and sensible solutions, but they must also constantly keep your differing political needs in view so that they do not simply indulge in hypothetical paper exercises that are of no real-world value to you. Every policy proposal must be judged not only on its merits but also in terms of its implications for the politics of governing (can it pass the Congress? will state and local governments accept it?), the politics of nomination and the politics of election. There is a delicate balance here: the policy people should not try to be too political or they will foreclose options before you or other key actors see them, yet they should not blue-sky it either. They should lay *their* preferences out in such a way that you can see *your* pitfalls.

The political analysis should be just as systematic as the policy analysis itself. Your political advisors should thoroughly understand the various political forces that may affect the policy. They should have enough understanding of substantive detail to be able to test out alternatives with potential allies and adversaries (and not just ask: "Do you like Policy X?"). They should also have the suppleness of mind to enjoy and move easily between the politics of governing, nomination and general election.

We cannot be too emphatic. If you want sensible decisions presented to you, you must insist that your political people and your policy people talk systematically to one another on a wide range of issues. This may require locking them together in a room periodically. If so, do it. But the better solution is to stock the key positions in your administration with an all-too-rare but hardly extinct species of governmental animal: political people with a well-grounded knowledge of and aptitude for policy, and policy people with a well-grounded knowledge of and aptitude for politics.

As regularly as the seasons change, you will read charges that you are too political or that you are not political enough—that you are bowing to unseemly political pressures in order to save the shell of a proposal, or that you are pigheadedly persisting in the face of overwhelming political forces. Whatever is said about you in the short term, there is one best combination of policy and politics in the four-year context of governing: significant *results* in policy innovation, policy implementation, crisis management or moral leadership.

In a very real sense, you face no greater challenge in functioning as the domestic president than to blend policy and politics properly. It is one of the most creative acts of your presidency, and one of the hardest to achieve. It is not too much to say that the question of whether you will find a role as a historic domestic president turns in large measure on whether you can find important policy themes and then move creatively to breathe into them political life.

## E. The Battle Plan

Not every strategic dimension of the administration can be reduced to writing, but there should be a concrete embodiment of the strategic approach to the domestic presidency, a carefully crafted and quite explicit plan of battle on the major issues that will give direction to your government. In simplest terms, this plan should point your administration where you want to go and describe the milestones along that path. But commonsensical as it sounds, a battle plan, an explicitly articulated strategy of governing on the major issues, is not usually developed at the beginning of a president's term (although administrations may have looked back three years later and wished they had done so).*

Articulating such a battle plan is often avoided because, while commonsensical, it is also devilishly difficult to craft. We recognize that, but believe that the discipline of the process is crucial, however painful and time-consuming it may be. Vague platitudes about a strategic approach are fine: but only an actual process that asks the complex of related questions—and then seeks answers that have operational force—can make it happen.

• *What is in it?* The strategy of governing should consider separately and then weave together the four basic elements of executive government with a constant appreciation of the relationship between aims, constraints and available resources. In outline form this means:

—All significant issues in policy innovation, policy implementation, crisis management and moral leadership that will face the administration should be identified to the extent possible. These will be policies you may want to initiate or policies you will be forced to confront because of external pressures (that is to say, a strong congressional push for a

---

*It is interesting to note, for example, that although Hamilton Jordan wrote his now famous how-to-get-elected-president memorandum to a then-obscure former governor of Georgia long before November 1976, there was not a comparable strategy memorandum on how to be president, despite the flood of papers produced for the President-elect's transition in the fall of 1976.[4]

particular bill). These policies should then be roughly divided into categories according to relative levels of policy importance: presidential, mixed presidential/secretarial and secretarial. The number of issues in all three categories may total up to two hundred, but as noted, only about five to ten should be presidential and twenty-five to thirty-five presidential/secretarial.

—This initial identification and ranking of the important substantive issues should then be tested against political considerations. Can these substantive issues be handled in the politics of governing? Can you assemble political coalitions inside the Congress and in the rest of the political system that will be able to drive your policies to completion, or near completion? Then, assuming that alliances can be identified for accomplishing first-order policy priorities within the framework of the politics of governing, those high-ranking choices ought to be tested against your political advisor's four-year plan for the next nomination and general election season. If you have to make choices between those different spheres of political concern—between, for example, an important bill that could pass the Congress but that would alienate an important group active in your nomination effort—these choices should be presented to you as sharply as possible as early as possible.

—Politics and policy should then be merged. You will, by your own lights, have to decide. Do you agree with the substantive preferences? How do you balance those preferences on what is desirable with an assessment of what is politically feasible as you govern? Given a choice of priorities for governing, what are the costs or choices in terms of both the politics of future nomination and general election processes? After this merger, the issues should be sorted once again into the three categories.

—On timing, you should then carefully plot out how the major issues—at the various levels of importance—will move in the four-year time frame. What is the order of battle? When do you plan to move what, where? What has to be accomplished initially before the second wave can be launched? And this exercise will turn mainly on the forums in which these issues will be determined. Overload of committees of the Congress in policy innovation or a single department in policy implementation must be avoided.

—At this point, you will also have to bring in the foreign policy issues—where a similar process should be taking place —and try to reconcile the foreign and domestic policy priorities.

—On structure, you should set forth how you want the Executive Office of the President (EOP) organized and how the EOP should, as a general matter, relate to the departments and agencies.

—Similarly, you will want to provide guidance on how you want the basic processes of executive government to work: among them, policy development, congressional relations, external political relations, budget-making *and* the updating of the battle plan itself.

—Finally, specific strategies for the various high-priority issues that will be deemed presidential should also be articulated. This means development of: internal timetables and processes for deciding specifics on those policies; methods of consulting and garnering political support before the policy is finally shaped and announced; steps to ensure that the policy is carried out—either successfully piloted through the legislative process or systematically embedded in the management of the departments and agencies. If you can't see quite clearly how these preeminent issues should unfold, think again about whether they deserve their first-rank status.

• *What form should drafts of the battle plan take?* Obviously the strategy of governing should be very closely held because of the sensitive questions it addresses. It can be summarized in writing for you and you alone by a top aide on your personal staff, presumably the chief of staff. But it must be shared with—and tested against the views of—the top officials in your administration, both in the EOP and the departments. This can be done at high-level meetings either through oral presentations or off outlines.

• *When to make it.* The strategy of governing should be crafted immediately after the election, and considered and revised during the less than ninety days until the inauguration. It is both most important and most difficult to do it then because you are least prepared and there are other tremendous pressures, primarily choosing (or replacing) key personnel.

• *When to update it.* Since the first cut at the battle plan is likely to be very rough because of time pressures between the election and the inauguration, the strategy should probably be reassessed three and then six months after you are sworn in. After that, reconsideration every six months is probably about right, unless there is a major unforeseen crisis.

*The strategy must be organic, not mechanistic.* You must be prepared to change and move with events, because dramatic developments over which you have no control may dictate what is wanted and expected from your office. But the strategy must not be blown off course by every gust of the political winds. The whole point is to give your administration direction for four years, and to be able to see the inevitable short-term crises in a larger time framework and from a broader perspective.

But if the strategy of governing should be updated every six months, there should also be a mechanism for day-by-day or week-by-week appraisal of its progress and the problems it is encountering.

• *How to make it.* Development of the strategy of governing is not something that you have to do personally, although your personal involvement is critical at the end. Your chief of staff, who unlike all other senior EOP officials and all the Cabinet secretaries is responsible only to you and to no other institution of executive government, is the appropriate person to drive the process, with the Vice President having a direct consulting role.[5] The chief of staff must seek the counsel of the senior staff and the Cabinet, develop different broad choices for you, seek your initial guidance privately, go back to the senior staff and the Cabinet and test out various options, and then frame the major questions for an open-ended discussion with the top members of the administration. After that, you can decide if you need additional work done or whether you can simply make decisions.

• *Who should know?* After decisions are made, you should communicate them to the senior staff and to the Cabinet. Presumably this should be done at a day or two of high-level meetings early in the administration, and then subsequently as part of the process of updating the strategy.

—As to the major policy issues, you will obviously have to make a public case for your priorities. This case should not be phrased in exclusive terms—that you are concerned about these issues and these alone. But you must indicate to the nation what your priorities are and why. As noted, this agenda-setting function is critical within the administration but also as a matter of highly publicized politics.

—But just as you must make a strong public case for the final choices about your substantive priorities, you must keep confidential within your official family your broad determinations about the reconciliation of policy and politics.

—On substance and process, you obviously cannot and should not write a constitution for the executive branch. You must, however, communicate the broad rules of the game to your key officials—the broad concepts about how you want the executive government to operate. Obviously, problems will develop. To the extent that you have to deal with these individually, you may want to send a written directive to the relevant parties (for example, setting out how you want a special initiative on the auto industry organized and carried out). But if you write down something as potentially explosive as the ordering of the power relationships within your administration—even on a discrete problem—the danger of a leak is extremely high. On the other hand, if you communicate orally, there is always fuzziness and ambiguity (not that a written document would remove all ambiguities). Nonetheless, providing a broad oral description of the basic organizing concepts and principles to your key people is the best you can do at the beginning of the term. Especially at that point, substantial goodwill should exist in your official family. Since you have just received the votes of tens of millions, your prestige within an administration you have just personally appointed will be unsullied by the trials and rivalries of governing.

We must emphasize one point: structures and personalities will inevitably not perform as expected, and patchwork arrangements building on strengths where they are to be found will become necessary. But even while acknowledging that improvisation will be necessary and that the strategy of governing should be reviewed and changed with the course of events, we cannot reiterate too strongly that you should explicitly articulate such a strategy for the limited audience at the top of executive government. It is a discipline that you and all the key actors who work for you should undergo.

## F. A Word on the Transition

The transition period is the bridge between running and governing, and the two should be differentiated. Indeed, as many have noted, running for office often undercuts the president's ability to govern because the themes struck, expectations raised, commitments made and relationships forged between the president and his immediate campaign staff may be ill-suited to meeting the demands of executive government.

The eighty days of the transition are thus key to the next four years. But they are especially crucial to the first six months, months that are in turn of signal importance to you. They are a period for launching some, though not necessarily all, major initiatives. And false starts here are extraordinarily costly. Some argue in fact that Carter's domestic presidency never recovered from a number of basic mistakes made in the first half of his first year.* The first six months will also create the first impression of you as chief executive. And, if you are to sustain the momentum from the election, first impressions are critical. You must give a sense of control and direction: to your immediate staff, to the rest of the administration, to Congress and the press, and to the public at large. Thus, you must use the transition period clearly to put running behind you.

*For example, the Carter administration was bedeviled for most of the first two years —some would say for the whole term—by a hastily conceived energy program that was developed by only a few of the concerned parties within the administration and launched in April 1977 without much consultation with key actors in the administration or the Congress or with those outside the government. That program led to an interminable and largely unsuccessful legislative battle during the 95th Congress that, with the exception of partial natural gas decontrol, not only failed to produce significant energy legislation—a substantial defeat in itself—but adversely affected all other administration efforts (such as social security financing, tax reform and welfare reform) in the Senate Finance and House Ways and Means committees. It was a strategic mistake of the first order, failing to join policy and politics, and undertaken with flawed processes of policy development.

The transition should have two distinct phases, but during both you should shun publicity. The two and a half months between the first week in November and the last week in January are the longest time you will have for reflection until you leave office (either on your shield or with the flags flying) or until the day after you win reelection. Take advantage of it—and let a little mystery grow about you.

The *first phase* of the transition should be devoted to personnel:

—Resolve the questions surrounding your personal staff immediately. Otherwise uncertainty and jockeying for position will create enmity and tension among those closest to you, deflecting the staffers from your concerns while they plot out their route to a cushy office with a suitable view. *But* the need for speed does not obviate the need to go outside. The tradition of youth on the personal staff and age in the Cabinet should be cast aside. If Jimmy Carter could get senior people of the caliber of Lloyd Cutler, Hedley Donovan and Bob Strauss to work in a close personal capacity toward the end of a faltering first term, you can get senior people to serve in the important positions close to you in the heady opening months of a new term.

—Choose the Cabinet quickly, too. Like you, they have an enormous amount to learn, no matter how involved they have been in some of the issues handled by their departments. And the Cabinet secretaries themselves have as many as thirty to forty top positions to fill immediately. If you wait until late December to designate your Cabinet, your administration will limp along with many key positions unfilled until late spring or early summer, five or six months into your term.

The *second* phase of the transition should be devoted to a single goal: developing the substantive and political strategy for governing. You will be pressed to start making immediate decisions: about the fiscal 1982 budget or about this or that issue threatening to break after the inauguration. Wait. Step back. Look at the four-year period. Decide what is important. Decide the order of battle. And consult widely—even with your adversaries. You will at least understand more clearly the arguments

that will be used against you. Working on the strategy now will
have costs. There are other urgent matters pressing for your
attention. And because time is short, the initial strategy will
only be partial—will, as noted, have to be updated soon. But if
you don't start the process during the transition, you may never
get around to this most critical task.

Two final notes of caution:

- Don't assume that just because something was done or
tried during the last four or eight or twelve years that it was
wrong. Be skeptical, but not condemnatory. New administrations may waste a great deal of time rediscovering the obvious.*

- Don't let your transition chiefs seek top-level jobs during
the coming term, except in unusual instances.†Rivalry between campaign and transition staffs can subvert the transition process, to your great detriment. The transition people
must be willing to serve you and you alone, and must not even
give the appearance of wanting to feather their own nests or
advance their own special causes.

## G. Some Limits—and Some History

The strategic approach to the domestic presidency and its
many companion suggestions are all beads on a very thin thread
of rationality. They represent not much more than an attempt
to apply common sense systematically to the task of orienting

*If you have been reelected, don't assume that just because it was done during the last
four years it was right.

†Ideally, you will have had top people working on alternative ideas for the coming
term's strategy of governing as early as six months before the general election. These
people should be outside the campaign structure. Preferably they will be headed by an
elder statesman with substantial executive branch experience who should not threaten
those within the campaign because of a clear desire to help you through the transition
and then return to private life.

*Alternatively,* the positions of your transition leaders in a new government could be
clear from the start. This is much more difficult, since you won't really know the shape
of the administration until the campaign is over.

While the transition staff should be concerned with the bits and pieces of executive
government, their most important task is to begin to bring alternative strategies of
governing into view. Only you can decide the initial strategy after you understand the
terms of your election, know who your key actors will be and consult with the Congress.
But the transition group can assemble some of the key building blocks of your initial
strategy.

yourself toward the presidential office—and toward executive government. But certain dynamics in the executive branch have frustrated realization of this practical ideal in the past and are likely to do so again in the future, absent an extraordinary effort on your part or on the part of those close to you.*

These include:

—*Integration or Incoherence?* Integrating all the competing and related aspects of substantive policy and then connecting that substantive overview with all the competing aspects of the disparate political worlds (the politics of governing by themselves are wonderfully intricate) is a task of supreme difficulty. Our description of this job, filled though it has been with warnings about complexity, hardly does justice to the challenge. And no matter how talented are those who attempt this task, you can be sure that the strategic coherence they recommend to you will be only a pale and imperfect approximation of the world as it is. Worse, you may discover that the world won't come together into a coherent view—that the conflicts between worthy objectives during your presidency are simply too profound or that an integrated, coherent position on policy is an utter impossibility in politics.

—*Presidential Personality.* Even to get part of the way through the fog of complexity will require ample intellectual and organizing will on your part or on the part of someone who is truly your other self—whom you trust completely. The strategic approach to domestic affairs requires, in other words, personal skills and temperament for which there is no training and on which the presidential selection process does not put a premium. You may have been a political executive before, but there is nothing like being the chief political executive. You are likely to have some of the requisite strengths, but not all. You will never succeed totally in integrating the various dimensions of executive government. And since presidential personality is a factor with an importance far beyond the space we give it in this memorandum, in the end you must

*In Chapter 2, we discuss the constraints that might prevent you from realizing your goals *even if* you were able to fashion a strategic approach such as the one we recommend. Here we are indicating the kinds of problems that will prevent you from even fashioning a very sophisticated strategic approach.

know yourself (maximize your strengths, compensate for your weaknesses) and do it your way (in a way that is comfortable for you, with people whom you trust). But you must ask yourself how far toward the practical ideal of the strategic approach will you get with your style, abilities and temperament.

—*Personnel.* Finding the right people to staff your administration is also extraordinarily difficult. They too must have an unusual collection of talents for which there is no particular training. Government—especially executive government—is a profession that requires its own special combination of skills. But your top appointees must also possess that mysterious capacity of being able to disagree without disliking one another, and must recognize that their ultimate interest lies in helping and supporting you. And choosing people is, like so much you will do, a roll of the dice.* You won't know how they will work out beforehand, although good personnel practices can reduce the problems. If 60 or 70 percent of your top appointments work out, you will have done very well. That still leaves you with some very serious problems, however.

—*Campaign Bias.* As noted, presidential attempts to manage executive government in the past have been hampered by the tendency to promote to positions of importance those who were close to the President during the campaign. Only rarely do top political aides—especially in this era of media and image politics—bring the requisite governing skills to your service as chief executive. Yet if you let it happen, these aides can skew executive government away from strategic balance and prevent others from doing what needs to be done.

—*Lack of Tradition.* The key offices and relationships of executive government are as changeable as the tides, and every administration has to learn how to structure them, but often at a tremendous cost.

—*Crises.* The old saw "The immediate is the enemy of the important" will continue to be applicable. The problems of the moment will always crowd out strategic thinking—if you let them. There are major crises and pseudo-crises. While you

*Said John Kennedy during the 1960 transition: "I must make the appointments now; a year hence I will know who I really want to appoint."

must deal with the former (some of the time), others can deal with the latter. But the pressures to chase down the blaring headline or the lead network news story can easily take up most of the day of most of your key people. At times you will feel that executive government is merely government by press release.

—*Fighting the Last Battle.* There is an iron law of institutions: successors have to be perceived as dramatically changing the practices of predecessors. Presidents may come in and fight the last battle—the one their predecessor lost—but it may not be the important struggle of the moment. Surely Carter did himself no good when, in an attempt to demonstrate his "integrity" and separate himself conclusively from the duplicity of Watergate, he tried to keep to the letter of many of his campaign promises, even though these were too ambitious, ill-suited to the temper of the times or in direct conflict with one another.

Of these limits, your personal style and the personnel you select are the most important. Indeed, to our verities of policy and politics, substance and process, we should add presidential style and personnel selection. Jimmy Carter promised a government as good as the people, and in a sense he was right. His government depended heavily on his key people.* Only they, and you, can bring the judgment, experience, intellect, sensitivity, humanity and will to huge, faceless and ponderous institutions and try to make them work, or at least work better. The right people can give the strategic approach a chance. But without them the thread of rationality and common sense will break, and the connected beads of the strategic approach will, like your support in Washington and the nation, tumble helter-skelter.

---

*In a 48-page memorandum to Jimmy Carter dated November 3, 1976, and titled, "Some Thoughts on Organizing the Executive Office of the President," Jack Watson concluded with the following:

> After all is said and done about how to organize governments and White House staffs, the success of your presidency and your reflection in history will be determined, not by organizational structures or management theories, but by people. In the final analysis, you really have only one initial task of overriding importance—and that is to choose wisely and well the men and women who will serve with you in this great adventure.
>
> God be with you.

• • •

It is for the historians to opine whether previous Presidents have tried to adopt the strategic approach—and whether they have succeeded. And an ability to join successfully policy and politics, substance and process with the right presidential style and administration personnel in the service of an articulated vision is certainly not the only standard by which to judge presidential performance. Surely, after the experience of Richard Nixon, one must also step outside the strategic approach and ask whether its particulars are appropriate to the times and to the traditions of the nation.

Nonetheless, it is our impressionistic sense that we are urging an essential quality that has eluded many presidents of the modern era.

Listen to James McGregor Burns describe Franklin Roosevelt at the end of his second, and in many ways his most difficult, term, and remember that Burns is discussing the most successful of the modern presidents, the man who, more than any of his successors, was able to join policy and politics and to get things done:

> . . . Roosevelt to a surprising degree was captive to the political forces around him rather than their shaper. In a democracy such must ever be the case. But democracy assigns a case for creative political leadership too. The forces handcuffing Roosevelt stemmed as much from his own actions and personality as from the unyielding political environment. He could not reshape his party, reorient foreign policy attitudes, reorganize Congress and the bureaucracy, or solve the economic problem largely because he lacked the necessary intellectual commitment to the right union of ends and means. . . .
>
> Roosevelt, in a sense, was captive to himself as well as to his political environment. He was captive to his habit of mediating among pressures rather than reshaping them, of responding eclectically to all people around him, of balancing warring groups and leaders against one another, of improvising with brilliance and gusto. . . .
>
> Roosevelt was less a creative leader than a skillful manipulator and a brilliant interpreter. Given the big decisive event—depression at home or naked aggression abroad—he could dramatize its significance and convey its import to the American people. But when the

*crisis was less striking but no less serious, and when its solution demanded a union of intellectual comprehension and unified and continuing strategic action, Roosevelt saw his efforts turn to dust,* as in the cases of court packing, the purge, and putting his country behind efforts towards collective security. He was always a superb tactician, and sometimes a courageous leader, *but he failed to achieve that combination of tactical skill and strategic planning that represents the acme of political leadership.* [6] [Emphasis added.]

When historic forces are not creating a unifying momentum for political action within the nation—as depression or war did— then the need for a strategic approach to the presidency is even greater. When the nation is confused, the conflicts are growing, and there is not a clear sense of direction, then the margin for presidential error is smaller, and your opportunity to have a substantial impact reduced.

To move from the first to the most recent of the modern presidents, Jimmy Carter had enormous difficulties in his term —difficulties for a man who was hardly Rooseveltian in his ability to communicate with the nation or to operate tactically. These troubles can be traced, in important part, to an absence of a strategic sense in general and a lack of one of the four basic strategic elements in the more particular failings of the administration.

Clearly, the results of the Carter domestic presidency were viewed by observers from all points on the political spectrum as less than good. The economic policies were not successful, as measured by almost every major indicator. Though a Democrat, he had difficulty working with a Democratic Congress; on most major legislative initiatives, in either social or economic policy, he suffered major defeats and could show few significant victories. He could not balance the budget, as he had pledged, but more important, he failed to articulate for the nation or for the Congress new approaches to the federal budget in a constrained period. In management, he emphasized reorganization when the real issue was efficiency and increased governmental productivity. There were also problems in managing crises, from Bert Lance in 1977 to the coal strike in 1978 to the gas shortages of 1979 to the remaking of the budget in 1980. He had great difficulty keeping his own house in order.

At best, the term left a very uncertain domestic legacy.

Clearly, executive government under Jimmy Carter during 1977–1980 manifested some basic problems. There was no overall strategy of governing in domestic affairs. Politics and policy were not effectively fused. There was little initial understanding of the constraints on the domestic presidency—from the Congress, the press, the interest groups and abroad—and this naturally precluded any strategic thinking. Despite the lip service paid to the role of the Cabinet, that role was not well defined. There was little appreciation of how to balance the competing needs of centralization and decentralization that are at the core of executive government. There was substantial confusion about how the immediate presidential staff and the larger staffs in the Executive Office of the President were to relate to one another and then to the major departments and agencies. Accordingly, there was enormous waste of time and confusion about what should be taken to the President for decision when.

Let us be clear. No direct cause-and-effect relationship exists between the disappointing results and the Carter administration's inability in the first term to manage a strategic presidency. The constraints that we will describe in Chapter 2, as well as many other factors, contributed significantly to the difficulties. But it is hard to believe that the record would not have been substantially better if some of the difficulties which were of the administration's own making had been avoided.

Perhaps most modern administrations have had similar difficulties—and have suffered from an inability to be strategic. Kennedy probably did not develop a sense of strategy—of how to link his substantive priorities in domestic affairs with the politics of the time—until midway through his third year in office. Johnson was brilliantly strategic in policy innovation, waiting like a fox for the 1964 election before his brief but leonine legislative moment in 1965–67, but was less able to deal with executive structure and process and left executive government incapable of absorbing administratively what he had wrought legislatively. Nixon probably did not develop a coherent view of domestic affairs until late in his first term—a budget-cutting, decentralizing vision that was substantively coherent but politically at odds with the still powerful liberal impulses of the period. In any event, coherence came too late to be tested, sunk as it was with Watergate. Ford probably never really had enough time; on the presidential calendar, the 1976 election season began late in the summer of 1975, leaving him only twelve months (from August 1974 to August 1975) to develop and implement a strategic approach. Perhaps Eisenhower came closest to having a strategic approach, with a clear (if pared down) domestic agenda and a sophisticated understanding of the workings of large executive institutions. But his minimalist view, while successful for him and on its own terms, left a legacy of unfinished national business that led to the convulsions of the 1960s.

Perhaps there is a tragic potential here. Crafting a strategic approach presents extraordinary problems. But beyond that is the unpleasant possibility that, however good your performance, we are at one of those points in our national life when the confusion and fragmentation produced by deeply rooted and historic forces will defy even the most outstanding leader and confound even the most brilliant planning. It is possible that a coherent and consistent set of policies appropriate for our times will be utterly lacking in political viability. Whether your task in the early 1980s is Sisyphean cannot be foretold. But the imperatives of seeking a strategic presidency in this age are inescapable. No other approach can work—unless fortune smiles and unexpected forces beyond your control propel you to the top of the hill.

# II·
# THE RIDDLE OF
# THE EIGHTIES:
# CONSTRAINTS ON
# THE DOMESTIC
# PRESIDENCY

To plan and manage a strategic presidency in domestic affairs, you must understand in considerable detail at the outset of your administration the forces that will limit your powers. These constraints—competing institutions and complex practices, available resources and public attitudes—have changed markedly during the past twenty years; so much so, in fact, that some argue you will attempt to govern in "a new American political system."[1] Only if you and your top aides can accurately assess these constraints can you develop a realistic set of expectations about what you can accomplish during your time in office. Indeed, realistic expectations are essential:

- to avoid deceiving yourself.
- to forge a strategy of governing that blends the inevitable high-risk issues you will have to take on with issues that have a greater chance of success.
- to develop a public rhetoric that deals with the real problems of governing, not just the pieties of your party or the unalloyed virtue of your ideals. This rhetoric should educate the politicians, the press and the public about those problems so that your performance can be more fairly evaluated when compared to that of other institutions and actors.

The Constitution, of course, prescribes a system of shared authority, setting forth the general powers and limits of the Congress in Article I, the President in Article II, and the judiciary in Article III. But the formal powers and limits defined in the Constitution are well known to you. They do not, in any event, give you a feel for the real nature of your power and the real constraints on that power.*

Rather, the system of shared powers, competing interests, limited resources and contradictory attitudes that you face is better understood in terms of the specific realities of the present. In the vastness of the executive branch and in its manifold activities, as well as in your personal qualities and the personal qualities of the top officials in the administration, you have significant resources at your command. For all the talk of presidential weakness, the fact remains: you administer a budget of more than $600 billion (approximately one-fifth of the GNP); you can, through your political appointments, bring some of the nation's most talented and energetic people into executive government; and to the extent that you wish, you can be constantly at the center of national political attention.

This is not to say you don't face significant obstacles. It is only to underscore that your problem is not lack of formal constitutional authority to shape events, nor even lack of more informal sources of influence. Rather, it is whether you can marshal strategically the powers mandated to you by the Constitution and the resources given to you by statute to work within the existing configurations of power—or to establish a new balance of power—as you push against existing constraints in dealing with the difficult substantive and political problems that you choose to face, or must face, as domestic president.

---

*To be sure, important constitutional questions may arise during the coming term (for example, is congressional inclusion in statutes of one or two house veto provisions constitutional?). But there do not appear to be any constitutional issues of extraordinary magnitude on the horizon—issues like the scope of the commerce clause (used by the Supreme Court to strike down New Deal legislation in the thirties); or the civil rights implications of the commerce clause and the enforcement clause of the Fourteenth Amendment (used to justify unprecedented extensions of federal, and executive, power in aid of civil rights in the sixties); or the questions of impoundment and executive privilege (which were resolved in part by the courts and in part by the Congress in the seventies).

Understanding the nature of present constraints is not easy, however.

*First,* putting present realities in perspective requires a sense of history. That sense is sorely lacking in most contemporary journalism and political discussion outside academia.

*Second,* in the manner of all candidates, you campaigned as if the powers of the president—and the ability to bend a host of institutions and actors to your will—are greater than in fact they are. Your campaign workers tried to portray you as a strong, decisive figure who could get the nation moving again or back on the track or whatever. This has created an unrealistic public expectation of a dramatic leap forward. A Rooseveltian hundred days may occur only once or twice in a hundred years. A sense that the end of the election season signals a dramatic shift in the conditions of national social, economic and political life exists even though the dominant public attitude about government is sour skepticism, not the buoyancy prevalent in that now distant age of the early 1960s.

*Third,* presidents before you have rarely (perhaps understandably) made an effort to explain the limits on their power to the people. After experiencing extraordinary difficulties in domestic affairs during his first term, President Carter started talking quite a bit about constraints, although not systematically.[2] He asserted that, facing difficult problems, he was not afraid to make the hard choices, but he did not often give a persuasive public account about why those problems were so difficult. Often it appeared that they were considered difficult because the President had not, in his first term, been able to deal with them successfully. As in so many other areas, the President's instincts were good, but his execution somewhat less than that. One of your tasks will be to lay out the problems, indicate the difficulties in effecting change, make a case for what you can and cannot do, and where appropriate, share some of the responsibility with others inside and outside of executive government.*

*Finally,* the traditional measure of the great domestic presidents in the twentieth century may not be very relevant to our time. These presidents—in part because of their personal skills

*It may be time for a major presidential speech, perhaps at a commencement, on changes in the institution of the presidency.

and in part because they arrived in office on the crests of historic tides—secured passage of a host of landmark bills that at the very least dramatically changed the structure of federal statutory law and at best actually changed underlying social and economic conditions. But these periods of dramatic legislative change—1913–15 under Wilson, 1933–35 under Roosevelt and 1964–67 under Johnson—are the exception, not the rule.

To give you a sense of present limits, we will discuss the broad constraining influences on your power to act by comparing key features of your domestic-affairs world with the world as it may have appeared to the president in 1965. There are differences— and the limits on presidential action are greater. For Democrats, a Lyndon Johnson without a war is not going to happen. For Republicans, the New Deal and the Great Society are not going to be rolled back. For both, we have entered a very different era —that much is obvious. But the comparison will highlight the reasons why.

Many of these constraining factors have been discussed in detail elsewhere, but we think it important to summarize for you in one place the most fundamental or structural realities, laying them side by side. Individually they are important limiting conditions, but cumulatively their impact is quite profound, constituting a significant challenge to your personal and governmental skills.

## A. The Economy

Fifteen years ago, the economy was a strong ally of presidential power. It appeared to respond magically to executive will, providing on a lavish scale the resources needed for a long agenda of social reforms. Today the economy is perhaps the greatest adversary of presidential power. It appears to mock all executive ministrations, provides insufficient resources for government's numerous objectives, and vexes presidents with choices between politically unacceptable evils.

You take office during a period of cyclical recovery. Over your first year, unemployment may be falling and—barring another oil shock—inflation may show some minor abatement. But do not be deceived: such a cyclical upturn is only sweet froth on a basically sour brew.

The economy you inherit suffers from long-term structural weaknesses. You have an obligation to work diligently at correcting these, *but the problems are very stubborn and your efforts will show few tangible results over the next four years.* If you don't apply yourself consistently to this thankless job, the whole economic edifice could develop serious cracks during your incumbency.

During the campaign, you did not discourage speculation that you would soon coax from the economy all the usual virtues of prosperity: rapid real growth, high employment, and reduced inflation. But that optimism will soon be tempered by a basic fact of economic life. Everywhere you look in the area of economic policy, you face major constraints.

**1. Then and Now.** Both John Kennedy and Jimmy Carter took office as the economy was emerging slowly from a recession. Kennedy cut taxes and launched the economy on a seemingly limitless sea of full employment, low inflation, and robust real growth. By 1965, the major economic problem was the wondrous tendency of the progressive tax structure to reap more revenue out of economic growth than the federal government could spend. What to do with this embarrassing fiscal dividend—whether to cut taxes some more, or think up new federal spending programs, or give it away to state and local governments (unblessed by progressive tax structures)—was the major source of controversy in economic policy.

The Carter term also began with a stimulus package comprised of both tax cuts and spending increases. As under Kennedy, the result was a prolonged expansion. But there the resemblance ends. The Carter expansion was storm-tossed by inflationary acceleration and financial crises (first with the dollar and then in the bond markets). Where the 1960s boom was ultimately consumed by the Vietnam War, Carter's self-destructed in a major new recession.

The story of the two recoveries is told by the table on page 58. Though by now familiar, the story is nonetheless sobering, and crucial to your own predicament—for your recovery will likely resemble Carter's far more than Kennedy's. Since the mid-sixties, price stability has given way to high and chronic inflation. Even during expansions, the economic system seems unable to keep unemployment low. The system has virtually

*Average Annual Figures*

| | 1961–65 | 1976–80 |
|---|---|---|
| Inflation | 1.3% | 8.8% |
| Unemployment | 5.5% | 6.7% |
| Productivity growth* | 3.5% | 0.7% |
| Trade balance | −$5.4 billion | −$27.1 billion |
| Oil import bill | $1.8 billion | $50.0 billion |
| Average federal tax rate on median-income family | 10.2% | 16.4% |
| Federal budget deficit | $4.6 billion | $50.0 billion |
| Federal budget deficit as percentage of GNP | 0.8% | 2.5% |

* The growth of real GNP per hour of labor effort in the private, nonfarm business sector of the economy.

ceased generating increases in real production per employee. Our international accounts have swung toward deficit, and oil imports have exploded, weakening the dollar. Tax rates have soared for the average family, but the resultant revenues have been insufficient to erase a large, stubborn deficit in the budget.

All of these economic problems are interrelated in complicated ways. Working to solve one often will make some or all of the others worse, at least in the short run. In no other area of domestic affairs will it be more important for you to fashion a realistic four-year strategy of governing—and in no other area will the options be less appealing. The fundamental constraints will arise in three dimensions:

- the inflation/unemployment dilemma.
- the productivity problem.
- the energy problem.

## 2. The Inflation-Unemployment Dilemma.

(a) **The basic issue.** The most difficult and critical presidential problem in economic policy remains what it has been for decades: whether to emphasize high employment or price stability. In the very long term, the two objectives are probably complementary. Over a four-year span, however, they are in conflict.

Your first year in office may present you a rare gift—a simultaneous decline in the inflation and unemployment rates. The 1980 recession will have left a reservoir of idle resources. This gap between the economy's actual and potential (that is to say, fully employed) flow of production will put some downward pressure on inflation. For a period you can put idle resources to work (reducing unemployment) without significantly weakening the downward pressure exerted on the inflation rate by the gap between actual and potential production. There will, however, come a point—much sooner than you would like—when further progress on the unemployment front will so narrow the gap of idle resources as to stop, and then reverse, progress on the inflation front.

Your dilemma is cruelly simple. If you wish to make the inflation rate fall significantly, you must maintain a considerable gap between actual and potential production—and thus maintain a high unemployment rate—for an extended period.* The dilemma is cruel because its dimensions are large. The unemployment rate needed for decelerating inflation is very high, perhaps greater than 7 percent, and the period you must hold it up there is excruciatingly long—almost certainly four full years, and quite possibly longer—to cut the inflation rate from its current 10 percent to about 5 percent.

Fifteen years ago, the economics of inflation was a simpler and more pleasant subject. It was thought then that inflation (*any* inflation) could appear only if the economy was heated up beyond "full employment," then generally estimated at about 4 percent unemployment, and that inflation (*all* inflation) would vanish swiftly if recession sent the unemployment rate much above 4 percent. This relatively simple trade-off between inflation and unemployment was the stuff of elementary economics textbooks, and events in the 1950s and early 1960s seemed to bear the theory out. But the economic turmoil of the last fifteen years has drastically altered professional views of the inflation-

*The discussion below assumes that changes in the inflation rate depend on the size of this gap between actual and potential production. There is some evidence that the *speed* with which the gap is narrowed or widened also affects changes in the inflation rate. We ignore this subtlety here to keep the exposition as simple as possible.

unemployment dilemma in three crucial respects.

*First:* Most economists now doubt that there is in fact *any* trade-off *in the long run* between unemployment and inflation. Rather, the trade-off is between unemployment and *changes* in the inflation rate. A high (low) unemployment rate makes the inflation rate fall (rise), while a particular pivot-point unemployment rate simply maintains inflation at its prevailing pace, *whatever* that pace might be—for example, 4, 6 or 10 percent a year. You will start with inflation in the 10 percent range. If you would like it to fall over your term, you must tolerate an unemployment rate above the pivot-point rate *until* you reach an inflation rate you can accept—at which point you can allow unemployment to return to that pivot-point level.

*Second:* This pivot-point level of unemployment—the level at which the inflation rate remains constant—is not full employment in any socially desirable sense.* More particularly, it is not 4 percent unemployment. The best contemporary research places it at about 6.5 percent unemployment. This means that, to cause a *decline* in the inflation rate, you must keep unemployment *in excess* of 6.5 percent, probably at 7 percent or more. The 6.5 percent estimate is very approximate (the guesses range between 6 percent and 7 percent), and it may fluctuate somewhat over your term. But there is no question that the pivot-point rate is at least half again as high as the 4 percent full-employment rate bandied about in the 1960s.†

*Third:* Economists are now convinced that it takes a very long time for high unemployment to bring about sizable declines in the inflation rate. The problem is attributable to *expectations* about inflation. In some markets—commodities, retail goods,

---

*In technical, economist's jargon, the pivot point is called the natural rate of unemployment, or the non-accelerating inflation rate of unemployment.
†For this, there are several reasons. The labor force now contains a higher proportion of women, minorities, and youth, groups that traditionally have higher unemployment rates than the adult white males who dominated the work rolls in the 1960s. Also, inflationary expectations may have become more sensitive, on the up side, than in the two decades of virtual price stability following World War II. It is also possible that liberalized social programs and the increased availability of part-time jobs outside the formal economy cushion some of the blow, making unemployment a less effective depressant on inflation. Finally, markets for many goods and services today may be tighter than in the 1960s, in the sense that increases in economic activity push more quickly against shortages of supplies and capital than in the past. None of these factors can be altered swiftly by federal actions. Over the next four years at least, you are stuck with an uncomfortably high pivot-point unemployment.

and some industrial products, for example—prices are very sensitive to the interplay of demand and supply. If actual production falls below its potential, creating a reservoir of unused assembly lines or supplies, inflation rates drop sharply in these markets. But in other markets—of which the labor market is the chief example—variations in demand and supply do not have a rapid impact. In these markets, prices are set over relatively long periods, and therefore tend to reflect the expectations of market participants about what the long-term inflation rate will in fact be. For example, firms and their workers usually set wages for 12-to-36-month periods. To promote a fair and stable working relationship, they try to keep these wage rates roughly in line with the long-term inflation trend—which means with their expectations about inflation. They will largely ignore short-term fluctuations in the inflation rate, whether up or down. Accordingly, to reduce the rate of wage inflation significantly requires a period of market slack sufficiently sustained to change long-term expectations—that is, to convince all involved, by results, that the inflation rate is itself on a permanent downward course.

This does not mean that wages or labor unions are the cause of inflation. In fact, wages have typically risen markedly less rapidly than prices over the past decade's several episodes of inflationary acceleration. But by the same stubborn mechanism, wage inflation will *fall* markedly less rapidly than other elements of inflation in any period of general market slack. Because wages constitute two-thirds of business costs, the inertial force of expectations makes a dis-inflationary policy one requiring many years.

No one knows how fast wage expectations would adapt to a sustained policy of high unemployment. Some economists think that after a year or so the change might occur relatively quickly, cutting perhaps 1.5 to 2 percentage points a year from wage inflation. Other economists doubt the decline would be as much as a point or so a year. Neither side can prove its case, for this painful course has never been followed in modern America.

Politicians—both liberal, big-spending Democrats and conservative, tax-cutting Republicans—are reluctant (to put it mildly) to face this issue candidly. Their evasiveness is understandable: to accept high unemployment for an extended period as an explicit tenet of policy is an almost certain prescription for human suffering and political disaster. The pain of unemployment is acute and tangible, especially for the poor and for minority groups: the unemployment rate for blacks is typically twice that for whites; for black youth in urban centers, the unemployment rate sometimes shoots over 50 percent.* At the same time, progress on inflation is undramatic—often proceeding at so leisurely a pace as to escape public notice (and praise). That politicians (whatever their rhetoric) almost invariably opt for high employment, rather than for a long, arduous campaign against inflation, is hardly mysterious.

But this choice has a major cost. Over the last twenty years, the government has methodically pushed up the long-term inflation rate by pushing unemployment below the pivot-point level. Accordingly, each recession has begun with inflation at a higher level.

| Last Year Before Recession Beginning In: | Inflation Rate (GNP deflator) |
|---|---|
| 1960 | 2.1% |
| 1969 | 5.5% |
| 1973 | 7.5% |
| 1980 | 8.9% |

If, like your predecessors, you choose not to take the cost in unemployment of moving the inflation rate down to a lower plateau, you will probably end up with a higher inflation rate as a result of the economic recovery that will follow the 1980 recession. The precise pivot point between maintaining the inflation rate roughly constant and moving it to a higher plane is hard to discern, and harder still to hold.

(b) **Complications.** Even if you hold unemployment at a high level, your progress in pushing down the inflation rate may be subject to major, dispiriting interruptions or reversals on two important fronts.

---

*Moreover, if you look at the number of workers experiencing unemployment at some time during the year, the unemployment figures become more dramatic. For example, during 1980, the number of workers experiencing unemployment may rise to a historic high of 22 million, or about 20 percent of the total labor force. With an average of 2.8 people per household, more than 60 million will be directly affected by unemployment.

• *Surprises and shocks.* Quite apart from the general degree of market slack in the domestic economy, the general price level can be bumped temporarily upward by any number of discrete, erratic explosions in the prices or costs of particular goods. From 1977 through 1980, the rate of wage inflation crept upward steadily from 7.9 percent to 9.6 percent, but *overall* inflation, as measured by the consumer price index (CPI), fluctuated much more widely, coursing from 5.8 percent in 1976 to 18 percent in early 1980, and back around 12 percent in late 1980. These gyrations in the CPI measure were caused by discrete shocks to the price level. The most notable villain was oil: even a minor interruption in oil supplies by OPEC can trigger an explosion in world oil prices. This raises the consumer price index, because oil and oil products (chiefly gasoline) play such a significant role in the U.S. economy. For every 10 percent rise in oil prices, the U.S. inflation rate rises about 0.5 percent over one year. Similarly, food prices often soar when harvests fail—or when government price support rules are liberalized. Business costs rise whenever payroll tax rates or minimum wages are increased by legislation. A tariff will raise the domestic prices of the goods subject to it (and of everything that competes with those goods). A rise in interest rates will cause a temporary explosion in the housing costs component of the CPI.

These discrete "shocks" do not directly increase the long-term inflation rate. They merely increase the price *level*—causing a temporary one-time rise in the inflation rate. But these price level increases can register psychologically on employers and employees, enter into wage bargains, and thereby creep into the long-term rate of wage inflation—unless met by a *general* policy of demand restraint across the whole economy. This is a formidable problem. In many cases, you can take action to avoid shocks—for example, to avoid tariffs, expensive regulations, or other policies that jack up individual prices—but such anti-inflationary decisions will invariably prove very unpopular with some powerful interest group. In all cases, you can minimize the aftereffect of shocks on the long-term inflation rate by keeping general demands on the economy in a restrained posture. This is how Germany absorbed the 1973 oil price shocks without a serious rise in its long-term inflation rate. But if shocks are large and frequent, the general demand posture (and the unemployment rate) required to hold down inflation is even more draconian than the already painful stance required in placid circumstances.

• *Trade and the dollar.* When the dollar sinks abroad, the domestic price of everything we import increases—and so does the domestic rate of inflation. Each 10 percent decline in the average value of the dollar (relative to other currencies) boosts the domestic inflation rate by about 1 percentage point after a year or so. Inflation effects aside, dollar stability is important to our economic and political posture throughout the world.

But the requirements of dollar stability will impose another stiff constraint on your management of the domestic economy.

—To keep the dollar stable, U.S. inflation rates must stay roughly in line with foreign inflation rates. But other nations —Germany and Japan in particular—have shown a remarkable determination and ability to keep their inflation rates low, even in the face of major oil shocks. On the inflation criterion for currency stability, therefore, the United States is likely to be at a relative disadvantage.

—Dollar stability also requires that the United States not run markedly larger international deficits than the other major currency nations. Unfortunately, our trade deficit tends to expand, relative to our trading partners' deficits, even when all of our economies are growing at the same pace. Why this is so, no one knows for sure—but it *is* so. Thus in order to keep our trade deficit in relative alignment, our real GNP must grow *more slowly* than the foreign average. This is what we did from World War II through the early 1960s. But in the middle and late 1960s, our GNP growth rate increased relative to foreign growth rates. This is one reason the old system of fixed exchange rates collapsed in the early 1970s, forcing a big, effective devaluation of the dollar. We also grew faster than the foreigners during the recovery period from the worldwide recession of 1974–75. And again the result (by 1978) was a collapse of the dollar. If you choose a fast recovery from the 1980 recession, you will likely have dollar woes by 1982.

—Finally, there exists abroad—in private hands and in the coffers of foreign central banks—a multi-hundred-billion hoard of dollars, built up over the long postwar period during which the dollar was as good as gold. These dollar holders can at any time diversify at least some of their holdings into other currencies or assets. If you give them the least excuse to do so —by letting the inflation or trade balance factors go sour—the slide of the dollar can be very swift and disorderly. This foreign overhang of dollars makes our currency's value inherently fragile and greatly limits your margin of error in making economic policy.

(c) **Policy complications.** Two sorts of policies are available to you to deal with the inflation-unemployment dilemma: so-called macroeconomic or demand policies, and wage-price policies.*

The two tools of macroeconomic policy are monetary policy (the manipulation of the money supply and interest rates) and fiscal policy (the manipulation of budget deficits and surpluses). These demand policies operate, in theory, in the same manner: they regulate total demand for goods and services in the economy, thus pushing actual production up or down relative to potential production, narrowing or enlarging that gap which determines whether the long-term inflation rate will move up or down. Monetary policy regulates demand by controlling the growth rate of the money supply, while fiscal policy does so by supplementing (detracting from) private sector demands with a budget deficit (surplus).

This sounds very tidy, but there are major complications:

• Economists increasingly believe that monetary policy, not fiscal policy, is the really influential determinant of total demands, and thus of unemployment and inflation trends, over the long term. And monetary policy is controlled not by you but by the Federal Reserve Board. On this theory, the Fed can largely or entirely offset the demand effect of a budget deficit by keeping money supply growth low—that is to say, by refusing to create new money to finance the budget deficit. The budget

*Your policies for raising productivity growth will also have an impact on inflation, but this impact has often been overstated, as noted immediately below.

deficit under such constrained circumstances will simply cause interest rates to rise, as the Treasury sells bills and bonds to finance the deficit with old money supplied by private lenders. The level of total demand on the economy over the long term will not be changed by the deficit. Rather, the money supply will determine the total level of demand, and the deficit's size will merely determine the mix of demands as among government spending, private consumption, and private investment. To the extent this theory is true, you in fact will have little to say about the long-term course of inflation and unemployment (except by lobbying the independent Federal Reserve Board).

This is not an academic consideration. The present Fed has embraced the theory and has been committed since late 1979 to a policy of methodically squeezing down inflation through tight control of the growth of the money supply. Each year the Fed plans to set targets for money supply growth lower than the year before. This may well guarantee that the next four years will see relatively high unemployment and (hopefully) declining inflation—whatever your fiscal policy.

• Even if we assume that fiscal policy has an independent effect on total demands—and it probably does in the short run —you will have a difficult time arriving at the proper fiscal policy. As we note later in this chapter, there are formidable institutional and political problems in manipulating the federal budget for macroeconomic purposes. But there is also a more basic problem: picking the proper budget deficit or surplus requires a series of steps that may well be impossible. First, you must decide how much decline in inflation you want, given the (uncertain) unemployment rate needed to attain it. Second, your economists must determine how much (or little) total demand is needed to attain that objective. Third, your economists must figure out how much of that total will be forthcoming autonomously from the private sector. Only then can your economists take the final step of recommending the budget deficit or surplus needed to adjust private demands to the desired total. In many respects, these final steps are the most difficult. Forecasting private demands, and the impact on them of budget deficits and surpluses, has become an ever more tricky enterprise as inflation and inflationary expectations have come to dominate private economic behavior. Your economists will have at their disposal all the sophisticated computer models of the economy developed over the last decade, some of which have close to a thousand complicated equations covering every market from oil to underwear. But the models have proven disastrously wrong in forecasting both inflation and sharp turns in economic activity—the two things most important to you as a fiscal policymaker.

Even if you navigated all these intellectually treacherous shoals with some confidence, you would still face the difficult task of selling your recommendations to a country and a Congress increasingly skeptical about the logic of the whole enterprise. The people would like you just to balance the budget. They may grudgingly accept apologies or excuses for failing to do so during a steep recession, but at other times you will have a very tough time explaining why a particular deficit or surplus is desirable on grounds of managing total demand in the economy.

• Wage-price controls or guidelines are in theory a way to shorten the period of unemployment required to work down the inflation rate. They do this by forcing down, through legal fiat or moral injunction, that component of inflation which takes a long time to respond to demand policies—for example, wage inflation. Most economists would concede that wage controls or guidelines have a certain logic, as a complement to macroeconomic restraint, but the option is not without serious problems.

The arguments usually lodged against controls and guidelines include the following: (a) You will still need fiscal and monetary restraint. Otherwise prices generally will not fall swiftly, and the unions will rebel. But once you have controls, or a well-observed program of guidelines, the rest of the political system will expect you almost immediately to reorient your fiscal policy toward reducing the unemployment rate. If you acquiesce in this, the resultant demand pressures may well blow the lid off the controls or guidelines scheme. (b) The unions will demand price controls or guidelines as well (even though prices generally respond quite swiftly to demand restraint), and price controls or guidelines will ultimately create so many inefficiencies and distortions in all markets as to worsen inflation by reducing the economy's productive potential. (c) Controls and guidelines will not help you prevent such shocks and surprises as world oil or food price increases; you cannot control prices on international markets. At best, controls or guidelines can keep the shock effects from passing through fully to wages. (d) Controls require legislative authority. Getting it from the Congress, and maintaining a political consensus behind a controls program, would consume virtually all of your time and political capital in domestic affairs. (e) Voluntary guidelines tend to disintegrate into massive evasion without your constant personal attention.

**3. The Productivity Problem.** The unemployment-inflation dilemma centers on the gap between actual and potential production in the economy—the gap of idle resources which simultaneously determines the unemployment rate and the degree of downward pressure on the inflation rate. Fiscal and monetary policies—the so-called demand policies—alter the size of this gap by manipulating the level of *actual* production. Recently, economists and politicians alike have focused attention on the level and growth of *potential* production. Potential production reflects the *supplies* of productive factors—for example, labor, capital, and technology—the growth of which are determined largely by forces other than demand pressures on the economy.

The reason interest has focused on the supply side is that the growth of productive potential has been stagnating in the United States. In the 1960s, our productive potential—that is to say, potential GNP, indicated by the resources available to generate real GNP—grew at about a 3.7 percent annual rate; in the early 1970s, at about 3.4 percent annually; and more recently at about 2.5 percent. The labor force, of course, continues to grow —indeed, at a record rate as women leave the home—but the growth of capital (plant and equipment and productive skills) and technology per worker has fallen off drastically over the last fifteen years.* As a consequence, real GNP per worker (so-called labor productivity) is growing far less rapidly than in the past.

Whatever its precise causes—still a source of controversy among economists—the collapse of productivity growth raises serious problems for you in four areas:

*In the 1960s, the labor force grew by 1.7 percent a year and the capital stock by 4.5 percent. In the 1970s, the figures were 2.4 percent and 3.2 percent. Thus the ratio of capital to workers has slowed its rise, growing at 2.8 percent in the 1960s and 0.7 percent in the 1970s. There is also evidence that technological progress has slowed over the last fifteen years.

(a) **More inflation.** A slowdown in productivity growth narrows the gap between potential and actual production, thus putting upward pressure on the inflation rate. For example, if productivity growth in 1979 had been 3 percent, as it was in the 1960s, instead of being slightly negative, inflation might have been lower by more than 3 percentage points.

This suggests that you can fight inflation by boosting productivity growth. Unfortunately, however, this unassailable proposition has been oversold. On the most optimistic reckoning, available policies (for example, big pro-investment tax cuts, summing to $25 to $50 billion in revenue loss by 1985) can raise the productivity growth rate by only 0.5–1.0 percentage point or so over a five-year period, which would cut inflation by about the same amount—0.5–1.0 percentage point. You have inherited an inflation rate of about 10 percent. Cutting it by *one-tenth* over five years would not constitute much of an anti-inflation program.* So working *solely* on potential production—on the supply side—will not solve your inflation problem. For that, unhappily, you will also need demand restraint, lower actual production and thus high unemployment.

(b) **Stagnating real income growth for the citizenry.** Productivity growth is the way a nation increases its real per capita income over the long term.† Per capita real income grew at 3.2 percent a year from 1960 to 1965, but has since remained below 3 percent and for extended periods below 2 percent. This stagnation of income growth is of direct concern to nearly all Americans, but particularly to the poor, near poor and middle-income working people. Furthermore, as income growth slows, the nation as a whole loses some of the native vitality and optimism which have in the past helped presidents maintain social civility and a measure of social progress in times of political, racial or cultural turmoil. Finally, long-sustained sluggish productivity growth will erode the nation's economic strength relative to that of other major industrialized nations. U.S. per capita

*Furthermore, wages often tend to rise in concert with trend increases in productivity, nullifying productivity's contribution to a lower inflation rate.
†In the short run, per capita income can be increased simply by running the economy with a smaller gap of idle resources—that is to say, making fuller use of currently available labor, capital, and technology resources.

income has already fallen behind Germany's, and Japan's growth will see her overtake us in the early 1980s. What weight a president should put on such mechanical rankings is, needless to say, unclear. But you cannot simply ignore historic trends which threaten to transform the general world position of the United States.

(c) **Less government—or more.** A government lives off the production of its citizens. When the nation's productive potential was expanding by 3.7 percent a year in the 1960s, the U.S. government's activities—public services and investment, income transfer programs, defense—could grow at that same robust rate without enlarging the federal sector relative to the private sector of the economy. As productivity growth has slowed, however, the nation has been gradually forced to choose between less *real* growth in federal activities or an expansion in the federal share of the total economy. The latter course has often been followed:

|  | 1960 | 1965 | 1970 | 1975 | 1980 |
|---|---|---|---|---|---|
| Federal Revenues as Percent of GNP | 18.6% | 17.8% | 20.2% | 19.3% | 20.8% |
| Federal Outlays as Percent of GNP | 18.5% | 18.0% | 20.5% | 22.9% | 23.0% |

Budget outlays and tax revenues have both increased markedly as a share of GNP over the last twenty years, outlays by more than 4 percent of GNP, revenues by 2 percent of GNP. As the nation's potential growth in real income has slowed, the government has kept real tax revenues growing at a swift pace by raising tax *rates*. In 1965, the median-income family paid an average 9.3 percent of its income to the federal government and faced a marginal income tax rate of 17 percent. In 1980, the corresponding figures were 17.6 percent and 24 percent.

The combination of rising tax rates and stagnating real income growth has put a severe squeeze on many Americans. During the 1960s, real incomes after tax rose by an average of 4.1 percent a year. For the 1970s, the average annual increase was only 3.4 percent, and much of that from a temporary increase in the growth rate of the labor force.

**(d) Policy conundrum.** The fourth problem raised for you by the slowdown in productivity growth is the difficulty of doing anything about it. The difficulty has three aspects.

• As noted, economists are uncertain about the causes of the productivity slowdown. Perhaps one-fourth to one-third of the slowdown can be laid to a falloff in the expansion of the nation's per capita stock of capital—of plant and equipment per worker. The rest has been attributed to a falloff in average skills and work experience in the labor force, to a decline in technical innovation, to sectoral shifts in the economy, and to myriad other factors. With the causes so unclear, proper solutions are obviously hard to formulate.

• Reversing productivity trends is a very slow process. Putting new capital in place takes a number of years. Altering the rate of technological advance may be a matter of decades. You cannot count on showing large results over your term in office.

• The chief policy tool available, business-oriented tax cuts to spur investment, raises several problems. Such tax cuts, unless offset by spending reductions or tax increases elsewhere, expand the budget deficit.\* Expanding the deficit may prove inconsistent with the fiscal policy stance you want for anti-inflation purposes. Furthermore, expanding the deficit may itself *inhibit* investment: the government must borrow in private capital markets to finance the deficit. Such borrowing competes with private borrowers—both corporations and individuals—and thus pushes up interest rates.† Higher interest rates, in turn, tend to choke off investment in many sectors. In this way, tax cuts designed to spur investment generally can end up merely shifting investment from one sector to another. Whether that will boost overall productivity growth is an open question.‡

Finally, pro-investment tax cuts are of necessity regressive in character: the cuts go more to high-income than low-income

---

\*By raising the economy's productive potential, such tax cuts permit a faster rate of economic growth in the long term, thereby recapturing *some* of the lost revenues. But this effect is partial and very much delayed.

†The Fed could keep interest rates low by pumping more money into the market, but this would add to inflation.

‡The answer is *probably* yes, because the net result would be to boost industrial investment and to curb investment in housing. Most economists suspect the United States overinvests in housing, due to tax subsidies in that sector, and that a shift of capital from housing to industry would raise overall productivity. But this is all somewhat conjectural.

taxpayers, because investment is practiced largely by the well-to-do. An aggressive and sustained campaign to use the tax system to promote productivity growth will therefore encounter stiff political resistance and may be feasible only if coupled with large tax cuts across the board, for everyone. Funding such large, sweeping tax reductions by expenditure cuts would be extremely difficult. Financing the resultant deficits by government borrowing could easily offset the investment incentives of the productivity tax cuts.

**4. The Energy Problem.** Dependence on foreign oil will cast a dark shadow over every aspect of economic management during the next four years. The United States now imports about half the oil it uses, at a cost of almost $90 billion per year. Four years hence, we will likely still be importing about half of our needs, at a cost of perhaps $150 billion. The economic impacts of foreign oil dependence are severe:

—Higher OPEC oil prices—particularly sharp increases caused by temporary interruptions of supply—can easily undo several years of progress on inflation in a matter of weeks.

—The mounting dollar value of the oil import bill, though suffered also by our European and Japanese trading partners, often tends to undermine psychological support for the dollar.

—The rising price of oil leads to premature obsolescence of the nation's capital stock—built to run on cheap oil—and thus places a damper on productivity growth.

—The mounting oil bills of the less developed countries could create major international financial crises during the next four years, into which you will be drawn because of the ramifications both for foreign policy and for our own banks (which lend heavily to these nations).

—A significant and prolonged interruption of oil from the Persian Gulf would cause serious dislocations in our economy.

The obvious answer is to do away with dependence on foreign oil. But substantial progress toward this goal is very unlikely over the next four years.

—OPEC is learning how to manipulate its oil production so as to keep oil prices on a rising curve. Accordingly, even if we were to cut oil import *volume* significantly over the next four years, our oil import *bill* would continue to soar. For example, our oil imports dropped significantly in volume from 1977 to 1980, but the import bill rose in dollars from $45 billion to $86 billion.

—In fact there is little prospect of cutting oil import volume by a large amount over your term. Conservation efforts, spurred by oil price increases, are moving along well, but domestic oil production continues to decline thanks to the picked-over geology of the country. Natural gas production is up, but the vagaries of federal regulation could impede that about halfway into your term. Nuclear energy is frozen in politico-theological controversy. Production and use of domestic coal and shale oil—greater in energy potential than all of OPEC's oil reserves—is mired deep in environmental disputes and bureaucratic red tape. Solar and fusion energy have promise, but these are twenty-first-century technologies. Virtually all energy experts both inside and outside the government expect oil import volume to remain constant or to rise slightly between now and 1985.

Your chief job in the energy field is to construct political coalitions capable of springing loose from environmental bottlenecks the orderly and safe development of nuclear, coal, outer continental shelf oil, and shale oil energy sources. This will take four years of bruising controversy and imaginative bureaucratic and political innovation. If you succeed, the 1990s and early 2000s could see the country move toward significantly lower oil import volumes. But during *your* term, the outlook is for undiminished dependence on foreign oil—with all the economic dangers that entails.

**5. Summing Up.** Economic management confronts you with exceptionally difficult choices and constraints.

• You face a brutal trade-off between reducing inflation and reducing unemployment. As soon as the economy heats up enough to bring unemployment below about 6.5 percent, the basic rate of inflation will cease falling and begin once more to rise.

• Whatever progress you make on the inflation front can be swiftly erased by oil price shocks or large declines in the dollar's value on the foreign exchange markets.

• The basic tools of macroeconomic management are blunt and not entirely within your grasp. Monetary policy lies with an independent Federal Reserve Board; fiscal policy is hostage to technical problems of economic forecasting and even more serious institutional problems of budget-making; and wage-price policy may well be unworkable, both technically and politically.

• A secular stagnation in productivity growth—which will take years to turn around—is adding to inflationary pressures, dragging down the growth of real per capita income, and making the public and private sectors bitter competitors for an economic pie that is no longer growing at its traditional pace.

• The dependence of the United States economy on insecure sources of foreign oil—which will also take years to turn around—is seriously aggravating all of your other economic problems: inflation, slow GNP growth, declining productivity growth and the weakness of the dollar.

By tradition, all presidential candidates pledge to get the country moving again, to reinstate healthy economic growth in short order. Once in office, however, the melancholy truth unveils itself: huge obstacles block the nation's path to prosperity, and they can be moved only very slowly, and with considerable pain.

## B. The Federal Budget

The budget confronts every president every year with two distinct, though related tasks: establishing a fiscal policy, by proposing a deficit or surplus of a particular size, and establishing a program with sensible themes and priorities out of the thousands of activities that make up the flow of federal spending. Both these tasks have grown enormously complex during the last fifteen years.

*Perhaps the dominant constraint associated with the federal budget is that despite its huge size—more than $620 billion in actual expenditures during fiscal 1981—it is an extremely unwieldy and unresponsive instrument of public policy.*

**1. Fiscal Policy.** After a year or so you will smile ruefully at the very notion that you or anyone else actually makes fiscal policy. Here are the main complicating factors:

**(a) Economic confusion.** Today no two economists agree on the theory, much less the practice, of fiscal policy. As noted in the previous section, doubts have arisen on every front: because economists cannot accurately forecast the course of private demands, they cannot really tell you how much, if any, deficit or surplus is needed; because the economy evinces both high inflation and high unemployment at the same time, fiscal policy is constantly torn between conflicting objectives; because monetary policy has grown more influential and determined, the influence of fiscal policy on the economy is now clouded in doubt.

Over the past year or so, two new complications in fiscal policy have assumed prominence:

—Supply-side emphasis. Even within this school there is dissension. One group urges consistent large budget surpluses, because a surplus adds to the nation's pool of savings from which investment is financed; the other urges big (deficit expanding) tax cuts for business, to increase corporate savings and investment, and letting interest rates rise to divert investment out of housing and consumer durables into capital equipment.

—Budget-balance fever. The notion that the budget should invariably show a balance has developed a broad constituency in the country. But you cannot meet this popular demand, even if it made economic sense: the budget deficit not only influences but is itself influenced by the largely unpredictable fluctuations of private economic activity. Every one point increase (decrease) in the unemployment rate will swing your budget toward deficit (surplus) by about $25 billion—a $20 to

$22 billion loss (gain) in tax revenues and a $5 to $7 billion increase (decrease) in unemployment-related spending. Likewise, every change in the inflation rate will affect revenues (as private incomes change) and outlays (due to inflation indexing in many federal programs). A balanced budget is, in brief, a highly mobile target.

**(b) Congressional process.** The budget you announce each January will have been locked up for the printers almost a month earlier—and won't go into effect until the subsequent October. Once you announce it, the budget will virtually disappear into the congressional budget process, where politics and unfolding economic events will typically combine to produce a fiscal policy different from the one you proposed. You will get the congressional budget in big pieces (usually during September), one appropriation bill at a time. Having no line item veto power, you will have either to accept or to reject each big piece. The resultant mosaic will hardly be what you had in mind in January. Once in place, in October, the budget will be subjected to a whole new set of economic influences. By consequence, it is a foregone conclusion that the deficit or surplus you proposed in January is not likely to happen, or if it does, the revenues and outlays will be different from those you proposed. Here are some examples:

*Budget Deficits*
*(in billions)*

| | *Fiscal 1977* | *Fiscal 1978* | *Fiscal 1979* | *Fiscal 1980* |
|---|---|---|---|---|
| President's January proposal | 43.0 | 61.8 | 60.6 | 29.0 |
| First congressional budget resolution (May) | 50.4 | 64.6 | 50.9 | 23.0 |
| Second congressional budget resolution (September) | 50.7 | 61.2 | 38.8 | 29.8 |
| Actual result (twelve months later) | 45.0 | 48.8 | 27.7 | 61.0 |
| | | | | (estimate) |

**(c) Hidden items.** Despite its talismanic significance, the federal unified budget excludes all manner of activities a true fiscal policy would logically encompass. In fiscal 1979, for instance, the unified budget showed outlays of nearly $500 billion. But off-budget loans amounted to another $17 billion, and private loans guaranteed by the federal government were another $60 billion. In addition, regulatory programs annually mandate tens of billions of dollars of private expenditures. Inventive bureaucrats and congressmen have learned how to use these off-budget devices to avoid the formal controls established to discipline on-budget spending programs. The effect of all the off-budget items on the economy is only dimly understood. While you are struggling to shave or add a few billion dollars on-budget, many more billions from federal activities will be sloshing about outside the normal budget process.

**(d) Stubborn trends.** An important reason why you cannot really make fiscal policy each year is that every budget is overwhelmingly dominated by programmatic trends which are simply impervious to annual tinkering. Your control over the spending side of the budget is very limited.

For instance, in FY 1980, more than 75 percent of federal expenditures was uncontrollable: either permanent statutes mandated the level of spending by means of entitlements formulas or these expenditures constituted prior-year commitments (contracts, interest on the national debt). These expenditures are not subject to the annual appropriations process. The uncontrollables were only about 60 percent of the budget in the mid-1960s. Many of the uncontrollable programs are indexed to inflation, and are thus subject to sizable and often unpredictable increases every year. You can of course try to change the authorizing statutes or the indexing formulas, but in each instance this would involve major changes in laws and would ensnare you in a political battle of gigantic dimensions.

About 25 percent of the budget—$140 billion out of $563 billion in fiscal 1980—is subject to annual "control" through the appropriations process. But, as we will discuss below, a large percentage of this amount is also virtually mandated by well-entrenched political coalitions in the Congress—and if not politically untouchable, is almost as hard to cut back as the entitlement programs. A key constraint lies in the defense area of the budget. Almost half the defense budget is formally uncontrollable—that is, committed by prior-year contracts or statutory entitlements—and the rest of the defense budget is subject to overwhelming bipartisan demands in the Congress for annual real increases.

On the revenue side, your flexibility is similarly constrained. Tax laws are permanent: they apply until changed by Congress. In 1980 the tax law provided subsidies—so-called tax expenditures that allow special credits, deductions or deferrals—of about $180 billion. These can be altered only by a major legislative exercise in tax reform. Similarly, revenues rise of their own accord, in response to inflation (as noted, about $5 to $7 billion for each point of inflation), without the least assist from your January budget message. Altering this trend also takes substantive legislative action by committees (House Ways and Means and Senate Finance) noted for their independence and their lack of interest in the executive agenda.

(e) **The structural deficit.** This is perhaps the key constraint on your role as maker of fiscal policy: over the 1970s the federal budget acquired a sizable long-term, structural deficit, which will strongly resist your annual ministrations. The structural deficit has four elements:

—The explosion of social program innovations in the late 1960s and early 1970s—in food stamps, social insurance, subsidized housing, welfare, education, medical care—has built into the budget a huge, politically entrenched segment of programs that for a variety of reasons (chief among them inflation) tend to grow each year.

—The decline in military spending relative to domestic spending in the early 1970s has built up political pressure for an increased defense effort over the next five to ten years.

—Tax rates in 1980—for example, tax revenues as a percentage either of GNP or of personal income—reached the historic highs registered at the peak of World War II. Political forces will almost certainly keep federal taxes from exceeding for any length of time, or by very much, the nearly 21 percent of GNP attained in 1980.

—The collapse of productivity growth has pushed down the curve of long-term real income growth from which the tax system sucks up its increased revenues. Congress and presidents put all those permanent social entitlement programs into the budget in the 1970s, expecting that they would be financed by an economy growing at 4 percent a year in real terms. The long-term rate of real economic growth for the 1980s now looks more like 2.5 percent.*

*Taken together, these four structural features mean that even before introducing your own new tax cuts or spending programs to the budget you are likely to face a four-year regime of sizable budget deficits.* Because you take office at the tail end of a recession, modest deficits in the near term are both inevitable and economically justifiable. But as the recovery proceeds—as private sector demands revive, as the gap of idle resources narrows, as unemployment falls—anti-inflation considerations will call for shrinking these deficits. Your problem is that the structural features in the budget—the entrenched entitlement programs, the pressures for increased military spending, the pressure against further increases in tax rates, and the sluggishness of real income growth—will be at war with the objective of reducing the deficit. For you, fiscal policy will not be a neat year-to-year exercise in calibrating the budget to your macroeconomic plans. Rather, fiscal policy will involve a painful four-year struggle to rein in powerful programmatic and political forces tending to create deficits well in excess of what your economists will recommend.†

**2. Budget Priorities.** The last fifteen years have seen major transformations in the size, composition and nature of the budget.

• *Size.* Federal spending has grown from $118.4 billion in fiscal 1965 to $563.6 billion in fiscal 1980, an absolute increase of 376 percent and an increase in real dollars of 86 percent.

---

*For the next year or so, the economy could in theory grow somewhat faster, by eating into the idle resources created by the 1980 recession; but concerns about reaccelerating inflation will in practice keep the growth rate from exceeding its long-term potential by very much.
†We return to this problem in Chapter 6.

- *Composition.* In 1965, before the Vietnam buildup, defense spending consumed $50.2 billion. In 1980, the bill was $131.3 billion. Defense expenditures grew 162 percent in absolute terms but only 2 percent in real terms over the period, slipping from 7 to 5 percent of GNP. By contrast, spending on social programs moved from $37.2 billion in fiscal 1965 to $299 billion in fiscal 1980, expanding in absolute terms by 703 percent and in real terms by 214 percent, and jumping from 5 to 12 percent of GNP. In 1965, social welfare spending was 31 percent of the total federal budget, but by 1980 it had almost doubled and was a striking 53 percent of the budget. By contrast, defense spending was 42 percent of the federal budget in 1965 but had declined to 23 percent in 1980. In brief, the last fifteen years have seen the evolution of the federal budget into an instrument of social support on a par with the centralized governments of Europe.

- *The uncontrollables.* The importance of the uncontrollables is reflected in the striking growth associated with domestic programs during the past fifteen years. The most dramatic dollar increases came in automatic payments to achieve income security (social security, AFDC, food stamps, supplemental security income, unemployment insurance and civil service retirement), which grew from $26.1 billion in 1965 to $178.7 billion in 1980, an increase of 585 percent in absolute dollars and a real increase of 168 percent. The second big jump occurred in health care (medicare, medicaid, and veterans' medical care), which grew from $1.6 billion in 1965 to $54.1 billion in 1980, an increase in absolute terms of 3,181 percent and a real increase of 1,222 percent. These uncontrollable domestic programs are likely to continue to grow due to a number of factors, including the following:

—*Indexing.* Of the nearly 80 percent of the fiscal 1980 budget that is uncontrollable, nearly 30 percent is indexed—that is to say, benefits are tied to an inflation index, usually the CPI, and the payments to which individuals are entitled automatically increase. With inflation running at or near a double-digit rate for the foreseeable future, indexing obviously has an enormous expansionary effect on the federal budget. For example, benefits under the social security program alone increased automatically in fiscal 1980 by about $15 billion.*

—*Demographic Shifts.* With the aging of the population over the next two decades, the number of individuals eligible for the basic entitlement programs like social security, supplementary security income and medicare will increase, driving up program costs. For example, between 1980 and 1990, the population aged sixty-five or older will grow by about 5 million persons, or 20 percent.

—*Participation Rates.* In many of the federal entitlement programs, the number of individuals actually receiving benefits may be significantly lower than the number eligible for those benefits. This ratio—called the program's participation rate by governmental planners—can increase unexpectedly, however. In the last decade, for example, we have witnessed a dramatic increase in the participation rates in the AFDC program—from 45 percent in 1967 to an estimated 94 percent in 1977, according to one estimate.

—*Utilization: The Health Cost Problem.* The federal cost of health care has also skyrocketed; in 1970 medicare and medicaid expended $9.8 billion, but by fiscal 1980 this sum had risen to more than $50 billion, or almost 12 percent of the federal budget. Part of this increase is due to the extraordinary rise in the cost of medical services, but part is due to the increased utilization of medical services by the poor and the elderly.

—*Unemployment.* Choosing anti-inflationary policies that create unemployment also has a dramatic impact on the federal budget because, as noted, it increases federal expenditures for such programs as food stamps, AFDC, unemployment insurance, medicaid, and disability insurance.

**3. Guns vs. Butter: The Sixties vs. the Eighties.** The economic expansion of 1960–65 was skewed by the refusal of the Johnson administration to choose between guns and butter: with the economy near full employment, the administration decided to pump up defense spending for Vietnam without

---

*This *increase* is, for example, about equal to the combined budgets of the Energy, Interior and Commerce departments in fiscal 1980.

offsetting the added budget costs with either a tax increase or a cut in the social programs of the Great Society. The enlarged budget deficit generated inflationary pressures which began a fifteen-year flight from price stability.

You also face the guns-versus-butter dilemma in a highly aggravated form. You start with inflation already at about 10 percent and with a budget already locked into a structural deficit which, perhaps by 1982 and certainly by 1983, will be raising genuine inflation worries. Your economists will be berating you almost immediately to begin cutting back on *existing* spending programs and/or to consider new sources of tax revenues (for example, a gasoline tax or a value added tax). At the same time, however, powerful forces will be driving you and your budget in the opposite direction. The military, and its congressional allies, will press for real growth in the defense budget beyond the "3 percent per year" pledge made by President Carter. Many existing domestic programs will grow automatically, and there is still the need for important expansions in the areas of health, welfare, social security and the like. Moreover, well-organized groups will stoutly resist any cutbacks in entitlement programs. In many areas of public research and investment (particularly in the energy field) you will face enormous demands for expanded spending. In the tax field, the pressures to cut taxes (that is to say, to enact tax expenditures) will if anything be even more fierce. And middle-income groups, with widespread congressional support, will clamor loudly for generalized relief from the highest income and payroll tax rates in the nation's history.

To put the matter baldly: You are confronting a long list of fiscal demands upon a budget already too far into the red for macroeconomic peace of mind. Your government faces a real resources crunch for which there is no easy solution. And yet the battle of budget priorities will be an unavoidable problem you must confront, in very constrained circumstances, during the next four years.

## C. The Federal Enterprise

There are today more than 1,100 separate domestic programs that spend two-thirds of federal tax revenues (or more than $400 billion in fiscal 1980) on some national problem: among them, income security, education, health care, transportation, energy independence, community development, middle- and low-income housing, environmental and consumer protection, or job creation. As Charles L. Schultze, head of the Council of Economic Advisors under Carter and budget director under Johnson, has written: ". . . in the short space of twenty years, the very nature of federal activity has changed radically. Addressed to much more intricate and difficult objectives, the newer programs are different; and the older ones have taken on more ambitious goals."[3]

Our discussion of the federal enterprise focuses briefly on the problems of implementing those programs—not developing and securing the approval of new ones. Management and implementation have always been important functions of executive government, even though they have received a disproportionately small amount of public attention. But if, as appears likely, money for new programs is not readily available, more attention will be paid to how the already mandated billions are being spent. As former HEW Undersecretary Hale Champion has said, "Bringing up the children is as important as making babies."* And just as the federal involvement in national life has expanded and changed during the past twenty years, so the federal role in managing programs has altered. To be sure, time-honored problems remain (lack of continuity at political levels, overlapping responsibilities between departments), but there is a new reality—the federal government often doesn't implement programs itself but tries to supervise others, either public or private parties, who are charged with carrying out federal purposes.

**1. Key Indicators.** The role of the federal government in social and economic affairs expanded dramatically during the

---

*Two important constraints on policy implementation and program management are noted but *not* discussed here: *first,* the profound problems in ordering the relations between your top appointees in the departments and your top appointees in the White House and the Executive Office of the President; and *second,* how those political appointees are affected by forces that cut across your chain of command—congressional oversight, interest group concentration at the lower levels of the bureaucracy, issue networks and other forces pushing your Cabinet officers and top departmental officials away from your direct influence. They will be discussed at greater length in Chapters 3 and 4.

New Deal. But the legislative and administrative changes undertaken in the mid-sixties worked a change of equally dramatic proportions.

- *The domestic share of the federal budget\** has, as noted, grown from $59 billion to $417 billion (an increase of 609 percent, or 177 percent in real terms).
- *The departments* have grown from nine in 1965 to thirteen in 1980 with the addition of Transportation, Housing and Urban Development, Energy, and Education.
- *The federal dollars paid directly to state and local governments has grown from $11.1 billion to about $90 billion in the fifteen-year period.* Direct federal funding, as a percent of state and local expenditures, has generally increased from 15 percent to about 25 percent in the 1965–80 period, and has dramatically increased as a percentage of state and local expenditures for such functions as welfare, education, health care, roads, airports and housing.
- *The number of pages of regulations issued annually* has more than tripled from 1970 to 1978. And the number of administrative law judges to hear disputes arising from these disputes has more than doubled from 1960 to 1980.
- *The number of functional responsibilities of the federal government has also grown dramatically.* Merely reading the table of contents of any recent budget submitted by the President to the Congress will remind you of the vast sweep of federal involvement in our national life: the federal government is responsible for providing everything from income security through a gigantic system of transfer payments to job creation for the hard-to-employ to stimulating scientific research to determining whether to regulate recombinant DNA research or test-tube babies to fusion research to mass-transit subsidies to export production. These changes are not due to some mysterious creepy-crawly bureaucratic force. Most are due to national laws passed by the Congress. For example, the number of grant-in-aid programs in domestic affairs has, according to the Advisory Commission on Intergovernmental Relations, grown from 160 in 1962 to 498 in 1978. After all, most regula-

---

*The nondefense, nonspace, nonforeign share.

tions, the eternal bugaboo of those who decry the executive bureaucracy, are merely an attempt to implement acts of Congress.

• Yet with all this growth, *the number of federal employees has only increased from 2.4 million in 1965 to nearly 3 million in 1980.* The tremendous growth in federal programs, expenditures and involvement has been made possible because the federal government does not directly administer many of its programs, using instead a variety of intermediaries—state and local governments, private contractors, grantees or consultants—to carry out its purposes.* As Frederick C. Mosher has observed, the federal civilian work force has grown more slowly than the American labor force and the American population it serves, and only about 15 percent of federal spending is for functions actually performed by the federal government itself.†

In trying to give meaningful expression to the laws filling fifty volumes of the United States Code and the regulations which fill approximately 80,000 pages of the Code of Federal Regulations, you will face extraordinary problems—beyond the obvious one that you personally will not know what is going on with respect to 80 to 90 percent of the programs Congress has legislated into your branch.

Briefly stated, the most salient difficulties are:

**2. Confusion.** Congressional enactments have noble goals—end age discrimination, provide bilingual education, increase youth employment and so forth. But one does not have to serve in the government long or to read very many pieces of legislation to realize that there is usually a fair amount of confusion about what the goal actually means. What is age discrimination? Is bilingual education to teach English to non-English-speaking children or to teach them about their cultural heritage? Should youth employment programs focus on those who have finished school or those who have dropped out of school—and for what

---

*From 1955 to 1978, for example, the number of employees of state and local government increased by 172 percent (from 4.7 to 12.8 million). During the same period, the federal work force increased by only 17 percent.
†And half of this amount is for the armed services.

kind of work opportunities? If goals are unclear when the bill leaves the Congress, then managing implementation is necessarily difficult until your subordinates attempt to define what the goals mean with some specificity. And then those in Congress and within the interest groups who disagree with the attempted definition may rush into the departments or back to the congressional committee or into court to halt implementation as being faithless to the underlying congressional intent.

**3. Judicial "Administration."** If executive government does not carry out congressional mandates (as was the case in the Nixon era with respect to a number of social programs) or if groups are unhappy with the executive's interpretation of vague acts of Congress—and cannot get satisfaction in the departments or with the congressional committees who wrote the laws —litigation is often the result. Program implementation can be enjoined, pending resolution of suits; executive resources can be tied up responding to suits; or executive resources can be directed, in quite specific detail, by district judges, not Cabinet officers. There is nothing improper about recourse to litigation, but the degree to which it affects major departments may not be fully understood.* The courts have

> become increasingly involved as administrative participants. Responding to a flood of lawsuits, contemporary judicial decisions not only enforce but direct executive actions in policies dealing with the environment, prisons, education, housing, welfare payments, civil rights, health, and many other fields. At the end of the 1950s, for example, the secretary of health, education and welfare had several hundred lawsuits pending against him; at the end of 1975, he faced approximately 10,000 lawsuits, a large portion of which challenged some use of executive discretion.[4]

**4. Continuity.** It is well known in Washington but perhaps less clearly understood in the nation that the top political appointees of the president and his Cabinet officers don't serve for

---

*For example, about 1,200 to 1,400 court orders affect the Department of Health and Human Services in any particular quarter. Of those, about 300 to 350 are continuing, in that they require recurrent departmental oversight. Of those, 10 to 20 may be considered major, involving significant direction of departmental resources by a judge in a particular case.

very long. Yet it is these administrators, deputy secretaries, assistant secretaries, and deputy assistant secretaries who must try to give direction to management and implementation. Yet very few Cabinet officers last for four years, and very few sub-Cabinet officials last three.* Rapid turnover makes it difficult to provide continuity to the career bureaucracy that must make the programs work.

**5. Civil Servants.** With confused program objectives and constantly changing political leadership in executive government, the top civil servants are understandably not always sure of their direction. Not surprisingly, they may take the line of least resistance: no or limited action may be safe action, especially when there are no clear incentives for—assuming there was a definition of—effective action. The Carter administration's legislation to reform the civil service sought to remedy some of these problems by providing greater mobility and cash incentives for the top civil servants. But it remains to be seen whether that reform can be closely tied into better program definition and implementation or simply becomes another elaborate paper process more concerned about the evaluation of personnel than the effectiveness of programs.

**6. Overlap.** Because of jurisdictional divisions within the Congress, laws dealing with related problems don't always get lodged in the same department for implementation. The lack of coordination between similar programs—and the need to manage integration between departments with overlapping responsibilities—is a significant, though hardly new problem. As a governmental study recently noted:

> New programs have been developed to deal with extremely complex and interrelated problems such as saving cities, reducing unemploy-

*"Few department secretaries stay the length of the Administration. Their average tenure in recent years has been forty months. In the first five years of the Nixon administration the entire cabinet was replaced with a total of thirty cabinet appointments. . . . At the subcabinet level the average tenure in office in recent years was only eighteen months. . . . Between 1960 and 1972 many officials averaged less than one year of service, including 16 percent of the undersecretaries, and 22 percent of the assistant secretaries."[5] Only 47 of the Carter administration's 106 original deputy secretaries, undersecretaries and assistant secretaries were still in office as of June 1980.[6]

ment and promoting economic development . . . administration
. . . requires new and highly specialized technical knowledge. This
necessary specialization has made it increasingly difficult to manage
program interactions, as for example, when environmental programs impact efforts under economic development and employment
programs.[7]

The answer to these problems, however, is not as simple as it
might seem: consolidation of similar programs and emphasis on
reorganization will require an enormous amount of time and
capital, and is not likely to meet with success. But you are then
left with managing integration, a task as awkward in practice as
it is in phrasing.

**7. Federalism.** Your ability to act as a manager and imple-
menter is sharply constrained by the federal system to a degree
not generally understood. The federal role runs the gamut from
a totally federal function (such as writing and mailing more than
30 million social security checks each month) to a partly federal
but largely state and local function (such as delivering social
services to the elderly). But generally there is a cumbersome
sharing of management responsibility between federal, state
and local actors and a state of continual intergovernmental conflict.

Indeed, to avoid a bloated federal work force, the primary
federal technique of giving assistance has *not* been to provide
services directly.[8] Rather it has been to leave actual service delivery or program implementation to others and then establish
guidance and accountability through regulations.

In the 1960s, a number of federal laws were passed and regulations promulgated which imposed detailed and stringent requirements on the states with respect to the implementation of
federal programs. This anti-state attitude was based on a worst-
case mentality, which assumed in many instances that states and
localities would resist federal initiatives. Thus they would have
to be tightly controlled if they were to be instruments of federal
purpose. The worst-case attitude was in large part an outgrowth
of the civil rights movement, and tied to the understandable
concern that programs primarily aimed at aiding the black and
the poor were likely to be frustrated by antagonistic state and

local governments, especially in the South, which had failed for decades to take adequate steps to ensure equality of opportunity.

In the early seventies, this trend was reversed. With general and special revenue sharing, and with other initiatives that emphasized decentralization of the management of major federal programs, the federal government sought to give the states and localities substantially greater control over the administration of federal funds.

During the eighties, as in so many other respects, the themes of the sixties and seventies in federal-state relations will converge. The federal government no longer holds worst-case assumptions about the willingness of the states and localities to manage federal programs, and more of a case-by-case approach has been adopted in determining the level of federal involvement in administering federal programs. *As a general matter, the trend is toward guiding the states and localities by measuring substantive results and providing incentives for improved performance, in contrast to the regulatory technique of the previous decade, which attempted to ensure conformance with federal aims by establishing elaborate procedural requirements and imposing penalties for nonperformance.* * The problem is increasingly being recognized as how to develop techniques of indirect management.

In sum, the federal system constitutes a very profound constraint on your ability to carry out many federal domestic programs. The question today is less whether the state and local governments have *the will* to implement federal initiatives—the days of outright obstructionism have largely passed—but whether they have *the capacity to manage complex and difficult programs.* Calls for a return of federal functions to the states and localities run headlong into two major problems. If the problem is national, why should there be less than national uniformity in implementing solutions? Why should one think that the state and local bureaucracies will function more effectively without

---

*The variation is illustrated by the Carter administration's attitude toward health—where it pressed for the complete federalization of medicaid because of continually poor state performance in the administration of this rapidly growing multi-billion-dollar program; education—where it sought to give states and localities increased responsibility for federal elementary and secondary programs and to relax federal restrictions; and welfare—where it sought to continue state program administration by introducing a greater degree of uniformity in eligibility, benefits and management and by providing financial incentives for good performance.

a federal check on program accountability than with one?*

In any event, it is commonplace to rail against the bureaucracy in Washington. But it is often the bureaucracy in Peoria or Topeka or Houston that will determine your success, even as your effective control over those state and local officials is severely limited. Executive government thus "tends to get the worst of both worlds—blamed for poor delivery by its public customers and besieged with bills from its middlemen."[9]

**8. Contractors and Consultants.** Increasingly the federal government has begun to utilize the private sector—through an elaborate system of grants and contracts—to carry out the work of the federal enterprise. For example, in fiscal 1979, private contractors and consultants in the domestic (not defense) programs are estimated to have received $75 to $100 billion in federal funds for services that ranged from processing medicare claims to providing day care to developing energy projects. (It has also been estimated that more than 80 percent of the Energy Department's $11 billion budget goes to outside contractors.) Absent a scandal, this system of private implementation is largely hidden from public view. And while regulations are a source of controversy, as they impose public costs on private parties in other areas of activity, their role here is to ensure that federal funds are being spent for public purposes—an important task but laden with obscurantist detail. In part because it has been so obscure, the system has not functioned as effectively as it should, which also makes for a constraint your administration must confront. Nevertheless, as long as it is politically popular to oppose growth in the federal work force, the use of outside contractors and consultants will continue.

**9. Lack of Knowledge.** In the years since the outpouring of Great Society legislation, there has been a growing sophistication about how social programs work (or don't work) and an increasing technical capability to predict what will happen if certain programmatic changes, both major and minor in scope, are implemented. Nonetheless, prediction and evaluation in ec-

*The percentage of state agencies that receive 50 percent or more of their budget from federal aid has risen from about 10 percent in 1965 to nearly 30 percent in 1980.

onomic and social policy is still more art than science, turning as much on the values embedded in the questions asked as in the uncertain answers to those questions. And the lack of knowledge about how programs affect the real world—coupled with the confusion about program objectives noted above—is one of the most profound constraints on the ability of executive government to manage programs effectively.

The need to evaluate last year's program—and improve its management—before proposing next year's has been a tenet of good government for decades, a precept that has gained special importance and attention in the last fifteen years as the federal domestic enterprise has grown so dramatically. And yet good evaluation techniques—an aspect of better program management, which would in turn lead to better program design—are all too rare in most of the departments and agencies of executive government, partly because they have to focus on formal programs that affect only a part of some larger problem,[10] and partly because your top appointees, like others before them, are likely to pay more lip service than attention to evaluation.

## D. The Congress

The problem of cooperation between Congress and the executive branch on major national issues has been a recurrent one for much of this century. Watergate aside, the historic tension has not been between different conceptions of constitutional roles so much as between the nationalism of the president's view and the pluralism that is the sum of the Congress' many diverse parts. As noted, it is a rarity, not the norm, when the particularism of the Congress coalesces into a set of attitudes consistent with a dramatically innovative national posture adopted by the president. This is illustrated by the evanescence of the cooperation between the president and Congress during the New Freedom, New Deal and Great Society eras. The basic question is whether the two institutions at either end of Pennsylvania Avenue can cooperate within a constitutional framework that shares formal power in addressing major problems that require national solutions.

During the Nixon-Ford years, the relationship between Congress and the presidency was especially heated—over both constitutional questions and legislative policy. With a resurgent Congress, very few major presidential initiatives were adopted, and in response, presidential vetoes became a commonplace, as a Democratic Congress sought to continue the reform agenda of the sixties. And out of the welter of constitutional and legislative controversy significant new congressional constraints on the Presidency emerged: among them, the War Powers Resolution of 1973 and the Budget and Impoundment Control Act of 1974.

But the congressional constraints on the executive were equally dramatic during the first Carter term. For the first time in eight years, the President and the Congress were of the same party, but they still could not work together on a presidential agenda in domestic affairs. As we have noted, many of Carter's major domestic initiatives—social security financing, the first energy program, comprehensive tax reform, comprehensive welfare reform, a major national health insurance proposal— were defeated, drastically altered or not seriously considered.

The record was due in part to the political, policy and, ultimately, the strategic failures of the administration. Moreover, major proposals aimed at completing some of the unfinished business of the sixties hit the realities of the seventies and a more conservative set of attitudes about the federal role and government spending. Some of the problem was due simply to confusion about how to reconcile a period of austerity with the items on an expansionist agenda and how to deal with intractable and related problems of inflation and energy.

But part of the stalemate reflected changes in Congress as an institution since the mid-sixties: congressional responsiveness to presidential leadership has been undermined. Mid-sixties' cooperation between the president and the Congress produced an outpouring of significant legislation, particularly in the 89th Congress of 1965–66: the Civil Rights Act of 1964; the Voting Rights Act of 1965; medicare and medicaid in 1965; the Elementary and Secondary Education Act in 1965; the Higher Education Act of 1965; and the Housing and Community Development Act of 1966, to name just some of the major bills enacted. The factors leading to legislative productivity included:

• an identification by members with party and with a coherent and consistent party position on major issues.

- the clout of the congressional leaders and committee chairmen.
- the executive branch's clear advantage in expertise on key issues and the Congress' consequent dependence.
- the political strength, until he was consumed by Vietnam, of a president who had run ahead of most members of the Congress in the 1964 election.
- a national consensus on the need to expand the rights, benefits and opportunities for a number of disadvantaged groups.

By 1980, much had changed.

Jimmy Carter must have wished privately that he could have dealt with a Congress like the 89th, rather than the balky, irascible and at times contemptuous 95th and 96th Congresses.* To be sure, Johnson's landslide in 1964 helped elect a large class of Democratic newcomers grateful to the president and sympathetic with his broad program. But that alone hardly accounts for the differences between 1965 and 1980.

**1. Lack of Roots and Reduced Importance of Party.** Most close observers of the Congress agree that members are different today than they were fifteen years ago—that they are less influenced by the party position than before. This can be traced in part to the decline of party and lack of a clear party legislative program, but other forces have also been at work to make the men and women elected to the Congress more individualistic and less predictable.

—Members of Congress—especially in the House—tend to be younger, sometimes better educated and almost always more independent on the issues. Said House Speaker Tip O'Neill in 1974: "Sam Rayburn used to be able to glare people down. These new members are brighter, better educated, more talented. . . . You just don't glare these people down." Many also object to being classified as liberal or conservative.

—Because many of the members are relatively young, they

---

*"President Carter's first term has not been one of the rare historic periods of fruitful collaboration, and the limited legislative output—as in the case of energy—has disappointed almost everyone. The effect on public confidence has been direct, and disastrous."[11]

may not remember the New or Fair Deal; some, not even the New Frontier. Most became interested in government during the Vietnam War–Watergate years.

—Party organizations at the local level have lost much of their importance. Members today are more likely to have personal organizations independent of the formal party organization.

—The rise of personal organization has been driven in part by the importance of the media and volunteers' attachment to particular candidates (rather than precinct workers loyal to the party and party leaders) as the key method of reaching voters.

—With the resurgence of special interests (about which more below), the politics of congressional districts and, to a lesser extent, of states have become more client- and problem-specific. Through franked mail and lack of in-depth ongoing press coverage, members can often control the information reaching their constituents.*

—Sources of campaign funds are more readily available because of the proliferation of political action committees formed by special-interest groups, especially on the corporate side. Politicians are less dependent upon campaign financing from just a few organizations or through the party.[12]

—Lobbying is much more sophisticated. In particular, corporate interests, once regularly outgunned by labor and liberal groups, have considerably increased their strength. Members of Congress who lack a strong ideological base tend to be more susceptible to the sophisticated lobbying techniques employed today, including grass-roots efforts by back-home friends and neighbors.

—The rise of single-issue groups has had the effect of making members more cautious than they would otherwise be, lest a wrong vote put them on a group's "enemies" list.

—Many members are less issue-oriented than their predecessors. They lack a strong ideological commitment that provides "answers" to a range of issues. Many seem more

*Said Speaker O'Neill: "Members are more home-oriented. They no longer have to follow the national philosophy of the party. They can get re-elected on their newsletter, or on how they serve their constituents." *Congressional Quarterly* (September 13, 1980), p. 2696.

interested in their own reelection than in changing public policy. They have also become preoccupied with process at the expense of substance. Such issues as the budget process, oversight, sunset proposals, regulatory reform and lobbying reform are far higher on the list of congressional priorities today than they were a few years ago. Process issues are almost always less costly than programmatic initiatives are.

—Regional rivalries on such critical issues as energy or social programs (which are often distributed by formulas that due to their complicated weighting systems favor one region or another) cut across party lines and tend to unite members of different parties. Regionalism in the Congress has always been important in our political history on issues from tariffs to bank regulation to racial equality. But renewed regional competition is an important phenomenon of the contemporary Congress.* There are also caucuses cutting across party lines on a variety of issues, from the auto and steel industries to women's concerns.

**2. Reduced Influence of Congressional Leaders and Committee Chairs.** A related system of accountability that has weakened over the past fifteen years is the power of the party's leaders in the Congress and of the chairs of the congressional committees. This weakening is clearly related to the decline of party importance and party discipline. But such a trend is also due to institutional changes that have taken place within the Congress itself. During the past fifteen years, major changes have occurred in the way congressional business is conducted, especially in the House (and especially among House Democrats).

—Fifteen years ago most of the votes on the House floor went unrecorded. Now almost all votes are on the record, and members can no longer hide behind anonymity to give a vote to the leadership or the president for the good of the party.
—Similarly, the practice of marking up legislation behind

*For example, a bipartisan Northeast–Midwest Congressional Coalition has been organized to deal with the problems facing the region. And it is of course possible to find northern senators Bradley (D-NJ) and Danforth (R-Mo) voting together often on energy legislation against southern and western senators Long (D-La) and Packwood (R-Ore).

closed doors (when the key legislative decisions are made) has for the most part been eliminated in both the House and Senate. Fifteen years ago, hearings were open but most mark-ups were closed. Today sessions are generally open to the press and public, including lobbyists representing affected interests. This is now also true of House-Senate conferences where differences between bills are reconciled.

—The trend toward democratization has weakened congressional leadership and the chairs of committees and subcommittees. No longer is seniority the only factor in selecting a committee or subcommittee chair. Seniority is still the most important factor, but the House majority party has demonstrated in recent years that it is prepared to deny a chair to the person next in line to become chairperson. And it has unseated sitting chairmen in favor of the next in line.*

—Committees have been enlarged and the process has been opened up and made more accessible to junior members of Congress. This was the intended, but not the only, result. It has also made the committee processes less controllable, less predictable and more difficult to lead.

—The number of House and Senate subcommittees has grown steadily. Today the Senate has 15 committees and 90 subcommittees, compared with 16 committees and 80 subcommittees in the mid-sixties. The same situation exists in the House, with committees increasing from 20 to 22 and subcommittees from 101 to 148 in the 1965–1980 period. In fact, there are now nearly 300 committees and subcommittees (including select and special committees), more than one for every two of the 535 members of the House and Senate. The growth of committees and subcommittees of course carries with it a proliferation of committee and subcommittee chairmanships. And the growth of the latter means a weakening of power for the committee chairmen and—since so much legislation is written in detail in subcommittee—a further diminution of the authority of the House and Senate leaders. It also means

*In 1975, for example, three committee chairmen were deposed: Agriculture's William R. Poage; Armed Services' F. Edward Hébert; and Wright Patman of Banking, Currency and Housing. At the start of the 96th Congress in 1979, Richardson Preyer (D-NC), the next in line to succeed the retiring Paul Rogers as chairman of the important House Commerce Health Subcommittee, was passed over in favor of Henry Waxman (D-Cal).

that members of Congress, particularly senators, serve on a larger number of committees and subcommittees, which means they are spread exceedingly thin.

These two trends—the weakening of party and the diminution of the strength of the leadership and the committee chairmen—mean that your ability, as either party leader or head of the executive branch, to cut a deal with a few key leaders in the legislative branch has been significantly reduced.* The reduced power of the leaders and the chairs is of course not all bad: it is easy to forget how a powerful chairman could hold up legislation decreed by a majority of the House or Senate for years. The flip side of dealing is blocking.

But as President Carter discovered, the institutional changes added momentum to the trend that began with the congressional reaction to the executive excesses of Vietnam and Watergate. The Congress today is often inclined to assert its own institutional prerogatives against the executive, even when the president and the Congress belong to the same party. Perhaps the discipline that supposedly existed in the past has been exaggerated, but there is definitely less party discipline and a more independent spirit than there was fifteen years ago.

The assertion of congressional prerogatives has been buttressed by two other developments. The bureaucratization of the Congress—the growth of staff and the establishment of new congressional centers of expertise—has diminished the importance of the expertise and sources of information in the executive branch.

**3. The Growth of Congressional Staff.** The past fifteen years have produced a dramatic increase in the number of Hill staffers, from about 6,000 in 1965 to approximately 12,000 today.

—In the Senate, the personal staff of the members grew from 1,749 in 1967 to 2,600 in 1975. Committee and subcommittee staffs reflected a similar increase, rising from 448 in 1965 to 1,120 in 1975.

*Could a president today call a few congressional leaders as Eisenhower did (Rayburn, Johnson, Martin and Knowland) or as Johnson did (Dirksen) to work out a compromise on a controversial civil rights bill?

—In the House, personal staff increased from 4,055 in 1967 to 6,115 in 1975. And committee and subcommittee staffs grew from 506 in 1965 to 952 in 1975.[13]

As staffs grow, a bureaucratic law comes into play: they prepare, or claim to prepare, their principals more thoroughly, giving the members a greater sense of autonomy and independence—from the chairmen, the leadership and the executive branch, and ultimately from you. At the nitty-gritty level where key legislative decisions are often made, knowledge—or apparent knowledge—is real power.

**4. Growth of Congressional Expertise.** Over the past fifteen years, new institutions and processes have also been established in the Congress to counter the executive branch's monopoly on information and analysis.

—The Congressional Budget Office has been established to perform the congressional equivalent of OMB's budget analysis functions. With a high-quality professional staff, CBO is a valuable *and* independent source for all members of the Congress, complete with its own computer capabilities and critiques of administration positions.

—The establishment of the congressional budget process and the creation of the House and Senate Budget committees in 1974 were an attempt to provide Congress with an overview of, and disciplined approach to, the federal budgetary process. No longer would OMB be the only comprehensive budgetary game in town.

—The creation of the Joint Economic Committee in 1946 was an attempt to provide for the Congress a systematic source of economic analysis comparable to the information and advice provided to the President by the Council of Economic Advisors (especially when it builds on the analyses of the Joint Committee on Taxation and CBO). And in recent years the prestige of this committee has markedly increased (although it still lacks authority to initiate legislation).*

*A similar but less successful attempt to provide the Congress with independent technological and scientific expertise was the creation of the Office of Technology Assessment in 1972.

—The Congressional Research Service, a unit of the Library of Congress, provides general research capacity to all members and their staffs.

—The General Accounting Office audits federal expenditures, but also provides general critiques of executive branch program management and effectiveness.

**5. Rivalry Between the Authorizing and the Appropriations Committees.** Some authorizing (legislative) committees looked for ways to create automatic entitlements that would ensure funding of their programs outside the normal appropriations process, a constraint on your power to this day. Gaining a measure of control over the federal budget will be one of the key issues of the 1980s. And if you seek budgetary reform, it is far easier for you to deal with two sets of committees—the budget committees, which have broad advisory power, and the appropriations committees, which can actually set spending levels in the discretionary programs—than with all the legislative (authorizing) committees. Yet the uncontrollable portions of the budget—the entitlements, the trust funds and the like—emerge from the legislative (authorizing) committees and can be passed on the floor of both houses without significant review by the appropriations committees. Moreover, alterations in the uncontrollable programs must be initiated in the authorizing committees, which decreases, at the outset, the probabilities of working real budgetary reform.*

**6. The Jurisdictional Thicket.** Changing the jurisdictional relationships in the Congress strikes at the core of a member's responsibility, since these are often the areas in which he or she has established a reputation. To change committee jurisdiction is almost as difficult as amending the Constitution itself. In the 1970s both the House and the Senate took a crack at bringing committee jurisdictions more in line with the real

*Before 1980 the congressional budget committees made recommendations and the preliminary budget resolutions were largely advisory. With the reconciliation process, however, which both houses approved and which *requires* authorizing committees to meet spending constraints, the ability of the authorizing committees to ensure spending through entitlements may be reduced. But it is an open question whether reconciliation is here to stay or was just a response to a one-time problem.

problems confronting the nation, without much success in the Senate—though a Committee on Energy and Natural Resources was created—and with notable lack of success in the House.[14]

As a result, many critical problems can only be addressed in several committees in each house. Jurisdiction over energy, for example, is split among nineteen committees in both houses, the most important split being between Finance and Energy and Natural Resources in the Senate, and Interstate and Foreign Commerce* and Interior and Insular Affairs in the House. Many health-care matters—such as national health insurance or hospital cost containment—face dual jurisdiction: Finance and Human Resources in the Senate, and Ways and Means and Commerce in the House. Similarly, Carter's initial comprehensive welfare reform proposal would have had to clear *three* committees in each house: Finance, Agriculture (because food stamps was being replaced by a cash-only program) and Labor and Human Resources in the Senate; and Ways and Means, Agriculture, and Education and Labor in the House.

The two tax-writing committees—Senate Finance and House Ways and Means—exercise complete or partial jurisdiction over a vast array of important domestic issues: taxes, trade, energy, social security, medicare and medicaid, welfare (AFDC) and social services (Title XX of the Social Security Act). Indeed, Finance has jurisdiction over about half of the federal government's annual expenditures as well as tax legislation. This has two fundamental implications:

—The tax-writing committees can be a bottleneck, severely limiting the number of important administration initiatives that can be moved through Congress during a four-year term. The problem is accentuated in Senate Finance, which does not use a subcommittee system to mark up, or draft, legislation before it is considered by the full committee. Similarly, in Ways and Means, major tax legislation is considered only by the full committee; other measures are marked up in subcommittees.

—If the chairmen of the committees are skilled politicians, they can, even in these days of reduced influence of the chairs,

*Its name will be changed to Energy and Commerce in the 97th Congress.

wield significant power—and significant control—over your domestic agenda. Finance Chairman Long has, of course, been a Washington legend for his ability to hold up committee action on major legislation until the waning days of a session, when under the press of time he can execute a series of dazzling compromises and deals to his own advantage.[15] Whether Bob Dole, Long's Republican successor, can duplicate his skill is an open question. But you have no choice: you must deal with the leadership of Finance and Ways and Means.

One expedient tried in both energy and welfare to cut through the jurisdictional thicket during the first Carter term was the creation of ad hoc committees comprised of members from the relevant legislative committees in each house. The theory in energy was that the special committee could report out legislation that would be referred directly to the floor. In welfare, the special subcommittee bill would go back to the full legislative committees, avoiding subcommittee consideration. But, for different reasons, neither special committee was able to avoid the congressional snares.* For the foreseeable future, the jurisdictional problems of the Congress will be your problems as well.

**7. Two Extremes in Legislative Technique: Overregulation and Buck-Passing.** Your ability to direct the federal enterprise will also be seriously affected by two congressional legislative methods.

—Another legacy of the Nixon-Ford era is Congress' continued distrust of the executive branch's ability to carry out a program consistent with congressional intent. Just as the federal government in the 1960s made a worst-case assumption about the ability of state and local governments to carry out federal mandates and at times imposed self-defeating regulations that drowned state and local officials in paper-

---

*The House ad hoc énergy committee, with the prodding of the Speaker, did move the first Carter energy proposal with swiftness, but to no avail, since it became deadlocked in conference. The House ad hoc welfare subcommittee labored heroically, but its product was never voted on by any of the full authorizing committees to which the bill was referred.

work, so the Congress in the last decade has had a tendency to overregulate the executive branch by passing exceedingly detailed legislation that attempts to limit executive discretion sharply. These bills either attempt to usurp management functions by specifying standards and procedures at extraordinary levels of detail or lodge functions below the secretary in a bureau or agency presumably friendly to congressional intent, seeking to remove a substantial supervisory role from the secretary or from you. This before-the-fact oversight tends to hamstring executive initiative and implementation, and can be a serious barrier to effective executive government.

—At the other extreme, the Congress has developed an unfortunate tendency to deflect political pressure on controversial matters by passing extremely vague laws, often with very little legislative history, in order to avoid coming to grips with difficult problems. As a result, the executive branch is forced to write legislative regulations that must construe broad mandates without the benefit of clear legislative intent. One- or two-sentence laws which proclaimed nondiscrimination in federal programs that affected the aged and the handicapped and restricted federal funding for abortions are striking examples of this problem. The Congress knows that these hotly contested issues will have to be resolved first by the executive and then probably by the courts.

Both overregulation and buck-passing occur with enough regularity that you may want to develop general policies on them in your dealings with the Congress.

**8. The Resurgence of Special Interest Politics.** Another constraining phenomenon, the resurgence of special interest politics, has been the subject of much comment in recent years. The basic facts have been widely reported:

—By most objective measures, the number of lobbyists representing organized interests has jumped dramatically over the past fifteen years. The number of lobbyists formally registered under the Federal Regulation of Lobbying Act has increased from 450 in 1965 to 1,800 in 1980.

—The number of trade or other organizations—special interests banding together to get strength (usually financial) through numbers—has also increased dramatically. In Washington, there are currently about 14,000 offices for trade associations or organizations of national scope—usually among the more skillful of the lobbying groups—as compared with about two-thirds that number in 1965. These are not just the traditional powerhouses—the American Medical Association, the American Petroleum Institute, the National Rifle Association, the AFL-CIO and the Tobacco Institute—but include such newcomers as the American Chiropractic Association and an association to ensure the nutritional value of infant formulas. Indeed, there is an American Society of Association Executives to provide guidance about the ways of Washington to other associations.

—One of the campaign reforms passed in response to the abuses of the Nixon era, the creation of political action committees (PACs) under the Federal Election Campaign Act of 1974, has had the unintended effect of increasing the power of special interests. The act limits traditional sources of giving and thus makes candidates more dependent on funds from PACs. Individuals can contribute only $1,000 per election, while PACs can donate $5,000. This in turn has led to dramatic increases in these political action arms of discrete interests (from approximately 350 in 1974, with contributions of $12.5 million, to nearly 2,000 in 1978, with contributions of $35.1 million). By targeting their funding on certain congressmen with appropriate records, PACs are having substantial influence.

The increase in special interest politics has a symbiotic relationship with other developments affecting the Congress in the last fifteen years.

—It nourishes the rise of personal (as opposed to party) politics in individual congressional districts (and states). Indeed, in its most extreme form, special interest politics becomes single-issue politics—where individuals feel so intensely about a single issue, usually as a result of special interest pressure, that they will vote for or against a candidate on the basis of that issue alone.

—It feeds on the fragmentation of the congressional committee structure into an ever-increasing number of subcommittees, since the special interest can obviously spend an enormous amount of time lobbying the few members of the relevant subcommittee—the place where many key laws will be drafted.

—It also feeds on the time-honored relationship between the committee (or increasingly the subcommittee) and the relevant bureau or agency inside a huge federal department, since it can, again, spend a great deal of time monitoring and seeking to influence those interstitial relationships that defy your control or the control of your top political appointments in the departments.

—Strong special interests can use the jurisdictional thicket to ensnare proposals they oppose. For example, the Carter administration's proposal to restrain the sharp increases in hospital costs would have had to pass through seven legislative subcommittees and committees, and the Rules Committee in the House, two floor votes, a conference and subsequent floor votes approving or disapproving the conference report. The American Hospital Association, the Federation of American Hospitals and the American Medical Association—three organizations with effective Washington lobbies—could wage a war of attrition, which they did, with ultimate success. In the 95th Congress, for example, hospital cost containment was considered for six straight weeks by the House Commerce Committee. The administration and other advocates of the bill fought off a series of killing amendments by one-vote margins, but finally suffered defeat in the sixth week on yet another amendment developed by the lobbyists for the hospitals and the doctors. In the end, one member switched his vote, under the continuing pressure, and the bill was gutted.

The growth in special interest politics has given new momentum to the particularism and pluralism that has always characterized the Congress. Small, well-organized, intensely committed special interests have always been able to overwhelm diffuse, poorly organized efforts undertaken in the name of the national (or majority) interest.

If you want to be detached about it, the restraint on presidential action exerted by congressional diversity obviously has its virtues. For your immediate needs, however, the growth of special interest politics only makes your already difficult task of working with the Congress on major national issues that much harder. You can proclaim an energy crisis or a crisis in rising health-care costs. But the grandeur of the goal and the drama of the problem can get lost, often forever, in the trenches, where technical details and obscurely worded amendments can distort or destroy your intentions. And you can be sure that the special interests will be in those trenches with their bayonets fixed.

## E. The Group Basis of Politics

In the 1960s, the president could count on a stable coalition of groups to support his programs. Labor, middle-class liberals, the poor, minority Americans—all tended to support not just a single proposal that advanced their particular interests but a *range of proposals* that advanced a range of interests. This kind of stable coalition is of course important to win election to office, but it is also critical to the presidential politics of governing. *A broadly based coalition that supports a broad range of proposals is a powerful instrument for working your will as the chief of executive government.*

But obviously such a coalition does not exist today—for a president of either party. Rather, we live in a time when single-issue groups have returned to prominence, and perhaps even more important for you, in an era of *single-issue coalitions.* In other words, for a major proposal requiring the assent of other major actors in the political system—that is, for virtually every presidential or mixed presidential/secretarial issue—you will have to develop, often from scratch, the coalition of groups and interests that can give you the necessary muscle in the politics-of-governing. To take a simple example, blue-collar workers and liberals, allied in the mid-sixties on virtually every Great Society reform, may now be split on other issues: increased support for production incentives versus the costs of assuring environmental protection, anti-abortion versus pro-choice, anti-busing versus pro-busing, increased protectionism versus greater international economic competition.

The implications of an era of single-issue coalitions for you are profound.

- *First,* knitting together such coalitions on a case-by-case basis can be a painstaking exercise. It will take an inordinate amount of time and attention to create a coalition and then to keep it from unraveling. Party no longer mediates between the president and the interest groups; you must deal with the groups directly, continuously and intimately—assuming that there are leaders in those groups who can actually lead.
- *Second,* you risk losing your support on one issue if, as is likely to be the case, you take, or are forced to take, a position on another controversial issue that cuts across the first. And your support on an issue important to a group may not gain the support of that group on another issue of importance to you. For example, organized labor pressed President Carter hard for labor law reform and for the Humphrey-Hawkins bill, but when he agreed to support those controversial issues, organized labor would not in turn moderate its views on national health insurance and back Carter's national health plan.

This is not the place to explore the reasons for the confusing, contradictory and atomized nature of America's group politics. Certainly the absence of a compelling public philosophy is one problem—what, for example, is the proper balance between the "expansionist" and "managerial" agendas and what level of government (federal, state or local) should have primary responsibility for domestic programs? A faltering economy is another reason (it sharpens the mind—and makes groups more aware of their narrow self-interest). And surely the tidal pull of renewed regional politics is a third.*

But the reality of fragmentation is inescapable. You will truly have to play chess to piece together political support on individual issues—and understanding how the group politics of that item on your agenda will affect, perhaps adversely, achievement of your other goals. You may be able to bring into being or to

*During the 1980s oil-producing states like Alaska, Texas, California and Louisiana will receive increased tax revenues of more than $100 billion as a result of oil decontrol.

take advantage of a broadly based coalition that supports a broad range of proposals. But that appears unlikely, at least for the near term.*

## F. The Party—and the Nomination

A commonplace about American politics: when broadly based, multi-issue coalitions exist within one of the major parties, the party can reduce the built-in tensions between the legislative and executive branches. But again, that is not likely to obtain in the near future, and in its present state of decline, the party is not likely to serve you very effectively as an instrument as you practice the politics of governing. Indeed, the party can actually become a constraint on your ability to govern.

As indicated, to govern effectively you must stay credible as a party leader who can control the nomination process—for yourself or for your chosen successor. Whatever its weaknesses, and they are multiple, the party is still a link to the source of sovereignty, the electorate. Keeping that link as strong as possible conveys a necessary aura of strength. Moreover, grass-roots organizations are still the key to electoral success: to turn out the vote, to win caucus states, to raise money, to provide workers, and to carry out a host of other campaign chores. But satisfying the party activists who will help you win the next nomination can cause you substantial difficulties as you govern, since they may not look kindly on compromises that attenuate positions in which they fervently believe and which may have motivated election-year efforts on your behalf.

## G. The Media

Reams have been written about the media and the presidency. But whatever else may be said, for the President the media environment of the early 1980s is strikingly different from that of the early sixties. Vietnam, Watergate and related attempts to

*There is the possibility, just over the horizon, that if the country was to swing force-fully and durably to the conservative end of the political spectrum—more defense spending, less domestic program spending, returning program authority to the States —and if the Republicans are able to run the Senate and win the House, such a coalition and governing mandate might begin to emerge in the middle of the 1980s. To some, the 1980 election signaled this conservative shift.

manipulate the media changed the way in which the press corps reports the presidency (and other major public institutions), certainly for the immediate future and possibly beyond that.

Although the media have traditionally been independent and critical of government, media attitudes now are unrelentingly adversarial, especially after Watergate, when the ethos of the media underwent a transformation. Never again would the press corps serve as flacks, the ultimate term of press opprobrium, for high officials. Every pronouncement and action would be scrutinized critically and the "real" motives or wellsprings of behavior uncovered. Given the unremittingly critical perspective that the press brings to the presidency, a disturbing but substantial question presents itself: namely, whether any president can be perceived as successful today unless his governing victories are overwhelming.

While the media should of course be adversarial and skeptical, they should also perform many other functions when they cover an institution as vast as executive government. The media are obviously the primary vehicles for informing the American people about the dimensions of the major issues facing the nation and about the realities you face trying to govern. But how many, even in the press corps itself, would say that the media do an adequate (not excellent, but merely adequate) job of covering the actual functioning of the presidency, let alone the much more complicated workings of executive government?

The eccentricities of the media toward you and the executive branch—eccentricities that will sharply constrain your ability to govern—are unfortunately many and will constitute a strong constraint on your ability to govern. A litany would certainly include the following:

—The media are preoccupied with personality, tending in particular to overpersonalize the presidency.

—The media are preoccupied with conflict, often mistaking normal good-faith debate within the executive branch as a life-or-death struggle that will devastate the loser, even if the participants recognize that the issues should be aired clearly and that the ultimate decision is a close call.

—The media are preoccupied with electoral politics, and often treat acts of governance as a series of events in the next campaign. Indeed, many members of the White House press corps are political reporters who may have had limited experience (or interest) in covering the excruciatingly detailed work of executive government.

—The media are preoccupied with results, and do not reflect upon how complicated and problematic are the processes of change.

—The media are ahistorical and do not customarily portray the development of issues as part of broader and deeper trends that are only partly within your control.

—The media do not articulate the nature of the constraints facing you, or the standards that they use in judging you, but judge they will: in the news columns and headlines as often as in the editorial pages and the columns. Increasingly, the subjective impression or interpretation underscored by an editorial adjective or adverb ("The President suffered a crushing defeat") is the staple of news stories or prime-time broadcasts.

—The media rarely convey the difficult trade-offs involved in important decisions. By focusing instead on the final result and the difficulties it may cause, they often fail to give a sense of the alternatives, and the difficulties or problems that may be associated with them.

—The media are concerned with the horse race in the Congress: will the president's bill pass largely in the way that he proposed it? Much less frequently do they examine the critical question of how the legislation is in fact implemented and administered after enactment.

—The media emphasize failures and scandal, and much less often report equally important phenomena: progress, under the circumstances, and exemplary personal qualities.

One other important constraint associated with the press is the obvious problem of leaks. On occasion (and sometimes more often than that), leaks come from the bowels of the big departments or the Executive Office of the President. They may stem from disgruntled members of the permanent government, upset by a development that runs counter to their personal views or disrupts their normal course of business. Such leaks are a fact of life in executive government, and they have very serious effects.

It is hard to negotiate with members of the Congress or powerful interest groups in a fishbowl. Leaks can be minimized only if your political appointees are able to win the loyalty and respect of their troops, and if they exercise great care in not letting the final shape of high-level decisions be discerned at too many removes from the top before the decisions are made public.

An equally serious problem of leaking occurs when your top appointed officials launch attacks on one another. The press is adept at parlaying even a casual aside into a major confrontation that can assume a life of its own. During the Carter years, there were regular news stories that high administration aides were displeased—or reported that the President was displeased—with Cabinet secretaries or other top officials. Similarly, whenever major policy was being made by the President, there were typically leaks about who was saying what and who was winning. Both types of leaks are bush-league and make the administration look the same. Again, these kinds of leaks cannot really be controlled by you. Perhaps they can be minimized if you make it unequivocable that you do not want the administration's dirty laundry aired in public, and if the phrase "White House sources" is not attached to sentences critical of other parts of your administration.

You should not permit sniping through leaks as a technique of imposing internal discipline on your administration. It is especially pernicious and self-destructive because it feeds existing antagonisms, breeds distrust, and reduces what is already in short supply: cooperation among extraordinarily busy people with overlapping responsibilities. Sniping does not produce creative tension but merely makes the administration look like what it is, in disarray. Internal discipline should be just that—internal.*

## H. Public Attitudes and Programmatic Themes

Vietnam, Watergate and inflation have all led to a declining belief in the ability of the president, and government generally, to deal with the problems facing the nation. To be sure, there

---

*Only after repeated internal attempts to discipline a top official have failed should you consider taking a public shot across his or her bow.

is a Dickensian "best of times, worst of times" dimension to all public opinion polling. A question can doubtless be framed that will obtain any public opinion result desired. But few will dispute that confidence in governmental institutions has declined.

With respect to the federal government, a major shift in public opinion has unquestionably occurred.

—As you know, the Gallup approval rating of every president since World War II has steadily declined during his term (or terms) in office. There may be some up-ticks on the approval chart, but the overall trend is inexorable: down.

—The number of people who said that they had a "great deal of confidence" in the executive branch dropped from 41 percent in 1966 to 13 percent in 1978.[16]

—The number of people who said that they had a "great deal of confidence" in the Congress dropped from 42 percent in 1966 to 13 percent in 1978.[17]

—The number of people critical of government has dramatically increased. The number who think government cannot be trusted to do what is right went from 22 percent in 1964 to 70 percent in 1978; the number who think that government is run by people who don't know what they are doing went from 28 percent in 1964 to 56 percent in 1978; and the number who think that government wastes a lot of tax dollars went from 48 percent in 1964 to 79 percent in 1978.[18]

Perhaps the most troubling indicator of citizen discontent with government is the drop in those voting for president: 62.8 percent of the eligible voters cast ballots in 1960, a figure that had declined nearly 10 percentage points to 54.6 in 1976.[19]

Nonetheless, despite the lack of confidence in governmental institutions, strong support still exists for the functions performed by the federal government, including the newer functions adopted during the 1960s.* Part of this phenomenon no

---

*"Support for economic or New Deal liberalism continues at a high level. In spite of the widespread speculation about a swing to the right, spurred by concerns about the level of government spending, there is as yet no indication of a widespread inclination to cut back substantially on the liberal, interventionist state. . . . When asked whether the federal or state governments should cut back on spending for public services, the public today overwhelmingly favors sustaining or increasing current spending. . . . People in all social classes, in all regions of the country, and of all political persuasions

doubt stems from the fact that the number of individuals who either are employed by government (federal, state, local), are employed because of governmental contracts to the private sector, receive governmental transfer payments or pensions or receive other governmental benefits has risen from 42 percent of the population in 1960 to nearly 54 percent of the population in 1977.[21]

—Despite the potential cost to the federal budget, nearly half of the population still wants a program of national health insurance fully paid by the federal government, although obviously that percentage might drop sharply if the question were posed with some of the cost implications included.[22]

—Although a striking 58 percent of the people in another poll opposed welfare spending in general, an even higher percentage—81 percent—favored cash assistance, food stamps and government health care for single-parent families and for others who were poor.[23]

—A 1976 national poll indicated that 61 percent of those surveyed favored increasing welfare expenditures or keeping them at the same level.[24]

A number of implications could be derived from these and from other survey data, but with respect to constraints upon your ability to govern, perhaps the most salient are the following:

• A substantial amount of confusion exists about the tension between the expansionist and the managerial agendas. People want to improve government effectiveness, reduce taxes and fight inflation, but people want to cut back very few of the existing governmental functions (when the survey question is posed without an emotive word like welfare).

• Absent a demonstrable national emergency, calls for sacrifice will fall on deaf ears unless there is a clear sense that all citizens will be treated equitably and unless there is a sense

now consistently endorse high levels of public expenditures for most social services. . . . The sources of public discontent with government performance . . . do not involve opposition to liberal policies. . . . what disturbs people is a sense of government incompetence and waste. . . ."[20]

that government itself can act with equity and efficiency. It is very difficult to hold people to higher standards than the government itself will accept—or can meet.

• The number of major new issues to which the public will pay attention—unless they are doorstep problems like civil disturbances, long gas lines or shrinking paychecks—is extremely limited.

• Given the general likelihood that your approval rating will decline over time and given the still poisonous public attitudes about government, it is all the more important that you think strategically, marshal your resources effectively and tackle problems that have a high probability of success. And given the constraints that we have been discussing, you must define those problems well and give the public meaningful standards for what would constitute success.

## I. Achieving Social and Economic Change

Our discussion of constraints has focused on resources and institutions, practices and attitudes. But we should make one last, fundamental point.

Most government activity in domestic affairs is aimed at changing economic and social conditions. And the ultimate test of government is not passing laws, changing policies and making organizations run efficiently. It is instead carrying out the broad purposes that have justified governmental action in the first place: to help people become healthier, better educated, more employable, better housed, more adequately fed and more secure in their retirement; and to help create an economic climate that maximizes private sector strength, reduces unemployment and creates stable prices while at the same time ensuring safe products, a clean environment and a healthy workplace.

Yet to say the obvious is simply to step back for a moment from government's preoccupation with things governmental and to recognize how extraordinarily complicated—and problematic—are the processes of using government to manage, or significantly affect, social and economic change.* Your "ex-

---

*Visualize, if you will, the number of separate steps in improving the health status of the 15 million poor Americans who do not have adequate health care—from the moment you charge the secretary of health and human services with the development of a plan

perts" will define problems and provide solutions, but despite their appearance of knowledge, they are operating on a very partial apprehension of the facts and very uncertain theories about how the world works—and will work after you adopt their position. Economics and other areas of social thought will spin out theories about the causes of problems, provide an apparently persuasive rationale for solutions, and then in the future systematically critique the intellectual bases for governmental action and find them wanting, a cycle Henry Aaron has skillfully detailed.[25]

The ultimate constraint, then, on the actions you take as president and on the government in general is the extraordinary difficulty of actually effecting social and economic change—*and* the problems you and your key advisors have in *understanding* how *limited* their knowledge is. Being skeptical, therefore, about what your experts are telling you will always serve you well.

We are not making an argument for a reduced governmental role. In most instances, a compelling case can be made for basic federal programs in the traditional social policy areas for the traditional reasons: because the market system has failed or because other private or public actors have neither the incentives nor the resources to address major national problems. We merely want to underscore that a major constraint and a major challenge of government is that so many decisions—in economic as well as social policy—have to be made in less than ideal circumstances thanks to time pressure, lack of information or, worse yet, lack of knowledge. Although the answers may be painful, you and your top aides must at least ask how the process of change is supposed to work; what the key points of uncertainty or difficulty are in the process; and what the probabilities of achieving the ultimate goal are.

Indeed, one of the key problems in public policy is the politi-

to the actual preparation of the proposal to its consideration and approval within the executive branch to its tortuous passage through the Congress to development of administrative structures to implement the new law, to hiring of appropriate personnel and establishing new relations with the private sector and with state and local officials, to delivering the prescribed services in an efficient manner to the right people, to ensuring that appropriate monitoring and evaluation systems are also in place and then over time achieving the goal: not just increasing the amount of health care received by the poor but their general conditions of health. *And* beneath each step are a host of theories about the nature of the present health-care system, the ways of financing and administering services, and the effects of certain activities on actual health status.

cal need to proclaim that a proposal is built on the rock of certainty (it *will* save the world by 1984) when instead it really rests precariously on the shifting sands of probability (there is a 20 percent chance it may save the world *if* our theory is right and if other factors don't come into play).

Changing policies or laws is one thing—and in the present climate of government that is hard enough. But to have a real effect on underlying economic and social conditions (and to have the persistence to remember last year's law and to see if it is having its intended effect) is, unfortunately, even more difficult.

The constraints on your ability to get things done are stubborn. But they are not immutable. Just as the processes that have produced the constraints have evolved over the years, so they are much more likely to be susceptible to evolutionary, not dramatic, change. That may be at odds with the breathless way we view our presidents and their pronouncements, but "that's the way it is." Only a strategic approach, rooted in messy reality and operating carefully on a number of fronts, can *begin* the necessary processes of change: institutional, technical, attitudinal—and ultimately economic and social.

Our recitation of the difficulties you face is not to counsel timidity or despair. Your task is to work with and change the world as it is, not as you would wish it to be. Whatever the constraints on the modern presidency, its task remains one of undiminished excitement. The problems may be difficult, but they are at least big. In any event, for a time they are yours.

# III·
# THE CRUX OF
# EXECUTIVE
# GOVERNMENT:
# THE
# DEPARTMENTS

## A. Conflicting Pressures and a Confused Tradition

T HE Cabinet officers are politically accountable to you. They carry out your orders, report to you and are removable in an instant if you will it so. Their first loyalty should be —must be—to you. But although Article II vests in you the "executive power" of the United States, the Cabinet appears nowhere in the Constitution.

Rather, the Cabinet departments and the Cabinet secretaries are statutory creations of the Congress—starting with State, Treasury and War during the First Congress of the Republic. The powers of Cabinet officers are given by the Congress. Their appointment is dependent on Senate confirmation. Their department's annual expenditures stem from congressional acts. And they are subject to continual congressional oversight—they will get in their limousines just as quickly for a conference on Capitol Hill with an important member of the Congress as to meet with you in the Cabinet Room or the Oval Office.

The contradictory pull of executive loyalty to you and legislative accountability to the Congress is mirrored in other tensions that propel your major Cabinet officers in divergent directions. They are your emissaries to but also your guardians against the important organized interests that surround their departments. They must contest suits but bow to court orders that challenge your authority. They must somehow manage, motivate and win over the permanent bureaucrats whom they nominally lead but whose interests and traditions, without strong leadership, may be different than theirs—and yours. They are constantly vying with your more immediate staff for their vision of what blend of policy and politics constitutes the presidential interest.

In many respects, the conflicting pressures that buffet the department heads are similar to the contradictory demands that are made upon you, as the chief of executive government, albeit on a smaller scale. Realizing that Cabinet secretaries stand between you and many of the conflicting pressures that play upon executive government is a key starting point for understanding the Cabinet's proper role. Like you, the Cabinet officers must carry out the basic tasks of executive government—policy innovation, policy implementation, crisis management and moral leadership—keeping in constant view the three levels of politics (governing, nomination and election). Like you, they are caught in the swirling demands of multiple inconsistent constituencies and multiple inconsistent objectives which make fealty to a simple and pure idea of presidential interest very difficult—*just as it is for you.*

Although much has been written on the Cabinet in the past decade—most of it urging, as we do, a strengthening of the Cabinet officer's role—there has been, and continues to be, substantial confusion about what the Cabinet should do, and how it should relate to your top aides in the White House and the Executive Office of the President. As a perceptive observer of the presidency has written, the Cabinet "is simultaneously one of the best known and least understood aspects of our governmental system" and the "whole notion of what a cabinet is needs rethinking."[1]

Some of the confusion stems from the ambiguous role of the Cabinet officers, poised as they are between you and Congress, the interest groups and the bureaucracy. Some of the confusion results from the unquestioned difficulty in reconciling the need for a central strategic direction and decision-making with the equally pressing need to delegate as much executive business as possible to the departments. Semantic problems add to misunderstanding. "Cabinet government" in the British sense means collective decision-making by a body exercising both legislative and executive power, a role that cannot be imported to these shores. In America, the Cabinet is merely a collection of individual executive appointments, and throughout this chapter, our emphasis is on the proper use of individual Cabinet officers as department heads or in small groupings and *not* on the Cabinet as a collective entity. Some of the confusion results from the White House perspective of those who often write about executive government—presidential assistants or scholars who spend much of their time interviewing presidential assistants.

The rhetoric and practices of the first Carter term did little to dispel any of this confusion. Carter promised a return to Cabinet government, both when he was campaigning and after he had been elected. But the concept was never defined. In practice, President Carter's view of the Cabinet departments was initially based more on a rejection of White House/department practices under Richard Nixon than on any positive conception of the importance—and the limits—of the Cabinet. Carter did not want his top personal staff giving orders to the department heads, and he wanted the Cabinet officers to feel free to speak directly to him. At an early press conference, the new President said:

> I believe in Cabinet administration of our government. There will never be an instance while I am President where members of the White House staff dominate or act in a superior position to the members of our Cabinet.[2]

He wanted, in short, to avoid the excesses and White House isolation created by Ehrlichman and Haldeman. For the most part, President Carter succeeded in these simple goals, which were more or less correct as far as they went. The problem, of course, is that they didn't go very far.

The result—aided and abetted by a press corps that played up the traditional departmental/White House conflict and rarely analyzed what the Cabinet should do—was a continuous emission of contradictory and bewildering signals about the meaning and status of the Cabinet officer's role in the executive branch. The senior White House staff grumbled on background that Cabinet government was coming (or should come) to an end. Yet President Carter invariably expressed his respect, admiration and support for all his Cabinet members and for the rejuvenation of the Cabinet in executive government—right up to July 1979 when he made major changes in his Cabinet. Indeed, with the first return from a Camp David retreat (in the spring of 1978) and then with the second, domestic Camp David conclave (in the summer of 1979), the press reported that the Carter experiment with an enhanced role for Cabinet officers had come to an end. Reports of the Cabinet's demise, however, are greatly exaggerated.

Our basic premise is that there will always be a significant role for Cabinet officers in executive government: because of the size and complexity of the federal enterprise; because of the limits on your time; because of the inability of the White House staff to run the federal government from 1600 Pennsylvania Avenue or the adjacent executive office buildings; and because of your paramount need to share, and deflect, responsibility for the myriad tasks that executive government is now expected to perform.

The question is not whether there should be a significant role for the department heads, but rather how to structure that role as it pertains to you and to your top staff in the Executive Office of the President (EOP). Our basic position is that the Cabinet officer's responsibilities should vary depending on the importance of the issue to you. You should determine which issues on your agenda are presidential in importance, which are mixed presidential/secretarial and which are purely secretarial. You must then define, for each type of issue, different roles for the Cabinet officer, different relationships to the staffs in the Executive Office of the President, and different relationships to you.

This basic set of questions must be answered. When they are, the answers will go some of the way (perhaps a significant way) toward reducing the eternal tension between the President's staff and his Cabinet. If allowed to burgeon unchecked, the rivalry can eat at the innards of your administration, enfeebling its basic functions and even paralyzing it. Many think that no set of decisions you will make is more important than solving this problem—certainly getting the relationships right from the start may be one of the four or five most important things you can do in the first year. Our suggested approach blends together the perspective of the departmentalists (who argue for strong Cabinet officers) and the presidentialists (who call for increasing, or at least continuing, the strength of your immediate personal staff). Such a balance is necessary, for the point of the exercise is to meet simultaneously the need for central strategic direction and decentralized responsibility and decision-making.

As we will argue in detail later, the suggested approach would work as follows:

- On presidential issues (for example, the economy), you will be deeply involved and a high degree of collaboration between the appropriate Cabinet officers (and their staffs) and your top staff is necessary. These are the first-order substantive issues of your domestic presidency, and before you decide them, you should consider a broad spectrum of views. On these matters, Cabinet officers are key advisors, but you will not defer exclusively to their advice.

- On the mixed presidential/secretarial issues (for example, the future of nuclear energy), a delicate balance must be established. Because they will be of great importance to your administration's record, these issues require some direction and management from you and the EOP. On the other hand, many of them possess a no-win character: a decision will involve pleasing some important groups but profoundly alienating others. It will often be far preferable for the secretary to absorb some of the political heat rather than have it come directly and immediately into the EOP, much less the Oval Office. Generally speaking, you should set the broad direction internally. Then the Cabinet secretary should keep you or key members of your personal staff informed about these issues so that you can in turn inform the secretary about particular concerns you may have. But, as a public matter and insofar as possible, the secretary should be at the point—responsible for publicly articulating the policy, defending it, implementing it and absorbing criticism that may be directed at it.

- On the purely secretarial issues arising in a single department (for example, a regulation implementing a law restricting funding for abortions), there should be much less White House involvement. On such issues, you should have almost no role and you should look to the Cabinet secretary to work out the problems within the broad framework of your strategy of governing. If he (or she) repeatedly fails to do so, he should be admonished or asked to resign. On these issues the Executive Office of the President should not continually second-guess the Cabinet officer. It is better to delegate to the secretary and judge him on a pattern of *results* rather than let the EOP interfere in the process of making of individual decisions.

As a rough guide, we would suggest that the presidential issues in domestic affairs be restricted to five to ten in number; the presidential/secretarial, to twenty-five to thirty-five; and the secretarial, to a hundred to a hundred and twenty-five. Taken together, these issues will constitute the basic record of the administration. Obviously, the three levels of issues do not exhaust all the important matters that the administration will confront. The issues are placed in these three categories as part of the priority-setting exercise that is an essential element of your strategy of governing. There will of course be hundreds of other issues, which we will simply call routine, that will be handled by the department or by major EOP offices. These, too, are important—and, as events warrant, they can be moved up onto the priority list monitored in the White House.

One other point by way of definition. For shorthand, we will refer to "subpresidential" decisions. This is an extraordinarily important concept, since so much of the business of executive goverment is—or should be—conducted without your direct involvement. The term subpresidential is simply a catchall phrase meaning decisions not made by you. As we will explain, there can be subpresidential decisions on mixed presidential/secretarial issues, on secretarial issues and of course on routine issues.

In this chapter we make the case for maximum delegation to Cabinet officers of those subpresidential decisions. Maximum delegation is likely to work most successfully where substantial overlaps of responsibility don't exist between and among departments. In Chapter 4 we qualify the case we make here by indicating those instances when key EOP players, rather than the Cabinet, should make subpresidential decisions—usually when issues are heavily interagency in character.

## B. The Case for a Significant Cabinet Role

Virtually all modern works on the presidency quote the statement of the first director of the Bureau of the Budget, Charles G. Dawes. "Cabinet members are vice presidents in charge of spending, and *as such they are the natural enemies of the President.*" Yet as a long-time budget bureau official has written:

> Dawes obviously was speaking from the perspective of the Budget Director. Cabinet members may be the natural enemies of the Budget Director, or the White House staff, *but they are the President's natural allies.* A President may not like his Cabinet members; he may disagree with them and suspect their loyalty; but he cannot destroy their power without seriously undermining his own.[3] [Emphasis supplied.]

The reasons for assigning your Cabinet officers significant roles in the next four years—for viewing them as your natural allies and not otherwise—are simple and, in our view, unassailable.

*First,* you have no choice but to delegate to others decisions on myriad questions regarding domestic affairs. With the growth of the federal enterprise, there are today more than a thousand separate federal domestic programs (three for each day of the year). Understanding the issues that are raised by that labyrinth requires substantial day-to-day contact with policy experts, political analysts, interest group representatives, congressional actors, and state and local officials. And you obviously cannot engage in the hands-on, nitty-gritty work entailed in making huge bureaucracies work better.

*Second,* the immediate White House staff and the more institutionalized staffs in the permanent Executive Office of the President cannot—and should not—directly and unilaterally decide many of these issues, whether they relate to policy innovation, policy implementation, crisis management or even moral leadership. The primary role of your top aides in the White House and the Executive Office of the President should be to coordinate policies that cut across departmental jurisdictions, to develop the broad strategy of your coming term, to update it as necessary and to advise you on the presidential and presidential/secretarial issues.

The White House and Executive Office staffs, with a few exceptions (one being the Council on Economic Advisers), do not have the technical skill and expertise to formulate (as opposed to review) innovative policy proposals. To the extent that the technical expertise for innovation resides in the federal government, it usually resides in the departments.*

The White House and Executive Office staffs do not have the direct management relationships with the key bureaucrats in the departments who actually run the key programs or who are charged by statute with making the key policy implementation decisions. The most recent attempt to manage the federal government from the White House—which briefly took place under John Ehrlichman at the end of Richard Nixon's first term —was a striking failure, leading to substantive confusion, unacceptable delays in making decisions and a resolve to abandon the approach during the second term.[4]

*Third,* talented Cabinet secretaries, who bring to the executive branch independence, intelligence, integrity and experience, can be superb and visible extensions of presidential authority. You can only attract the kind of top-quality people who should be in the Cabinet if you can assure them that they will have significant responsibility and visibility. Development of policy is—or should be—heavily dependent on policy implementation: what has happened in the past administration of similar types of programs, and what will happen in the future? With specialized policy staffs and substantial departmental experience in program administration at his disposal, the Cabinet officer is properly situated to ensure that policy innovation is closely tied to questions of policy implementation.

The Cabinet secretaries are also in the best position to defend publicly many of the administration's basic decisions because they are more directly in contact, on a regular operating basis, with the relevant experts, federal managers, state and local offi-

*Whether the EOP should be strengthened in this respect is a question that has been debated for several decades. We think not. The capacity should be built in the permanent staffs of the department, but as we will discuss, the White House/EOP staffs should be able to draw on that expertise in a systematic fashion.

cials, private sector actors and members of Congress. Again, the Cabinet officer who must defend a decision should participate deeply in making it. The quality of many of your key decisions in both politics and policy will turn on the equality of the key political appointees in the departments—the deputy secretaries, undersecretaries, assistant secretaries, commissioners and administrators, and the division heads who serve at the discretion of either you (presidential appointees) or the secretary (secretarial appointees). And the Cabinet secretary who is given substantial responsibilities is in the best position to attract the kind of top sub-Cabinet talent necessary for quality performance by the executive branch.

*Fourth,* strong Cabinet officers are lightning rods: they can absorb some, though not all, of the political voltage on a host of controversial issues that executive government must, under the law, address. There will be enough controversy surrounding you on the first-order presidential and the presidential/secretarial issues that you cannot escape. If you try to be identified with all other hot items facing executive government, you will court disaster. Moreover, it is unwise to allow your immediate, top-rank personal staff to assume too visible a public role in explaining or defending controversial decisions. That will bring issues in too close to the Oval Office.

## C. A Short Course on the Anatomy of the Executive Branch

As you start to focus on the Cabinet officer's role, there are several do's and don'ts in thinking about the structure of executive government.

• *Don't view executive government in formal, organization-chart terms as comprised of thirteen separate departments* (including eleven departments whose jurisdiction, in whole or in part, is domestic affairs) and seventy-three permanent agencies (including sixty-four that relate to domestic affairs). That will tell you nothing except that it's a big government.

• *Don't view the Cabinet as a single entity* that will sit around the Cabinet Room discussing great issues of government. Calls for a more collegial presidency in which the Cabinet secretaries as a group should meet regularly with the president to *provide advice* on the broad range of important issues facing the administration—issues that are outside their immediate purview—have very limited utility.[5]

The Cabinet *as a whole* should probably meet every two to four weeks in the first year of the administration and every four to six weeks thereafter to exchange information on the major policy and political questions before the administration and to give your top appointees a sense of shared responsibility for the administration's fate.* The Cabinet as a whole should also meet once or twice a year with the President and top presidential staff to discuss and *give advice* on the general political and policy themes of the administration and how they should be integrated and synthesized in the strategy of governing. But such meetings, while important, are hardly central to a practical conception of the Cabinet's proper role, which is instead built on the importance and limits of delegation.

The basic argument for collegiality in the Cabinet as a whole —that Cabinet secretaries can bring important perspectives to bear on specific policy questions outside their own jurisdiction —flies in the face of reality. Most substantive issues are too complicated and too rooted in difficult technical concepts and specialized political settings for a busy Cabinet officer to find time first to get briefed on a subject for which he has no responsibilities and then to make a meaningful contribution in a group setting. And holding meetings with a collection of so many high-level, often competitive individuals present is hardly likely to advance the debate or to augment your understanding.†

---

*Too often the Carter Cabinet meetings did not discuss the issues of real political concern to the President. In part this was due to a fear of leaks, but in part it was a result of the failure to synthesize politics and policy. The inside political thinking of the White House was often not shared with Cabinet officers.
†Some would argue that on particularly momentous but discrete decisions you would be well advised to get general reactions from the broad-gauged but uninvolved members of your official family. But it is hard to imagine the President convening a meeting of the Cabinet to discuss something extremely sensitive—like the planned raid to free the American hostages in Iran. Again, the danger of leaks and the lack of relevant information is likely to make such meetings risky and frustrating. A better way to gain the benefit of the experience and wisdom in the Cabinet would be to consult, on an individual basis, those Cabinet officers whom you grow to trust on decisions outside their purview—not to seek their *advice* (they are not likely to have enough information to give substantive advice on the crucial details) but to find out what *questions* they might ask if they were in your place.

• *Don't view the Cabinet secretaries as falling into one of two broad groups, an inner Cabinet and an outer Cabinet.*[6] The inner Cabinet —State, Defense, Treasury and Justice—supposedly act as counselors to you because of broad jurisdictions and multiple functions. The outer Cabinet—Agriculture, Education, Commerce, Health and Human Services, Housing and Urban Development, Transportation, Interior, Energy and Labor—supposedly relate to you as advocates for their more particularistic, more client-oriented, less presidential interests.

To be sure, you will probably spend more time with the attorney general and with the secretaries of state, defense and treasury (and possibly energy) than with the other members of the Cabinet due to the broad sweep of their responsibilities. But the so-called inner-group secretaries will not necessarily get along any better or worse with the senior White House staff and with you than the so-called outer-group secretaries. Indeed, the conflict between the State Department and your immediate National Security Council apparatus has been a recurrent theme of foreign policymaking in the executive branch for the past twenty years.[7] And to take a specific example, the Justice Department's initial position on the most important legal question of the Carter administration's first term—the constitutionality of affirmative action in education that the *Bakke* case presented—was bitterly opposed by top White House officials, as well as by other senior members of the administration. Internal debate subsequently altered Justice's position in several important ways.[8] Nor was Treasury Secretary Blumenthal considered a Carter administration insider despite the centrality of his responsibilities to the administration's political standing.

Conversely, if you view the outer group of Cabinet secretaries as mere advocates for the interest groups that their departments serve, you may needlessly create a self-fulfilling prophecy. To the extent that these secretaries are kept away from important decisions affecting their responsibilities and are treated with distrust, they may indeed gravitate to their client or congressional constituents and away from the central themes and concerns of your domestic presidency.

If, however, you give the Cabinet secretaries in the more

client-based departments significant responsibility, autonomy and visibility—as part of a strategy of governing having your imprimatur—you can effectively use them to develop or implement necessary presidential or mixed presidential/secretarial policies that may in fact arouse opposition from the client and other interest groups with a heavy stake in the operations of the particular department.*

• *Do view the Cabinet secretaries as crucial links in an attenuated and vulnerable chain of command that extends from you down to career civil service managers in the bureaus and sub-bureaus of the major departments.* Your chain of command is characterized by alternating levels of political or noncareer appointees (approximately 1,600 persons who serve solely at your pleasure or the pleasure of the Cabinet officers) and career employees, the nearly three million civilians who compete for protected positions in the civil service ranks regardless of party affiliation or political views—the so-called permanent government.

In effect, executive government is like an Austrian chocolate cake, with many finely graded layers of political and permanent employees. An outline sketch of the layers of loyalty reveals the following:

• *The Executive Office of the President (EOP)*†

—Senior White House aides. These are the top non-career employees appointed directly by you and numbering 19 in the Carter White House. Some head offices created by statute (for example, the chairman of the Council of Economic Advisors), and others head offices you create (for example, the chief of staff).

—Middle-level White House aides. These are noncareer employees appointed directly by you or by senior White House

*For example, Interior Secretary Cecil Andrus was willing to confront a powerful segment of his department's natural constituency when he sought to cut back water projects during the Carter first term. Similarly, in an effort to restrain the enormous and often wasteful increase in federal expenditures for health care, HEW Secretary Joseph A. Califano, Jr., acting with the direction and approval of President Carter, was willing to confront the extremely powerful hospital and medical associations in pressing for legislation to contain rising hospital costs.

†This description applies to the executive branch during the middle of 1980.

aides. They serve as deputies to the senior staff in such positions as deputy director of the Domestic Policy Staff or deputy director of the Office of Management and Budget or as members of the Council of Economic Advisors.

—Junior-level White House aides. These are noncareer employees appointed by the senior White House staff. Taken together, the middle- and junior-level White House aides numbered approximately 440 in the Carter White House.

—Senior career officials in the Executive Office of the President. These are the highest civil servants in the EOP's permanent government, with such titles as OMB division directors or senior staff economists with the Council of Economic Advisors, and they numbered approximately 360 in the Carter EOP structure.

—Junior career officials in the Executive Office of the President. These are all other members of the EOP's permanent government, with such titles as budget examiner and junior staff economists. They numbered approximately 960 in the Carter EOP.

- *The Departments*

—Thirteen Cabinet secretaries, nominated by you and confirmed with the advice and consent of the Senate. The Cabinet officers are at the pinnacle of those presidential appointments requiring Senate confirmation (the so-called executive-level appointees).*

—Approximately 600 other executive-level presidential appointees who also are nominated by you and confirmed with the advice and consent of the Senate. This group is the sub-Cabinet—the deputy secretaries, undersecretaries, assistant secretaries, and commissioners who are the top noncareer, political appointees in the executive branch.†

—Another 1,200 noncareer employees appointed by the secretaries and who are usually assistant commissioners or associate administrators or special assistants to Cabinet officers or

*There are others in the executive branch with Cabinet-level status—for example, the ambassador to the United Nations and the special trade representative.
†The Cabinet officers are executive level I and get paid more than the sub-Cabinet, who are executive levels II–V and are paid at slightly different rates, depending on the level.

to other presidential, sub-Cabinet appointees in the departments.

—Approximately 8,000 top-level career officials who cannot easily be dismissed, but who can be placed in their positions by the Cabinet secretary and who have major managerial responsibility in the departments. This top level of the departments' civil service is now designated as the senior executive service and includes such positions as the assistant secretaries for budget or assistant secretaries for personnel in most of the departments and many of the formal deputies to the assistant secretaries and commissioners and administrators. Although these individuals are nominally members of the civil service, many of them are attracted to an administration by their immediate supervisors and leave the government when an administration or top personnel change.*

—The middle-level managers of the permanent departmental government. These are the division heads or bureau directors who usually have the immediate operating responsibility for many governmental programs. They tend to remain on the job much longer than their immediate supervisors. They have such titles as director, Office of Indian Education, Interior Department, or administrator, U.S. Employment Service, Labor Department.

—The rest of the departments' permanent government: the analysts, program operators, budget examiners. This group constitutes by far the largest proportion of the professional federal work force.

The Cabinet officers are thus poised at the top of the departments' permanent government, having formal responsibility over the hundreds of civil servants, who in turn have key policy and operating responsibility in the executive branch. And it is through the Cabinet secretaries—and the immediate political, noncareer employees who serve under them—that your administration's themes will be given meaning or key items on your agenda carried out. The crucial position that the Cabinet

---

*You should consider placing high qualified members of the senior executive service in positions usually reserved for political appointees. They may have greater knowledge of government—and be able to move faster—than political appointees.

secretaries occupy in the chain of command can become either a point of cleavage that leads to ever-widening fissures in your administration or a link between the strategic center of the administration in the White House and the hundreds of thousands of people who at least nominally work for you.

But we must emphasize:

• The chain of command is hardly a straight top-down matter. The permanent government in the Executive Office of the President does not, as a general matter, relate directly to the Cabinet secretaries and their inner circle. The White House senior staff, often the top officials in the Office of Management and Budget and on the Domestic Policy Staff, have direct relationships with the secretaries and their top staffs. The EOP career staff has a direct relationship, however, with the departments' permanent government. It is extremely important for you and your top political employees, *both* in the White House and in the departments, to make sure that wars are not fought or treaties negotiated between these permanent staffs without the knowledge of top officials. Your top political appointees must also make sure that they don't go to war because of shots fired by the permanent staffs. In short, the political levels in both the EOP and the departments must deal with each other on the important issues, rather than letting the permanent staffs pound away at each other. Better that there should be star wars (between the top political appointees) than staff wars (between the members of the permanent government) if war it is to be.

Nonetheless, the two permanent governments—one in the EOP and the other in the departments—are a strong potential force for working your will. But this potential can only be realized if the political appointees in the White House and the departments work together in defining your strategy and priorities and then in giving the permanent government the necessary direction and leadership.

• Not only does the chain of command zigzag within executive government, but as we have indicated, it is constantly being intercut by the Congress and its committee and subcommittee system, by the pressure groups, and by the courts. Yet it is the Cabinet secretary who must balance all these competing forces and do the best he or she can in maximizing achievement of your objectives. In other words the chain of command, like so much else in executive government, is an ideal that cannot be fully realized; but it can be realized more fully if you pick the right Cabinet officers—people who can understand your needs just as you must understand theirs.

• *Do view the Cabinet departments as falling into three main substantive groups that correspond to the broad way in which you will perceive the problems that confront you—foreign policy, economic policy and domestic programs.* But, and this point cannot be stressed enough, you must be prepared to integrate views among these three subgroupings on both general and particular problems. The central cluster encompassing economic policy (Treasury, Labor, Commerce, Energy) has a set of core concerns, primarily fiscal and monetary policy and inflation, unemployment and energy. But to an increasing extent, that cluster must be closely related *both* to foreign policy (State and Defense) and to domestic programs (Agriculture, Education, Health and Human Services, Housing and Urban Development, Interior, Transportation and, to a much lesser extent, Justice).

Obviously national problems do not fit neatly into the functional boxes called departments. Heedless of organizational niceties, issues cut across existing jurisdictional and organizational lines. These so-called cross-cutters (to use the rather artless government term) require a high degree of integration among differing departmental views.

To the extent that you meet with groups of Cabinet secretaries, the three clusters—and the mixing of the economic group with either foreign affairs or domestic programs as appropriate —are likely to be the most common and most useful way to relate to collections of Cabinet officers. As particular crosscutting issues arise, deliberative processes involving the appropriate Cabinet officers and their staffs and the White House/EOP staffs will coalesce and dissolve. For example, a debate about a wheat deal with the Soviet Union could conceivably take in Cabinet officers from the foreign, economic and social policy spheres.

Especially in the foreign policy and economic policy areas, special problems come up because the major departmental actors have substantially overlapping jurisdictions. *You will thus have to structure relations not only between the departments and the*

*White House but also among the departments themselves.* The jurisdictional overlaps are less pervasive in domestic programs per se but do rise with some frequency nonetheless.*

Although the foreign, economic and social policy labels have some usefulness, the problems caused by cross-cutters and the need for ad hoc clustering and integration must also be clearly understood at the outset. This means that the structure of delegation must operate within a matrix of interagency coordination and communications. You must simultaneously meet the need to integrate agency views and contributions and the need to push as much business as possible back out into the departmental structure.

## D. The Meaning of Presidential Perspective

The charge most often leveled at the Cabinet secretaries is that they do not act with presidential perspective. While that phrase, like the grand phrases "national security" and "public interest," is used with frequency, it is rarely analyzed with care.

**1. Two Problems.** When asserting that the Cabinet will not, or cannot, act with presidential perspective, observers of the executive branch usually refer to two types of alleged failings.

*First,* the Cabinet secretaries will supposedly become captives of their bureaucracies, which have a very limited perspective on things due to the well-known laws of the iron triangle. John Gardner described the phenomenon succinctly nearly a decade ago:

> As everyone in this room knows but few people outside of Washington understand, questions of public policy nominally lodged with the Secretary are often decided far beyond the Secretary's reach by a trinity consisting of representatives of an outside body, middle-level bureaucrats and selected members of Congress, particularly those concerned with appropriations. In a given field these people may have collaborated for years. They have a durable alliance that cranks out legislation and appropriations in behalf of their special interest. Participants in such durable alliances do not want the

---

*For example, on problems relating to provision of jobs for those on welfare, Health and Human Services must work with Labor.

Department Secretaries strengthened. The outside special interests are particularly resistant to such change. It took them years to dig their particular tunnel into the public vault, and they don't want the vault moved.[9]

Recent observers have suggested that the phrase *iron triangle* connotes connections that are too stable, and that *issue networks* is a more accurate descriptive phrase for the subterranean relationships between executive operating bureaus, special congressional interests and active pressure groups. Individuals with long-standing involvement in a particular area—education for the handicapped, for example—move back and forth between Capitol Hill, the executive branch and the interest groups. No matter. The argument is still the same: Cabinet officers will be trapped in iron triangles or ensnared by issue networks. The Nixon White House was especially concerned about the Cabinet secretaries going native and being taken over by their own bureaucrats.[10]

*Second* is a related problem. Even if Cabinet officers are not controlled by the departmental bureaucrats, they will decide to make an independent name for themselves by pleasing the pressure groups and the congressional actors who are constantly at the door rather than the more distant and general interests represented by you and your men and women. The temptation for a Cabinet secretary to become a dominant feature on the political landscape by sacrificing more long-term presidential interests for immediate, though parochial, departmental concerns is viewed as a clear and present danger by White House staffs.

**2. Three Nonsolutions.** To counter the centrifugal forces that may push a Cabinet secretary out of your orbit, several solutions have been advanced or tried in recent years. None, however, will work.

• Some argue that the essential quality you must look for in a Cabinet secretary is strong personal loyalty to you, often a loyalty demonstrated in the past. Loyalty is an important quality in a Cabinet secretary—one of about ten important qualities. But loyalty is better earned by you—through clear delegation and clean decisions—than by simply importing a crony from your past. Obviously, the job of secretary is simply too important and too complex to make loyalty the litmus test for selection. The pool from which you choose the Cabinet cannot be limited to your prior associations. Also, loyalty in the past is no guarantee of a willingness to submit to the White House staff. For example, neither Griffin Bell nor William Rodgers acted with special deference toward the White House.

• To avoid the parochialism of client departments, study groups have recommended the consolidation of existing executive departments into larger super-departments:

—President Johnson first proposed that the Commerce and Labor departments be combined. When this failed, he subsequently appointed a high-level behind-the-scenes task force to make reorganization recommendations for his second term. This study group recommended a dramatic consolidation of the existing departments into four super-departments.[11]

—President Nixon asked Roy Ash to follow up on the work of the Johnson reorganization task force. Ash's reorganization team also proposed super-departments,[12] and the reorganization plan was sent to the Congress in 1971, where it was promptly dismembered and buried.

—President Carter also considered creating super-departments of National Resources and of Community Development. National Resources was promptly withdrawn in the face of congressional opposition; and the prospects for Community Development were so grim after a trial balloon was floated that it wasn't formally proposed at all.*

The theory behind these consolidations is simple. They seek to integrate in one place all the disparate though related pieces of government that require frequent coordination and balancing. If a Cabinet secretary has diverse, sometimes competing responsibilities—if a secretary heads a super-department that serves or affects a host of different even if functionally related interests—he or she will have to make the same kind of integrating, balancing decisions, involving difficult trade-offs, that those close to the

---

*The Education and Energy departments were of course created during Carter's first term. Education moved away from the consolidation theme and toward a more client-oriented conception. Energy was the symbol for a new problem, like the other departments created since 1960, HUD and Transportation.

President, or that you yourself, must make. Therefore, the argument goes, heads of consolidated departments are less likely to become mere advocates for their constituents. This is a thesis analogous to the one advanced by those who would like the Cabinet divided into inner counselors and outer advocates.*

There is just one thing wrong with the proposals: a decade of experience indicates that they are not politically viable. To restructure the existing executive departments in any major way requires legislation.† The creation of a super-department scrambles the existing jurisdictional relationships between the congressional committee and subcommittee system. And there is no subject dearer to the congressional heart than preserving the jurisdictional turf of the present committee system. Moreover, the two departments that could be likened to a new super-department—HEW and Defense—were not smashing administrative successes. They cannot therefore be cited as examples of the benefits that would flow from additional equally massive consolidations.

In short, whatever one may think of the merits of major consolidation through reorganization, structural changes of the sort proposed simply are not going to become a reality. Accordingly, they are not worth the colossal fight which you would have to wage to succeed—and which, absent the emergence of a major problem like energy requiring an organizational symbol, you would in the end probably lose anyway. In other words, super-departments do not present a real solution to the problem of making sure that Cabinet officers operate with presidential perspective.

• A third nonsolution to the supposed problems of Cabinet parochialism is to try to run the government out of the White House or the Executive Office of the President. For the reasons we have discussed, that is both infeasible and undesirable.

*There are of course other reasons advanced for consolidations. These include a belief that placing similar governmental functions under one roof and one command will lead to more efficient performance.
†Lesser reorganizations—usually involving a change within an existing department or moving some functions from existing departments to other existing departments—can be accomplished either with complete discretion or by submission of a reorganization plan to the Congress. These reorganization plans then become effective if neither house of the Congress disapproves within a given time period (usually sixty days, depending on the reorganization plan legislation giving you that lesser power). But formal legislation is needed to create or abolish existing departments.

**3. Presidential Perspective in Perspective.** Ensuring that the Cabinet operates with "presidential perspective" must confront a basic problem: deciding what the presidential interest actually is. *Most of the time, the debates between the Cabinet officers and your top personal staff are over what is good for you.* And the standards for making that judgment are extremely variable and complex. The secretaries have their own strong conceptions of what is in the presidential interest. Moreover, they often question, and properly so, whether members of your top staff, when purporting to speak for you, do indeed represent your actual views or, even if they don't actually speak for you, truly appreciate what will advance your goals. And the secretaries may especially question the wisdom of the White House or the Executive Office of the President when pronouncements come from second-, third- or fourth-level staffers who may not even be speaking for the senior White House staff, let alone for you.

Determining whether a Cabinet secretary is acting with the presidential perspective must obviously turn on the objectives of your administration and the broad strategy for achieving these objectives. A budget aide may claim that a spending proposal runs against your budget themes, but that proposal may also meet a particular substantive need about which you have expressed great concern or placate an important interest group or member of the Congress who is important *to you* for other reasons. Until there is some understanding of the balance you want to strike, for example, between policy innovation and policy implementation, between the expansionist and managerial agendas, between the politics of governing, of nomination and of the general election, between your desire to push items through the Congress and the Congress' ability to deal with them, almost no framework exists for making the individual decisions that will arise on an almost daily basis within executive government. There is no meaningful way to determine what the presidential perspective is on a host of discrete matters.

If the Cabinet officers are given a role in formulating the strategy of governing and, whatever the result, if they are kept fully informed about your policy and political themes, then they can try to act in good faith with your perspective in view, both when working on the administration's major issues and when dealing with those lesser but still important issues that should be largely delegated to them. Without such a strategy, your administration will try to develop one in an ad hoc, contentious fashion—by bruising battles on virtually every issue of importance and some that are not so important.

## E. Important Distinctions: Decision Maker, Advice Giver and Process Manager

In the following sections, we will describe the differing implications of designating issues presidential, presidential/secretarial and secretarial, focusing on your role and those of Cabinet officers. The discussion will be built on the distinction between three elementary aspects of governmental process.

- *Decision-making* is, obviously enough, making the basic call on an issue. You will make some decisions, but your key subordinates, both within the EOP and the departments, will make others. Some of the decisions made by others can in theory be appealed to you, but in practice, few of them will be. For this reason, it is always important to specify—and at this point is not as simple as it seems—who in your official family has decision-making authority on which types of issues.

- *Advice-giving* is making informed recommendations to the person with the decision-making authority. Again, it is important to specify—and this point is also not as simple as it seems —who will advise at what point in the decision process and on what issues.

- *Process management* is the responsibility for preparing the issue for decision. It entails establishing a timetable for the decision process, ensuring that all advisors are fairly consulted, sharing the information from the various advisors with others performing that function, and preparing the basic materials for the decision maker. The essence of the process manager's role is fairness and efficiency.

These three roles are often confused—to the point of combining them in a single individual, which creates a classic conflict of interest. Rare is the official who can manage a decision process fairly when he also has an advisory stake in the decision. Rarer still is the official who can manage issues, among actors of comparable status, in a balanced way for his own decision.

## F. Presidential Issues: The Cabinet Officer as Presidential Advisor

**1. The Test of Your Domestic Presidency.** In simplest terms, the presidential issues of the coming term will be those matters which are of great substantive importance to the nation and great political importance to you, and on which you wish to stake your personal reputation. These issues will therefore become the major tests of your success or failure, both during your term and in the history books. You cannot have too many of these first-order issues in domestic affairs. Indeed as we have argued, the presidential issues in domestic affairs should number no more than five to ten because they will claim so much of your time.

If you become too involved personally in too many matters, your image will become blurred. You will stand for everything, and therefore for nothing. Although you will find it difficult to restrain yourself from playing in the hundreds of games available to you, you must restrict yourself to these first-priority items. These items will become an important signal to the rest of your administration—and to the larger political world beyond. But they will be an important guide for *you*. While this observation applies at all levels of the executive branch, you especially must remember *that you are better off doing a few important things very well than handling a greater number of matters with reduced skill.* To the extent possible, it is absolutely necessary for you to take a clean line by choosing your key issues, defining your position on them clearly and then bringing the issues home successfully. To do that, you must learn these issues well so you can operate tactically as well as strategically. You must, in other words, touch bottom by understanding the basic choices that lie at their core (and that may be inadvertently hidden from you by your experts) and by understanding in depth the political and policy positions of those who will oppose you.

You and your key advisors will have to make the initial cut at these presidential issues in domestic affairs. But a short list might well include the following:

—general economic policy—primarily the continuing tension between inflation and unemployment and the major problem of lagging productivity growth.

—energy policy—primarily reducing dependence on overseas oil through conservation in the near to middle term and developing alternative energy supplies for the longer term.

—a key item on the managerial agenda, such as developing a restrained yet humane budget policy that recognizes the enormous amount that goes each year to the indexed entitlement programs as the key issue in shaping the federal budget to meet other social, economic and national security needs.

—a key item on the expansionist agenda, such as expanded health care for the poor and for those without protection against the costs of catastrophic illness; measures to meet the financial needs of the social security system; steps to assure equity for women in the social security system; or rebuilding the infrastructure of our major cities.

—a major effort in moral leadership, perhaps an attempt to start a major rethinking of our nation's total income security effort, including the issues surrounding public and private retirement plans; the uses of savings from those plans; and the effects of work effort by the elderly.

**2. The Importance of the Rules of the Game.** You will make most of the *decisions* on these first-order domestic issues facing your administration. The fundamental role of the Cabinet secretary on presidential-level issues should be as direct personal *advisor* to you. The secretary should be brought directly into your inner circle and should be urged to provide you personally with the best advice based on available resources. The key, quite literally, is personal proximity and a direct personal relationship with you on these issues. A Cabinet officer who is isolated in his or her department on presidential issues that affect that department in a central way will be a very discontented and underutilized member of your administration.

With respect to process management on key presidential issues, Cabinet secretaries can act in one of two ways. They can have the lead on the issue: that is, they can be the process manager and be responsible for preparing the options and gathering the political and policy data that inform those basic choices. As the process lead, the Cabinet officer would both manage the process and provide advice. Alternatively, Cabinet officers can offer advice merely by participating in the formulation of the decision. They can, that is, suggest options, provide policy information or political intelligence, and critique the materials that will eventually go to you as part of a decision process managed by someone else.

But whether Cabinet officers have the lead role or a participating role in the process of developing presidential decisions, they will not be the only ones to advise and their views will not always prevail. On these first-order issues, it is obvious that top officials in the EOP—the director of OMB, the assistant for domestic affairs, the chairman of the Council of Economic Advisors, your top political advisors and possibly the Vice President —will also participate as equals. One of the absurd misconceptions about the Cabinet is that the secretaries actually make the decisions on presidential issues affecting, or within, their domain. When reporting that the Carter experiment with Cabinet government was ending, the press would at times cite the experience of a Cabinet officer whose views had not been accepted on some important issue. But that is not what the role of the Cabinet, properly conceived, is about. It is instead obvious: on the presidential issues *you* will make the decisions, after hearing the advice of all top advisors with a relevant perspective.

In other words, on the presidential issues, the Cabinet secretaries can hardly expect to hold sway within the inner councils. But *only if the Cabinet secretaries believe in the fairness of the process by which you make presidential-level decisions can you expect that, once a decision is made inside the administration, the Cabinet secretary will give it strong support outside the administration, whatever the result.* *

The rules of the game—the processes by which these critical matters are presented to you—are thus of utmost importance to the effective functioning of the Cabinet in your administration. No Cabinet secretary with any experience will expect that you are going to follow his or her advice on every major matter. But

---

*Of course, some positions on presidential issues are so important to the secretary that if you do not accept that position they may resign. But as Cyrus Vance's resignation over the Iran raid showed, this is very rare.

each must feel that he or she has had a fair chance to present his or her views, and that you have been given all the available information in a soundly structured framework before you actually make the choice. Frustration and anger often arise less from the President's making a particular decision—since reasonable men and women recognize that most of the important decisions are tricky judgment calls that could go any one of several ways —than from a sense that the whole process was cockeyed, that you couldn't have known what you were doing, or that the important decision wasn't made at all. It is this corrosive atmosphere that must be avoided.

### 3. The Strategy of Governing and the Budget Strategy.
On these two critical presidential-level issues, it is clear that the role of process manager should rest with a senior advisor close to you and not with a Cabinet officer.

The person who manages the process for devising the strategy of governing—and most importantly, in updating that strategy —should be your chief of staff, a figure whom we will discuss more fully in Chapter 4. Someone with a view as broad as yours, with no direct responsibility for managing a department or an EOP staff unit, and with close connections to both your policy and your political advisors, should be directed to undertake to manage that process. And the only individual who can fit that description is the chief of staff.

The lead role in developing your broad budget strategy should of course rest with the director of the Office of Management and Budget. By broad budget strategy, we mean determining a fundamental threshold question: basic areas of reallocation within the existing budget that you might propose.* If there are to be significant cuts, what broad areas they will come from; if there are to be significant increases, what broad areas they will go to. By broad budget strategy we do *not* mean the fine-grained department-by-department program determinations that characterize the final stages of the annual budget process in December.

---

*The treasury secretary, as part of his responsibility for economic policy, should have the lead role in preparing for your decision materials on a closely related question: the size of the budget deficit or surplus.

But Cabinet secretaries should have a central role in developing positions on these two fundamental sets of issues. With respect to the strategy of governing, the Cabinet secretaries should participate on at least two levels. They should generate a list of issues that will be of consequence to the administration, provide a ranking according to importance (presidential, presidential/secretarial, secretarial), give a rationale for that ranking and detail a timetable for dealing with the matter. The secretary should also provide an analysis of the broad political and policy themes that would guide the administration over the next few years. Then once the chief of staff has put all the major pieces of a tentative battle plan together in draft form, the Cabinet secretaries should critique it. And if there are significant disagreements, those should be reflected in either a memorandum or a briefing for you.

*We cannot emphasize too strongly:* you must share with the Cabinet secretaries your understanding of how you wish to strike the balance between the policies of governing, nomination and general election. If, as was the case with the Carter administration, these competing spheres are not reconciled or are kept hidden in a black box to which access is extraordinarily limited, the Cabinet members simply cannot do what is central to their role: try to act with your perspective in ultimate view and guide their actions within a broad policy *and* political framework that you establish.

With respect to the budget strategy, there are two critical points in a budget cycle before the flurry of paper in December that arise during the specific department-by-department appeals. The first is during the so-called spring review, when preliminary spending levels are set for the government as a whole and for each department. The second comes in the fall, after the departments have put together their preliminary budgets, when OMB passes back "marks" that form the basis for specific appeals to the director of OMB and if necessary, to you. Both the spring review and the period of the pass-backs (usually in mid- to late November) involve broad political/policy choices. The fundamental issues that OMB and the other economic advisors are debating should be shared with the Cabinet officers, and their views sought. The Cabinet should have an opportunity to critique and raise issues on the budget strategy as a whole, rather than have to deal with more discrete matters piecemeal later on.

Although the inclusion of the Cabinet in the overall budget strategy will undoubtedly require more time earlier in the budget process, doing it that way presents several important advantages. The budgeteers will have a chance—in a context less adversarial than the December reviews—to hear alternative strategic perspectives. And the Cabinet secretaries will feel that they have had a fair chance to make their views known on the larger questions involved in the budget. Moreover, to the extent that you should make broad political policy calls on the share of the budget, it is better to have a preliminary sense of the debate and for the Cabinet officers to feel that they have expressed their views to you.

**4. The Special Case of Economic Policy.** Because of the broad range of matters affected by economic policy and because of the large number of departments and EOP units directly concerned with its formulation, it must be treated as a special case. As we will detail in Chapter 4, *you* must make the broad framing decisions. Your treasury secretary should be your *chief* advisor and spokesman: at the same time, there must be a more neutral process manager lodged in the White House who works closely with the treasury secretary but who ensures that the views of the other economic departments and EOP units are fairly represented.

The domestic program departments are not as directly responsible for the formation of economic policy, but they should, on an individual and often limited basis, have the same kind of advisory role that we recommend they have with regard to the overall strategy of governing and the strategy of budget policy. At appropriate points, these other domestic-affairs secretaries should be briefed on major presidential options and given a chance to comment. As a general matter, no one should expect that they have deep substantive expertise, but their departmental perspectives on certain dimensions of economic policy can be important.

The secretary of health and human services, for example, is responsible for the Social Security Administration, which sends out more than 30 million checks a month and expends about 20 percent of the federal budget each year. The financial viability of these trust funds is sensitive to economic conditions, and the methods of financing the funds (for example, the payroll tax) in turn contribute to the shaping of economic conditions. Obviously a close link must exist between the secretary of health and human services and the economic policymakers in the formulation of an economic policy that will affect the Social Security Administration.

**5. Policy Innovation.** Policy innovation, as we have said before, can be viewed as having two distinct phases: (1) the process of policy development inside the administration, which ends with final decisions made by you on the shape of a particular proposal and its relationship to other major items of administration business; and (2) the process of securing as much agreement as possible from actors outside the administration.

Except for cross-cutting issues that involve a number of departments equally, we recommend as a general rule that the department with the predominant (or total) responsibility have the lead role in managing the processes of both developing internal positions for your decision and securing external acquiescence. But a key White House advisor—usually the assistant for domestic affairs on internal development and your top political advisor for external agreement—will be available to ensure the fairness of these processes.

• The lead in internal policy development means that the Cabinet officer is responsible for developing the basic factual information that defines the problems; for developing the various options that address these problems; for articulating the criteria by which the options can be judged; and for formulating a strategy by which the favored options can win approval. On complicated policies—energy, health care, income security, housing, manpower programs—developing positions is an extraordinarily complex task involving highly technical analytic work as well as subtle and detailed political consultation with members of the Congress, congressional staff, interest group representatives and other governmental officials.

Giving the lead to the Cabinet secretary on major presidential issues of policy innovation does not in any way mean that the major actors in the other departments or in the Executive Office of the President should be excluded. Your assistant for domestic affairs should be a single focal point within the EOP on such issues of innovation. He or she should be deeply involved at a number of important points in the policy development process: defining the initial set of issues and agreeing on a work plan with the secretary; establishing an internal timetable for the administration's work; coordinating the responses of other Cabinet secretaries and other EOP actors (like CEA and OMB) to both the work plan and subsequent pieces of analysis. Working with the lead Cabinet secretary, the assistant for domestic affairs should also decide when issues need to be taken to you for preliminary guidance. In other words, although the Cabinet secretary can manage and drive the process on presidential issues, the assistant for domestic affairs should oversee it.* In sum, the domestic policy advisor is a process check on the fairness of the Cabinet officer's process management role.

In the end, you may be best served if a *single short* memorandum—fairly reflecting agreements and disagreements on the relevant facts, policy choices, political reactions and strategic elements—goes to you drafted by the Cabinet secretary (and staff) in close consultation with the other affected staffs but *under the signature* of all the main actors in both the departments and the EOP. Rather than having a purely argumentative memorandum from a Cabinet secretary which is then covered by countless other memoranda from different actors which are in turn then covered by a shorter memorandum purporting to synthesize all the divergent views, it is far better for you—and a far better discipline for your subordinates—if all the arguments and disagreements are laid end to end in a single document. A joint memorandum of this type is a final guarantee of a fair presentation of views and minimizes the end runs, secret memos and introduction of last-minute information that are time-honored bureaucratic techniques for manipulating the process. A joint memo serves to reduce the ambiguous roles of both the lead

*Under President Carter, Stuart Eizenstat, advisor to the President for domestic affairs, sought to play this type of role which was formally established in a 1977 reorganization of the Executive Office of the President. But there were two major problems. *First,* the degree to which the domestic-affairs advisor could request that the lead Cabinet secretary include options and information desired by others in the administration was not clear. *Second,* overseeing a taut process, with clear deadlines and tasks, was not uniformly a strength of the members of the domestic policy staff.

secretary and, to an extent, the domestic policy chief, who must both give advice and run a fair process.*

On cross-cutting issues of presidential importance that impinge on a host of departmental interests, there will probably be no lead in the Cabinet. The advisor for domestic affairs will be the sole process manager and the Cabinet role will be to provide advice and information into that process, sign the kind of synthesizing memorandum described above, and then argue his/her position before you.

• As Cabinet lead in securing enactment of a major proposal or agreement from actors outside the administration, the Cabinet officer is the visible advocate for the policy and prepares various tactical and strategic issues for your decision. Moreover, the department's legislative and policy staffs will usually have close working relationships with the relevant congressional committees and subcommittees and with the important interest groups.

But very close connections must also exist between the department and the Executive Office of the President. Just as the head of the Domestic Policy Staff should be your main link with the Cabinet secretary during internal policy development, so also should there be a person who commands the resources of the Executive Office of the President and who relates to the Cabinet secretary during that phase of policy innovation in which outside approval is sought. In most instances, that person should be either the assistant for domestic affairs (if heavy substantive revision of the proposal is necessary) or the head of a consolidated White House office of political affairs, about whom more later.

Although the Cabinet secretary will have a key role in the external phase of presidential-level policy innovation, three aspects of the process will require broader White House consideration and decision.

First, and most important, is the question of how to use your public time. Since you are going to be closely identified with the

*An additional safety mechanism—the chief of staff—is discussed in Chapter 4. It may also be desirable to let each of the major actors—whether in the departments or in the EOP—write a two-page advocacy memorandum that would go behind the joint memo. These advocacy memos allow the EOP staff or Cabinet officer to give special emphasis or color to the elements of decision he or she considers crucial.

presidential-level policy innovations, how you should be engaged—speeches, press conferences, interest group meetings, congressional meetings, one-on-one lobbying, television events —is an important matter that should be resolved by your key personal staff. How much time, for example, should you devote to a general media strategy, and should you limit the degree of your public exposure? The lead Cabinet secretary can advise you on how your efforts are best deployed with respect to the particular issue, but final decisions must take place in a broader context.

A second question here is how a particular piece of policy innovation may relate to other matters that the administration has on Capitol Hill. When the time comes to woo key members of the Congress, it is especially important that bargaining take place in the context of the administration's overall dealings with that member. Otherwise, you will make the mistake that plagued the Carter administration during the first term: dealing with a member on a single issue of immediate concern, making a concession to get the vote and not having the internal discipline to understand how other seemingly unrelated administration business might be used to secure the vote without the concession. It is often forgotten in the heat of battle, especially when a proper system of political intelligence does not exist, that if you offer goodies to swing votes at the last minute and don't deal with members as part of a broader pattern, many people will just hold out until the end of the legislative process and exact a high price when you need the votes.

A third question is how any particular piece of innovative policy, as well as other administration concerns, might affect the interests of important pressure groups. As with congressional relations, the White House can be brought to bear to mobilize or neutralize interest groups. But this can only come from a capacity to see whole the administration's entire range of relations with the politically organized sectors of American life.

In sum, the Cabinet secretary will be one of several important advisors who present issues for *your* decision. Care must be taken to resolve the ambiguity between substantive advice-giving and procedurally fair process management. *But* however that problem is worked out, the Cabinet secretary must have a vital role advising you on these issues.

**6. Policy Implementation.** Presidential-level issues of policy implementation are somewhat easier to structure. The threshold question takes us back to your strategy of governing: which management issues should be of first-order importance to the administration? Obviously an issue here should not get presidential-level treatment and exposure unless the probabilities of concrete and dramatic success are high or unless substantial risk is worth taking because you want to demonstrate personal commitment to an especially important position.

But once that decision is made, the Cabinet secretary should generally have the decision-making responsibility for carrying out the major management initiatives, subject to constant reports to you.* And just as the head of the Domestic Policy Staff is the process focal point for EOP development of a key piece of policy innovation, so the director of OMB should provide EOP oversight of the department's efforts to manage a presidential-level policy implementation issue short of you.

**7. Crisis Management.** The proper role for Cabinet officers and their relationship with the EOP will turn on the nature of the problem and the strengths of the top personnel in the administration. You will simply have to ad-hoc it. But at the very least, the affected Cabinet secretaries should function as participating advisors. And, as appropriate, they should be given the role of lead process managers with a second, checking process manager in the EOP.†

---

*For example, if reducing waste in the major public assistance programs were to become a presidential issue, the lead should be the secretary of health and human services (because DHHS has jurisdiction over social security, medicare, AFDC, medicaid and the supplemental security income program), working closely with other Cabinet officers such as the secretary of agriculture (who has jurisdiction over the food stamps program).
†A national labor dispute that threatens to upset the economy could, for example, quickly become a presidential-level issue requiring an enormous amount of your time and attention. But the secretary of labor would be given the lead process and advice responsibility for presenting the decision to you and then actually carrying it out. Yet as in other policy innovation or implementation areas, there should be an EOP process check—presumably the domestic policy advisor—who ensures that the views of other actors are taken into account as the labor secretary drives the decision toward you.

**8. Meetings.** Every president develops his own personal style in dealing with the important matters of his administration, especially the presidential-level issues. And regardless of style, there is no substitute for concise, well-structured memoranda to give you the essence of complex questions in brief compass.

But you can only do so much off paper, especially on the complicated presidential issues that should absorb much of your time. Gerald Ford did not like memos, and was reported to have gained much of his information from meetings. But in the first term, Jimmy Carter spent an inordinate amount of time plowing through reams of overly long memoranda.

At some point, you must get a feel for the people and the issues, and this means meetings. Given the press of time, such occasions are not always going to be well structured. They may in fact give you a more acute sense of just how messy the underlying problem is than you want. Yet rather than letting a paper process grind slowly toward you, you might find it better to have an early meeting of key, trusted players, listen to the debate, even if it is somewhat unformed, and then provide initial guidance by raising the questions and concerns that occur to you.

The presidential-level issues will require your best judgment, and there are a number of ways to get the feel of what is really at stake—what values are in conflict, what ultimately you are choosing. But getting that feel is most important of all. You will have to live with those judgments, and mucking around in the confusion that usually lies behind the neatly typed, respectfully written memos is a vitally important exercise.

## G. Mixed Presidential/Secretarial Issues: The Cabinet Officer as Sword and Shield

Matters of second-level importance to you—what we call the mixed presidential/secretarial issues—are nonetheless of extraordinary significance. They can be national or regional in scope or issues that affect an important group. The issues should number about twenty-five to thirty-five—you must not let them grow beyond that. They should be consciously chosen as part of your battle plan. And they can of course arise with respect to the basic presidential functions.*

But despite their importance, presidential/secretarial issues need not be seen by the press or public as controlled by the White House or as constantly on your desk. Indeed, they should not be. Keeping these issues at some remove, even while they are high priorities of your administration, is important for a number of reasons, including:

—*Overexposure.* If you are the point man too often on bitterly disputed controversies, you will needlessly dissipate precious political capital that you should hoard by holding back, as a decision maker only of last resort.

—*Danger.* Many major issues have precipitous down sides. You can let someone else share—or even take most of—the risk.

—*Time.* Our constant theme. These second-level concerns will be as intricate and complex as the presidential issues. You cannot give them all enough personal attention, so don't try.

Of modern presidents, Dwight Eisenhower appears to have been the most sensitive to the need to delegate; to shield himself from controversy; to enhance the dignity and stature of his office by so doing; and to retain strong policy direction behind the scenes nonetheless. Unlike presidents who wished to be constantly seen as at the center of events, perhaps exemplified most strikingly by Lyndon Johnson, Eisenhower used "[c]overt or *hidden hand* leadership as an alternative political tactic to seeking to enhance one's professional reputation [emphasis supplied]."[13]

It is often exceedingly difficult for the key White House and EOP staff to understand that discretion is often the better part of valor, that it may be in your interest to let someone else in the administration, someone outside the Executive Office of the President, fight the battle. Those close to you possess an inherent activism and will want to range widely over issues of obvi-

---

*These presidential/secretarial issues can be matters of policy innovation, as, for example, the Carter administration's effort in 1978 to reauthorize the federal elementary and secondary education laws, to defeat a move for a tuition tax credit and to increase funds for the existing higher education grant programs as part of the tax credit fight. They can be matters of policy implementation, such as the Carter administration's first-term effort to make the wage and price guidelines work. They can be matters of crisis management, such as the sudden eruption of concern over the financial troubles of the Chrysler Corporation or the influx of Cuban refugees.

ous significance, especially if members of Congress or of power-ful interest groups set phones ringing. Harness those activist instincts, and don't let outsiders bring issues too close to you, unless you are ready.

**1. Two Types of Mixed Issues.** It is helpful to see mixed presidential/secretarial issues as one of two types:

• *Positive Issues: Secretary as Sword.* These involve objectives that the administration *affirmatively* wants to achieve. If they can be carried out successfully, they will be trumpeted as ad-ministration accomplishments and will become a solid part of the record of your term. They are not, however, first-order presidential matters because of their number and their relative importance and also because:

—*The mixed issues may involve a high risk relative to the gain.* Civil service reform legislation, for example, was perceived as being very important to the Carter effort to improve the man-agement of the federal government, but it was also, at least in the beginning, seen as very difficult to achieve. Accordingly, the administration in effect treated it as a mixed presidential/ secretarial issue which President Carter announced and sup-ported but which in most of the important particulars was managed and identified with Scotty Campbell, the head of what was then the Civil Service Commission. Campbell was built up by the White House as the spokesman on the issue and was essentially acting as a person of Cabinet rank.

—*The mixed issues may not be clearly formed.* The administra-tion may want to act, but may have to feel its way into the problem. Until the issue has ripened you should stay away publicly, even though you are privately aware of its existence. The risk of a swine flu epidemic is a clear illustration of a problem that potentially had national significance, but that should not have been publicly identified with President Ford. It should instead have been handled at the departmental level until the nature of the problem was more clearly understood and a sensible response developed.[14] Had President Ford kept his distance, even as he followed developments with care, he would not have suffered the personal defeat he did on the issue.

*—The mixed issues may not have much publicity value because they are so technical.* Credit can be gained after the fact if the administration's efforts are successful. The work of Robert Strauss in pressing for congressional approval of the trade agreements of 1978 is a good example. As the President's trade representative with Cabinet status, Strauss maneuvered the complicated trade legislation skillfully through the Congress; kudos for Strauss and for President Carter came after the task was completed.

*—The mixed issues may be more effectively handled if they are not given presidential status.* If they are seen as absolutely top priorities of the administration, they may draw more partisan fire than necessary, making congressional action more difficult.

• *Negative Issues: Secretary as Shield.* A number of critical issues will ignite intense debate, and alienate important groups or important blocs of voters. Such no-win issues have existed for every president, but the number may be increasing today because economic constraints lead to decisions involving painful trade-offs.

You cannot dodge ultimate responsibility for no-win decisions, but your Cabinet officers can shield you from some of the ensuing explosions. If they, not you, can be seen managing these fiercely controversial issues, they, not you, will become the focus of attack from those who will vehemently protest the decision made. Delegation thus has obvious value: keeping you above the battle.

Some of these no-win issues may be the fallout from a conscious economic and budgetary path you will choose for the next four years. But others will land on the administration's agenda not by your choice but because of an action-forcing event.

—Litigation can force your hand. For example, during the Carter administration's first term, HEW's controversial efforts to desegregate higher education in southern states that had previously practiced de jure segregation were carried out pursuant to court order. A U.S. district court in Washington had ruled during the Nixon-Ford years that the department was required to undertake desegregation activities as mandated by Title VI of the Civil Rights Act of 1964. The department therefore could not finesse the problem. After seeking negotiated settlements, it became clear that actions of the administration were either going to enrage an important southern state, North Carolina (seen as the keystone of the President's southern reelection strategy), or an important constituency of the Democratic Party, the civil rights groups.

—The Congress can also force you to respond at a time and in a manner not of your choosing. For example, when Catholics and other groups eager to support private, religious schools pressed in the Congress for a tuition tax credit, the Carter administration decided it had to act. Having opposed the credit on substantive grounds (bad education policy), the administration had to offer an expensive alternative to deflect the pressure, and in the process angered many who were otherwise its supporters.

—Pressure to interpret regulations can also push you into an unwanted decision. For example, in 1978, HEW was forced to issue elaborate regulations construing the Hyde Amendment, which restricts the use of federal funds for abortions under medicaid. The Congress had simply failed to resolve clearly a number of critical issues—including the precise circumstances under which medicaid funds could be used for an abortion if the pregnancy was the result of rape or incest (and did not just pose a threat to the life of the mother). The resulting regulations, whatever their form, would anger either the pro-life or pro-choice advocates.

In order to serve as an effective shield, the Cabinet secretaries must have a strength and independence of character, which does not mean lack of loyalty to you. But only if they are perceived as being a force in their own right can they be truly credible in managing controversial questions with your broad approval. In other words, if the Cabinet secretaries are to serve as lightning rods on these no-win issues, they must be strong. Weak ones melt when hit.*

---

*During the first Carter term, the political elements of the White House staff did not appreciate the shielding role of the Cabinet officers, although the policy staffers did. The political staff heard the unhappy reaction from some important, usually vociferous quarter after decisions were made, without fully understanding that the problems had

**2. Your Role.** On the presidential-level issues, you will be continually involved making strategic and tactical decisions and closely following both their internal development and then their external progress. With respect to the mixed presidential/secretarial issues, your role should be different.

• *Internally,* you will of course initially decide which issues should be classified as presidential/secretarial, and then review that decision at regular points during the term. But your basic role with respect to the second-level priorities is to make the decision that unmistakably establishes the policy direction. Once the broad decision is made, you should leave important details (not just technical ones) for resolution by the Cabinet officer and, if necessary, the Cabinet officer and your top White House advisors. Most subsequent decisions ought to be made within the framework of your guidance on the issue itself and with reference to the strategy of governing. Only if a subsidiary question threatens the general way you have chosen to approach the presidential/secretarial issue should you be drawn back into decision-making.

• *Externally,* your role will also be important, but limited. You will probably be involved in announcing some of the basic decisions—at least the affirmative ones that you have placed on the administration's agenda (as opposed to those, like interpreting a statute through the regulations process or responding to lawsuits, that are forced upon you). You will on occasion speak publicly in support of the issue, if it is a positive one. You will probably be asked to intervene at a *few* key points in the legislative or negotiating process. But the essence of your effectiveness may be to hold back and let the issue ripen before you personally become involved. Of course if the effort is successful, you will surely bring all the parties to the White House to herald the outcome and bathe in the warm glow of victory.

Beyond that involvement, your role in presidential/secretarial issues should be limited to succinct periodic briefings on their status. In fact you must avoid being drawn into these issues. At press conferences, you may have to state simply that

---

to be faced, decisions made, and important interests upset, and that protection for the President depended on a Cabinet officer's credible prominence.

Secretary X or Secretary Y is handling the issue, that you have delegated it to him or her, that the basic posture of the issue is thus and so, that you have approved that posture and that you will go no further at this time. By setting the overall direction here, you can be properly perceived as in control. Whether you can educate the press and the public to the need for delegation on the subsidiary dimensions of those issues is another matter.

**3. The Role of the Executive Office of the President.** To the extent that decisions regarding the mixed presidential/secretarial issues come to your desk, the EOP staff offices should work just as they do on presidential issues—direct personal advisors, equal in status to the Cabinet officer. But once a general agreement is reached on the general approach, and if the second-level issue is not heavily interagency in character, a presumption of regularity should exist that accords the Cabinet secretary significant autonomy in day-to-day management or in decisions under the broad framework. Only you can impress upon your top EOP officials that you genuinely want them to honor the presumption. Many subsequent disagreements between the Cabinet officer and your top EOP staff can be worked out through discussion. On those that can't, the chief of staff should conciliate, before taking the decision to you, and should, whenever possible, support the judgment of the Cabinet officer.

The partial delegation on the mixed presidential/secretarial issues does not impinge on the traditional functions of the Office of Management and Budget. If cost is an important component, you personally will have to make the decision about expenditure levels in the context of your four-year budget strategy. The regular processes for estimating costs and deciding cost levels, meanwhile, remain unchanged. Nor is OMB's traditional legislative clearance role affected. Again, you are likely to make the major controversial decisions on the shape of a presidential/secretarial bill. Subsequent questions, when the actual legislation is drafted, should be guided by those decisions or worked out between the staffs or the principals. A more complicated problem arises when administration legislation is being marked up in committee or subcommittee, forcing the administration to take positions on specific amendments. OMB should determine the cost of those amendments, but the agency should not make the unilateral political judgment on whether the amendment should be accepted. Again, in instances where the issues relate largely to one department, the secretary should make the decision after close consultation with the OMB director and your top political advisors. If the amendment is of great consequence, the decision may have to be taken to you.

It should also go without saying that the Cabinet secretary with the lead on a second-level matter should be able—as appropriate—to receive assistance from the EOP: lobbying should be carried out in close coordination with the White House congressional office; media efforts by the departments should be coordinated with the White House Office of Public Affairs; approaches to interest groups should take advantage of the broad view held by the head of White House political affairs. Thus, on the more important presidential/secretarial issues, it may be appropriate to set up a White House task force, paralleling the department structure, to focus White House assistance for the effort. But the technique should not be used except on the most important mixed second-level matters. Otherwise, the task force mechanism will be devalued, as it was in the Carter administration, simply because there is not enough time in the day for key White House or EOP staff to sit on many task forces; and second- or third-level White House staffers have much less clout in the world beyond.

**4. A Word About the Hill and the Interest Groups.** Your immediate subordinates may have difficulty dealing with the interest groups and the Hill on the important presidential/ secretarial issues. Once you have made the broad strategic decision, the Cabinet officer should handle the external negotiations and publicity surrounding the issue—and this means dealing with the interest groups and the Hill.

If the members or Hill staffers or interest group representatives do not get immediate satisfaction through the lead department, they will often start calling around the White House until they find a sympathetic assistant to the president or deputy assistant to the president or assistant to the deputy assistant to the president. The White House or EOP aides cannot simply ignore the Hill staffer or the congressperson or the interest group representative on these issues, but they can respond in an appropriate way.

The inappropriate way is to start second-guessing the Cabinet officer without the facts, and then to try to solve the problem for the caller directly, going over the Cabinet officer's head. The temptation to do this, especially for lower-level White House staffers, is hard to resist because it gives the staff aides a sense of importance, both in their own eyes and in the eyes of the caller. The more appropriate way to respond is to listen, say that either the White House or the secretary's staff will be back to the caller, and then determine, after consulting with the secretary or the secretary's staff, who should handle the matter. Normally, the departmental staff should then deal with the problem. If the caller is especially important to you, your staff and the departmental staffs can decide who in the administration should formally respond.

To resolve most public policy issues requires hard bargaining and negotiation. And unless you have a single negotiator or bargaining point for an issue, the person out front will be continually undermined; your administration will appear confused; and it will, in fact, be much less effective. The Carter administration was often not disciplined enough to lodge clear negotiating responsibility in the departments. Instead, outsiders with access to the White House telephone directory played dial-a-staffer, calling around until they could find an aide, at whatever level, who would be willing to take up the cudgels on their behalf. As George Reedy has observed: "There is, on the part of White House assistants, a tendency to bring to the White House problems which should not properly be there, frequently to the disadvantage of the President."[15]

This is not a minor problem. And it is one likely to occur with some frequency on important presidential/secretarial matters until the administration indicates clearly that it will not allow wedges to be driven between the White House and the departments.

## H. Secretarial Issues: The Basics of Delegation

Most of the important decisions made by your administration will be secretarial or routine in nature. As we have indicated, secretarial issues should be distinguished from routine issues as part of the strategy of governing: they put the top officials on notice that they have priority importance, they constitute a likely list from which the administration's accomplishments will be drawn, and they will be monitored (but *not* controlled) in the White House. When secretarial issues do not cut across departmental lines, they should be largely delegated to the Cabinet secretary, and the Executive Office of the President should limit its involvement as the issue is decided and implemented.

Secretarial issues should be evaluated by the *results* produced. If the program isn't cleaned up, if avoidable political crises hit the administration unexpectedly, if mistakes are made which undermine passage of a third-level piece of legislation, and if some or all of these problems recur with any frequency, then you can decide that the Cabinet officer's performance is inadequate. *But the key here is to give the secretary room to maneuver without having a White House or EOP aide—most often from the second, third or fourth echelon—peering over his or her shoulder or over the shoulder of a top presidentially appointed sub-Cabinet official (like a deputy secretary or an undersecretary).* You should, in short, be much more concerned with results than with processes.

**1. Your Role.** Compared with your role on presidential or even presidential/secretarial issues, your role on these third-order matters should be extremely limited.

—You should decide which secretarial issues are important enough to carry on the working agenda of administration business for purposes of devising the overall strategy of governing. This simply means culling out of a very long list of potential issues facing the administration those matters that, while of third-order importance, are important enough to become the focus of special secretarial attention. *These are issues for which you will hold the secretaries personally responsible.* The broad cut at issues should probably be made at the beginning of each of the two Congresses that will serve during your coming four-year term; but as you continually review the strategy of governing, you may determine that events have forced issues onto the priority lists before scheduled review meetings take place.

—A few of the more important secretarial matters may be of special interest to you, and you may want to set goals with respect to them. Where possible, this can be a one-shot setting of standards that will form some basis for judging whether or not the Cabinet secretary has performed well. For example, the secretary might be asked to reduce error rates in a major domestic program by a certain percentage or to try to stimulate a certain number of health maintenance organizations in a given time period. But even this goal-setting by you will be rare—unless the goal is fairly obvious. Otherwise you will get into too much detail. An alternative route: after you have identified the secretarial issues, you may want to ask the Cabinet officer to establish goals you will review. In any case, your main role is to identify the issues as being of some importance —and of potential value to the administration's record of performance.

To be sure, you will have a few "hobbyhorses"—smallish issues in which you take a large interest because of your personal background or that of the First Lady. But don't let the hobbyhorses grow into a herd.

**2. The Role of the Executive Office of the President** will be discussed in detail below. Suffice to say here that the role of the EOP on the more important secretarial issues—the ones that you will look at closely in judging the performance of the Cabinet secretaries—should run parallel to the role you perform on the mixed presidential/secretarial issues. Generally speaking, the head of the relevant EOP staff unit (most likely OMB) should concur in the broad approach to the particular problem. Any dispute should then go to the chief of staff. And once the issue is resolved there should be nearly complete reliance on the Cabinet secretary. The senior EOP aides should make suggestions and provide their perspective on the important secretarial issues when reviewing the overall approach. They should only rarely try to force a different approach down the throat of the secretary (by taking the issue to the chief of staff for resolution). In general they should keep their hands off.

But EOP aides will want very, very much to keep their hands on. The only real solution to this pervasive problem is to have a tough-minded and politically savvy group of top political appointees in the EOP complex, especially in OMB. This group must control staffs, not be controlled by them, and work out problems with the top-level political appointees in the departments. For example, the undersecretary or assistant secretary for either management and budget or planning and evaluation in the department should work out a solution with the deputy director of the Domestic Policy Staff or the deputy director or associate director of OMB. Rarely should such matters even rise to the secretary and the heads of OMB and your domestic-affairs staff. Even more rarely should they be taken all the way to the chief of staff for formal resolution. And they should almost never find their way to your desk.

But if you have weak people at the political levels—in either the departments or the Executive Office of the President—you may find the permanent staffs in perpetual disagreement, even if they are in effect speaking through one of your political appointees. And once it gets up to the political appointees, then brush fires can become conflagrations that must be put out by even higher political appointees, leading to the bitter feelings often engendered when the need for formal dispute resolution arises.

You must therefore initially choose the right independent-minded people for the key political appointments in the EOP, *especially in OMB*, and then make sure that, unless secretarial decisions are clearly controlled by a larger strategy call (like the overall level of spending for specific governmental functions), deference is given to the Cabinet secretaries, *especially on decisions that are essentially operational or managerial in nature.* A good example of how this can work is the budget practice of providing a department with a lump sum within a final spending level and then allowing the secretary, after consultation with his top advisors, to decide how to allocate the sum among various departmental requests rather than having the budget examiners in OMB try to impose their will on very fine-grained decisions.

**3. The Cabinet Role.** The essential role of the Cabinet secretaries on secretarial issues is to *make decisions* (not advise or manage processes) and to produce results. That, at least, is their function, properly conceived, as seen from your perspective.

But when operating within their own departments, the Cabinet secretaries will have a different general role:

—to question departmental experts sharply, and not be bamboozled by them.

—to work with, but stand up to, the interest groups surrounding the department, as necessary.

—to work with, but not always please, the key committees and
subcommittees.

—to delegate, as you do, to their chief operating officials charged
with managing major domestic programs.

To perform as an effective political executive in a department
requires a special combination of personal skills.

**4. Summary Chart.** On pages 162–163 we summarize our
approach to delegation when the priority issues do not involve
competing jurisdictional claims from a number of departments.

## I. The Cabinet Officer: An Abbreviated Job Description

Looking at their departments, Cabinet officers confront the
same kinds of problems that you do when deciding how to
structure your administration. They will find the same tensions
between line and staff functions; between policymakers and
program managers; between the complexities of policy and the
imperatives of politics. And there are the same needs to set
priorities, to think strategically, to delegate effectively and, most
of all, to provide leadership.

Service in the executive branch of federal government is a
profession unto itself. No past professional experience is a sure
guide to an effective Cabinet secretary. Lawyers, businessmen,
administrators in the nonprofit world, or state and local officials
—all can be highly successful secretaries, or abject failures.

One can recite a litany of the qualities a political executive
must possess. The ideal secretary should have a sense of history
and a sense of humor; a feel for ideas and for numbers; an
abundance of courage, integrity and loyalty. But in keeping
with our view that resolving the tension between policy and
politics in a strategic context is *the* creative act of executive
branch governance, we would isolate two characteristics.

*First*, the secretary must have a strong and independent mind.
In many respects, the greatest challenge in government—given
the astounding time pressure—is to make sense out of an overwhelming amount of information, to ask the right questions

*Delegation on Major Domestic Affairs Issues*

| | *Presidential* |
|---|---|
| Number | 5–10 |

| | |
|---|---|
| President's Role | —Intense in both internal development and external effort<br>—Strategy *and* tactics |

| | |
|---|---|
| Role of Top Executive Office of the President (EOP) Staff | —Intense advisor role in both internal development and external effort for both EOP and Cabinet<br>—Process lead can be in *either* Cabinet or EOP<br>—If process lead in Cabinet, EOP coordinator ensures options and data requested by others are developed by lead department<br>—Others participate fully in presentation of all decisions to President |
| Role of Cabinet Officer | |

| | |
|---|---|
| Dispute Resolution | President |

| *Presidential/Secretarial* | *Secretarial* |
|---|---|
| 25–35 | 100–125 (if successful, become part of administration record) |
| —Sets broad policy direction only<br>—Sparing use of negotiating or tactical role<br>—Occasional public events | —Identifies issues on secretarial list<br>—May set goals for individual issues (rarely)<br>—Disciplines Cabinet if results are poor |
| —Major officials participate intensely as advisors on presidential decisions<br>—Then only single EOP contact for Cabinet, either assistant for domestic affairs or Office of Management and Budget | —Routine OMB processes<br>—But presumption of regularity and deference accorded Cabinet on policy innovation *and* especially on policy implementation |
| —Process lead on policy development issues headed for President, but subject to EOP participation<br>—One among equal advisors to President on major, direction-setting decisions<br>—Decision-making authority on other aspects of problem, subject to EOP review but with presumption of deference to Cabinet officer | —Substantial decision authority, subject to EOP concurrence in broad approach |
| *Broad Direction*: President<br>*Other*:<br>—Negotiation between secretary and EOP; *then*<br>—Concilation by chief of staff; *or*<br>—Decision by chief of staff (or President if chief of staff thinks it necessary) | —Negotiation between political appointees in EOP and secretary or his/her political appointees<br>—Conciliation and then decision by chief of staff (but deference to Cabinet officer key) |

quickly and to structure problems in a powerful and productive way. It is especially important that the secretary be independent-minded because most policy is too important to be left to the experts. A secretary doesn't have to be a talented generalist, but he or she should be able to question the fundamental assumptions hidden in the assertions of policy experts. Fighting with one's own experts—not being dominated by your staff—is of incalculable importance if a secretary is not to be manipulated and if he is to serve you well. You can only have confidence that our tripartite priority-setting scheme will work if you have confidence that the Cabinet secretaries possess that essential independent cast of mind.

*Second,* the secretary must have an innate sense of politics—of the bureaucratic politics of the executive branch; of the very different politics of the Hill; of the electoral politics that gave you, and the secretary through you, the legitimacy of power; of the politics of the contemporary media, which, out of its strange, semi-conscious symbiosis with government, shapes and limits the potential for governmental action. Obviously, not every potential member of your Cabinet will initially possess knowledge in all those spheres. But he or she must have that intuitive ability to understand those different political worlds and, before very long, to work within them.[16]

Finally, a thought on management. Although we have stressed the importance of effectively managing the departments, of questioning policy experts and setting standards for program managers, the Cabinet secretary need not be a direct manager. He or she will in any event be spending an extraordinary amount of time outside the department: working on major problems in the White House; testifying or lobbying on Capitol Hill; speaking to and meeting with the press, the interest groups and state and local officials. But the secretary must have an appreciation of the management dimension of running a department and must be able to find a top-flight manager—usually the deputy secretary or the undersecretary—who will oversee day-to-day operations. Like you, the Cabinet officer need not actually manage, but he or she must have an understanding of what it is to be a manager and how to set management directions, especially in a period when increased effectiveness has to be a dominant concern for all who serve in the federal government.

## J. Special Problems

**1. The Thorny Question of Sub-Cabinet Personnel.**
Substantial tension often exists between the White House and
the Cabinet secretary over the selection of key departmental
personnel: the sub-Cabinet presidential appointments (the deputy secretaries, undersecretaries and assistant secretaries) and
the other political appointments (those made at the discretion of
the secretary). Indeed, it became an article of conventional wisdom at the political levels of the Carter White House—and
among the political writers—that the first-term Carter administration gave away the government by allowing the Cabinet
secretaries to pick the sub-Cabinet and the top nonpresidential
departmental employees. But we think that view was incorrect.

Subject to several qualifications that follow, Cabinet officers
must have great discretion in choosing their most important
subordinates.[17] The top twenty to thirty people in each department are essential if that department is to move according to
your priorities and the priorities of the Cabinet secretary. As the
connecting link between your strategic world and the operational world of the department's permanent government, the
Cabinet secretaries must have subordinates they trust and with
whom they feel comfortable. And the only way in which they
can get such subordinates is to make important personnel
choices themselves.

If you are going to hold the secretary to account and are going
to obtain loyalty from the secretary because you delegate important responsibilities, then the necessary corollary is that you
must give the secretary control over the key people who will be
working in the department. If you want to please interest
groups, let them judge you on the results of governing, not on
the placement of people in key departmental positions. If you
need to reward campaign workers, find jobs less important than
the top sub-Cabinet jobs in the major departments. If you think
you need loyalty, focus on the Cabinet secretary's loyalty—that
will ensure the loyalty of his subordinates. To be sure, the
Cabinet secretary will have to pay attention to the political
needs of his department, and may have to compromise on some
jobs accordingly. But let him make that decision. He, much

more than you or your staff, has to live with the result. An assistant secretary for legislation or planning, a key commissioner or administrator may technically be your appointment. But you will see him or her five or ten times a year, if that often The Secretary will be talking to him as many as five or ten times a day.

There are two qualifications to our basic approach:

—The White House personnel operation should set, and monitor, affirmative action goals for the executive branch as a whole and for each department. Those goals should provide firm guidance for the Cabinet secretaries, and they should live within them.

—The White House personnel operation should be able to recommend that you exercise a *personal* veto on the important jobs. Although the secretary should be able to pick individuals he or she wishes, so you should be able to conclude that, for political or other reasons, the designated individual is not suitable. That still leaves the secretary substantial room to find someone else who will be satisfactory.

The White House personnel operation can play a valuable formal role in generating the names of possible candidates for key positions and an important informal role in discussing the merits of various candidates with the secretary's own personnel staff. But that operation should not dictate to the departments. You must hold the secretaries accountable for the performance of those whom you appoint but who work for the secretaries. But the secretaries, not the White House personnel officers, have to produce results.

**2. Length of Service.** Jimmy Carter was right in theory when he exacted a four-year pledge of service from those whom he selected for the Cabinet. Major jobs in the federal government are enormously complicated, and it takes a good deal of time to learn the position and to begin to make a difference even when individuals start with some knowledge of the policies and politics of their areas. Directing a major department is like steering a supertanker; it takes an agonizingly long time to turn the monster even a few degrees. And staying power is important because the civil servants have correctly come to expect that they can normally outwait the new people and their "unrealistic" ideas. Moreover, changing the head of a major department can cause a dramatic disruption and waste precious time by bringing work temporarily to a standstill. The four-year commitment is a good one to seek. Indeed, even that time period would seem brief to those in the private sector, given the complexities of government positions.

A related question is the grounds for divorce as you might see it, since, inevitably, all your appointees will not work out to your satisfaction. Two obvious reasons for a firing are manifest incompetence or statements undermining one of your positions by the Cabinet secretary. But as to the second point, you should have strong evidence: Iagos will always lurk in your inner court waiting to play on rumor. And the cost of publicly firing a Cabinet officer can be great because it is often difficult to find a credible public explanation that does not cast doubt on your previous judgment or your existing policies. A more subtle ground for severance is that a key appointee is not working well with the constellation of advisors or Cabinet officers with whom he must constantly deal—is not interlocking in a productive way. If you feel that one of your appointees is not performing, the best course is quietly to work out a resignation schedule.

**3. Access to You.** You should consider whether you ought to meet alone, on a regular basis, with those members of your Cabinet whom you do not see regularly—at least at the beginning of the term. These informal sessions would not involve decision-making and need not be lengthy. They would also help cement personal relationships and would provide the Cabinet secretary with an opportunity to give you his sense of the problems in his department that are of particular concern to you. This is not directly useful time, but such meetings could easily constitute an investment that will pay off in the long run.

**4. Access to the Department.** The White House staff is often tempted to go around the Cabinet secretary and begin to use the department's staff for its own purposes. This should not be permitted. If EOP officials want the departmental staff to perform important (nonroutine) tasks, they should clear these through the Cabinet secretary or his top subordinates. Otherwise the secretary will simply be unable to command his own troops. If the political appointees in a department are not being responsive to the EOP, the chief of staff can address that situation. But the common problem is that low-level White House staffers, without your knowledge or even the knowledge of their bosses, issue requests or orders to departmental staff that sharply cut into their time to perform tasks required by the secretary. On the major issues, there should be an immense amount of traffic between the secretary and his staff and the top White House staff.

**5. Coalition or Congressional Cabinets.** To help bridge two fundamental gaps in the political system, you should at least consider Cabinet appointments from the congressional ranks and from the ranks of the opposing party.

—A key congressional appointment or two can, at least in the near term until the inevitable scars start to show, informally create a higher level of executive-legislative partnership in key areas, based primarily on the appointee's understanding of and goodwill in the Congress.

—A key appointment or two from the other party may also be useful in giving the administration the centrist cast necessary for governing. Customarily, appointments from the opposing party do not involve people active in partisan politics. But they will have enough contacts in their own party to be informal emissaries to your adversaries and to help you in consensus-building. Other administrations have done it, and it may be a tradition worth reviving.

We do not, however, unequivocally recommend either course. There are definite problems associated with both: the members of Congress may bring with them from Capitol Hill the antipathy of their enemies as well as the goodwill of their friends; and the appointment from the opposite party will not be much use on the partisan matters of nomination and election. And such appointments will hardly solve the problems of improving executive-congressional relations or achieving consensus on major national problems. But they may help.

## K. Can Delegation Work?

Many forces can throw into an unseemly snarl our proposed use of Cabinet officers. Reconciling the need for centralization and the imperatives of decentralization in decision-making, advice-giving and process management may fail for a number of reasons. They include:

- *The Media.* It is an open question whether you can reverse the trends of the past twenty years and simply say: "My secretary of the treasury is handling that." To the extent that you are able to find strong, powerful and credible figures to serve in your Cabinet, the media may find them sufficiently newsworthy to accept them as your surrogates when they speak on major mixed presidential/secretarial issues. Certainly a Henry Kissinger or a Jim Schlesinger, a George Schultz or a Joe Califano, were strong enough figures to find media acceptance as figures standing in for the President on important matters.
- *Rivalries.* The issues of executive government involve high stakes, and the internal politics of your administration can easily sink into a Hobbesian world of unmitigated conflict. Because powerful personalities will be bumping into one another under tremendous pressures of time, rivalries will develop just as inevitably as thunderstorms sweep across Washington on humid summer afternoons. Fairness in process and firmness in final decisions can ameliorate the problem, but they can't solve it.
- *Splintered Structure.* Much as you may want to decentralize, the frustrating jurisdictional overlaps of executive government—which give many Cabinet officers a piece of numerous policies—can force many issues up to the White House/EOP. Indeed, managing integration is a serious obstacle to our preference for decentralization on second- and third-order issues. Giving the process lead to the dominant secretary, having a process check in the EOP and establishing a chief of staff to conciliate or resolve disputes short of you will help—but that, too, won't solve all the problems.

• *Staff Size.* Your key White House and EOP staff—the OMB director, the CEA chief, the presidential assistant for domestic policy—will all find their hands full with the presidential and presidential/secretarial issues. But it is those who serve three or four levels down on their staffs who will pull more matters into your house than should be there. Here a simple expedient will help. To the greatest extent possible, keep the political appointees on those staffs small in number.

Formal structure is important in trying to solve these problems. But of equal importance is how you instruct those who serve you, how conscious you are of these difficulties and how serious you are about not letting them undermine executive government.

Although delegation is aimed at keeping your attention focused on the essential, you must pay attention to the structure of delegation. You cannot simply decide once how it should work, and then ignore how in fact it is working. This will require an informal feel and an informal intelligence system about executive government. Some, like FDR and LBJ, had it: they loved gossip, knew everyone and had their tentacles everywhere. If you don't have this innate feel for the government, you will periodically need more formalized meetings with your key officials in the EOP and the departments to get a sense of how executive government is working, beyond what you personally are seeing. Without that sense, you will be too divorced from the delegation scheme that you have sought to impose.

You can make it work, at least better than it has. *But you must want to make it work, and you must adopt a strategy of governing that provides a framework for resolving the inevitable disputes before they land on your desk.*

## L. Addendum: Policy Development

To illustrate the relationship between the departments and the EOP and to give a hint of the procedural complexity, we will describe in outline how a presidential initiative on energy conservation might be developed inside the administration. The initiative would involve both legislative changes and changes under existing law. The Department of Energy obviously has a dominant interest in the issue, but other departments, agencies and EOP units will also demand to play in the game—for example, the Environmental Protection Agency, Transportation, Treasury, Commerce, Labor, the Council of Economic Advisors, OMB and the assistant for domestic affairs.* The Energy Department would have the process lead. The assistant for domestic affairs would have the process check and would be responsible for ensuring that views of others are reflected in the work done by the Energy Department and in the papers that go to the President. But the assistant for domestic affairs would also have to consult closely with the EOP's economic policymakers. The broad steps would be as follows.

## 1. Problem Defined and Different Approaches Outlined

—High-level EOP officials would discuss with Energy and other departmental officials tentative placement of the initiative in the overall strategy of governing.

—The Energy Department would develop a paper defining the problem to be addressed with as much precision as possible and outlining broad approaches for its resolution (tax incentives, new regulations, voluntary program for enhanced efficiency, etc.).

—This paper would be circulated at a staff level to interested parties within the executive branch for comments, criticisms and additions.

## 2. Private Consultation Outside the Executive Branch

—Energy Department draws up list of key people to consult: in the Congress, state and local government, industry, labor, public interest groups, etc.

—List is checked with key people in the EOP: domestic affairs advisor and political advisors, for example.

—Informal, private discussions held between administration officials and selected outside parties on problems, approaches and politics.

---

*And possibly State, if direct action, such as tariffs or quotas, is proposed against foreign-produced energy.

### 3. Key Technical Issues Identified

—As a result of Step 1, the Energy Department staff would work with staffs in the other departments and agencies to define the critical technical issues that would have to be addressed before various approaches and options could be evaluated: cost estimates, supply and demand projections, incentive effects, etc.

### 4. Work Plan Developed and Agreed Upon

—The Energy Department would prepare a work plan for the development of options, resolution of technical issues and more formal consultation.

—This plan would be shared only at a high staff level (assistant secretary or deputy assistant secretary) in other departments and agencies.

—Domestic affairs advisor would ensure that there was agreement on tasks and who was to perform them and on timetable.

### 5. Presidential Event

—President might give speech, meet with business and labor, travel to dramatic site to begin process of publicly defining and dramatizing the issue.

—President might also talk personally to key people outside the executive branch about the problem.

### 6. Second, More Focused Round of Consultation

—After developing a sense of what groups, interests, actors are likely to be key in either the legislative or the administrative contexts, a second round of consultation would take place between key administration officials and important people on the Hill and elsewhere, focusing in on a number of broad options (approaches reduced to general proposals).

—Domestic affairs advisor would convene group of high-level actors from the administration, including the White House political advisors, to discuss the results of the consultation.

### 7. Preparation of Options Paper for the President

—Basic drafting done by energy secretary/staff, according to options identified in work plan.

—Circulation for comments to core departments/agencies (with major interest in issue) and to EOP.

—Staff level meetings to highlight and define carefully key technical, judgmental and political differences.

—Final draft signed by key departmental and EOP principals, with opportunity for short, personal papers from the principals attached to coauthored options paper.

—Domestic affairs advisor, political advisor and energy secretary discuss how to present political questions to the President if they are too sensitive to put in memorandum, including place in strategy of governing.

## 8. Presidential Decision Meeting

—President is briefed on broad options and there is debate among principal actors before him.

—If he can, President makes tentative decision about options he prefers. Otherwise, if he raises questions, these must be resolved.

## 9. Intense Technical Work Continues

—After presidential guidance, staffs dig in on preferred options to see if there are underlying technical problems and to begin preparing basic arguments, facts, and legislative specifications in support of the proposal. Centered in Energy Department, but interdepartmental work group cooperating at this stage.

## 10. Third Round of Consultation

—At greater level of detail, with key technical people outside the administration, but not revealing presidential preference, although options reduced in number.

—If necessary, at broader conceptual level, with number of influential people outside the administration.

## 11. Second Round of Presidential Decision-Making

—After broad guidance, there will be a host of second- and third-level issues of importance to the conservation initiative.

—Process of preparing them for the President as in Step 7 above.

## 12. Detailed Decision-Making

—After this round of presidential decision-making, there will still be a host of technical and fourth-level decisions to be made. These are secretarial in nature. If relating only to a single department, Cabinet officer makes them, after decision process within department. If cross-cutting part of the initiative, domestic affairs advisor makes them after consultation with OMB and economics types. Appeal to chief of staff on either kind of decision, if others feel it necessary.

## 13. Presidential Curtain Raiser

—Another scene-setting event.

## 14. Preparation of Strategies for the Issue

—Although these have been discussed in decision-making, now quite specific strategies for securing acquiescence or implementing the various components of the initiative are devised, primarily by the Energy Department, but with involvement of key EOP units, chief of staff and then President.

—Media approach for announcement of issue clarified.

## 15. Preparation of Basic Documents

—Drafting and approval of fact sheets, legislative specifications, actual bill language and presidential message. These are carried out in departments, with EOP review.

## 16. Final Pre-Announcement Consultation

—On eve of announcement, out of courtesy to most of those who have been consulted before. With less important actors, can also be done immediately after formal announcement.

—Statements of support solicited from those inclined to approve, and these people may be brought into White House for announcement.

## 17. Announcement

## 18. Working Group Established for Legislative Process

—To coordinate work between the departments and the EOP, there will be working group to focus on the precise details of the strategy here in a precise time frame. President continually informed/involved.

## 19. Secretarial Issues
—The regulatory and other administrative components of the initiative are now secretarial issues which are the responsibility of the Cabinet officers to carry out. How they fit into the broad initiative should now be clear.

## 20. Updating
—Domestic affairs advisor, political advisor and energy secretary establish schedule and method for continually reporting to President on various aspects of initiative.

—Presidential involvement at tactical level on important elements of initiative as it moves forward.

# IV·
# PROVIDING
# STRATEGY
# AND COHERENCE:
# THE EXECUTIVE
# OFFICE OF
# THE PRESIDENT

O<small>N</small> the morning of Inauguration Day—after an old administration has effectively expired, before a new one takes office—the West Wing of the White House and the Old Executive Office Building next door stand virtually empty. Desks are clean, walls are stripped of photos and plaques. This fleeting moment of calm reveals the distinguishing property of the top echelons of the Executive Office of the President (EOP)—total subservience to you.

Here will reside your top personal staff and the elite of the EOP's institutional staff—your appointees all. These discretionary appointments are at the core of your presidency. The people who fill them will provide you with day-to-day support; they command the permanent civil servants of the EOP; and they will become vital channels of communication between you and the rest of executive government. Here, in short, you have a chance of truly governing, not merely presiding. That you succeed in governing here is vital to your presidency, because the EOP is your chief instrument for converting the executive branch into a coherent administration, responsive to your strategic goals.

Unfortunately, the EOP was not designed for this role. In fact, it hardly seems to have been designed at all; it just grew. Even its name is deceptive: the EOP is not an executive office.

Rather, it is a bloated and disorderly grab bag of separate and mutually suspicious staffs, units, councils, boards and groups with strikingly different histories, purposes and problems. It must struggle, in turn, to bring some coherence out of the jumbled structure of executive government, which has also grown haphazardly and remains jumbled because the Congress wills it so. Even more perplexing, the EOP must impose at least some order on the obstreperous world of domestic affairs that, of course, defies the neat organizational lines by which government tries to cage national problems.

To pursue a strategic presidency, you will have to restructure the EOP and manage its work with a good deal more skill, discipline and imagination than your recent predecessors have been able to muster. If you can't make your will felt here, you cannot succeed as president.

## A. A Cook's Tour of the EOP

Like so many institutions of the executive branch, the EOP owes its contemporary contours and powers to the bureaucratic creativity of the New Deal. In the late 1930s, Roosevelt sought to wrench the tired and rather impotent Budget Bureau out of the Treasury Department and to convert it into his personal instrument for controlling the funding requests to Congress of all executive departments and agencies.[1] In 1939, the Congress approved Roosevelt's reorganization plan and established the Executive Office of the President, with the Bureau of the Budget at its core.[2] This set the vital precedent of a central staff concerned as much with the substance of governing as with servicing the President's daily needs.

Over the ensuing years, the EOP has grown explosively. Today even publishing a telephone book for the EOP is difficult (it is always out of date). Similarly, an organization chart that would show how the units actually mesh with one another is literally impossible to construct. No overall structure to the EOP exists. All staff units are suspended in the fluid medium of palace politics, and the currents and eddies of the medium vary a great deal from president to president.

One way to understand the confusion is to look at the organization of the EOP in terms of proximity to you. The West Wing of the White House houses the Oval Office; the *Old* Executive Office Building (the OEOB) is just across West Executive Avenue from the West Wing; and then come a host of structures, including a New Executive Office Building (NEOB), scattered within a block or two of the White House itself. Put all these together—the West Wing of the White House, the OEOB, and the other sites—and you have in them the people who comprise the Executive Office of the President (the EOP—not to be confused with the EOBs, old and new).

Historically, the top personal staff occupied the West Wing; the elite of the institutional staff, the Old Executive Office Building; and the lesser lights of both institutional and personal staffs, the outer geographic reaches of the EOP. But today it's not quite that simple, in important part because the distinctions between the personal staff, the institutional elite and the institutional staffs have become increasingly confused. There should of course be institutional dimensions of the EOP to provide continuity from administration to administration and to guard executive traditions and prerogatives. But the concept of a strategic presidency is built, in part, on the need to integrate operationally in the EOP that which in the past has often been distinguished conceptually—"personal" and "institutional" staffs, politics and policy, "budget" and "policy" considerations and economic and social issues.*

**1. The West Wing.** Within a few steps of the Oval Office sit a dozen or so assistants to the President who manage (or at least mix intimately with) the events, issues and crises requiring your personal attention.

During the Roosevelt and Truman years, the West Wing was primarily a personal staff office for the President. With some colorful exceptions (among them, Harry Hopkins and Clark Clifford), West Wing aides were infrequently seen and even more rarely heard, and had no acknowledged role in governance outside the White House. In the 1950s, however, and very rapidly throughout the next two decades, West Wing aides began to specialize and to focus on governing, extending bureaucratic

---

*And, we should add, foreign and domestic concerns, although as we have noted, that critical connection is beyond the scope of this memorandum.

tentacles throughout the rest of the EOP and, from there, into the agencies.[3]

The 1960s and 70s witnessed a dramatic accumulation of bureaucratic fame and power on the domestic side of the West Wing. These personal staffers began to preside over ever larger institutional responsibilities—and ever larger staffs, comprised of either political appointees or civil servants.

—A series of White House domestic advisors succeeded in building up a large EOP staff, parallel to the National Security Council, for coordinating interagency development of domestic policies or developing domestic policies itself with outside help. The evolution began with the small, relatively informal support staffs assembled under Kennedy (Theodore Sorenson) and Johnson (Joseph Califano). In the early 1970s, the Nixon administration formalized and enlarged the handful of aides into a Domestic Council staff managed from the West Wing by John Ehrlichman.[4] This became the Domestic Policy Staff, under Stuart Eizenstat, in the Carter administration, with its chief in the West Wing and its staff across the street in the Old Executive Office Building.

—The press secretary's office, with a professional staff of three in Truman's time, has grown over the years into a large EOP media bureaucracy, replete with pollsters, PR specialists, TV experts and the like—a trend that cannot be reversed given the number of staffers needed to service the electronic media.

—The congressional liaison—the President's personal lobbyist on the Hill—has acquired an EOP staff of specialists on House and Senate activities, so he could oversee legislative tactics for the key items on the administration's agenda and could coordinate agency lobbying efforts on a number of other issues.

—Various assistants for interest groups or constituency affairs have gathered a sizable staff of contact people to hear the demands and grievances of blacks, chicanos, women, owners of small businesses, and so on.

—In recent years, an assistant for intergovernmental affairs has built up a staff to coordinate administration relations with —and federal grants to—the nation's governors, mayors and county commissioners.

—The counsel to the President, your personal lawyer, now has a small coterie of attorneys to oversee legal work and problems throughout the EOP, but also to help you with the inevitable spot assignments.

—Finally, in the last three administrations, following a precedent set by Eisenhower, a senior assistant has served as chief of staff or staff coordinator. The duties of the office have varied importantly from president to president, but have usually included running a small secretariat to impose at least the semblance of procedural order on the creeping empire of the West Wing and overseeing presidential schedules and appointments secretaries. In some instances, the chief has also been the President's top naysayer and most intimate political advisor.

In short, during the past fifty years the West Wing has become a strange, hybrid institution. On the one hand, it has housed the President's own personal mafia of inner-circle aides and advisors—helping him get through his day, loyal only to his immediate political purposes and insulated from the bureaucratic grind of governance. On the other hand, because so many senior presidential assistants head up sizable EOP staffs charged with coordinating agency policies and practices, the West Wing has also become a strategic center of sorts for the entire executive branch. This hybrid status is an uneasy one. The West Wing—the White House to the press and public—has acquired more power and visibility than is necessary or healthy for its traditional role of providing personal staff support to the President, but the West Wing's focus is still too political and short-term, and its structure too haphazard, to serve as a true strategic center. The White House—which because of proximity to you is an institution in both a real and symbolic sense—thus shelters actors playing two distinct roles, their separation reflecting its past, their synthesis (*not* merger), in our judgment, presaging its future.

**2. The Old Executive Office Building.** The old EOB—a huge gray fin de siècle edifice that once provided shelter to the entire departments of State, War and Navy—today contains the top management of the major staffs, councils, boards and offices established by statute, reorganization plan or executive order over the years to coordinate or advise you on the interagency development of administration policy. This has been a self-serious place, far more enmeshed in substance and somewhat less politically charged than the West Wing.

For the domestic presidency, the key units in the Old EOB are:

*—Office of Management and Budget (OMB).* The old Budget Bureau was enlarged by President Nixon in 1970 to oversee executive branch management practices and by Carter in 1977 to oversee departmental and interagency reorganizations (hence the M in its current title), but OMB's main job remains what it has been for almost half a century. It seeks to exert control over the annual budget cycle for the government and thus to serve as the central clearinghouse for your domestic program which takes shape annually from the thousands of spending and legislative requests directed at you by the departments and agencies of the executive Government.

The Old EOB houses the *politically appointed* management of OMB—the director, deputy director, and four associate directors (dividing among them the federal budget's whole array of policies). These officers serve at your pleasure and, while rarely in public view, are critical in welding together the disparate pieces and programs of the administration into a recognizable whole. But the budget shop consists of 470 civil service examiners, just as it did in 1965. Most of these civil servants are consigned to anonymous office space a block north of the Old EOB on the far side of Pennsylvania Avenue.

*—Domestic Policy Staff (DPS).* As noted, the director of this unit traditionally sits in the West Wing, as assistant to the President for domestic policy, but his staff works out of the Old EOB. The staff members specialize in particular areas of policy, attempting to cover the whole range of domestic issues, large and small, ranging from natural gas pricing to DNA research. Unlike OMB, DPS has no civil servants to support it. All its members are political appointees, and by Washington's inexorable process of title inflation, each is at least an assistant director of the DPS. (That is to say, this is

a staff in which no one is staff.) Set up under the Domestic Council rubric by the Nixon administration, the unit was supposed to provide expert long-range planning for Cabinet-level committees in major policy areas. The committees rarely met, however, and the council concept was formally abolished by President Carter.[5] Long-range planning has given way to relatively short-range coordination of interagency policy development and congressional politics.

—*Council of Economic Advisors (CEA)*. Established by the Full Employment Act of 1946 and given its present form by Arthur Burns under Eisenhower, the CEA consists of three senior economists (the members of the council, of whom one is chairperson) and twelve to twenty staff economists. Chosen for one- and two-year rotations from the best economics graduate schools around the country, the staff here is neither political nor civil service in origin or bias. The CEA is the embassy of the academic economists (a position envied by other professions and shared by few). Its role is to provide expert economic analysis of domestic policy options going to the President and, working with OMB and Treasury, to advise the President on the general macroeconomic policies he should pursue. Occasionally the CEA is drawn into the coordination of interagency task forces, but its chief function is to provide advice and analysis, rather than to manage a policymaking process.

—*Economic policy committees*. For at least twenty years economic policy has been made in the executive branch via a Cabinet-level committee (or committees), usually chaired by the treasury secretary.[6] The committees have had no statutory base and have varied dramatically in size, composition and mandate. Generally the committee is considered to be, at least informally, a part of the Executive Office of the President. In the Ford administration, the Economic Policy Board had an actual coordinating staff in the EOP, reporting to a West Wing assistant to the President for economic affairs. The Carter administration's Economic Policy Group, by contrast, was staffed out of the treasury secretary's office and was not considered part of the EOP. Whatever the technicalities, however, the coordination of economic policy is viewed as a major function of the EOP.

—*Office of Science and Technology Policy (OSTP)*. Like the CEA, OSTP is a creature of statute and serves primarily as an advisory body-cum-embassy. It consists of a senior science advisor to the President (the director of the office) and a meritocratically selected staff of associate and assistant directors expert in various scientific disciplines.

—*Inflation Advisor's Office*. Created in 1978 by President Carter, the "inflation czar" is a free-lance advisor (to whomever will listen) on the problem that has dominated economic policy for the past decade. Technically he or she is the head of the Council on Wage and Price Stability (a statutory cabinet committee with a staff resembling CEA's but housed outside the Old EOB). Under the only two incumbents, Robert Strauss and Alfred Kahn, the advisor's own office included a small staff of bureaucratic infighters, trying valiantly to specialize in particular areas of domestic policy which posed inflationary risks.

**3. Other Voices, Other Rooms.** As one moves beyond the Old EOB and thus farther from the Oval Office, the EOP grows more specialized, bureaucratic, and parochial. The looming red brick office blocks along 17th Street and the handsome old Georgian buildings on West Jackson Place, adjacent to Lafayette Park, house the civil servant staff of OMB and the staff overflow from other major policy units in the Old EOB. Administrations have also regularly consigned to this netherworld a large number of less essential operational and advisory units. From time to time, one or another of these units manages to sneak into the Old EOB or to secure a reporting relationship with a major Old EOB policy unit or even with an assistant to the President. For the most part, however, these are operations peripheral to the President's main preoccupations.*

---

*Council on Environmental Quality.* Patterned on the CEA, the CEQ is a statutory board of three members—usually prominent environmental activists—and a technical staff charged with reviewing the development of environmentally sensitive policies in the agencies.

*Council on Wage and Price Stability.* The statutory successor to the agencies that operated President Nixon's wage-price controls, CWPS is a staff of technical economists—the Cabinet-level council never meets. The staff splits its time between commenting publicly on the inflationary impact of government actions and operating whatever wage-price guidelines program is in place at the moment. In the Carter administration, titular chairmanship of CWPS shifted from the treasury secretary to the CEA chairman and finally to the inflation advisor. De facto control of the staff rests with its director.

*Executive Office of the President (EOP): Domestic Affairs*
*(as of July 1980)*

| Year Formed | Unit | Employees | | Location | | |
|---|---|---|---|---|---|---|
| | | Political | Career | West Wing | Old EOB | Other |
| * | VP and Staff | 19 | 0 | X | X | |
| * | Chief of Staff | 21 | 0 | X | | |
| * | Assistant for Domestic Affairs (DPS) | 50 | 0 | X | X | |
| * | Assistant for Intergovernmental Affairs | 18 | 0 | X | X | |
| * | Assistant for Congressional Liaison | 26 | 0 | X | X | |
| * | Press Secretary | 30 | 0 | X | X | |
| * | Counsel | 9 | 0 | X | | |
| * | Assistant for Interest Groups | 10 | 0 | X | X | |
| * | Assistant for Media | N/A | N/A | X | X | |
| * | Office of Speechwriter | 6 | 0 | | X | |
| 1921 | Office of Management and Budget | 6 | 567 | | X | X |
| 1946 | Council of Economic Advisors | 22 | 14 | | X | |
| 1974 | Economic Policy Board (under Ford) | N/A | N/A | X | | |

| Year Formed | Unit | Employees | | Location | | |
|---|---|---|---|---|---|---|
| | | Political | Career | West Wing | Old EOB | Other |
| 1978 | Inflation Advisor and | 1 | | | X | |
| 1974 | Council on Wage/Price Stability | 8 | 225 | | | X |
| 1976 | Office of Science and Technology Policy | 1 | 23 | | X | X |
| 1978 | Office of Administrator | 14 | 125 | | X | X |
| 1974 | Office of Special Trade Representative | 8 | 108 | | | X |
| 1978 | Regulatory Council | N/A | N/A | | | X |
| 1969 | Council on Environmental Quality | 14 | 18 | | | X |
| 1965 | Consumer Advisor | 19 | 0 | | | X |
| 1977 | Aging Advisor | 2 | 0 | | | X |
| 1972 | Office of Federal Procurement Policy | 1 | 44 | | | X |
| | Etc.† | 162 | 140 | | X | X |

Total Employees = 1,700
(approximate)

* A staff office in spheres traditionally considered personal to the President or Vice President, with precursors of various kinds running back to FDR or earlier.

† There may be, in addition to the "etceteras" located beyond the White House/Old EOB complex, a certain number of senior White House advisors playing the role that Hedley Donovan was intended to have performed for Carter: senior advice giver with no day-to-day responsibilities. Historically such people do not last long unless they are personal friends of the President who eschew titles.

In short, by the middle of 1980, the Executive Office of the President included the offices listed at pages 184–185.

## B. Functions

To operate a strategic presidency, you must make this sprawling bureaucracy into more than the sum of all these disparate and disjointed parts. You must discipline it into a supple and efficient headquarters for your administration. The EOP's precise role should vary according to issues—from intense involvement in presidential issues to a somewhat lesser role in presidential/secretarial issues, and primarily a clearance and consistency function (chiefly within OMB) for purely secretarial issues. But whatever the intensity and depth of its participation, the EOP must provide you with four basic services.

*First, process management.* Coursing through the corpus of executive government are basic processes that have to be either managed or overseen by the EOP. Although these processes result in policy innovation, policy implementation, crisis management or moral leadership, they are, because of routines estab-

---

*United States Trade Representative.* This office was created by Congress to handle the negotiation of trade agreements with foreign governments and to coordinate the work of Commerce, Labor, State, and Treasury in the development and implementation of trade policies.

*Regulatory Council.* A creature of a Carter executive order, the council consists formally of the heads of all regulatory agencies, but the actual work is done by a small staff and consists of coordinating regulatory agendas along with reform efforts everywhere in the government. Cross-cutting tasks are also undertaken from time to time by OMB, CEA, DPS and the counsel to the President—a source of considerable confusion and occasional acrimony.

*Counselor on Aging.* This office is a direct voice into the EOP of the nation's elderly —a non-professional embassy—even though the primary operational components (social security, medicare and the administration on aging) are all found in the Department of Health and Human Services.

*Consumer Advisor's Office.* An outpost of the consumer movement, this office proselytizes (in the name of the White House) throughout the executive branch for more consumer involvement in policymaking and for policies that in some sense favor consumers.

*Office of Federal Procurement Policy (OFPP).* A statutory body loosely tied to OMB, OFPP sets the standards by which about $20 to $30 billion of federal contracts are let every year.

*Etc.* The EOP also contains numerous commissions, committees, and offices on virtually every problem deemed by someone to be of presidential significance. At one time or another, there have been EOP units (and staffs) concerned with space policy, drug abuse, acid rain, pensions, agricultural land, spying on Daniel Ellsberg, urban renewal, refugees, coal exports and sex education. Sometimes, but not often, these units disappear when the problem at issue is either solved (unlikely) or forgotten (likely).

lished over time, perceived differently by the EOP itself. The basic processes include: legislative development (leading to an annual legislative program, to major initiatives within that program, and to signature or veto of enrolled bills); the annual budget cycle; economic policymaking; government-wide management initiatives; oversight of regulations with government-wide implications (a new, controversial area); handling of crises that rise to presidential or mixed presidential/secretarial significance; development of presidential words, either to accompany the basic processes described above or to accommodate such free-form appearances as speeches and press conferences; and a host of other support activities (appointments, personnel, hand-holding with interest groups, advancing trips, internal administration).

Although we have argued for substantial delegation down into the departments in Chapter 3, there is, as we have also indicated, a problem that is most evident from the perspective of the EOP. A large number of issues, even smallish ones, are interagency in character, requiring both the solicitation of views from different departments and agencies and *then* the melding of those views into a coherent policy. For example, in deciding whether you should recommend a cut in the social security payroll tax by 0.3 percent, you will need the views and expertise of the departments of Health and Human Services (which oversees the Social Security Administration), Treasury, Labor and Commerce; and in the EOP itself, of OMB, CEA and DPS, and of the political types. Managing this process of integrating views is a critical part of the EOP's business.

*Second, advice-giving.* Obviously, however, the major EOP actors—OMB, DPS, CEA, the various political aides—will not be content simply to manage these basic processes. They will be eager to give advice as to their appropriate resolution. The EOP actors will bring different and important perspectives to bear on problems, but that doesn't mean that their views are somehow disinterested and the views of the actors in the departments and agencies are biased. Nor will denizens of the EOP be any more capable than their brothers and sisters outside the EOP complex to resolve the basic tension between the roles of process management and advice-giving.

*Third, delegated decision-making.* On the presidential and mixed presidential/secretarial issues, you will make basic decisions. But there will also be the subpresidential decisions. Some may involve details after you have made the broad strategic call on a presidential or, more likely, on a presidential/secretarial issue. Some may involve differences of views on secretarial issues that you will never see. Some may even involve routine program and budget details that are not even within the view of the secretary or deputy secretary in the departments.

While your in box cannot (and should not) accommodate all these issues, these matters must be decided, or executive government will either lurch along in fits and starts or grind to a halt. And as the work of the executive branch grows inexorably, as new agencies are created, as reorganizations consolidating departments fail, and thus as issues more and more overlap and crisscross departmental and agency boundaries, the need to make subpresidential decisions grows ever more important. The Constitution creates no subpresidential decider. Only you can establish the structures and processes required to secure such decisions, either by the EOP or by the departments. And, consistent with your constitutional responsibilities, only you can monitor your delegations and assure that over time they reflect what you would have chosen if you had had the time.

*Fourth, strategic thinking.* The EOP's most important task is to pull all the relevant aspects of policy and politics together into a genuine strategy of governance. This applies not only to the overall battle plan but also on a daily issue-by-issue basis for matters of presidential or presidential/secretarial importance. Only in the EOP can the often competing factors of short-term policy, long-term policy, congressional tactics, press impact, interest group relations and party politics be brought within a single coherent focus and disciplined to your ultimate objectives.

If it can accomplish these tasks—process management, advice-giving, subpresidential decision-making and strategic thinking —the EOP will provide a brain and central nervous system to the body of the executive government. When the EOP operates properly, innumerable ideas and bits of information are synthesized into workable plans, and complex signals of direction and control flow smoothly from the center of your government to its many appendages. In recent years, however, the executive branch has too often resembled a witless giant, unable to take the simplest step without falling down in an inglorious heap. In important respects, the blame rests with the structure and management of the EOP. Each president has made his own peculiar errors here, but six generic problems recur from administration to administration.

## C. Failures

**1. Overpopulation.** The EOP is too big. There are too many units, and nearly every one of them has too many people. This is a common criticism, but its usual thrust—that expansion has brought excessive power to the EOP—turns the truth on its head. As with the ships of the Spanish Armada, size is a crippling handicap, not a source of strength, for the EOP. The EOP is powerful to the degree it can clearly and cleanly mobilize the rest of the government into formulating plans and executive actions responsive to your strategy. The EOP is currently much too big even to discern your will, much less to act upon it. The EOP's many chiefs and indians must spend most of their time and energy maneuvering with, around and against each other, rather than providing coherence and strategy to the rest of the government.

The proliferation of third-, fourth- and fifth-tier staffers in many EOP units may gratify the egos of their superiors, but these tyros can do very little useful work for you. Senior departmental officials quickly sense that inflated titles (for example, assistant director of the Domestic Policy Staff) do not carry with them a direct understanding of your purposes or the capacity to invoke your support or wrath. Accordingly, junior EOP staffers often spend their time creating nuisance work for lower-level agency officials, inventing projects and hatching intrigues unrelated to your objectives. The result is simple mischief. The White House suddenly finds itself associated with some cause or controversy of which even your Cabinet secretaries and senior EOP aides are (quite properly) ignorant.

Similar mischief usually attends the creation of a special EOP advisor, counselor, ambassador, consultant, or assistant to worry about a problem of undeniable significance: for example, inflation, refugees, peace in the Mideast, ghetto riots or world hunger. Typically, these czars find themselves without access to bureaucratic levers and spend their time throwing into confusion whatever established procedures already exist within the EOP for coordinating policy.*

The spreading size of the EOP irritates your Cabinet officials, *but its chief victim is you.* The EOP is unmanageably bulky. Unless shrunk and streamlined, it will resist all efforts to make it into an effective instrument of your governing strategy.

**2. Functional Confusion.** The EOP is now cluttered with units designed to do things other than provide the basic services of process management, advice-giving, delegated decision-making and strategic synthesis. The additional tasks are rarely unimportant, but they do not logically belong in the President's house. (You will not find them, for instance, in the main offices of your fellow chiefs of government in Europe and Japan.) These extraneous tasks fall under three headings.

• *Line or operating programs.* When Congress or the bureaucracy invents a new program that deserves prominence and fits awkwardly within the existing framework of agencies and departments, everyone's favorite solution is to put it in the EOP. If you don't complain, no one else will. That is why you will find under your wing the wage-price guidelines program (CWPS), the Office of Federal Procurement Policy, and many other small to middling bureaucracies which, however essential to the Republic, bear to you a relationship indistinguishable from that of numerous other agencies and bureaus in the executive branch. These operating units suck minor controversies into your house, and the EOP locale tends to overpoliticize the programs themselves, in substance or appearance. Their work may not reach you, but these offices will surely eat up more of the valuable time of your top EOP subordinates than they should (or would if located elsewhere). As a general matter, the EOP

*You may need special fire fighters if a crisis hits: but as soon as possible the problem ought to be pushed back into a more structured environment—either within the EOP or the departments.

should not operate programs. Its task is to synthesize administration policy from programs operated elsewhere.

• *Special interest outposts.* Throughout our history, the nation has been witness to a well-organized politics of grievance, but especially since the mid-sixties, every organized grievant has demanded a room or two in your house, in the name of compassion, equity and open government. Thus you will find that CEQ belongs to the environmentalists; the Consumer Advisor's Office represents the consumer movement; the Office of Science and Technology Policy often wields a lance for science grantees; and so forth and so on.

These days, it is inevitable that executive government provide redoubts and staging areas for powerful interest groups. These groups almost literally camp out around the bureaus and administrations of the major departments. But you need not give them a place at strategic headquarters. The EOP's function is to help you discern and dramatize the national interest, and this of course involves understanding the pleading of discrete, specialized interests. But far too often the Washington lobbyist now has not only his agency but also his EOP staff unit or person. This duplication of lobbying opportunities undercuts the usefulness of your agency heads as intermediaries to—and buffers against—the constituency groups.

• *Finance ministry functions.* Two of the oldest and most important offices in your EOP—OMB and CEA—are in a sense extraneous to its proper purposes. In most democracies, such units are lodged within a cabinet department, generally the ministry of finance. Control over public spending (OMB) and expert analysis of economic trends and policies (CEA) are functions that other nations typically place at one remove from the head of government, merging them with such related functions as tax policy, domestic finance and international monetary policy—which is to say, the roles presently vested in our Treasury Department. What the United States has done, in effect, is split up its finance ministry, leaving the bulk in the Treasury but placing two vital pieces in the EOP.

This makes the EOP far larger and far more detail-oriented than the usual staff office of the prime minister in other countries. The American practice forces the chief executive to be a part-time finance minister, a function for which he rarely has adequate time or training; which, unless carefully controlled, embroils him more than is healthy in the minutiae of the budgetary process; and—perhaps most important—which robs his economic policy of clear and continuous direction by a single senior officer in the Cabinet.

**3. Jurisdictional Conflict.** Whenever it attempts to integrate the conflicting views of the rest of the government— whether to develop policy options for you, or to decide below your level on a plan of action, or to facilitate execution of your decisions—the EOP typically exhausts itself with its own particularly enervating brand of turf-fighting. Although one of the EOP's primary jobs is to create a coherent government policy on related problems out of differing agency perspectives, too often the EOP is itself paralyzed by internal conflict. This is largely because there are no accepted lines of jurisdiction between the various EOP units. Everyone here has ample excuse to nose into everyone else's business, and it is rarely if ever clear from the formal structure of the EOP who is in charge on any particular issue or problem—who is deciding, who is advising and who is managing the decision process. As a result, issues may proceed through the EOP at a glacial pace; meetings and draft papers move in lazy circles from office to office; and departmental officials find their requests for central guidance converted into weapons in the eternal wars of attrition which low-level EOP staffers wage against each other.

Jurisdictional conflict is most acute in the two broad areas of policy dominating the domestic presidency: economic policy and domestic program coordination.

• *Economic policy:* Economics is everything and nothing, a term lacking natural boundaries. Virtually *every* issue entering the EOP is arguably the responsibility of whatever economic policy coordinating machinery may exist. This creates chronic friction between that machinery and the parallel devices (that is to say, DPS and NSC) set up to coordinate the rest of domestic and international affairs. Days have been spent in theological quarrels about whether a particular issue is really a part of economic, domestic or international policy. Setting up a coordinating apparatus for economic policy is itself an exercise in jurisdictional conflict. Since history has deprived us of a finance ministry, the EOP has had considerable difficulty reconstructing workable linkages among these core economic agencies. Which of these core economic agencies should be first among equals? If an EOP staff is needed to coordinate them, what should be its relation to the President, the lead agency and the other agency staffs? While questions like this fester, the EOP finds it cannot go the next step and smoothly coordinate the policies and operations of the many other agencies with a major stake in economic policy, whether they be inside the EOP (for example, Inflation Advisor's Office, Council on Wage and Price Stability, and U.S. Trade Representative) or scattered about the Cabinet (for example, Commerce, Labor, State, Energy).

• *Domestic program coordination*: Before the EOP's explosive growth in the late 1960s and 70s, interagency work on most domestic program issues was coordinated by the Old Budget Bureau, with White House aides intervening only when matters of very high policy or sensitive politics were at stake. This implicit jurisdictional understanding has been totally eroded by repeated waves of organizational innovation. Four organizational trends have proceeded simultaneously:

—*First*, after its creation in 1970, the DPS has expanded into a staff of thirty to forty issue experts intent on taking over from Budget Bureau bureaucrats the task of coordinating interagency policy formulation.

—*Second*, upon being transformed into OMB (also in 1970), the budget office acquired a new high-level tier of politically selected associate directors, who inevitably aspired to supplant White House (and DPS) staffers in coordinating development of important domestic policies.

—*Third*, during the 1970s, the EOP acquired specialized policy offices—for example, the Council on Environmental Quality and the Office of Science and Technology Policy—which took as their mandate the coordination of interagency policies relevant to their specialties.

—*Fourth*, as the nation's economy sank into stagflation and concerns arose about the inflation and employment effects of large domestic programs, the economic units of the EOP—CEA and CWPS—began to maneuver forcefully for a major role in the coordination and analysis of many domestic policies. Today, in the vast area of domestic program coordination, the EOP often has more trouble pulling itself together than it does in composing whatever differences may exist throughout the whole rest of the government.

**4. Procedural Disarray.** Lacking structural neatness, cluttered with inappropriate functions and suffering a chronic overlapping of coordinating jurisdictions, the EOP obviously and rather desperately needs procedural discipline. If the EOP is to supply you with advice, decisions and strategy, it too needs firm and precise rules of the game to make it clear who gets to participate in what, under the process management of whom, for decision by whom, by what date. Ordering relations within the EOP is just as important as ordering relations between the EOP and the departments.

But the EOP has proven remarkably resistant to orderly procedures. Most large executive agencies (and some EOP units —for example, OMB) have permanent secretariats whose sole function is to set up and run an orderly process of decision-making. These institutions have developed a certain tradition of bureaucratic regularity. But for the White House proper, and the EOP as a whole, each new administration must totally rediscover the virtues of procedural discipline. This is rarely done well, for no one of sufficient eminence (that is to say, sufficient access to the President) wishes to spend his time making the trains run on time—although the issue is as much keeping the trains on the track as on time.

Typically, the EOP displays a strange balkanization in its procedures. Each particular area of policy or practice—international economics, energy, regulatory reform, health, environment, speechwriting, lobbying, constituency liaison—evolves its own peculiar procedural routine, as the interested parties, in and outside the EOP, get to know each other and learn how to push business haltingly forward through an elaborate exchange of favors. Sometimes these informal mini-networks attain a semblance of efficiency. But they are rarely linked together, and there is nothing to ensure any of the networks against a massive brown-out at some critical moment.

The absence of overall procedural discipline deprives the EOP of two organizational virtues of which it has abundant need and which—in a properly run administration—the EOP would itself be lavishing upon the entire government.

- *Due process.* Without procedural rules, the game of government can get extremely rough. Victory is often most easily attained by seeing to it that likely bureaucratic opponents do not get a fair hearing. Knowing this, everyone becomes highly suspicious of everyone else. This produces comic results, but it is a serious matter. In the EOP, power derives not from money or programs, of which the EOP has little and few, but from access to the President and the policy deliberations of his top aides. This is why otherwise sane officials spend entire days trying to find out what meetings are being held to which they have not been invited and what papers may be circulating without their review or comment. The absence of due process exacts a huge cost in time and morale. More importantly, it virtually guarantees that you will get distorted information and an incomplete range of views, and that the officials excluded from participation will resort to press leaks and cocktail-party rumors to strike back at their bureaucratic foes —and at you.

Providing due process is a giant headache. The top levels of government are today overpopulated and scandalously leaky. Providing full access to every official who has an arguable interest in the matter at hand is neither feasible nor desirable. But the EOP too often lacks even a primitive code for determining who should be involved in what.

- *Peripheral vision*: Lacking overall procedural discipline, the EOP is very bad at creatively fusing the many aspects of its expertise—economic analysis, budgetary analysis, domestic policy planning, congressional tactics, media planning, constituency group tactics and so forth—into a synoptic view of the issue at hand. During the Carter administration, an issue too often reached the President's desk as a large pile of memoranda, one from each relevant department and each of the EOP advisors, and the President was left to apprehend the connections and gaps between their specialized views and to attempt some imaginative synthesis of the competing perspectives.

Perhaps the most important integrating job the EOP should, but does not, do for you involves our favorite fusion: between policy and politics. As we have noted, every issue has both aspects, and each aspect is itself usually a compound of contrary hunches, estimates and considerations. And policy is itself a field of combat for many antagonistic EOP offices. In the political area as well, there are strong institutional rivalries between the offices responsible for congressional affairs, constituency group relations, media strategy and state and local government affairs. As an issue slowly and contentiously bumps its way through the EOP maze, most of the important factors get some consideration, but they are rarely considered *together*, with the relevant trade-offs and compromises receiving sustained attention. Because EOP procedures are sloppy and weak, the political staffs and policy staffs are rarely forced into creative cooperation. The adversary and disorderly character of EOP life leads each staff to exaggerate its own biases and preoccupations. The policy people lampoon many of the political types as hacks, while your political aides dismiss the substantive difficulties of policy as academic irrelevancies. Very little useful dialogue occurs to bridge the gap, leading to many failings and not a few disasters.

**5. Indecision.** You cannot decide all the disputes and problems that flood into, and well up within, the EOP. But the need for orderly dispute resolution at the center grows more acute each year. The need is aggravated by the factionalism of the EOP itself: even if the rest of the government magically relapsed into harmony, the EOP would need some mechanism for settling its own disagreements.

But the EOP has rarely been structured or run to provide for orderly subpresidential decision-making. Far too many third- or fourth-order issues get themselves resolved at the President's desk or in a haphazard fashion—either through interagency logrolling ("I'll back your bad policy if you'll back mine") or through a conspiratorial abdication of executive responsibility (letting Congress settle the matter, with each executive agency lobbying for its own distinctive position). These methods totally undermine the strategic coherence of executive government.

Like any venerable and complex social institution, executive government has its own peculiar traditions of deference and hierarchy—the expectation, in other words, that someone short of you can make final decisions. For instance, certain Cabinet officers expect—and are expected by the bureaucracy, Congress and the press—to have the final say on certain types of subpresidential issues (that is to say, subject only to personal countermand by the President). Prime examples are the treasury secretary in the area of tax policy, and the secretary of state in the active conduct of diplomatic negotiations. On other kinds of issues, certain EOP officials are considered legitimate issuers of the last word, short of the President—for example, the OMB director, for small and middle range disputes about program spending levels; the CEA chairman for official economic forecasts; the congressional liaison for daily tactical arrangements with the House and Senate leadership.

These rules of legitimacy are vague, shifting and unwritten, but they can be upset only at the risk of confusion and resentment throughout the permanent government or the returning veterans of former administrations' wars. But the EOP has usually shown far too little sensitivity to these rules in fashioning procedures for dispute resolution. Second-level aides in EOP policy offices are tapped (or self-appointed) to usurp the traditional prerogatives of Cabinet officers; the press secretary steps in to interpret the economic outlook; political aides try to settle budget disputes; a Cabinet officer is granted authority to bargain with the congressional leadership about scheduling votes on programs outside his department; and so on. By proceeding in such fashion, across the grain of expectations held throughout the executive branch, the EOP actually undermines its ultimate goal of containing the centrifugal forces that threaten coherent presidential government. To be effective in the long run the EOP's mechanisms for decision-making short of you must instead clearly build upon traditional centralizing forces already at work in the executive branch.

There is a related problem: lack of accountability. President Truman's slogan, "The buck stops here," has no application in the EOP. Because everyone has a claim to be involved in everything, no one is ultimately accountable for anything. Office labels are no help. Under President Carter, DPS had putative responsibility for all things domestic, but most of these things involved spending (and thus OMB), legislative planning (the Congressional Liaison Office), economic policy considerations (the EPG, CEA, the inflation advisor, and CWPS), and constituency problems (the offices responsible for interest groups and state/local relations).

The absence of accountability greatly impairs the quality of individual performance in the EOP. It is not that people here need the fear of blame as an incentive to excel; most EOP staffers work murderously long hours out of a mixed sense of duty and self-importance, and many perform with great skill and intelligence, under the circumstances. But without accountability, no one feels called upon to take charge of anything. Those who try soon give up in frustration. Accordingly, the EOP lacks the extra dimensions of decisiveness, judgment and imagination even a talented and conscientious person can draw from himself only when he knows that an enterprise truly depends on his efforts. And that means understanding whether his role, or the role of his office, is process management, advice-giving or decision-making. For example, when procedural integrity is set at war with policy decisiveness, the typical result is the collapse of the coordinating process and a chaotic rush to your desk by all the disputing parties on issues that should *not* concern you.

**6. Lack of a strategic center.** Owing to its centrality, to its relative detachment from the great agency bureaucracies and to its proximity to you, the EOP should impose—or try to impose—strategic coherence on the rest of the executive branch: it can help you develop and regularly enforce a set of interrelated priorities which integrate the major aspects of policy and politics inherent in a genuine governing strategy. That you should demand this service from the EOP is a major theme of this memorandum. But as traditionally structured, the EOP will not be able to respond effectively. *The EOP has no strategic center.* As an institution, it is incapable of surveying the whole terrain of the domestic presidency, let alone of plotting a four-year path across that terrain. The EOP is full of units and staffs charged with overseeing large areas of domestic policy and politics, but *there is no mechanism for bringing all these perspectives into a strategic focus.*

The West Wing has not evolved into a strategic center for the government for three broad reasons.

First, Presidents have persisted in filling many West Wing positions on the domestic side with trusted cronies and campaign loyalists. This invariably creates a wide cultural gap—a gap of talent, knowledge, experience and preoccupation—between the West Wing and the rest of the executive branch (including the rest of the EOP).

Second, the West Wing's bureaucratic links with the rest of the EOP and the agencies are partial and haphazard. For instance, the head of the DPS is typically here, but the OMB director is not, and the Carter West Wing did not house anyone with responsibility for making or coordinating economic policy (although the Ford White House did). The West Wing has gathered to itself sufficient governing authority to preclude the ascent of any *other* strategic center within the EOP, but it has failed to integrate all the bureaucratic elements necessary for a comprehensive view of the domestic presidency.

Third, the central importance of the strategic approach—and the need for formulating and reformulating a battle plan in the broad sense—has not always been recognized per se, although every administration has obviously had bits and pieces of something that could be called a strategy. And there has not usually been clear responsibility lodged in someone for actually developing and updating our conception of a strategy of governing.

The West Wing is not just a convenient symbol for the need to bring the diffuse threads of the EOP and the administration together to create a strategy of governing, and to ensure that the personal and institutional pieces of the EOP work together. Proximity to you *and to each other* is a surprisingly important dimension of that basic EOP task—providing strategy and coherence to executive government.

## D. Staffing

In the rest of this chapter, we suggest ways to cure the EOP's ills by reforming its structure and procedures. But none of these suggestions will do much good without the right kind of people to implement them.

While the various slots in the EOP obviously differ—your CEA chairman and legislative liaison will not be interchangeable—the essential requirements for top-level appointees do not vary much from position to position. You need to find talented generalists or very broadly gauged specialists to counter the centrifugal tendencies of parochial expertise and constituency bias that constantly threaten the EOP with civil war. Keep in mind that from *your* perspective all these officials will really have the same job: to convert dispute and uncertainty into government—whether the dispute is between agencies, Cabinet egos, ideologies, technical projections or political hunches. They must know how to get things done. Producing concrete action that fits your governing strategy is the job of both your CEA chairman and your legislative liaison.

For each post you are looking for the same peculiar constellation of talents. As we have noted in discussing the Cabinet, government is a unique profession, with its own strange set of skills.

**1. Experience.** Bureaucratics require practice. The most effective EOP officials have usually served at least one substantial tour in an earlier government. Age and professional seniority are reasonably reliable sources of the skepticism and prudence that will prove essential in the crisis atmosphere of the EOP. Furthermore, gray hair and a certain worldliness are needed for the frank, easy liaison EOP officials must regularly conduct with Cabinet officers, congressional leaders, corporation executives, union presidents, faculty deans and other keepers of America's power structures. When the White House calls, the nation's elite expects to encounter substance and accomplishment—not a brash whiz kid or some water carrier from your campaign. Your first- and second-tier EOP officials should be longer in both professional accomplishments and the tooth than has recently been the case. There are literally hundreds of distinguished former government officials who secretly yearn for another tour of duty. You can get excellent people for your EOP, embodying years of invaluable training. Don't settle for less.

**2. Camera shyness.** Franklin Roosevelt said that White House aides should have a "passion for anonymity." His superb dictum has been forgotten. In recent years, top EOP officials have increasingly taken to the morning talk shows, the Style Section of the *Washington Post* and even *People* magazine. Second-tier aides have run about producing "background" for reporters covering every major area of policy. This is all justified as necessary to get the President's views displayed prominently and accurately in the media, but the practice is thoroughly pernicious. Once he becomes a public personality, with publicly stated views, an EOP official loses much of his raison d'être—which is to help you quietly broker and compose the views of contending public figures in the agencies. Publicity makes an EOP official part of the problem you hired him to solve. Though background or off-the-record jabber may make the aide feel important, chances are great that the transmitted information will be much more helpful to the reporter than to you.

When it seeks the limelight, the EOP savagely undercuts the credibility and press appeal of the Cabinet secretaries, who are the administration's proper day-to-day policy spokesmen. The secretary must be trusted to enunciate policy with flair and accuracy—and not be upstaged by your assistants. Where presidential nuance or context is needed, by way of supplement, a *top* EOP official can readily provide it on a background basis. This age-old practice is consonant with the EOP's necessary role of managing some of the government's drama behind the scenes, so long as the backgrounding does not itself create an appearance of disagreement between the EOP and the Cabinet secretary in charge. But, at all costs, you will want the vast preponderance of your EOP aides to stay discreetly in the wings. Find people for the EOP who genuinely disdain the publicity side of public policy.

**3. Fairness.** By this capacious term, we mean to invoke all the gentle virtues—modesty, honesty, openness, courtesy, decency, tolerance, etc. To have fair-minded people in the EOP is not merely nice, it is also efficient. A top EOP position is the wrong place for the arrogant genius, for the ideologue who places policy objectives ahead of fair procedures, or for the paranoid master of sharp practice. Anyone who feels badly used, deceived or insulted by EOP officials will invariably retaliate by withholding information and cooperation from you. This will weaken your grip on policy and isolate you.

Your agencies, the Congress, the press and every other institution important to you must come to trust your EOP as a basically fair instrument for processing information, for reporting contending opinions to you and for resolving disputes. Your substantive policies will inevitably be biased—that is what policy means—but your people, and the procedures and manners they deploy, should positively reek of open-mindedness and balance.

Fairness is also wholly consistent with firmness and decisiveness. Indeed, to make things stick once they are decided requires that everyone with an interest goes away persuaded that the processes of decision were fairly run. You personally can instill fear; your staff must win respect by straight dealing.

**4. Strategic intelligence.** Your main job as president is to set the main themes and pace of executive leadership. In the welter of crisis and detail, you will need help doing this job. In the top EOP jobs, you will need men and women who think the way presidents do (or should)—namely, those who pay attention to the connections between policy and politics, who understand the historical forces at work and who can place issues within the context of a long-term strategy for accomplishing broad public objectives. They must, that is, be able to get outside their own roles—even as they work slavishly to do them—and see as broadly as you must. Your top EOP aides should be able to address intelligently the vital question of where the whole enterprise of your administration is going. They should instinctively assess an issue not only on its policy merits and political appeal but on its relationship to everything else flowing across the desks of the EOP.

Strategic intelligence of this sort is a very rare quality in government. Tactical skills or narrow expertise are easier to find, but the top EOP jobs should not be wasted on people whose talents run only to maneuver or technical analysis.

## E. Structure: The Channels of Activity

If the EOP is to bring strategic coherence to your presidency, you must first bring some measure of organizational coherence to the EOP itself. And the first step is to consolidate the related functional pieces now strewn about the EOP into clear, broader channels of activity monitored by key presidential aides. Here we describe the basic structure, arguing, without detailed discussion, that particular aides should be the focal point for EOP activity in particular areas. In the next section, we then explain how these aides and their staffs relate to the basic processes of process management, advice-giving and decision-making with respect both to other EOP actors and to the departments and agencies on presidential, mixed presidential/secretarial, secretarial and other routine issues.

Although we generally counsel against wasting time and resources on reorganization, the EOP is an exceptional case. Given the genuine problems the present EOP causes, bringing a measure of order out of the chaos has a genuine premium in this instance. Furthermore, the political and bureaucratic costs of reorganization are somewhat attenuated here. This is, after all, your office, filled largely with your own people, all of whom are concerned with according some deference to your organizational desires.

Nonetheless, we advise you against ripping up the EOP and starting from scratch. If you *were* starting afresh, you could shrink the EOP drastically into a very simple staff mechanism for presidential coordination and control of the strategic direction and major disputed issues of your administration. You could shift OMB and CEA to the Treasury Department, thereby creating a strong finance ministry capable of bringing discipline to the bulk of your domestic program and your economic policy, as is the pattern in most European governments. You could similarly farm out to the agencies or extinguish all the other advisory and operating units which presently clutter the EOP. This would leave you with a single presidential support and coordinating staff—of perhaps thirty to forty professionals—which you could organize along simple lines to pull together the politics and substance of major issues (presidential and presidential/secretarial issues) in the economic and domestic arenas, drawing upon the resources of all the agencies and structuring the appropriate delegation of authority to Cabinet officers.

But we shall not pursue this fantasy. It would entail major reorganization in the *departments* (especially Treasury), and that would not be worth the effort. Congress would not sit still for it, and you presumably have more important things to do over the next four years than fight a thousand political wars in order to create a theoretically tidy structure for the EOP.

You will have to structure carefully here by low-visibility efforts. Tact and an eye to practical consequences will serve you better than fancy theory publicly flaunted.* *You must start with what exists and attempt to reorder the internal relationships so that a workable design emerges.* The point is not to make a pretty design —a symmetrical organization chart on paper—but to create an organization that is substantially free of, or at least minimizes, the six great defects of the current EOP we have described above.

*In short,* what we recommend is less messy, not demonstrably neat. But we believe it has a practical chance of success.


In essence, there should be four major channels of EOP activity, headed by a senior official who will at different times be the focal point for the activity within the EOP. These major channels of administration revolve around:

---

*You should not overplay your cards with respect even to the minor, client-oriented EOP subunits. Many of these units were created by Congress and have gathered about them entrenched constituency groups and elaborate traditions. Keep in mind that President Nixon turned a generation of professors and engineers against the GOP by abolishing the Science Advisor's Office (it came back, with reinvigorated staff and self-importance, under Mr. Ford); and that Jimmy Carter nearly undercut his very considerable environmentalist credentials by merely *considering* a proposal to move the CEQ out of the EOP (he rejected the proposal after assessing the political costs).

In general, you should use working procedures, rather than formal organization charts, to shove peripheral staff units—those generally housed beyond the West Wing and the Old EOB—from stage center: if you deny a particular unit regular access to you and your top advisors, and quietly make agency heads aware they need to pay the unit no particular heed, its role will wither away in substance, if not form. This takes longer than formal abolition or the noisy shuffling of organization boxes, but it will save you much pain. An exception: depending on your anti-inflation plan, you may want to move CWPS back to Treasury.

—an assistant for political affairs (including broad media strategy) who gives coherence to the fragmented world of executive branch politics.

—an assistant for domestic affairs who oversees formulation of the most important and politically sensitive domestic program issues (chiefly of presidential or mixed presidential/secretarial status).

—an assistant for economic policy, who is the treasury secretary acting as the chair of the Troika (Treasury, CEA and OMB), and who is responsible for the coherence and direction of economic policy.

—an assistant for budget/management—i.e., the OMB director —who runs the budget process and is responsible for oversight of the bulk of the domestic program—that is to say, all the secretarial issues and routine issues requiring EOP guidance and coordination.

In addition, there are three other key EOP aides who are not part of the four main channels of activity but who have access to you and who can be used by you to act in those channels (usually to give advice or handle crises) as appropriate:

—the Vice President.
—the President's counsel.
—the press secretary.

*And* sitting above them all (except the Vice President), and acting for you much as an effective deputy secretary would act for a secretary in a Cabinet department, is a chief of staff who functions in effect as an executive director of the entire Executive Office of the President.

There is nothing magical about the four main channels of activity. The lines between these areas are obviously flexible and unscientific, and it will be necessary to assure efficient integration at all levels between the channels. But these four groupings build in a practical way upon the responsibilities of the existing, major units in the EOP and give you a good prospect of eliminating most of the functional confusion and jurisdictional conflict which paralyze day-to-day operations in the EOP.

**1. Assistant for Political Affairs.** The White House is overstocked with political advisors, each supported by EOP staffs expert in some isolated aspect of the political game. Under Carter, there was a separate presidential aide for each of the five arenas in which that game is played: the Congress; the interest and constituency groups; the political party, or more accurately the politically active groups within the party that may prove crucial to the politics of renomination; the governors and mayors, who can strongly influence your ability to lead national opinion, the Congress, your party and even your own domestic agency bureaucracies; and the world of middle- to long-term media strategy—involving polls, the print and electronic media, and public opinion—by which your advisors seek to create a favorable political climate of opinion for your actions.

As the political game has grown more complex, the EOP has had trouble keeping activity in these arenas synchronized with one another and with the flow of policymaking within the administration. The political staffs tend to fly off in contrary directions, each stressing its own view of the political forces bearing down on you. The situation calls for a major organizational innovation—a single assistant to the President for political affairs, with an integrated staff.

Most presidents have had West Wing aides concerned chiefly with their political well-being; Hamilton Jordan played this role for Carter, Haldeman for Nixon. But as these examples demonstrate, the role has varied enormously—from free-floating guru without management responsibilities (Jordan during Carter's first two and a half years) to absolute dictator of the White House staff (Haldeman). Our proposal is to create a senior *political* aide with explicit responsibility for the major EOP staff functions in the political area: congressional affairs,* constituency group liaison, party relations, state-local government relations and media operations. Each of these areas in turn would

*Some may argue that a person who is a deputy assistant for congressional relations will have less clout on the Hill than an assistant to the President for congressional relations. But to the extent the head of congressional relations speaks for you, and makes good on his word when it is given in your name, we think this a problem of form, not substance. In any event, to help ameliorate this problem, this deputy would have a parallel title: director, White House Congressional Relations Office, and would have an office of his own in the West Wing. See pp. 243–247, below.

be headed by a deputy to the political advisor. The political aide would coordinate all these functions, both with each other and with the policy staffs. He or she would be responsible for synthesizing political intelligence and pressures arising from all sources into an integrated political advice that would be keyed to your long-run interest. His recommendations would balance the politics of governing, nomination and general election, and would provide a coherent and comprehensive political perspective to your strategy of governing.

Without a single aide at the apex of all these political channels, the advice you receive will be fragmentary and ill-digested. Depending on the relative strength of the personalities involved, politics will degenerate into an obsession with congressional tactics or with poll-watching or with interest group alliances. You are a first-rate politician, but you are now too busy to practice the art full-time. You need someone to help you pull together the disparate, conflicting considerations and to assess for you the subtle trade-offs between them, and the potential for imaginatively playing forces and interests off against each other to create new political opportunities.

Moreover, a single aide is also needed to help effect a fusion of politics and substance in your high policymaking councils. Your chief policy officials have enough problems integrating the various dimensions of policy. They won't want a large bloc of political aides fluttering about their deliberations with conflicting political advice. But they will welcome an ongoing relationship with an assistant for political affairs who can join with them in reconciling politics and policy—or at least seeing clearly what the choices are—on the major administration issues.

**2. Assistant for Domestic Affairs.** You need a single, relatively small staff (ten to fifteen people) to coordinate (with the Cabinet agencies and other EOP units) the development of the twenty-five to thirty-five major domestic policies—typically innovative in their substance, and controversial in their politics—that we have called presidential or presidential/secretarial. These issues are so important to your presidency that they ought to be handled, in a substantive sense, by a streamlined unit that has no other responsibilities. This unit is headed by your assistant for domestic affairs.

This redefinition of the role of the assistant for domestic affairs has several different rationales:

*First,* it will eliminate some of the problems that were created by the growth of the Domestic Policy Staff. DPS has consisted of forty to sixty people who specialized (though they were infrequently expert) in a variety of substantive areas. They attempted to manage great numbers of interagency issues and to maintain close liaison with all manner of constituencies. Too often, DPS has been a complicating factor throughout the government, an institutional rival of OMB in the routine business of government below what should have been the presidential and presidential/secretarial issues, and a powerful magnet for interest group pressures on the White House and thus on the President.

*Second,* the top domestic affairs issues of your presidency are so important to you—and so complicated in their political and technical detail—that you need a staff, and staff leadership, that will devote all its energies to those matters, and not be bothered with all the other controversies in the government that a broad jurisdictional mandate creates. To be sure, the big issues are related to the little ones, but these big matters will usually involve a substantial break with the past, while the little ones can be more routinely handled by OMB as part of the existing flow of executive business.

*Third,* no other office in the EOP can really handle this task. As we note below, the economic channel should review a number of domestic-affairs initiatives with economic implications, but the top actors in that channel will be so consumed with the basic issues of macroeconomic policy that they cannot pay enough attention to the other high-level issues in domestic affairs. Similarly, the Office of Management and Budget has its hands full with the budget process, with general management responsibilities and with running the more routine processes of executive government.

*In sum:*

—The jurisdiction of the assistant for domestic affairs should be restricted to the major domestic initiatives of the administration. On those, he should either be the process lead (interagency issues) or the process check (Cabinet lead).

—His staff, which can continue as the Domestic Policy Staff, should be reduced in number.

—His staff should be more clearly expert in its areas of concern (health, income security, education, etc.), but broad enough to work closely with the political advisor and his staff and with the departments and agencies both in developing policies internally and securing agreement for them outside the administration.

—His staff should not be in direct competition with the flow of business through either the economic channel or the more routine budget-management channel, because his lead responsibilities will be restricted to the presidential or presidential/secretarial issues not in those channels.

—He should have the ability to draw on the expertise of other EOP units and the departments and agencies as necessary in the handling of these major issues—rather than building up an elaborate analytic apparatus himself. Since his primary task is in fact working with the other EOP units and with the departments and agencies in defining issues, identifying needed information and establishing timetables, he should be able to work out cooperative agreements on the use of staff with the principals. If you can make his role clear and identify your priorities for the rest of the government, you can make this happen.

**3. Economic Policy, the "Troika," and the Treasury Secretary.** Economic policy obviously needs its own channel. Only a small number of *particular* economic programs or initiatives will be of presidential-level importance, but the general direction and coherence of economic policy will be perhaps the most significant aspect of your domestic presidency in the early 1980s. To formulate and impose a coherent economic policy, you will need a strong and efficient EOP mechanism, for the economic game has many players: Treasury, Commerce, Labor, Energy, Agriculture, HUD, Transportation, among others in the Cabinet, and OMB, CEA, CWPS, and the U.S. Trade Representative in the EOP. The centrifugal forces here are enormous. Even if it does not directly develop an issue, the economic channel should have clear authority to participate in the review of proposals which arguably could have a significant impact on the economy (on GNP growth, inflation, unemployment, investment flows, the balance of payments, etc.). The only way you will get a coherent economic policy is to build a mechanism that can in fact move all the levers and buttons of executive government that influence the economy.

Recent experience has amply demonstrated the problems of fragmenting or constricting the economic channel. President Nixon made the error of splitting the channel in two, creating separate EOP coordinating mechanisms for domestic and international economic policy. The international channel (called the Council on International Economic Policy) came under a relentless, turf-jealous attack by bureaucrats at the NSC, the Treasury, and State. President Carter, by contrast, allowed issues of major economic importance to move through the Domestic Policy Staff without detailed review in the economic channel, the Economic Policy Group (EPG), on the theory that energy, agriculture, environment, regulatory reform and the like were domestic rather than economic issues. This practice too often robbed the Carter administration's economic policy of coherence or theme.

To avoid this kind of fragmentation, and to assure a measure of coherence and consistency to economic policy, you need an economic channel in the EOP which has a broad jurisdiction and a compact organizational core. The channel's jurisdiction should be as broad as your economic advisors desire. Virtually every issue, domestic and foreign, should be open to thorough review by the economic channel. In many areas—for example, fiscal and monetary policies, trade, energy, agriculture, employment programs, incomes policies, regulatory reform—the economic channel itself should provide process management for the issues within the EOP. But even when process management is instead provided by DPS or OMB (or at times the NSC) the economic channel should have the clear right to review the issue's progress and to advise you on the implications for the shape and thrust of your overall economic policy. The EOP should not treat economic policy as a narrow subcategory of domestic affairs. Rather the EOP's structures and procedures should treat economic policy as an overarching discipline on the development of programs and policies across the whole sweep of the presidency.

Though its sweep across policies and departments should be broad, the economic channel should be streamlined organizationally. The channel should be centered on the so-called Troika agencies—Treasury, CEA, and OMB. And the chair of the Troika should clearly be the treasury secretary. You cannot formally reorganize CEA and OMB back into the Treasury, but you should set up this channel to create a similar de facto result. It is true that the Troika agencies share conservative biases— toward spending restraint and reliance on private market incentives and mechanisms. But the economic conditions likely to prevail over the next four years make it important that these agencies have their views fully aired and presented. To fight inflation, revive productivity growth and find room for tax relief, you will need a consistent economic voice which only the Troika can provide (even if it doesn't always prevail).

The Troika arrangement, created informally by President Kennedy, has withstood the test of time. Like a ministry of finance, it can weave together all the central threads of economic policy: spending policy (OMB), tax policy (Treasury), dollar policy (Treasury) and general principles about the effects of policy on sectors of the economy to guide program design across the government (CEA). The Troika should be in virtually continuous session, at Cabinet, sub-Cabinet and staff levels, so as to fuse Treasury, CEA, and OMB into a single organism, capable of withstanding frontal assaults from the rest of your administration. These three agencies should keep no secrets from each other. A de facto fusion of the Troika agencies will occur with spontaneous enthusiasm, if supported by you, because their respective bureaucracies share a mutual respect, a mutual desire to keep the government on a coherent economic path, and a mutual appreciation of the extraordinary power which their agencies can wield in concert.

There is a certain tension between giving the economic channel a very broad jurisdiction and limiting its permanent membership to just three agencies: Treasury, CEA and OMB. Powerful arguments will be made to expand the Troika by regularly including, among others: your domestic and national security advisors, to facilitate their coordination with the economic channel; the labor secretary, to provide liaison with the labor unions and to heighten sensitivity to employment issues; the secretary of state, to provide a fuller understanding of the international dimensions of economic policy; the commerce secretary, to reflect the insights of his business and trade bureaus; and so on. None of these arguments is frivolous, but accepting them would mean creating a giant and cumbersome Cabinet committee. Unless your administration is marked by an unusual (and probably undesirable) ideological consensus, this committee will be unable to fashion a consistent economic strategy. Accordingly, some other mechanism—a secret core committee or some particular advisor—would have to evolve as the de facto center of economic policymaking. The better approach is to retain a small core committee and involve the non-Troika agencies in economic policymaking through two special procedures. First, the core Troika committee should regularly, frequently and fully advise all other major economic agencies about the agenda of its actions, deliberations and concerns, inviting suggestions and criticisms. Second, whenever an issue is of legitimate interest to another agency, that agency should be drawn into the core committee on an ad hoc basis to participate as an equal partner in developing options *for that issue*. By these procedures, all of the government's many economic actors and agencies can be kept fully abreast of the general flow of economic policymaking and can be assured of fair participation in all actions of interest to them. At the same time, however, the Troika can retain its peculiar and vital integrity at the center of the process.

**4. Director of the Office of Management and Budget.** The channel over which the OMB director presides—program coordination and budget control—should in certain respects be the busiest: it would absorb all the budgetary and interagency policy issues neither big enough for the restricted presidential and presidential/secretarial agendas of the Domestic Affairs Staff nor sufficiently crucial to overall economic strategy for management within the interagency economic channel. We recommend that oversight of this residual traffic be lodged in OMB. This was the normal practice until about 1970. Thereafter, the creation and expansion of DPS (and of CEQ, OSTP and the like) confronted OMB with fierce institutional competition in the business of coordinating medium-level interagency disputes and of assuring that each agency's programs and practices conform to overall presidential strategy.

OMB lost its monopoly in this business because Republican

presidents thought it too liberal in orientation and Democratic presidents thought it too conservative, and because various scholars and constituency activists became convinced that budget bureaucrats lacked the vision, creativity and expertise necessary for broad-ranging social reform. There was and is something to these criticisms, but none of the attempted institutional solutions—in particular the expansion of DPS—did anything by way of a cure; these innovations merely created jurisdictional conflict and forced OMB into a more rigidly parochial (green eyeshade) attitude.

OMB should regain its role as the EOP point of contact and review with respect to the vast terrain of subpresidential domestic policy remaining after DPS and the economic channel have scooped off issues of major presidential and presidential/secretarial importance and of importance to the overall coherence of economic policy. To be sure, the OMB director occasionally has EOP responsibility for major presidential or mixed issues too, particularly the annual budget process. But leaving OMB to be the EOP focal point for the bulk of the domestic program conforms to the usual practice in other nations, where the expenditure division of the finance ministry settles out most issues with the other Cabinet agencies without troubling the prime minister's own staff. International comparisons aside, the role is justified by what *should be* OMB's institutional strengths: efficient, fair procedures for tapping agency views and staff work; historical memory of programmatic knowledge; strong secretariat procedures for spotting interconnections and trade-offs among program areas; the clout to force the pace of agency program development; an appeals procedure for raising disagreements swiftly to a political level capable of resolving them; a measure of legitimacy in deciding interagency disputes short of the President; and a layer of politically appointed officers who should (though don't always) have a broader policy/political view of your interests. Admittedly these attributes are the ideal —actual practice has fallen away substantially for a variety of reasons—but it is an ideal you should strive for again.

**5. Other Key Channels.** Our scheme elevates four institutions to coequal primacy within the EOP structure. The notion is quite simply that all the other units in the EOP—CEQ,

OSTP, CWPS, STR, the consumer advisor, and so forth—should work within these channels and find access to you only through coordination and decision processes established and run by the four major units.

To preserve the integrity of the four-channel structure, you should rigorously avoid creating free-lance EOP advisors, consultants, task forces, etc., outside the structure. You may wish to bring talented people into the EOP for short-term projects or assignments, but in each instance they should be attached to one of the channels and instructed that access to you will be available only through that channel and its established procedures.

Having said that, we immediately note three major exceptions. These are men or women who should be free to roam among and outside the channels and to enjoy independent access to you:

• *The Vice President*: If possible, the Vice President should be your senior advisor on everything. This is how Carter used Mondale, and it proved a brilliant innovation, rescuing the office of vice president from two centuries of waste and humiliation. As senior advisor, the Vice President needs a West Wing office and free access to all meetings, deliberations, memos, etc. Unfortunately, this innovation depends to a great extent on whether you and the Vice President have the right personal chemistry. If you do, you should also mimic the Carter practice of salting staff members personally loyal to the Vice President in prominent second- and third-tier positions on the domestic, economic, national security and political staffs. This avoids rivalry and distrust between your staff and his, the typical source of bad blood between presidents and their running mates. It can also prove invaluable when, as in the Carter-Mondale case, the President and his personal staff had less Washington experience than the Vice President and his staff.

Do not, however, give the Vice President managerial responsibilities. He cannot and should not function as your chief of staff or as a deputy president or in any position with a day-to-day operational role. His utility is as a personal advisor, confidant, spokesman, representative or lobbyist for you on important matters. To put him in charge of a middling task force or council of small import (as, for instance, when Johnson was given the

Space Council) detracts simultaneously from his constitutional dignity and, ironically, from the dignity of the enterprise in question, since it no longer can pretend to presidential importance. Putting him in charge of a major policy review (Mondale, for instance, was occasionally handed economic policy reviews by Carter) undercuts the lead Cabinet or EOP official who should be in charge and will make for a procedural awkwardness. Vice presidents are in far too precarious a position within your administration to make final decisions or to boss around your Cabinet members or senior aides. And the biggest problem with giving a Vice President explicit management tasks is that, unlike other personal staff, you can't fire him. Moreover, the tension between you is likely to be too great if the Vice President is publicly perceived as running significant pieces of your presidency. The Vice President's views are best given to you in a quiet advisory role.

• *The legal counsel*: The President's lawyer, backed by a small staff, must handle parochial EOP legal problems and work with the Justice Department on major statutory and constitutional issues affecting presidential power. But like many chief executives, you should come to rely on your lawyer as an intimate advisor without portfolio. The counsel is ideally placed to take on quiet solo assignments for you when a matter of policy or practice involves special complications or sensitivities. Put another way, he or she should be a highly valued fire fighter, picking up tough problems that your other key people are too busy to handle.

• *The press secretary*: The press secretary should report directly to you, independent of (though usually in tandem with) the political advisor. This is necessary to his credibility with the press corps. Reporters will expect the press secretary to put matters in a favorable light and to volunteer embarrassing information rarely if at all, but his usefulness to you requires a certain level of trust and roughhouse affection from the press. If the reporters decide that he routinely shades the truth into propaganda, you will be guaranteed press coverage of uniform snideness and cynicism. A good press secretary will live a double-agent existence—being almost, but not quite, at home in both the press and governmental communities, loyal in his fashion to their seemingly contradictory codes of behavior. Forcing your press secretary to be a simple apologist or flack would in effect impair his usefulness as your spokesman. For this reason, the press secretary should not run your media affairs office. That is a propaganda operation and should report to the political advisor.

On the other hand, the press secretary should coordinate the handling of breaking stories with his colleagues in the agencies. Each departmental press officer should regard your press secretary as his second boss, of an importance at least parallel to the department's secretary. When the White House and a department sing a different song, it is invariably news, however trivial or understandable the mix-up. It is the press secretary's job not merely to interpret you to the press (and the press to you) but also to make your administration appear unified day by day in its verbal reaction to the flow of events. This is a feat requiring lightning reflexes and considerable luck.

## F. Process: The Problem of Subpresidential Decision-Making

Consolidating EOP activities into four broad channels will help make clear which office—political affairs, domestic affairs, economic policy or OMB—is to be the focal point of EOP activity on an issue. At a minimum, this means that the lead office is the process manager *for the EOP,* and other EOP units must offer their advice through the lead office. But two other key questions remain:

- How does the lead EOP agency—in a process-manager sense —relate to the departments and agencies?
- Who makes the inevitable decisions that must be made short of you?

What follows is a sketch which is a companion piece to Chapter 3, the case for delegation, and which lays out when there must be centralized, not decentralized, decision-making within the EOP channels.

Dividing the key issues of your administration into the presidential, presidential/secretarial and secretarial categories has the distinct advantage *for you* of focusing your attention on the critical domestic issues of your administration and keeping less important ones from eating up your precious time. But as we have indicated, the system doesn't solve the problem of who should decide interagency questions of a subpresidential type. These questions are not too likely to occur on the key presidential issues when, by definition, you will make the big decisions personally. But, we must emphasize, tricky subpresidential, interagency issues can arise with respect to: mixed presidential/secretarial issues after you have made the broad strategic decision; secretarial issues that involve many departments without a single department dominating the issue; and routine issues that may be below the sight or interest of the top political appointees in the departments but have an interagency dimension nonetheless.

In essence, when a single department dominates an issue—as HHS dominates health—the discretion accorded the secretary should increase as the importance of the issue to you decreases. And it will be an important piece of administration business for you to make this clear, especially to your OMB director and the top political appointees, who are most likely to be concerned about reviewing the secretarial or routine matters.

But where there is a splintering of responsibility, with no single department or agency clearly having the lion's share of responsibility, we recommend a two-part solution to subpresidential decision-making.

> —The main actor in the particular channel—the assistant for domestic affairs for subsidiary questions arising out of presidential/secretarial issues; the treasury secretary for subsidiary issues of economic policy; and the OMB director for budget, management and routine programmatic questions— should try to conciliate with the relevant actors in the departments to see if a mutually satisfactory result can be obtained.* Failing that, the key official in the channel should make the decision, *even if there are different views in the departments or the EOP itself.*

*This was one of Stuart Eizenstat's strengths as President Carter's domestic affairs advisor.

—This obviously can cause strain. The key actors in the channels of activity are being forced to combine three roles— process manager, advice giver and, if necessary, decision maker. As a check on this in the economic policy area, where a Cabinet officer is elevated above his peers, we recommend an independent process manager located in the White House to ensure fair presentation of views for the other participants on a particular issue. But the more important check, which we discuss below, is the delegation of some provisional decision-making authority on these subpresidential issues to the chief of staff. After the key EOP actor has made a subpresidential decision, it may be taken on appeal to the chief of staff. Nominally, the chief of staff will be deciding whether it is something you should decide, since you will not want to foreclose decision formally. But the reality is that the chief of staff will usually decide either to let the decision stand, to conciliate between the parties, or to resolve the issue himself.

In what follows, we are most concerned with issues developed internally within the administration. On these, the assistant for political affairs will constantly *advise.* However, once an issue emerges into the political world, then the political advisor may have a more dominant role vis-à-vis the other EOP units or the departments and agencies on those tricky cross-cutting issues where a Cabinet officer cannot be the main official charged with gaining approval for administration policy.

By this explicit approach, you have a chance of rescuing the whole notion of subpresidential decision-making, which has acquired a tainted reputation. Unable to structure an acceptable system for the delegating of decision authority, everyone involved—presidents, White House aides, and Cabinet secretaries —has kept up the pleasant fiction that the President himself decides every interagency disagreement. Meanwhile, the actual decisions get made in all manner of secretive or haphazard ways, a system devoid of accountability or the capacity to conform the decisions to an overall strategic plan.

We emphasize that, here too, our solution is less than tidy but that it draws upon patterns of procedure and decision that have worked reasonably well in the past and that have an aura of legitimacy because they accord with existing lines of bureaucratic tradition and authority. There is no reason to create a whole new subpresidency of coordinators and decision makers in an EOP already bloated with coordinating staffs and senior officers. This would merely cause additional confusion and resentment. The goal instead should be to bring out in bold and clear relief the strongest elements of coordination and decision lurking beneath the surface chaos of the EOP and of the executive branch generally.

The chart on page 220 sets out our approach in schematic form. It is followed by a brief word on the processes in the three main channels.

- *The domestic affairs channel*: Because it deals with major issues —presidential or presidential/secretarial in nature—this channel will properly seek most of its big decisions on substantive policy from you. Accordingly, the emphasis within the channel should be on providing a fair and efficient means of coordinating the policy and political views and analytic work of all the appropriate departmental and EOP players into plausible options. Your domestic advisor will typically have views of his own, which you will want to know, but his main task is to bring order and due process to the interagency mechanisms operated by his staff. On matters of procedure, the domestic advisor and his staff should have the last word, although a Cabinet secretary can have the process-management lead when he works in close conjunction with the assistant for domestic affairs. By contrast, substantive questions of insufficient import for your attention (or for that of the chief of staff) should whenever possible be left to the Cabinet secretary most intimately involved in the issue. Before work on an issue commences, this allocation of responsibilities should be set out clearly for all involved.

When the substantive issues are heavily interagency in character, however, the domestic advisor must himself play a larger subpresidential decision-making role than he usually would. Even if the domestic advisor actively seeks to conciliate before deciding, his decisions may ruffle Cabinet feathers, or threaten the actual or apparent objectivity of the DPS as a procedural policeman. The procedural problems of who does what should, on almost every issue of a cross-cutting nature, be discussed with all key players in both the EOP and the departments and

*Subpresidential Decision-Making Authority*

| Type of Issue | Single Department Dominant | Heavily Interagency in Character |
|---|---|---|
| Presidential | 1. President decides on all but technical<br>2. Cabinet and EOP advise | |
| Presidential/Secretarial | 1. President decides broad direction<br>2. Cabinet officer decides rest if no agreement after consultation with EOP<br>3. Chief of staff conciliates if EOP appeals disagreement; decides if necessary, but deference to Cabinet<br>4. President resolves disputes from Steps 2 and 3 in rare cases | 1. President decides broad direction<br>2. Head of channel—domestic affairs, economic, OMB—decides rest if no agreement after consultation with EOP/Cabinet<br>3. Chief of staff conciliates if appeals of channel decision; decides if necessary, but deference to channel<br>4. President resolves disputes from Steps 2 and 3 in rare cases |
| Secretarial | Steps 2 and 3 in presidential/secretarial<br>Chief of staff stops virtually all subsequent disputes short of President, although formal right of appeal to President | Steps 2 and 3 in presidential/secretarial<br>Chief of staff stops virtually all disputes short of President, although formal right of appeal to President |

Subpresidential

resolved at the beginning of the policy formulation process, by the chief of staff if necessary.

• *The economic policy channel*: Here the structure must discriminate clearly between procedural regularity and decision-making.

The subpresidential decision maker should be your treasury secretary. You should rely heavily and explicitly on him to develop and implement an overall economic strategy, and you should delegate to him the authority to resolve all questions of economic policy of subpresidential magnitude. The treasury secretary's lead role may on occasion irritate the CEA chair, the OMB director, the domestic advisor, the labor secretary, the commerce secretary, the special trade representative and others. But you desperately need a *primus inter pares* in the economic game; it has far too many players to be run on the one-man one-vote principle. A president who treats all his economic advisors as equals will never get himself a coherent economic policy.

The treasury secretary is the best choice to lead the pack. He is the senior member of the Troika, which must stand squarely at the center of the economics channel. He is the sole Cabinet official with wide-ranging economic responsibilities in both the foreign and domestic fields, a vital credential with the economy ever more dependent on international events. He is the natural link to the powerful tax-writing and banking committees of Congress, through which most economic legislation must pass. Foreign governments traditionally view the treasury secretary as your senior economic official, on a par with their powerful finance ministers; and the key constituency groups—not only businessmen and bankers but also labor leaders and party officials—typically look to Treasury as the natural power center in economic policy. With this kind of leverage, the treasury secretary will either dominate economic policy or succeed in preventing anyone else from doing so.

The CEA head should not take the lead role in subpresidential decision-making here. For several years in the early 1960s— when neo-Keynesian economics, the wonders of econometric forecasting and the compelling logic of cost-benefit analysis were seen as the trinity of a new religion—CEA was arguably the natural center for economic policymaking. Treasury then seemed a stodgy backwater for complacent bankers and old-fashioned budget balancers. But that era has largely passed. Keynesianism and econometric forecasting hardly can claim all wisdom; the tricks of cost-benefit analysis have proliferated more swiftly than nuclear secrets; with a weakening dollar at home and abroad, the economic judgments of markets—and of the bankers and businessmen and international financiers with a good feel for markets—have gained renewed respect. CEA's narrow base in academia is not sufficiently sturdy to support a lead role.

When presidents have ceded decision-making authority to the treasury secretary—Nixon's effective delegations of power, for example, to George Schultz and John Connally—economic policy has typically been made with boldness, consistency and dispatch (whatever one may think of its merits). When presidents have accorded their treasury secretaries less clout, economic policy has been stale pudding, without a theme. Find yourself a sympathetic treasury secretary—one with good bureaucratic skills, native leadership abilities, and a flair for conceptualizing and strategy—and rely on him or her to mold an economic policy from the babel of views through the government.

But the treasury secretary should not take personal charge of the *mechanics* of process management in economic policy. His unique role as the *one* domestic affairs Cabinet officer who operates in effect as a senior EOP official—with cross-agency decision authority—will create problems with his fellow Cabinet officers. It is thus imperative that there be a due process mechanism with a bit of distance from the treasury secretary. You should create a very small EOP staff, anchored by a White House economic policy coordinator (not assistant) to manage the interagency process and to oversee the preparation of options papers for review by the Troika, either operating alone or when, as it will continually on specific issues, it expands into a broader Cabinet-level economic committee.

Economic policy typically rises to Cabinet level because the issues here can rarely be resolved deeper in the bureaucracy. The treasury secretary's lead decision-making role can stop many issues from moving beyond the Cabinet-level review—if that review is itself orderly, balanced and well-informed. Too often, under recent presidents, Cabinet-level committees have made economic policy virtually on the run, well out in front of careful staff work. A small White House–based coordinating unit is needed to assure that the professional analytic work at Treasury, CEA, OMB and the other economic agencies is keeping one step ahead of the Cabinet-level policymakers.

To preserve the distinction between coordination and decision, the White House coordinating staff should be very small and very low-profile, a true secretariat concerned solely with procedural mechanics, not with influencing the outcome of policy debates. The staff should have no policy views and should do little or no technical analysis of its own. You definitely do *not* need another group of substantive economists. The professional staffs at CEA, Treasury, OMB and the other economic agencies are perfectly adequate in supplying substantive analysis and advice across the whole range of economic policy.

Finally, the director of the coordinating staff, while formally working for you, must be acceptable to the treasury secretary, with whom he will have to deal intimately on a day-to-day basis. In economic policy, coordination and decision should be distinct functions.

It is difficult to create and maintain a purely objective, procedurally oriented coordinating staff in the EOP, particularly one anchored in the White House—difficult, but not impossible. President Ford seems to have created such a staff for the Economic Policy Board.[7] The treasury secretary chaired the board, but the supporting staff was attached to the presidency, not to the Treasury. This is the proper model.

- *The budget/management channel*: In many respects, the trickiest problems—because they are more numerous and less visible —will occur in the relations between OMB and the departments and agencies, and between OMB and the rest of the EOP units. If you adopt our recommendation to reduce dramatically the breadth of the Domestic Affairs Staff's jurisdiction, then OMB will be the main EOP focal point for a vast amount of administration business. Indeed, other than the overall budget process itself and a few across-the-government management issues,

OMB is not likely to have the process-management lead within the EOP on very many presidential or presidential/secretarial issues (although it will surely provide advice and staff support on all of them).

It will, however, sit athwart most of the secretarial and the routine issues. And here the problem of reconciling the desire to decentralize subpresidential decision-making through delegation and the desire to assure a coherence of approach and consistency of strategy through central review is most difficult. Through its budget and legislative clearance processes and, on a more ad hoc basis, through its management arm, OMB has the authority to review most dimensions of executive government's inner workings.

The best way to understand how OMB should function is to look at the handling of the secretarial and routine issues (a) where a single department has authority over the matter at issue —here delegation should work best—and (b) in an interagency context, where OMB must have an active decision-making role in resolving disputes as well as in running its basic review processes.

**(a) Single department.** OMB's relations with a single department should not be too difficult (although they will never be free from friction).

—On issues of policy innovation that require either program expansion, through increased expenditures, or new legislation, OMB review is vital to assure consistency with the President's budget and his overall substantive program. But the political appointees in OMB should defer to the judgments of the political appointees in the department, once the issue of consistency is no longer an issue. The top OMB officials should only rarely have their staffs generate alternative program innovations and repudiate the departmental judgment, especially when a top political official in the department has closely reviewed the matter (as is likely to be the case on secretarial issues but may not be the case on the more routine issues).

—On issues of program implementation and operations, OMB should rarely intrude its judgment and should leave those decisions in the department,\* *unless* it is seeking an across-the-government change.

If suggestions are informed by a presumption that the department should be accorded deference on these lower-level issues, most problems probably can be resolved by discussions between top officials without formal decision-making.

**(b) Interagency.** In instances where there is a splintering of jurisdiction and responsibility among the departments, there is little choice. The OMB career staff must act as the process manager and work with the departments involved in preparing the secretarial and routine issues for decision. Key OMB political appointees—usually the program associate directors—will then try to resolve the matter with the departments, usually with an interagency group of assistant secretaries or deputy assistant secretaries. If conciliation fails, the OMB official must make the decision. On routine matters, that is usually the end of it. On secretarial-level issues, an undersecretary or secretary may take the issue to the OMB director himself. Again, if conciliation fails, then the OMB director must make the decision— with a nominal right of appeal to you through the chief of staff.

Although this schema can work, it won't unless your top OMB officials—the director, deputy director and program associate directors—are sensitive to the importance of delegation, to the political forces that are at play on the Cabinet secretaries, and to the need for conciliation before using the decision-making authority that is necessary if government is not to be paralyzed by interagency disagreement. The political appointees must be strong enough to control their staffs and intelligent enough to understand that the conservative bias of the OMB staffs is a beginning, but not the end, of a problem's consideration.

You may hear the objection that an arrangement of the sort recommended would make OMB's political staff too powerful within the EOP. But the whole point is to get final decisions from *someone* in the EOP, since the interagency questions can't

---

\*This may be less true to the extent that general principles of regulatory reform emerge at the center of the administration. But their emergence will be an issue of elaborate debate and discussion—and will probably constitute a second-level, presidential/secretarial issue coordinated by the domestic affairs advisor.

be decided by a departmental official. OMB's political appointees, who are chosen by the director and serve at your pleasure, are the logical locus of this kind of power. The other EOP units are already accustomed to defer to OMB's decision-making in the budget process except on major issues of concern to you. You should build on the traditional clout and legitimacy of the institution to bring a measure of order and finality to consideration of the more routine cross-cutting issues within the EOP.

## G. The Chief of Staff: The Deputy Secretary Model

Throughout both the literature and folklore of the presidency runs a strain of hostility to the very idea of a chief of staff. A really first-rate president, it is sometimes argued, should be able to run his own staff. The chief of staff is seen as a Rasputin-like figure, isolating the President from both reality and dissenting opinion. But this is all nonsense. No president can be his own chief of staff and still have the time and energy left to do the myriad tasks required of him. Presidents are isolated only when they wish to be, and any president is free to pick a chief of staff of real distinction and experience.

Moreover, if you choose to operate a strategic presidency, you will need a chief with more responsibility and power than has typically been the case. The job should come to mean a virtual deputy president for domestic affairs. In fact, *this is the most important appointment you will make on the domestic side of the government*—more important than the treasury secretary, attorney general or OMB director. But you must understand that by so viewing the appointment, you are *not* giving away your power; you are using your top personal staffer to extend your power.

You should not apply the deputy president label to the job, as this will only cause confusion and produce allegations that you are somehow altering the constitutional design. Perhaps you should call him a staff coordinator or something similarly bland. But, as noted, he should be to you what an effective, top-flight deputy secretary is to a secretary—a person who stands above the competing staff and operating units, who sees the whole terrain, and who is able to resolve issues that should not go to your desk.

We reach this conclusion after considering all the things that need doing at the apex of the domestic presidency. Remember that much of your schedule will be consumed by ceremonies, public meetings, speeches, trips and decision-making on the major domestic issues, and by the unpredictable and endlessly seductive machinations of foreign affairs. Meanwhile, the agenda of the domestic presidency will (if past is prologue) be growing ever more complicated technically and ever more byzantine and intractable politically. If you do not have an operational second on the domestic side, that agenda will simply pile up on your desk. You will find yourself disposing of it in fits and starts, leaving important issues to fester, missing key opportunities to connect issues to one another, dissipating your political capital on trivia—in short, undermining any prospect for strategic coherence in your domestic program.

We must make clear that the chief of staff does not stand between you and rest of the government. *You* will set the broad strategic direction of the administration in consultation with your top officials. On the first- and second-order issues (presidential and mixed presidential/secretarial) you will make the decisions directly, with key principals—both in the departments and in the EOP—having direct access, both in person and on paper. The major choices on those issues you cannot and should not cede to the chief of staff.

A chief of staff can protect the integrity of the domestic presidency if you permit him to assume true executive responsibilities in three areas.

• *Strategy:* From his perch close to you and atop the whole executive apparatus, the chief of staff is ideally placed to sense the gaps and the interrelationships in the policy and politics of the administration and to keep everyone involved, including you, alert to the strategic direction of your presidency. The chief should not be a mere administrator. You should look to him to compel your other top advisors to subordinate near-term crises to your long-term objectives. He should be responsible for seeing to it that a four-year strategic plan is developed, constantly updated and consistently implemented.

As issues come toward you through one of the three policy channels, it is especially important that the chief of staff ensure that the assistant for political affairs be adequately consulted and involved. In short, the chief must continuously bring the political and policy people together,* first to ensure overall strategic coherence, and second, to ensure coherence between and among the discrete strategies adopted on the major issues.

• *EOP management:* He or she should not only be the chief strategist but should also manage the EOP, acting as the executive director of the EOP. At the trivial level, this means that the EOP administrative officer reports to the chief of staff, and also means that your schedulers, appointments and personnel staff will work under his charge. But more important, the executive director will have three critical process roles:

—The chief of staff must decide through which channel a particular piece of business—especially presidential or presidential/secretarial business—should be routed. The line between the economic policy and domestic affairs channels is especially arbitrary. Fiscal policy clearly lies in the economic channel; health policy, clearly in the domestic affairs channel. But what about energy policy, or efforts to save the auto industry? Under our conception, most very major domestic program issues should go through the assistant for domestic affairs, but there will clearly be hard calls.† The chief of staff should make them. With most, it is less important where the issue goes than that it goes somewhere with dispatch and finality. And he must ensure that there is proper review and communication between the channels.

—The chief of staff should ensure that process management within each channel is working well and in concert with the overall flow of business of the administration. He will have a tiny secretariat of his own to keep track of the strategy of governing, but he will be available to hear grievances if due process on major issues is not being accorded critical actors within the channels.

*In this role, the chief should have responsibility for your speechwriters. You will want to deal with them directly, but they also need a staff anchor to give them a strategic overview of administration policymaking. The chief provides the logical anchor.
†On energy, for example, a synfuels initiative might go to the domestic affairs advisor; oil price decontrol to the Troika; and research priorities of the Department of Energy to OMB.

—The chief of staff will be the person responsible for either setting up or recommending to you the arrangements for crisis management within the administration.

• *Decision-making:* This is a key function, and certain to be the most controversial.

We do not of course suggest that you make an irrevocable delegation of power to the chief of staff. That would be neither legal nor practical. Any senior EOP or Cabinet official dissatisfied with the chief's decisions must have the clear right to appeal to you. How often this happens will depend on how often you overrule your chief; if you do so habitually, you should find someone else for the job.

Nor do we suggest that the chief make *all* of the subpresidential decisions in your administration. On the contrary, our overall recommendation for structuring the Cabinet and the EOP aims to create a practical and complete hierarchy of delegated authority. For issues arising chiefly out of a single agency, the proper subpresidential decision maker is the secretary involved. For interagency issues, each of the several channels of activity in the EOP should provide for decision-making short of the chief of staff. The chief of staff thus sits atop a system of carefully decentralized power. If he attempts to usurp all power here, he destroys the entire design. Indeed, he must act with great care not to overturn too many decisions of either EOP or Cabinet subpresidential deciders. He must push decisions back down into the EOP-departmental structure or he will be overwhelmed, taking the system down with him.

Nevertheless, our system of delegated power leaves an important residue of high-level disputes that must be decided at the very center of the government. A strong chief of staff is needed to take a portion of this burden off your shoulders. You will not have the time or inclination to get involved every time your most senior officials—key Cabinet officers, your domestic advisor, political advisor, OMB director, and chief economic policy maker—find themselves in conflict on a matter of policy or tactics. The ready availability of an alternative referee—one who has your full trust and support—will make all of the processes of the EOP run more swiftly and smoothly and will guarantee that your strategic objectives are not lost through underground processes of compromise, logrolling, or back-stabbing among your senior officials.

To the extent possible, the chief of staff should seek to conciliate, rather than to decide himself (or decide that the issue be resolved by you). Genuine compromises can emerge when he sits down with the key actors and hears the disputes. But he cannot be afraid to decide. He must move the matters, or fatal indecision will quickly develop at the center of the government, indecision that will hurt *you*.

The chief of staff should, we must emphasize, have no staff that duplicates the other EOP staffs. If he needs substantive work to be done or wants to pose substantive questions, these should be handled by other EOP (or departmental) staffers. He has a lien on the best people when he needs them. If he finds that they are shading materials that go to him for their own advantage, they should be fired in an instant. The creation of another large staff for the chief of staff will only repeat, in a different form, many of the problems that our suggestions aim to solve.

As to personality, it should be self-evident that the qualities of experience, camera shyness, fairness and strategic intelligence must be his in abundance. Camera shyness is especially important. He cannot be what James Byrnes was to Roosevelt during World War II—known as deputy president for domestic affairs; absent an emergency, you will not want to cede formally that prominence to him. Your chief must derive satisfaction from knowing that he is the linchpin of the domestic side of the administration, not from cultivating celebrity status. Publicity of course can't be entirely avoided: when he makes decisions unpopular inside the administration, he may become the subject of leaks and gossip. But it is very much in your interest, and in the interest of the administration, that he be totally your creation—your shadow—doing what you want without attracting attention to himself.

The chief must also be someone whom you trust totally, and who can quickly learn your preferences and style. But that does not mean that he must come from the campaign, and you may well have to go outside your immediate circle of political aides to find him. You probably have a broad enough range of contacts in the nation's professional, commercial or governmental life to find the kind of senior aide who can do the job.

The chief's role in foreign affairs poses difficulties. Here he should have no subpresidential decision-making authority. Nor would he have a direct role in assuring that appropriate processes are being followed, *except* insofar as domestic and foreign issues are connected. Those matters will have to be structured between you, the head of the National Security Council and the secretaries of state and defense. *However,* the chief, as keeper of the strategy of governing, must be continually involved in assessing the connections between foreign and domestic priorities and in integrating into the battle plan those foreign items that are going to have substantial domestic impact (such as a treaty or a major shift in defense spending).

The Reagan and Ford forces at the Republican convention in Detroit were proceeding correctly when they looked for a way to create a role for a person above the Cabinet and the main EOP offices who could keep the EOP's house in order and provisionally make the more routine decisions in your name. But under the press of time they were not able to define that role carefully, and they were, in our judgment, wrong to consider giving it to the Vice President. Making the Vice President chief of staff in the sense we have described would raise controversial and unproductive constitutional, political and personal questions. The chief's job is, essentially, a direct, personal staff function. The person who performs it must be under your complete control, and operate in your shadow. A chief of staff is absolutely necessary in modern executive government, but for all its importance it must never be advertised as anything more than a staff job being performed for you by someone extremely close to you.

In that respect, the deputy secretary analogy is not apt, because the chief of staff does *not* perform duties that should be defined by statute. And unlike a deputy secretary, the chief of staff should not, therefore, be confirmed by the Senate. The job is wholly personal to you; the person is totally your creature. However important he becomes, it is only because you decide it is to be so—and because you can in an instant reverse that decision or send the chief back to his university, business or law firm.

Finally, we recognize that a very real conflict exists between devising strategies and making individual decisions. The second can eat up enormous amounts of time even if the chief of staff decides not to decide. But the first also requires time to reflect and consult and conceptualize. Being chief of staff is, no doubt, a killing job. But better him than you.

## H. The West Wing as Strategic Center

To provide a strategic center for the EOP, and thus for the executive branch, you should complete the historical evolution of the West Wing. It should become a genuine headquarters, linking you directly to the main lines of decision and influence in your government. The point is not to superimpose a White House mini-government onto the rest of the executive branch; that, in fact, is the major defect of the mafia model. Rather, the point is to draw into the West Wing the most important centralizing influences operating in the government. This will strengthen those influences, and provide you with the means of weaving them into the strategic design of your administration. The West Wing should connect you with the realities of the government, not serve as a buffer of loyalty between you and what you are in fact confronting and accomplishing.

The makeup of the West Wing headquarters follows logically from our other organizational recommendations for the EOP. In brief, you want here the men and women who will command the four EOP channels of activity, plus those few senior White House advisors whose job is to operate across or outside the channels. In somewhat different form, this was tried during Richard Nixon's second term. And it has one major problem: it separates principals from their staffs. The solution to that problem—which is most acute with Treasury and OMB—is to give the heads of the economics and management/budget channels a West Wing office but also an office in the department and the EOB respectively. There is value to the West Wing proximity, but there is equal value in having these individuals close to their own staffs for the daily informal conversations and meetings that are the real stuff of government.

This plan puts the first few lines in the EOP organization chart into the West Wing, and puts your Oval Office within a few steps of all our EOP subpresidential deciders. We do as much not simply for the sake of symmetry, for if the plan is to be effective, all deciders must be in close proximity. Tradition-

# The West Wing Headquarters

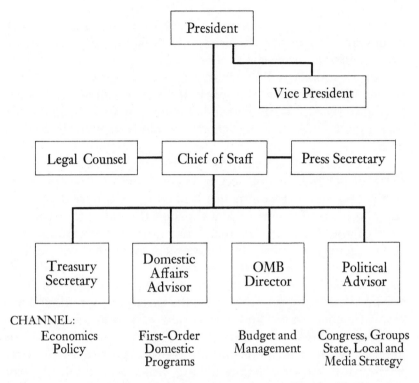

ally, neither the treasury secretary nor the OMB director has enjoyed a West Wing perch, the theory being that the West Wing was a place for presidential assistants, not the heads of statutory or Cabinet agencies. But this is a tradition without the support of any governing logic. The West Wing should be the locus of day-to-day governance on the major matters influencing the fate of your presidency, and you cannot give governance a strategic focus without encompassing economic and budgetary factors. If you exclude these two officers from the West Wing, both the economic policy channel and OMB's program/budget channel will lose touch with you and with the strategic deliberations that should occupy the West Wing. The domestic advisor will find himself usurping large parts of these two channels, simply because they will be unrepresented at crucial moments, and the basic organizational scheme of the EOP will begin to unravel.

The economic coordinator and your congressional liaison are two more officers who for quite different reasons belong in the West Wing.

The economic coordinator is here to assure the clout, efficiency and fairness of the economic policymaking machinery. He can also staff the economics desk during the many hours the treasury secretary will be across East Executive Avenue, attending to his departmental chores. If the coordinator is instead lodged in the Old EOB, liaison between him, the treasury secretary and other West Wing officials would be needlessly complicated.

The congressional liaison is here because his effectiveness on the Hill depends on his access to you—and on perceptions of that access. In our recommended scheme, the congressional liaison and his staff report to you through the political advisor, as part of the political channel. That is how the arrangement should generally work. But matters congressional will bulk so large in the West Wing's deliberations that the liaison's full-time presence will be convenient for you, as well as good for him.

The West Wing we recommend is tilted far more than usual toward a concern for and connection with substantive policymaking. The treasury secretary, the OMB director, the domestic affairs advisor, and the economic coordinator are all full-time participants in vital policymaking processes. Typically, the West Wing leans much more heavily toward politics: the domestic advisor is usually the only substantive aide present on the domestic side, with the other offices taken up by aides specializing in various areas of political, constituency and media work. This is one reason that the White House in recent years has been so obsessed with interest group pressures and short-term imagery. We have no moral qualms with such an emphasis, which bespeaks no corruption or deceit. But those offices symbolically (and at times in fact) skew your presidency away from its basic mission and strategic enterprise. In the end, we are convinced, a stress on substance will make for better political results.

## I. Special Problems

Even within the context of the structure and processes we have outlined, a host of problems will arise. Here we briefly alert you to some of the major ones in the central channels of activity.

## 1. Economic Policy

• *Forecasts:* The Troika publicly forecasts the course of the economy at least twice a year, as a guide to constructing the budget. These forecasts are *invariably* shaded toward the optimistic side to avoid destabilizing reactions by the private sector (and sometimes to make the budget appear less in deficit).

In the confusion, the Troika may even start giving *you* misleading forecasts. Put an end to the charade. Try to work out a deal with the Congressional Budget Office (CBO) whereby the Troika and CBO will issue consensus economic forecasts on a quarterly or twice-yearly basis *without* your approval and *without* consideration of the political or budget fallout. Even these honest forecasts will turn out to be wrong. But the process will save everyone endless hours of demeaning worry about just how much you should reveal of what your economists think may happen. You—and they—have better things to do.

• *The Federal Reserve Board:* A number of factors—the decline of Keynesian economics, the virulence of inflation, the fragility of the dollar abroad, the internationalization of capital markets —have united to make monetary variables a, perhaps *the,* critical element in economic policymaking. But you have no control over the monetary variables (except foreign exchange rate intervention policies, which are controlled by the Treasury). The independence of the Federal Reserve Board is real. Because it is sensitive to your democratic mandate and loath to make a fuss, the Board will not lightly engage you in noisy public controversy; but by the same token, it will not take direction—or sometimes even advice—from you or your economic officials.

You should leave daily liaison with the Fed to your treasury secretary. The Treasury and the Fed have a tradition of exchanging views in a candid, professional and confidential manner. Keep your other economic and political advisors at a discreet distance from this daily collaboration. However, the Fed chairman should be invited frequently to meet with the Troika and with you, so he may fully understand where you wish to take the economy. The chairman cannot properly act as a full member of your economic team, but close consultations are possible.

The best public posture for you is one of generalized support for all of the Fed's policies, acting as if so much were beyond dispute. This will suitably reassure international central bankers of your soundness and discretion, a valuable foreign policy asset, and will help set the stage for those occasions when you and the Fed chairman must in fact join forces to steady the financial markets. Except in such crisis situations, you should leave detailed comments on monetary policy to the treasury secretary—who will wisely choose to say nothing in most instances.

At some point in 1981, the Fed's policy of constraining money supply growth to particular targets will make the economic recovery stutter or stall. Interest rates will charge upward. Some of your political aides will counsel you to attack the Fed, at least obliquely, by railing against expensive money. And at other times during the term, you may find the Fed a tempting scapegoat for the economy's ills. High interest rates have been a standard target for presidents, going back to the Republic's birth. The dollar's international status is today too fragile for such broadsides. A modest suggestion: resist the temptation.

- *Inflation czar:* Don't have one. The Troika agencies and the Fed have their hands on every monetary, fiscal and programmatic policy available to the federal government for establishing an anti-inflationary course for the economy. A separate inflation advisor has minimal bureaucratic leverage to do anything.

The only policy instrument available to an inflation czar would be wage-price policy—that is to say, the guideline-setting bureaucracy of CWPS. If you must have guidelines or controls, someone must of course run the system. But that someone need not be an inflation czar. Guidelines and controls should never be the public centerpiece of your anti-inflation policy: even advocates of strong wage-price measures concede that those measures should be regarded as mere supplements to restrained fiscal and monetary policies and to microeconomically sound decisions across the range of domestic programs. Accordingly, the head of the wage-price program should be merely an efficient bureaucrat, subject to policy direction by your senior economic advisors. Organizationally, the tidiest arrangement is to make the treasury secretary the chairman of CWPS, thus merging it with your main economic policy committee, and to have a competent but anonymous executive director of CWPS actually run the operation day to day.

**2. International Economic Policy.** Once confined largely to foreign trade and international monetary questions, the border region between economic policy and foreign policy is growing steadily wider and more hotly contested. It now includes agriculture policy (international commodity agreements, embargoes, food aid), energy policy (relations with OPEC and with the oil-consuming countries), environmental policy (acid rain control, exports of toxic substances, nuclear proliferation, law-of-the-sea matters), and business regulatory policy (bribery laws, antitrust enforcement abroad, inward investment controls). International economics is an area already overstocked with contending bureaucracies and staffs. Creating a new unit would merely create more rivalries and confusion.

The best solution is to recognize that international economic policy—while a hot topic in the press and the academy—is in fact a polyglot concept of very limited utility. It cannot stand on its own. The large global issues—e.g., international monetary, trade, energy and agricultural policy—should go through the EOP economic policy channel, because the issues have a substantial impact on the domestic economy and its position in major world markets. Other, more particularistic issues—e.g., foreign aid, military sales, science exchanges—should go through the NSC, because these are intimately bound up with country-specific diplomatic policies. Still other issues—e.g., law of the sea, international environmental agreements, export embargoes—will require thorough cross-review by both your economic and foreign policy advisors. This sounds awkward, and as with so much else, it is the best that can be made of the situation. But our proposal can be made to work. If you give the treasury secretary full NSC membership (as Kennedy did), he can serve as a natural bridge and arbiter between the economic and foreign policy channels.

**3. The Budget Process.** Budgeting is by nature inelegant. A budget office can often hold its own against the spending agencies only by hoarding information or perpetrating bluffs and feints of less than complete nobility; and budgets inevitably resemble less a seamless fabric of policy than a jumble of disparate program decisions. More important, as we noted in Chapter 2 and will discuss more fully in Chapter 6, the budget is a very limited instrument in the near term for effecting major programmatic change.

Despite these qualifications, the more routine budget process is one of the few methods available to try to impose your priorities on executive government. Your proclamations, speeches and executive orders may wash over the bureaucracy like surf over a rock. But by turning your thumb up or down in the budget process, you can directly determine policy. Accordingly, you will want to develop major themes for the federal budget if possible, but you should also spend time improving and supporting the budget process itself.

There are several milestones on the road to a better budget process.

- *Your early and consistent support:* You need to discipline existing programs (that is to say, cut or slow the rate of increase) if you hope to reduce taxes or to effect even a modest expansionist agenda on the domestic side. Therefore, especially early in your term, you should strive to keep spending restraints in place, for old programs affected by the annual appropriation process—including superfluous defense expenditures—or for new spending initiatives. There is no scientific test for the right level of spending on any program; everyone in the budget process—department bureaucrats, constituencies, congressional committees, and budget examiners—works against a background of arbitrary expectations, formed largely by the general climate of fiscal discipline and by what the spending trends have been in the previous year or two. If OMB starts out your term by leaning hard on departmental requests, expectations will be lowered at a steady rate throughout the political system. If the pressure is relaxed, expectations will soar. It is greatly in your interest to get expectations down quickly and then to keep them there, which will not only create budget room for any expansionist initiatives but allow you to wring very large political benefits out of very small spending increases in the future. We will discuss later where restraint might come; the point here is simply that restraint will be necessary and it must have your support.

• *A superior director:* With the exception of your chief of staff, the OMB director is perhaps your most important appointment on the domestic side. Good ones have shared four qualities: a very close relationship with the President; a superhuman appetite for hard, dull work; an accurate, unsentimental feel for the political system's tolerance; and an ability to say no to important people. Moreover, look for a virtue not often associated with the post: a knack for conceiving of domestic policy in a strategic four-year perspective and an ability to understand quickly your political as well as your substantive needs. You need a director who can help you develop a sophisticated sense of what you can and cannot accomplish on the domestic front over your tenure. With such leadership, OMB's career bureaucrats can save you more than money; they can help you preserve the core and conscience of your presidency throughout the protracted trench warfare of the budgeting and appropriating processes.*

• *Superior political appointments:* The OMB deputy and the other key political appointees under them (for example, the program associate directors) are crucial positions because they are involved in so much of the day-to-day operations of executive government. These individuals must have extraordinary sensitivity and skill. They will have much of the contact with the departments and agencies on a regular basis. And they must use, but not become mere mouthpieces of, their own civil servants. They are placed to become extremely valuable expediters who can help get huge hunks of business done without ruffling too many feathers. But if you choose badly, the appointees can cause executive government endless trouble. Although much

*It is questionable whether a layer of political appointees introduced during the Carter administration—the two associate directors for budget and management—should exist. This additional layering means, for example, that civil servants have to go up three levels (program associate director, associate director, deputy) before they get to the director. High-quality appointees both in the program associate director positions and in the director and deputy positions would allow elimination of the associate directors.

less visible, these jobs can be as important to you as a deputy or undersecretary in a major department.

- *Better examiners:* You will rarely see a budget examiner. But the quality of OMB's career staff will determine in large measure the analytic strength of your EOP and, in consequence, the credibility and coherence of your domestic program. Be alert to any gesture that can boost the morale, prestige—and thus the drawing power—of OMB's career bureaucracy. These, too, are high-pressure jobs, with an *unfortunately high turnover,* but OMB should be able to recruit the best graduate economists, lawyers, and public policy analysts in the country for five-year stints of service. An industrious budget examiner may have more influence on programs and policies in his area than some presidential appointees and junior members of Congress. Also, if you can, meet the examiners. If you insist that they come to review (not necessarily decision) meetings, you can give them an extraordinary morale boost.

- *Long-term strategy:* Putting the budget on a formal multi-year cycle—a perennial good-government idea—has no practical prospect of adoption by Congress. But as your term begins, ask OMB and the Troika to generate for you a sophisticated four- or five-year profile of the budget and the economy and to repeat the process regularly. The exercise will be fraught with uncertainty and guesswork, but it can elucidate for you the severe interlocking constraints you will face from the momentum of existing programs, established tax laws, and probable economic and demographic trends. It can also alert you to the major problem areas that will complicate your domestic agenda —the programs soaring wildly in cost, the public needs shuffled to the bottom of the deck by your predecessors, the major breaking points in the tax rate structure. Most importantly, the exercise will bring home to you the meagerness of the resources available and the difficulty of changing the established course of policy, and will thus encourage you and your advisors to choose objectives with care and pursue them relentlessly. It may also suggest presidential or, more likely, presidential/secretarial issues regarding basic budget themes. We return to this very important point in Chapter 6.

• *Putting more of government under budgetary scrutiny:* The government commands the nation's economic resources not only by directly spending tax dollars but also by making and guaranteeing loans, by providing tax expenditures (credits, exemptions, deductions and the like), and by issuing regulatory mandates to impress private spending into the service of government objectives. OMB has been developing procedures to deal with these new methods of public intervention in the economy, but progress has been slow and halting. Speed it up. You need budgeting procedures for credit programs and tax expenditures, and at the least, a better budgetary understanding of regulatory programs. What is not understood and reviewed, you cannot influence.*

• *Giving the Cabinet a more significant role in the process:* Cabinet officers typically resent the budget process, in part because OMB does not consult them when determining overall budget strategies, and in part because OMB insists on reviewing and revising agency budgets in exquisite and painful detail. As we have discussed in Chapter 3, both difficulties should be met—by including the Cabinet officers in the formation of budget strategy and by deferring to them more on the finely grained decisions that are within broad spending limits.

**4. Politics and Congressional Relations.** Working with the chief of staff and the other senior officials in the EOP and the departments, the assistant for political affairs must be continuously worrying about and mediating between the overlapping but competing spheres of the politics of governing, nomination and general election. To handle the enormous task, he must rely heavily on his four deputies—all of whom have important jobs but none of whom will be able to see the complicated politics of your presidency with the breadth of the assistant for political affairs. Without discussing the deputies' roles in depth, we offer a few reflections about key problems in each office, with special attention to congressional relations.

*But do not let new budgetary concepts and mechanisms dilute the talismanic force of the budget deficit, as currently defined. It is a very imperfect concept, but perfection is not possible in this business. You will need a simple symbol and test of budgetary discipline to hold back the appetites of the government's clients and beneficiaries.

**a. Deputy for constituency relations:** He or she should be a great deal more than a contact person for interest groups. Indeed, routine matters of contituency contact should be bucked over to the departments. To succeed on the Hill, and to build organized support around the country, the White House must continuously build or rebuild interest group coalitions around its many policy initiatives—an extremely important and difficult task in an era of single-issue coalitions. At the same time, and somewhat inconsistently, the deputy must also develop a permanent coalition of support for you at the grass roots of your political party. Without a core of party support—founded upon state and local politicians, some of your congressional allies, and amateur political activists—the long-term fate of your presidency and its strategic design will be seriously at risk.

The deputy has three very hard day-to-day jobs.

- He must work with the deputy for congressional relations to build and use coalitions in support of the presidential and presidential/secretarial issues that are on the Hill. With these totaling as many as twenty-five or thirty, the deputy's work is enormously complicated.
- He must be involved in the formation of policies within the administration *before* you make basic decisions. Too often under Jimmy Carter, the considerable talents of Anne Wexler and her staff were not brought to bear on issues before they were formulated. That was a clear mistake.
- He must, within the limits of propriety and our strong preference for delegation to the departments, give selective hearings on more routine matters that affect the key members of various coalitions. But the deputy must not free-lance—and simply make promises for continued support. When and how to do that should be worked out with the assistant for political affairs and the relevant departmental officials.

**b. Deputy for intergovernmental affairs:** This person also stands at a delicate juncture between politics and government. His *political* job is to maintain your good relations with governors and mayors of your party, a constituency of considerable influence in the nominating process and vital to maintaining a sense of legitimacy about your presidency at the grass roots. The deputy's *governmental* job is to improve the working relations between federal programs and the state and local governments that use them, a highly significant area of policy innovation and implementation for the domestic presidency. His dual role sets up a potential conflict of interest, for the surest way to please a governor is to manipulate federal programs for his state's benefit. But it is necessary to risk potential conflict—the two functions are unworkable in isolation. You need a person of extraordinary integrity here, however, and you need to impress on him that his first loyalty is to sound government.

**c. Deputy for media affairs:** He is quite simply your propaganda chief—the keeper of your image, the watcher of the polls and the mobilizer of media campaigns in support of administration policies. The press, which has made this job vital to the modern presidency, will heap scorn on whomever holds it, about which you should not lose sleep. Image-making remains a risqué subject in modern politics. However, you should advise the deputy to keep a very low profile.

Do not ask the deputy to manage either speechwriting or day-to-day press relations. To fuse either of those tasks with your image-polishing operation would tend to cheapen both and rob them of credibility both inside the government and with the press.

Do, however, insist that the media advisor, working through the assistant for political affairs, talk at length with your policy people when developing media strategies. Thematics without substance as you govern are an invitation to savage press debunking. Also, you should instruct the assistant for political affairs to include the latest polling data when the Cabinet meets as a whole to discuss the strategy of governing.

**d. Deputy for congressional relations:** He or she will oversee your lobbying efforts. While most of the legislative liaison work of the executive branch should be entrusted to the departments, each of which has an assistant secretary for legislation, *your* congressional relations staff will inevitably set the tone of the administration's general relations with the Congress.

If these relations go sour, the departmental staffs can do little to repair the damage. What they can and will do is work overtime to separate themselves and their departments from the overall legislative program and strategies of the White House. It is therefore vital that your staff be as professional as possible. Do not make the mistake of viewing these people as mere lobbyists. They are your hour-by-hour ambassadors to members of Congress. If you choose hacks for these jobs, the Congress will draw unprintable and irreversible conclusions about your judgment and about the overall quality of your presidency.

• *Structure.* Although the deputy for congressional relations works for the assistant for political affairs, he has a special status because of the importance of his job. He should clearly have an alternative title: director, White House Congressional Relations Office.* He will also relate much more often to you directly than the other deputies in the office of political affairs.

The Office for Congressional Relations should be trim and fast-moving, and include: a full-time deputy responsible for co-ordination with the departments' assistant secretaries for legislation; a deputy for the House of Representatives (with a staff of four or five); a deputy for the Senate (with a staff of three or four); and a staff person responsible for coordinating significant grant and contract announcements by the departments and agencies. An extra complement of lobbyists should work for the CRO staff during budget season before the Budget and Appropriations committees, since the departmental staffs suffer a difficult conflict of interest (their clients want more than OMB saw fit to grant) and may be better off representing the departmental position routinely but letting the White House lobbyists carry the heavy lumber on the budget.

• *Personal qualities.* Obviously the deputy for congressional relations must relate closely to you—and to the members of the Congress. He must also have a broad understanding of national policy, because the breadth of the job is awesome and because

---

*You may decide that all the deputies need dual titles. Hence: director, White House Congressional Relations; director, White House Intergovernmental Relations; director, White House Constituency Liaison; and so forth.

of the ever-present need to bridge the policy/politics gap. Congress is an institution like no other—and understanding its folkways, its history, its procedures and the particular problems of its members would seem of self-evident importance. It also requires a person of deft touch to know when a member really cannot go along, when a request is too much, and how to communicate an understanding that all wisdom does not reside in the executive branch without giving away a bargaining position.

• *Basic tasks.* The deputy for congressional relations has four basic jobs: win passage of presidential legislation; work closely with the departments to achieve similar success on presidential/secretarial issues; understand the interrelationship of all legislative business before the Congress, no matter how routine; and understand how these different levels of activity relate to each other over the four years of the coming term. Although it is an extraordinarily complicated undertaking, the deputy must also develop the basic patterns of bargaining and negotiation with members—usually on voting patterns—so that you are not held up for grants or hospitals or personnel placement every time you need a vote.

• *The departments.* With their own congressional staffs, the departments will do an enormous amount of business for the administration on Capitol Hill. Normally, the departments would have the lead on second- and third-level issues, as well as the more routine business, but would be able to call on the deputy for congressional relations for help, especially in presidential/secretarial areas of concern. It is obviously important, however, for the CRO to meet regularly with the departmental congressional people to ensure full coordination and exchange of information and to be able to maximize the bargaining possibilities facing the administration.

• *The EOP.* Other than formal appearances at hearings, the key actors in the EOP who are regularly called to the Congress —for example, the OMB director or the CEA chairman—should have informal Hill contact only in coordination with the Congressional Relations Office. This precept applies especially for the second- and third-level staffers in the other units. To maximize leverage and to ensure that the administration speaks with a single voice on important matters, the deputy should be apprised of all major contact with members or the key Hill staffers by the rest of the EOP. Normally, the Cabinet secretary should be the main high-level contact on the Hill, working through his congressional staff and the CRO. If exceptions arise, the deputy should monitor them. And there will be an especially close working relationship between the deputy and the assistant for domestic affairs and his staff.

- *Consultation.* Although advance consultation can be risky—it can cause leaks and thereby unleash lobbying groups before the administration wants to move—such consultation is obviously a critical piece of the CRO's business. As with the deputy for constituency relations, the CRO office must be involved in the development of policy within the administration as well as in the attempts to secure enactment in the Congress. The degree to which it is necessary to have detailed readings on the Hill's likely response will have to vary from case to case. But a general rule would be to err on the side of consultation.

- *Don't abandon your friends.* You or your political advisor sometimes will ask your stalwart supporters in the Congress to act against their interest or to put out a special level of effort. Whatever you do, don't abandon these core supporters without consulting with them in depth and explaining why you think it advisable to change positions. The Carter administration made a number of very important people in the Congress unhappy by failing to practice this elementary rule.

- *Casework.* Most casework should be handled in the departments, but a system should exist for identifying members who will be key during the coming session and making sure that the announcement of grants or contracts in their states or districts is clearly communicated to the CRO. The director of the CRO can then decide whether a particular announcement should be orchestrated with a bit more care than normal.

- *Overload and early warning.* Clearly the CRO must make sure that the press of administration business is not too heavy for the

Congress to absorb. But it must, as part of the task, ensure that it has an effective early warning system to gauge which major issues the Congress will press forward regardless of the administration. Legislative initiative hardly rests with the administration alone—especially today. And effective strategic planning that involves the Hill should be very sensitive to what is likely to be put on the calendar whether the administration acts or not.

• *Personal involvement.* Personal relationships count for a lot in government. Accordingly, you should act on this truism by having frequent informal contact with members who are key to your overall strategy. There was much criticism of President Carter for having many members of Congress "to breakfast for a sermon" rather than routinely having five or six to the White House after dinner for a drink.

**5. Long-Term Planning.** One task of your administration more likely to benefit future administrations than your own is longer-term planning—that is, for problems that will emerge five to fifteen years out. Periodically, someone will recommend establishing such a planning office in the EOP and developing a staff to populate it. The first half of the proposal is sound; the second is not.

There clearly ought to be a longer-term planning mechanism that does not get swept up into the daily brushfires or bent out of shape by policy crunches. It should look out into the future and across the government. It should determine if appropriate resources are being devoted to developing a factual and analytic base for future decisions. It should ensure that those resources are put in place, if they do not presently exist. It should, in other words, plant seeds that will bear fruit for someone else.

The best way to do this, in our judgment, would be to establish a tiny planning office in OMB, chaired by the deputy director and staffed by one or two superstars. The office would convene a small working group comprised of representatives from the economic channel, the staff of the assistant for domestic affairs, other EOP offices as appropriate, and the assistant secretaries for planning from the departments. These will all be committed professionals who recognize that they are standing on the shoulders of those who have gone before. They will not be too parochial about their own department's concerns because they are broad-gauged and because they won't be around when the projects come to fruition. An agenda of longer-term items should be developed, and at some point a higher-level meeting (perhaps once a year) should be held by the key departmental actors (secretaries or undersecretaries) with either the EOP deputies or principals to decide what the worthy projects are and where the resources for longer-term policy development should go.

To the greatest extent possible, the actual analytic and data-gathering functions should be built back into the planning staffs of the departments. If projects cut across departmental lines, so much the better: there ought to be preliminary cooperation between the analysts on development of information long before there is a policy fight over options. If the projects are reasonably well defined at the beginning, cooperation on these long-term projects should not pose the same kinds of tensions between departments that occur with greater frequency on short-term policy problems. Indeed, early cooperation at the research and data-gathering end may lessen friction at the policy end.

**6. Media Relations.**  For press secretary, you will presumably find a skilled practitioner of the media arts who will bring to the day-to-day contact with the media the proper appreciation of telling facts, cutting opinion and gallows humor to make him respected by those who deal daily in those commodities. Presumably, too, that person will be able—or will have a deputy who is able—to handle the managerial aspects of daily press relations. He or she will also be capable of bringing the customary tricks of the press relations trade into play: making sure that you are not upstaged by an announcement the same day from a Cabinet officer; making sure that you, not a Cabinet officer, have the first opportunity to get credit if your administration is successful in something important; arranging to have the specialty press briefed in depth on background when there is a major policy announcement (the White House press corps itself is much more accustomed to the play of personality and politics than to the heavy details of policy, and in any event is forced to cover subjects as vast as those considered by you); making sure that departmental press officers have reviewed answers to possible press conference questions and have submitted their own zingers that might actually prick you; playing national reporters against each other with selective leaking; cultivating out-of-town press; and the like.

Still, you are bound to be disappointed by the press coverage of you and of executive government. Herewith a few thoughts on how to make a disappointing situation marginally better.

• *Problem definition.* The press and your adversaries will be skeptical about your solutions to major problems, which are necessarily prescriptive. But you also have an enormous opportunity to define the problem that gives rise to the solution—problems that may be more "fact-bound" and more dramatic than the solutions. Indeed, your ability to use the press as a vehicle for communicating your definition of national problems can, if artfully done, have real impact on the solution. It will focus national debate and generate substantial subsequent comment. Too often the Carter administration put out a fact sheet announcing a problem in several summary pages as a perfunctory prelude to a complex and controversial solution. Laying the groundwork by defining the problem is a critical first step with which you can engage the press. Indeed, other than finding official corruption and simply communicating, however imperfectly, the day-to-day happenings of government, the most creative role for the media is also uncovering and defining problems in the society. If the reporters and pundits merely tout your solution, their peers may label them flacks, but if they dig into the problems and report on them, they can help you indirectly by building momentum for a solution, without having to give even indirect support to that solution itself.

• *Alternatives.* Sometimes you and your top aides may want to let the press know what were the alternatives that you considered in making decisions. Especially in an age where there may be only least worst alternatives and no clear solutions, it may be extremely important for those who are communicating to the nation to report what the choices were, what the trade-offs were, what the problems were with the alternatives that you rejected. Without such a discussion, your ideas may be picked apart without being stacked up against the alternatives. Discussing the alternatives might be something done explicitly in the public papers supporting various administration proposals, rather than done informally and haphazardly by top officials on background the day the initiative is announced. If a proposal is controversial, it will draw fire anyway. Dealing with the alternatives straightforwardly at the beginning is not likely to induce that fire, and may help deflect some of it.

• *Previewing.* This is a cousin of the trial balloon, but relates closely to the last point. Sometimes it is advantageous to give selected reporters a sense of the dimensions of the debate within the administration before you make a decision. The dangers are that the practice will get out of control, that it will set off a winners/losers mentality among your aides that will cause friction and create animosity. But previewing presents some real advantages. It will get public opinion and important actors focused on some of the alternatives, which will help you decide which of several paths to follow. It may also help the consultative process with the Hill, since they too will be able to gauge public opinion before you make the decision and give more concrete advice. This technique may remove some of the surprise from the final announcement, and surprise does enhance the news value. But if it is a major decision, and if your position has not earlier been made clear, it will be major news nonetheless.

# V·
# CAUTIONARY
# TALES

 I N this chapter, we present two case studies. Drawn from the Carter administration's first term, they demonstrate the difficulties of governing in domestic affairs—and the perils of not managing a strategic domestic presidency. We will take up, first, the making and unmaking of economic policy and, second, the administration's inability to enact either welfare reform or national health insurance legislation. Returning the economy to acceptable levels of unemployment while holding prices stable and passing major pieces of domestic legislation were top priorities of the Carter administration. Yet both efforts failed. Both demonstrate, for different reasons, why a four-year strategy is absolutely essential if you are to increase the probabilities of success on controversial high-risk issues. But they also illustrate the substantial difficulties of forging such a strategy and the treacherous problems of joining sound policy and plausible politics.

 Our case studies are not intended as rounded histories of these massive subjects. Nor are they opening shots in a war of words about who was at fault.* Suffice to say, many factors, beyond the

*All within the administration who were involved in these matters would in retrospect acknowledge a measure of responsibility. Those less close to events will have to judge what that degree should be.

quality of its decisions, frustrated the Carter administration. Our point, rather, is that the case studies illustrate a number of our basic themes. They are thus set out for their prospective value to you—as cautionary tales.

## A. Economic Policy: Retreating Before Events

Under President Ford, the economy suffered the worst cyclical collapse since World War II and fell into an election-year rut: 7 to 8 percent unemployment, 5 to 6 percent inflation, a $66 billion budget deficit, and budget outlays at 22.6 percent of GNP. Upon taking office, President Carter promised to set all this right in a single term. By 1981

—The budget was to achieve balance.
—Outlays were to be reduced to 21 percent of GNP.
—Full employment was to prevail.
—Inflation was to fall to 4 percent.

Instead, President Carter entered *his* reelection season in the wake of a severe recession, with the economy in a rut even deeper than 1976: 7 to 8 percent unemployment, double-digit inflation, a $60 billion budget deficit, and budget outlays at 23 percent of GNP. The first-term targets had slipped far over the horizon.

But the real disappointment of economic policy in the Carter term was not so much the final results as the absence along the way of a coherent overall strategy for dealing with the obdurate and volatile reality of the economy. That the administration failed to attain its initial economic goals is not surprising, at least in retrospect. The goals were far too optimistic; no set of policies could have met them. What sapped the nation's confidence in the administration's economic management was a sense that it lacked confidence in itself. Instead of marshaling the tools of policy and the forces of politics behind an understandable plan of attack on the economy's major problems, the administration seemed more often to retreat before events— changing its mind, resorting to half measures when firm decisions appeared necessary.

In fact many of the decisions of the Carter term were courageous and right, but they were very often formulated in reaction to crisis. The decisions enjoyed the support of no long-term plan or philosophy specifying what needed to be done, why, how, and with what likely consequences.

Why did the Carter team conduct its economic policy more through tactical retreat than through strategic planning? Our conclusion is that economic miscalculation—a fatal misperception of the inflation problem early in the administration—was a major factor, but that thereafter, tactics were elevated over strategy by very powerful political forces. For a domestic president, economic management in the late 1970s was inevitably subject to a tremendous tension, perhaps an utter incompatibility, between ideal policy and feasible politics. To have pursued a coherent, persuasive anti-inflation strategy, President Carter would have had to set aside the coalition that elected him and sustained his party and to have created from whole cloth a new political majority committed to undertaking grave sacrifices for remote benefits. The administration was unwilling, or unable, to mount this political effort because it was not willing to risk the costs, which were obviously substantial. Perhaps the key economic question for the next four years is whether the task is now politically doable. But our purpose here is to demonstrate how intractable it was during the last four years.

**1. The Failure of Results: Accelerating Inflation.** Up to the onset of the recession of 1980, the administration had made some progress toward all but one of its professed economic goals. But the exception was inflation, and failure here was devastating; inflation led to recession, which in turn meant regression on all the other fronts. The chart below tells the story in simple terms.

Why did inflation accelerate so alarmingly during Carter's first three years? Economists will debate the matter for years, but the major factors are clearly visible: demand pressures in the economy in 1977 and 1978 produced an overly buoyant recovery from the 1974–75 recession, converting a gently falling inflation rate into a gently rising inflation rate. The rising rate of inflation was in turn given rude upward kicks by a number of special factors.

*Carter Administration Economic Goals and Results\**

|                  | 1976          | End-of-term targets | 1979          | 1980          |
|------------------|---------------|---------------------|---------------|---------------|
| Budget deficit   | $66.4 billion | 0                   | $27.7 billion | $61.0 billion |
| Outlays/GNP      | 22.6%         | 21%                 | 21.3%         | 23.0%         |
| Unemployment     | 7.8%          | 5%                  | 5.7%          | 7.8%          |
| Inflation (CPI)  | 5.9%          | 4%                  | 12.1%         | 12.4%         |

\* Formulated in 1977, the targets were variously mentioned as applying to calendar 1980, FY 1980, and FY 1981. The budget figures given here refer to fiscal years; the unemployment rates refer to rates obtaining in July; the inflation rates refer to changes in prices between September and September of successive years (i.e., the end month of the fiscal year).

(a) **Overly swift recovery.** During the Carter years, the economy's long-term productive *potential*—its basic supply of productive resources (labor, capital, technology, etc.)—was expanding at about 2.5 to 3.0 percent annually. But *actual* production (real GNP) rose by 5.5 percent in 1977 and 4.8 percent in 1978; dropping the unemployment rate from 7.5 percent in early 1977 to 5.8 percent in late 1978. By growing faster than its long-term potential rate, the economy was burning away idle resources—market slack—at an exceptionally rapid rate. Until well in 1977, market slack was still sufficient to keep the rate of wage inflation declining. Thereafter, however, the rate began to creep up.

The general heating up of the economy created inflationary pressures in many markets. As unemployment dipped into the 6 to 7 percent range in mid-1977, wage inflation began slowly to accelerate. High GNP growth rates in the United States helped tighten the world commodity markets—particularly the food and oil markets—and higher commodity prices coursed back through the U.S. economy via the channels of international trade and finance.

These basic macroeconomic forces would have carried the inflation rate to about 8 percent in 1978, would likely have pushed it to about 9 percent in 1979 and, unless abated by policy, into double digits in 1980. However, this basic inflationary process was *further* accelerated, pushing the CPI to 12 percent in 1979 and to 18 percent in the first quarter of 1980 (when the fever finally broke under the weight of recession) by special factors: a dollar crisis in 1978, a worsening slump in productivity growth in 1979 and 1980, the "Iranian" oil price explosion in 1979, and various microeconomic decisions throughout the four-year period.

## (b) Special factors

*—Dollar decline.* The speed of the recovery, and its attendant effect on inflation, precipitated an extraordinarily sharp and disorderly depreciation of the dollar against foreign currencies in late 1977 and 1978. In Carter's first twenty-two months in office, the dollar on average lost 20 percent of its foreign value against other major currencies. This pushed up the prices of all imported goods and added at least 1 percentage point to the basic inflation rate in 1979.

*—Stagnating productivity.* Real output per man-hour generally rises very strongly early in an economic recovery. This tends to offset inflationary wage pressures by giving business firms a cushion between wage increases and the price increases necessary to cover them. But the Carter recovery was superimposed on a decade-long decline in American productivity growth. The recovery was also accompanied by an unusually fast expansion of the labor force, which further depressed per worker productivity growth. In all, productivity grew at only a 0.7 percent annual rate during the 1976–79 expansion, compared with a 3.2 percent annual rate in the 1960s. In 1979, productivity growth was actually negative, making inflation perhaps several points higher than it would have been with the kind of productivity growth which obtained in the 1960s.

*—Rising oil prices.* The Carter expansion was cursed with the worldwide explosion in oil prices triggered by the Iranian Revolution in 1979. World oil prices executed a doubling during that year. This oil price explosion added at least 3 percentage points to the U.S. inflation rate in late 1979 and early 1980.

*—Microeconomic decisions.* The rest of the inflationary acceleration can be traced to a series of microeconomic policy decisions that raised business costs and the prices of particular products. A portion of these one-time cost and price increases

became embedded in the ongoing spiral of wages and prices, in part because stimulative macroeconomic demand encouraged the process. The microeconomic decisions contributing to inflation included: the four-year Farm Bill, enacted in 1977, which fattened up farm price and income supports; the new Minimum Wage Bill, enacted in 1977, which boosted the minimum wage from $2.30 in 1976 to $3.10 in 1980; and a variety of new regulations in the areas of environmental protection and workplace health and safety. In isolation, none of these policies added more than a few tenths of one percent to inflation. Together, however, they had a tangible impact.

**2. The Strategic Disarray.** Conducting economic policy strategically during this period would have meant concentrating almost singlemindedly on preventing an acceleration of inflation. Inflationary acceleration is a terminal disease for any economic recovery. To have prevented the disease, or at least to have put it into remission, was clearly the most important business before the government in the last half of the 1970s. Policy should have been structured to deal persuasively over the long term, at least four years, with the major forces pushing up the inflation rate—excess aggregate demand, dollar weakness, stagnating productivity growth, dependence on foreign oil, and microeconomic policies. Each of these problems was a major headache in its own right. By dealing with them in a coordinated fashion, the supreme headache—inflationary acceleration—would also have been relieved.

Unfortunately, in each of these areas, the Carter administration began with a serious misstep and, even after discerning the right direction, the administration often resorted to a strange shuffling motion—edging forward through elaborate sideways maneuvers. Having begun in 1977 by focusing economic policy on everything *except* inflation, the administration had a change of heart which itself seemed half-hearted.

• *Macroeconomic policy.* In retrospect, it is clear that fiscal and monetary policies should have moved decisively toward restraint as soon as the President took office—so as to moderate the surging recovery into a gradual and sustainable process, consistent with constant (if not falling) inflation. The new administra-

tion instead moved to liberalize macroeconomic policy. The first
program Carter sent to the Congress was a stimulus package of
tax cuts and spending increases. The Carter advisors also embarked immediately on a gentlemanly campaign to persuade the
Federal Reserve Board (and its holdover chairman, Arthur
Burns) to refrain from interest rate increases that might slow
down the recovery.

As the underlying inflationary pressures began to show their
true strength, the administration did retreat from stimulus. But
retreat does not always make for a coherent strategy, in either
style or substance. In its belated embrace of fiscal and monetary
restraint, the Carter team often showed vacillation, uncertainty
and regrets.

Fiscal policy was put on a seesaw. The $50 tax rebate proposal
was yanked from the stimulus package without prior notice in
the spring of 1977. In January 1978, however, an FY 1979 budget
was proposed with sizable spending increases for many domestic programs and a $25 billion tax cut. Six months later, the
President abruptly reduced this tax-cut proposal to $20 billion,
for anti-inflation reasons. In January 1979, an FY 1980 budget
was proposed with an emphasis on spending restraint and with
a projected deficit under $30 billion. But roller-coaster economic
conditions—high inflation in 1979 and recession in 1980—gave
an ironic twist to the fiscal results: the expansive FY 1979 budget
came in with a deficit under $30 billion, while actual FY 1980
spending escalated about $50 billion beyond the initial target
and the FY 1980 deficit ballooned to $61 billion. Fiscal policy
vacillated most during the 1980 election year, as we have noted
in Chapter 1.*

Monetary policymaking showed a similar lack of steadiness.
The jawboning for easy money ceased abruptly in the fall of
1978, when the Treasury launched an emergency dollar-rescue
operation based in part on raising interest rates. Throughout
early 1979, however, the administration conducted an inconclu-
sive, semi-public debate with itself and with the Fed about the
advisability of tightening the interest rate screws another notch.
In August 1979, as part of his Cabinet shake-up, the President
moved Fed chairman G. William Miller to the Treasury. To

---

*See pages 26–27 above.

calm nervous financial markets, the administration then appointed a tough monetary conservative, Paul Volcker, to replace Miller as Fed chairman. Oddly, this was probably one of the most important substantive results of the July actions—one that was in essence forced on an unprepared administration. Within several weeks, Volcker embarked on a major new policy of targeting the money supply and letting interest rates swing freely upward in the markets to check inflation. The administration supported the new policy formally, but various economic advisors let their private doubts about the policy leak into the press. In the spring of 1980, with inflation soaring, the administration moved back into an activist stance on monetary policy by invoking the Credit Control Act, which helped trigger a credit squeeze, which then helped precipitate the 1980 recession. By the fall of 1980, however, the President was criticizing the Fed's monetarist policies as a threat to the nascent recovery.

In brief, starting in mid-1978, the administration's rhetoric invariably lauded the virtues of fiscal and monetary restraint. But the actions beneath the rhetoric reflected considerable indecision about precisely what operational policies those words should entail.

• *Dollar policy.* An anti-inflation strategy would have placed a high premium on dollar stability and strength. Instead, in 1977 and early 1978, the administration campaigned semi-publicly for the Germans and Japanese to allow their currencies to appreciate against the dollar. The administration thought rightly that, by making U.S. goods more competitive on world markets, dollar decline would help stimulate the U.S. recovery. Further, the new Carter team was ideologically opposed to the management of exchange rates in which Germany and Japan were engaged. By almost any objective test, the Germans and the Japanese were keeping their currencies at artificially low levels against the dollar; the administration advocated allowing the rates to float freely on the markets.

By mid-1978, however, it was obvious that the U.S. policy of rapid economic recovery, coupled with talking down the dollar, had helped create enormous instability on the foreign exchange markets. The dollar was declining at an alarming pace, and the decline was powerfully feeding the inflation psychology at home. In November 1978, the administration executed a historic U-turn and adopted "managed floating" as U.S. policy for the dollar: thereafter, official intervention in foreign exchange markets and general monetary policies were mobilized to avoid large declines in the dollar's value. A strong dollar became, and thereafter remained, a major element of Carter economic policy.

• *Productivity policy.* To counter the stagnation of productivity growth would have required a policy strongly promoting business investment. The administration largely ignored the productivity problem in 1977. In 1978, the administration's proposed tax reduction did include a sizable corporate tax rate cut to stimulate investment. But still wedded to the populist rhetoric of tax reform, the White House chose to downplay this aspect of the tax proposal—emphasizing instead opposition to existing tax loopholes favoring business (for example, the three-martini lunch) and to any liberalization in the capital gains tax. Congress went ahead and cut the capital gains tax anyway. The President signed the bill, but with a statement of disapproval.

During the next two years, the administration talked more and more about productivity and the need for additional investment, but it abstained from proposing tax incentives aimed at the problem for fear that a large, inflationary tax cut for individuals might result. That is, the administration's late start on the problem of inflation had led to a Hobson's choice between deficit restraint and productivity tax cuts. Only in the late summer of 1980 did the administration address the productivity issue directly, proposing that the next Congress enact a tax package tilted heavily toward investment incentives.

• *Energy policy.* The major flaw in the nation's energy policy as inherited by the Carter administration was the structure of federal price controls, which led to severe underpricing—and thus overconsumption and underproduction—of petroleum and natural gas. So long as those price controls remained in place, any sizable expansion of our economy was destined to generate a great surge in oil imports and thus tighter world oil markets, a mushrooming U.S. trade deficit, and a declining dollar—that is to say, to events guaranteed to accelerate our inflation rate. Administration policy did not, however, reflect this connection between inflation and energy price controls. The administration moved immediately to heat up the general economic recovery but proposed to tackle the energy pricing problem through an extremely complex and controversial legislative program involving a very gradual and partial rise in petroleum and natural gas prices to world market levels.

The legislative program—the national energy plan—became bogged down in Congress for eighteen months. Finally the petroleum pricing provisions were jettisoned by the Congress, and natural gas price decontrol was put on a slow and complex phase-out schedule.

Throughout this whole period, the world oil markets were slowly tightening, the U.S. trade deficit was exploding, and the dollar was sinking. But to avoid angering the Congress, and prejudicing the legislative prospects of the national energy plan, the administration refused to take steps—by means of tariffs or quotas—to hold down oil imports. Several months after Congress served up the greatly weakened energy bill, the Iranian Revolution intervened, putting world oil markets into a speculative panic resulting in a doubling of oil prices in less than a year. This drove up the inflation rate by about 30 percent in 1979 and early 1980.

In mid-1979, after prolonged and bitter internal debate, the administration decided on its own to begin a phased decontrol of oil prices. This courageous decision was of momentous long-term economic significance, but its inevitable short-term effect was to raise an inflation rate already out of control. The complex link between price decontrol and long-term anti-inflation objectives was largely obscured by a public debate in which OPEC and the big oil companies were blamed for the nation's economic problems.

• *Microeconomic policymaking.* A committed anti-inflation strategy would have disciplined all of the administration's major programmatic and regulatory decisions to avoid significant impacts on business costs or the price structure. The Carter team did not embrace this discipline. The Cabinet Economic Policy Group and the inflation advisor lobbied internally on most of the issues—but found themselves squarely confronting a Domestic Policy Staff whose primary interest lay in accommodating the policy views of the various constituency groups making up the Democratic coalition. As a result, inflation consequences were accorded little weight in many of the final decisions.

• *Wage-price policies.* As inflation accelerated, the administration reluctantly embraced wage-price guidelines as a token of concern. The Carter team knew that this program could provide only limited and temporary relief from inflationary acceleration, but once started, the program was inevitably seen by the press as the centerpiece of the President's anti-inflation program. The administration itself never made up its mind about how seriously to take the guidelines effort. Formulating the wage-price guidelines in the summer of 1978 was an exceptionally laborious and leaky operation. The surprise proposal in late 1978 of a real wage insurance scheme—guaranteeing workers at least part of the difference between wage agreements under 7 percent and the actual rate of inflation—bombed in the Congress largely because it threatened to widen the budget deficit. Throughout 1979, the President alternately embraced and ignored the wage-price program, uncomfortably aware both of its relative impotence and of the political need to show leadership in its implementation. In late 1979, the program was in a sense kicked upstairs—embedded in an elaborate national accord with organized labor, which involved weakening the wage standard to the point of impotence. By 1980, the program was pretty much forgotten.

**3. Why the Disarray?** What explains the zigzagging and uncertain approach of the administration to the stark crisis of inflationary acceleration? Why did the Carter team so often rely on tactical retreat and so studiously avoid a comprehensive strategy of attack on the problem? At each stage, two factors were at work: miscalculation and politics.

**(a) Miscalculation.** Like many—probably most—private sector economists, the Carter team misperceived the inflation problem for well over a year. Through 1977 and much of 1978, the team found it difficult to believe that inflationary acceleration could occur in an economy still a long way from full employment.

The team relied very heavily on large private* econometric computer models to forecast the results of the policy options it was considering. All these models said much the same thing: the economy had an enormous amount of slack generated by the 1974–75 recession; until unemployment fell to about 5 to 5.5 percent, macroeconomic stimulus would generate large increments in real GNP growth and employment with little if any worsening of the inflation rate. Because the administration did not expect unemployment to fall below 5.5 percent for at least several years, the team assumed that the first term could be given over to relatively rapid demand-generated growth. The computer models were wrong, in four respects.

—The models under-forecast the strength of economic activity throughout the private sector in 1977, 1978 and 1979.

—The unemployment rate pivot point for inflationary acceleration in this period was not 5 to 5.5 percent, as the models assumed, but very probably about 6.5 percent. Because productive potential was growing very slowly in the economy, there really was not all that much slack left by late 1977.

—The models neglected the complicated but crucial interconnections between the pace of domestic economic activity and price movements on the international commodity and currency markets. The fact that domestic *labor* markets were still somewhat slack did not mean that prices in the volatile *international* markets would behave meekly when pressured by stimulative U.S. fiscal and monetary policies. And indeed, these international markets became the great engines of inflationary acceleration over the period (just as they did in 1972–73). Like most American economists, the Carter advisors were insufficiently sensitive to the macroeconomic consequences of floating exchange rates, foreign oil dependence and a growing international trade in commodities.

—Finally, the models could not of course forecast the collapse of productivity growth or the Iranian Revolution—and the Carter team failed to provide a margin of error in its plans for such contingencies.

*The executive branch does not have its own computer model of the economy. It relies on the large models produced by professional econometric forecasting firms.

In all, it took the Carter team until the spring of 1978 to appreciate the reality of inflationary acceleration, and it took the dollar crisis of November 1978 to hammer the point home. By then, it was too late to wring out the added inflation before the 1980 election. Indeed, it was almost inevitable that a recession would be needed prior to the election to halt the inflationary acceleration.

To some degree, the problem of misperception continued throughout 1979. Like virtually all private economists, the Carter team expected a recession to begin at any moment and thus resisted severe shifts toward restraint in macroeconomic policies. In retrospect, however, it is clear that the economy was being driven forward by consumer and business spending, in advance of expected inflationary acceleration: only decisive restraining action could stop it, and that was not forthcoming through monetary tightening until late 1979 and early 1980.

The lessons of this history for your presidency are rather simple:

First, don't put too much stock in the seemingly scientific forecasts of computerized economic models. These models are no more prescient than the men who develop them. Very often you can get a better feel for the likely consequences of policy options by talking to sophisticated businessmen, labor leaders and financiers who have an informed, unscientific intuition about the workings of and interconnections between the many markets that make up the U.S. economy.

Second, encourage Cassandras among your economic advisors. Economic advisors possess a dangerous tendency to compromise their differences of view and to present you with a bland, united front. They may expect that you are too busy to hear out their arcane disputes. Insist on knowing who thinks what and why. You may be confused, but that is far better than being carried away by a phony consensus.

Third, don't take any chances with inflation. Once it accelerates, the price of rolling it back is extremely high. When an advisor assures you that he can deliver all manner of wondrous things—jobs, growth, new programs, tax cuts, votes—at the risk of only a tiny up-tick in the inflation rate, keep in mind that the bargain may be Faustian.

**(b) Politics.** By late 1978, the Carter economists knew that they had miscalculated, that inflation was rising dangerously, and that a plausible strategy for halting the rise and then for reversing the trend over time would require bold, sustained, and mutually reinforcing steps in macroeconomic, dollar, energy, tax, and microeconomic policies. Some of the necessary steps were taken, but others were not. Why the waffling? As noted above, the computer models continued to send out false signals throughout 1979. But by then the operative constraint on policy formation was less technical than political.

A persuasive anti-inflation strategy would have imposed a huge political price immediately, and would have reaped an undramatic political benefit very slowly. At each step, the political price was vivid and tangible, while the economists had to admit that following their optimal course might not make things appreciably better in the short run. Consequently, the Carter team tacked back and forth. They took strong action when forced to do so by events—the dollar crisis of November 1978, the oil price decontrol decision of spring 1979, the Volcker monetary policy initiative of October 1979, and the balanced budget initiative of March 1980—but between crises they often temporized and sought refuge in claims that the economy was something about which mere presidents could do little.

No one in the administration was happy about the image of flip-flopping which this course made inevitable. But the alternative was to confront intractable political problems.

- Monetary restraint sufficient to halt and begin reversing inflationary acceleration would have brought on very high interest rates, recession, and high unemployment. The Carter team shied from this prospect until forced to action by the financial panic of early 1980. As predicted, the resultant recession ceded the liberal wing of the Democratic Party to Senator Kennedy (mild budget restraint had caused many to bolt before then) and blue-collar Democratic voters to consider Governor Reagan in a new light.
- Genuine fiscal restraint would have required deep cuts in dozens of social programs much beloved in Congress and in the President's party. Even the moderate efforts in budget-

cutting made by the President in FY 1980 earned him a skin-flint's reputation. To have gone further would likely have precipitated a complete revolt by the center and left of his party in Congress and the country.

• Tax cuts to stimulate investment would have been highly regressive: the tax savings would have flown predominantly to high-income taxpayers. This course would have sat un-easily at best with the President's populist and tax reformist image. The administration was able to solve the problem only in the summer of 1980, when popular fascination with rein-dustrializing the country permitted the President to support pro-investment tax cuts as part of a program to create long-term jobs. Even then, the liberal wing of the party demanded that various public works and unemployment relief programs be added to the budget as a counterweight to pro-investment tax cuts.

• Decontrolling energy prices more swiftly or thoroughly would have imposed an immediate and severe hardship on poor and working-class citizens—and on politically potent middle-class consumers of gasoline. Americans had come to regard artificially cheap energy as a semi-constitutional right. When the President proposed a new 10¢ gasoline tariff in 1980, the Congress rejected the measure overwhelmingly and overrode his veto of their action—the first veto override for a Democratic president in thirty years.

• Microeconomic policy decisions of an anti-inflation char-acter would have triggered bitter opposition from many pow-erful interest groups—for example, farmers, labor, environ-mentalists, the elderly.

In brief, moving boldly to deal with the fundamentals of inflation would have alienated huge constituencies at the core of the Democratic Party. The administration felt itself perpetually torn between the demands of economic policy and political sur-vival. The result was a wavering path between the two.

Aggravating the dilemma was the unhappy fact that no strat-egy, however bold, could have returned inflation to its 1976 levels in time for the 1980 election. It will take years to turn around productivity growth or cut the link between domestic economic growth and oil imports, and "macro" restraint itself takes years to work its will on the wage inflation rate. Reducing inflation is much harder, and takes a lot longer, than losing control of it.

A committed anti-inflation strategy presents itself to the American people in exceptionally dour terms: "We must do all these awful things so that matters won't get any worse. Someday —but not for several years at least—the economy may actually get better." The administration found itself incapable of conveying such a message.

From all this, there is an obvious lesson for the early eighties —obvious in articulation, perhaps impossible in execution. To undertake a strategy of winding down the inflation rate, you will have to accomplish two enormous political tasks. First, you will have to educate the people to the dimensions of the task— its difficulty, the time needed for even small successes to manifest themselves, and the importance of undertaking the distasteful effort. Second, you will have to create a powerful new constituency for making the necessary long-run sacrifices, because all existing constituency groups will fight you. You must join policy and politics here, as elsewhere, to be successful. But here it may simply not be possible.

Whether you or anyone can do the things necessary to preclude inflationary acceleration, much less to engineer a true *dis*-inflationary process, is far from clear. Economics poses by far the harshest challenge to conducting a strategic presidency. But the example of the first Carter term proves that the other alternative—retreating before events—is not a whole lot easier, or any more successful.

## B. Social Policy Failed: Welfare Reform and National Health Insurance

**1. Background: Commitments and Constraints.** Although both issues had complex and controversial histories going back much before 1976, the seeds of difficulty here for the Carter administration were sown during the 1976 presidential campaign. From his experience as governor of Georgia, Jimmy Carter became personally committed to a complete overhaul of the nation's welfare system.[1] From political necessity, he became publicly committed to national health insurance, making a promise to press for a universal and comprehensive plan to gain credit with the powerful United Auto Workers.[2] The contradictions of candidate Carter were never more apparent than when he campaigned for fundamental welfare reform and comprehensive national health insurance while also promising to balance the budget by 1980. Dealing successfully with this glaring inconsistency, which running for office had produced, would elude Jimmy Carter as he governed during his first four years as president.

Welfare reform and national health insurance were logical outgrowths of important New Deal and Great Society reforms. Welfare reform meant everything from eliminating waste to expanding benefits depending on whether the audience was blue-collar workers or welfare rights advocates. But for most people it entailed simplifying and making more uniform the major components of the complex array of needs-based (income-tested) transfer programs that had been enacted or expanded in the past fifteen years. It also meant placing a standard income floor under those receiving assistance and providing benefits for millions of poor people still not covered by federal programs. National health insurance would build on the expanded health protection for the elderly and the poor that had been achieved by medicare and medicaid. It would seek to ensure that *all* Americans were protected, in some significant way, against the increasingly high costs of health care.

As seen from the executive branch perspective, these reforms were in a sense above partisanship—were a response to genuine, deeply felt national problems. Richard Nixon had proposed the Family Assistance Plan (FAP) in 1969, building in part on concepts that had emerged in the last years of the Johnson administration.[3] In the waning months of his presidency, Nixon also proposed the comprehensive health insurance plan (CHIP), his response to increasingly intense (but ultimately unproductive) congressional deliberations about national health insurance. Neither FAP nor CHIP had, of course, been enacted,[4] although the supplemental security income (SSI) program, which federalized and made more uniform benefits for the poor aged, blind and disabled, was passed as a result of the FAP debate.

With the accession of a Democratic President who could presumably work with a Democratic Congress, there was hope, especially among liberal Democrats, that these major unfinished items on the expansionist social policy agenda could become law, perhaps in a form more generous than FAP or CHIP.[5] Nonetheless, there were significant constraints in January 1977 that would work against the enactment of either one of these major social policy proposals—let alone both.

—For reasons that now must be painfully clear, the economy was much less vigorous than during the mid-sixties. With erosion of real incomes, an increasingly pinched middle class was thus much less likely to support major new programs that were in large measure directed to help poor people.

—With the economy's poor performance and the absence of a significant fiscal dividend, very little room existed in the federal budget for significant new social policy programs, a fact that became more and more apparent as the administration's economic and budgetary planning failed to deal with the problem of inflation, as the President had pledged and as the economic planners had hoped.

—Concern and skepticism about dramatic new federal spending or greatly expanded federal programs were increasingly prevalent both in the Congress and among the public at large.

—Program costs had been underestimated and administrative skills overestimated in some of the major health and welfare programs, despite their successes.[6] These problems had in part resulted from a lack of commitment in certain quarters of the Nixon administration to make those programs work well, but whatever the causes, they fed a general skepticism about the efficiency of governmental action in the social policy area.

—After serious attention to the issues, the Congress had failed to take action on either welfare reform or national health insurance during the early 1970s. FAP had twice passed the House before dying in the Senate Finance Committee in 1972. And only one congressional committee, Senate Finance in 1971, had even reported out a national health insurance proposal, and that one never made it to the floor. (CHIP never made it out of a committee.) The divisions within the Congress that had prevented action during the

Nixon-Ford years could easily do so again under a new president.

In the euphoria following the defeat of President Ford, the Carter team also could not foresee that two shocks would send tremors through the administration in the middle of the first term: an emerging national consensus in which inflation replaced unemployment as the central economic problem facing the nation, and increasing national pressure to reduce government spending—however generalized the form that pressure took—following passage of Proposition 13 in California in the spring of 1978.

**2. Problems and Policies: The Dilemmas of Choice.** Despite these barriers, there was, after nearly a decade of relatively intense debate, an emerging national understanding of the problems in the nation's health and welfare systems.

*Income Maintenance.* Although expenditures in the needs-based federal programs had increased from a total of $3.7 billion in 1965 to $25.3 billion in 1975 and were expected to rise to $50.6 billion in 1980, millions of Americans still have incomes below the poverty threshold. According to the latest available data from the Bureau of the Census, 24.5 million persons (11.5 percent of the population) are still in poverty.* Of these individuals, about 9.8 million were in male-headed (primarily two-parent) families; 9.3 million were in female-headed (primarily single-parent) families; and 5.4 million were single individuals. Beyond the millions still in poverty, other problems with the needs-based programs were (and are) the following:

- Among the poor who can work, there are simply not enough job opportunities to make work requirements mean-

*There is a significant debate about: (a) how to measure poverty, and (b) how many Americans are in poverty after receiving various types of cash and in-kind benefits. The census definitions include only cash benefits in determining the number of persons in poverty. But a 1977 study by the Congressional Budget Office indicated that the number of families in poverty would drop by 16 percent if food stamp and child nutrition benefits were counted as income and by another 24 percent if medicare and medicaid benefits were counted. Even if this alternative method of estimating poverty is used, millions of Americans still live below the poverty line. See Martin Anderson, *Welfare* (1978).

ingful. For example, of the 5.3 million family heads under the poverty threshold in 1978, about 1 million worked fifty to fifty-two weeks, but only 800,000 of those worked full-time. Another 1.6 million worked less than fifty weeks, and of those, 600,000 spent most of their time looking for work when not employed.

• The coverage in existing income maintenance programs has irrational gaps that need closing. These include: aid to families with dependent children (AFDC), supplemental security income for the aged, blind and disabled (SSI), food stamps, the earned income tax credit (EITC), and general assistance (financed totally by state and local governments in certain areas). For example, only twenty-four states exercised an option under AFDC and provided cash assistance to two-parent families when the primary earner is unemployed.

• Even under existing programs, benefit levels in various parts of the country—even between neighboring states—differ substantially, variations that are not merely the result of cost-of-living discrepancies. For example, a family of four in Mississippi received $3,500 from AFDC and food stamps in 1979, while a family of four in Illinois received $5,328 and a family in New York $6,528 from these same two programs.

• Unnecessary administrative complexity and confusion exist for recipients, officials and the public because the programs have widely differing and extremely complex rules and eligibility standards.

• Because of its administrative complexity and the lack of uniform rules, the welfare system is unduly susceptible to errors and waste (practices which are much more widespread than the intentional welfare fraud, which despite high publicity accounts for a tiny percentage of misspent funds). For example, error rates in AFDC—defined as the percentage of total outlays that constituted overpayments or payments to ineligible individuals—averaged 8.4 percent during the period 1976–78.

• The current system places severe fiscal burdens on certain state and local governments. For example, New York, Massachusetts, Michigan and Pennsylvania have relatively generous AFDC programs, and provide general assistance for single individuals and childless couples not covered by AFDC. These four states alone had about 25 percent of the families receiving AFDC in 1978, and spent about 34 percent of the benefits nationwide. And while public welfare expenditures in the nation as a whole averaged 0.8 percent of personal income in 1978, in these states such expenditures averaged about twice as much (1.7 percent).[7]

• Inflation has continued to erode the value of the welfare benefit in those programs not indexed to inflation. For example, in the state of New York, the basic AFDC benefit for a family of four was $4,800 in 1975 and $5,712 in 1979, an increase of 19 percent. But given the rapid inflation during that period, the real value of the benefit had declined 12 percent.

General agreement existed on the principle that should guide welfare reform efforts: jobs for those in poverty able to work and cash assistance or other in-kind aid for those unable to work. Yet despite agreement here, sharp dilemmas were posed by the policies aimed at solving the acknowledged failures in the existing welfare system:

• Job creation for the very poor was necessary, but such a program had not been tested for this hard-to-employ population, and a jobs program for the very poor would, in a period of budget restraint, require significant new federal expenditures (for training, job search, creation of public service jobs or tax credits for businesses that employed the very poor).*
• Expanding coverage and increasing benefits were necessary for those who could not work, especially when inflation reduced the value of existing benefits, but how could benefit expansion be reconciled with the popular pressure to hold down welfare costs?
• Fiscal relief for state and local governments was necessary, but such a goal also ran headlong into pressures to re-

---

*Moreover, although a public jobs program for the very poor would reduce welfare dependency, such a program would be more expensive than a needs-tested program providing the poor the same income; would, if limited in size, provide employment for the best qualified, who had the least relative need; and depending on wage rates, might attract workers who could get private sector jobs.

strain federal spending, especially at a time when many state governments had begun to develop budget surpluses.*

• Raising benefit levels was necessary, especially in the southern states, where the combined benefits from AFDC and food stamps were in many cases below two-thirds of the poverty threshold.† But increasing the level of benefits was likely to lead to controversial results: increasing the number of individuals on the welfare rolls and creating work disincentives.[8]

• Making a host of eligibility and accounting procedures tighter and more uniform was needed to achieve greater efficiency. But these reforms, if applied to existing recipients, could result in significantly reduced benefits for hundreds of thousands, even millions—an unfair and unpopular result.[9] Yet if existing recipients were grandfathered in—that is to say, protected against the effects of prospective changes—new elaborations would be added to a system the reformers were trying to simplify.

Such complex and painful dilemmas prompted HEW Secretary Joseph A. Califano, Jr., to call welfare reform the Middle East of domestic politics. And a seasoned veteran of the welfare reform wars, Senator Daniel Patrick Moynihan of New York, warned in 1977 that the "best should not be the enemy of the good" in this area, implying correctly that any welfare reform proposal would have to be a delicate compromise between important values necessarily in conflict with one another.

*Health Insurance.* As with welfare reform, years of debate and analysis in the executive branch, the Congress and outside the government had produced general agreement on a set of problems in our nation's health-care system.

*In 1979, for example, state and local governments had revenues of $354 billion (including federal funds) and expenditures of $330 billion, for a net surplus of $24.4 billion. Most of this surplus was in state, not local, governments. And a recession is likely to alter this picture, since it leads to a reduction in revenues from sales taxes and to an increase in expenditures for social programs.
†The poverty threshold was $7,400 in 1979. In the same year, the combined AFDC/food stamp benefit was $6,528, or 88 percent of the poverty line in New York.

- *First,* despite the achievements of medicare and medicaid, a dramatic lack of coverage affected the lives of tens of millions. In 1980, out of a total U.S. population of over 230 million, about 22 million individuals were not covered by public or private health insurance, many below or just above the poverty line.[10] About 20 million individuals lived with inadequate health insurance (in other words, did not have basic coverage that paid for the costs of hospitalization, physician services, X-ray and laboratory tests). An additional 41 million did not have adequate protection against the cost of major illness—i.e., costs that in a particular year exceeded either 15 percent of gross income or $2,500.
- *Second,* there was dramatic and corrosive inflation in health-care costs. Total health costs rose from 5 percent of GNP in 1965 to nearly 9 percent of GNP in 1975 and, without cost restraint, would skyrocket to more than 10 percent of GNP by 1985, increasing in absolute terms from $43 billion in 1965 to $132 billion in 1975 and to an estimated $438 billion in 1985. Federal health costs rose from 5.1 percent ($6 billion) of the federal budget in 1965 to nearly 12 percent ($37.1 billion) of the federal budget in 1975 and, without cost restraint, would grow to nearly 15 percent ($132 billion) in 1985.
- *Third,* agreement existed that other systematic reforms in health care were long overdue. Competition had to be increased, since nearly 90 percent of all health-care bills were paid by public or private insurers—so-called third-party payers—thus eliminating any incentive for efficiency by either the consumer of services (the patient) or the provider of services (the doctor or hospital). Prevention and outpatient and primary care services had to be emphasized and increased. Geographical maldistribution (not enough doctors in underserved areas), specialty maldistribution (too many specialists, not enough general practitioners) and an overemphasis on doctors altogether (physician assistants and nurse practitioners could perform many functions as effectively and more inexpensively) had to be rectified.

But as with welfare reform, agreement on the problems did not imply a consensus about the solutions. And the policy choices in health insurance were just as fraught with peril as the choices in welfare reform. Indeed, the complexities and contradictions of the subject were truly mesmerizing because a national health plan would affect every American, including 40 million poor and near poor and 156 million employed and their dependents. It would to some degree restructure the nation's third largest industry, which employs 6 percent of the nation's work force. Among the most salient dilemmas were the following:

- How could controlling costs be reconciled with expanding coverage and benefits? With the expenditures for existing health care coverage gobbling up an ever bigger share of both the GNP and the Federal budget, did it make sense to institute major benefit expansions until effective cost restraints were in place? But how could effective cost restraints affecting two of the most powerful lobbies in Washington, the hospitals and the doctors, be enacted unless that bitter pill was coated with coverage and benefit expansions that created a broadly based coalition for action?

- What was the proper balance between public and private programs? Dramatic expansion of *public* programs to cover the middle class—as the comprehensive proposals of the early seventies required—would be extremely difficult in a more conservative time, because it would result in major new public expenditures and a significantly reduced role for private insurance companies. Yet if coverage for the working poor and the middle class was to be mandated through private sector mechanisms—by imposing nationally legislated, legally mandated requirements that employers provide a core health insurance package—then many businesses (especially smaller ones with low-wage workers) would bear significant new costs and new responsibilities.

- If a significant private component was to have a place in a national health plan, should it be financed by additional payroll taxes or by premium payments? A flat payroll tax would be simpler and more equitable. Yet in a period when payroll taxes were being raised merely to keep the social security system afloat and were the subject of enormous controversy because of their potential inflationary impact, use of the payroll tax seemed to have about reached its limits.*

• What kinds of cost controls were proper? A regulatory approach—imposing limits, for example, on increases in expenditures for hospital care or doctors or both—would be effective immediately. But that approach would run up against strong anti-regulatory sentiment in the Congress and the nation. But no other viable near-term alternatives existed, with substantial waste in the health-care sector and with health-care costs running out of control. Some advanced the idea of competition as an alternative option, but that was more properly seen as a complement to—not a substitute for —cost limits for the immediate future.[11] Meanwhile, some type of cost containment was an essential predicate for action.†

• Should the states or the federal government have primary administrative responsibility for a new national health program? The federal government runs medicare through the private health insurance industry, while medicaid is publicly operated by the states. In an era deeply concerned about improving governmental operations, a unified federal program, combining medicare and medicaid and increasing the role of the private sector as administrative agents of the federal government, might make the most sense. But strong currents of

---

*Amendments to the social security laws in 1977 had imposed significant new payroll taxes to keep the system fiscally sound. But in the late seventies—at least until the 1980 recession hit—there was much public talk about rescinding those payroll tax increases rather than adding a significant new tax for health purposes.

Mandated premium financing would, however, be much more complicated to administer than payroll tax financing because it would have to be based on more varied considerations for each firm (i.e., the type of work force, the type of work and the nature of the coverage). It also would impose greater burdens on the working poor, who would have to pay a fixed percentage of a premium (and this percentage of premium was likely to be higher than a payroll tax), and on small businesses, which generally did not provide health insurance coverage (and would be faced with dramatic new premium costs that were likely to be higher than the employers' share of a payroll tax).

†Another difficult issue was whether cost containment techniques should apply just to the public programs or to health-care services provided in both the public and private sectors. Obviously, it would be easier to impose limits on medicare and medicaid. Yet this could drive providers out of the public systems and cause even greater health cost inflation on the private side (since limits on revenues from the public programs would cause providers to increase charges for private patients in order to make up the difference). On the other hand, the Carter administration would discover in its unsuccessful attempt to enact hospital cost containment legislation that imposing across-the-board limits on hospitals was fraught with difficulty. Establishing system-wide restraints that would affect doctors' fees for *both* publicly and privately insured patients would be even more difficult, if not downright impossible, politically.

opinion were (and are) running against further federalization of important social policy functions, even if federalization in effect meant a significant implementing role for the private sector.

**3. The Politics of the Issues: On the Eve.** In welfare reform, the administration would face three committees in each house if, as the President had hinted during the campaign, it was to send up a comprehensive proposal that included a substantial new jobs program for the poor and a cash-out of food stamps (consolidating it with AFDC and SSI in a single cash assistance program). The House and Senate tax-writing committees, Ways and Means and Finance, would have jurisdiction over the cash assistance portions of the bill;* the House Education and Labor and Senate Labor and Human Resources committees would have jurisdiction over jobs;† and the Agriculture Committee in each house would have jurisdiction over a legislative provision replacing food stamps with cash.‡

---

*The biggest hurdle would be Ways and Means and Finance. In both committees there was an activist public assistance subcommittee chairman (Jim Corman, of California, on Ways and Means and Pat Moynihan on Finance), reined in to varying degrees by more conservative committee chairmen (Ullman and Long). Chairman Ullman was opposed to a major welfare reform proposal in part on spending and in part on philosophical grounds. He initially opposed a guaranteed annual cash assistance income—a negative income tax—even though the food stamp program already provided a guaranteed annual in-kind income for the poor (albeit it on a level far below the poverty line). Because he did not exercise strong control over his committee, Ways and Means would be a question mark. Long was a long-time and steadfast foe of the cash assistance component of welfare reform, and despite pro-work rhetoric would be less than enthusiastic about a new jobs program for the welfare population because it would be expensive and because jurisdiction for that portion of a bill would go through Human Resources and not through Finance (unless it involved tax credits for businesses). Even with Moynihan as an ally, any progress in the Senate was likely to come by getting a modest bill through Finance and then attempting to liberalize it on the Senate floor or in the House-Senate Conference Committee. That at least had been the pattern for most social policy reforms to emerge from the Finance Committee earlier in the decade.

†On the jobs component of a welfare bill, the administration could look to both Senate Human Resources and House Education and Labor, chaired respectively by Senator Harrison Williams of New Jersey and Representative Carl Perkins of Kentucky, as inclined to work closely with the administration in developing satisfactory provisions. Williams and Perkins were staunch Democrats who, after the Nixon-Ford years, were ready to cooperate with a President of the same party. Unlike Finance and Ways and Means, their committees had solid liberal majorities.

‡The Agriculture committees were more problematic. Representative Tom Foley of Washington, chairman of the House Agriculture Committee (and fourth-ranking Democrat in the House), was likely to be a strong friend of the President's but might not be sympathetic to a food stamp cash-out because it would mean diminution of his committee's jurisdiction. Senator Herman Talmadge, chairman of the Senate Agriculture Com-

Outside the Congress, the strongest supporters of a major welfare reform proposal were likely to be the governors, mayors and county executives (recently organized into a political action group called the New Coalition)—so long as there was substantial fiscal relief. They had to live on a daily basis with the incrustations and frustrations of the welfare nonsystem and had watched their welfare costs escalate with rising case loads in the early seventies. The state and local officials, Democratic and Republican alike, were prepared to support sweeping change that would simplify the programs, improve benefits, provide jobs for the hard-to-employ *and* include significant federal assumption of state and local costs.

But beyond the state and local officials, only question marks could be found when it came to developing grass-roots support to exert pressure on the Congress. Welfare reform had ceased to be a burning issue for the labor movement (the most powerful liberal union, the UAW, was more concerned about health insurance), and some within labor had serious doubts about touching the food stamps program. But labor might help if the right jobs component were part of any welfare package. Business was largely silent on the issue, or opposed to it. The welfare rights organizations, which had played an important role in the FAP debates, had been much weakened by time and the nation's more conservative mood. And the once-powerful civil rights coalition that included the civil rights, church and consumer groups, along with the elderly, had other priorities and did not appear likely to provide energetic support.[12]

In sum, except for state and local officials, not much of a constituency seemed to exist for a comprehensive and expensive proposal that would have to be taken to an increasingly conservative Congress and that would be opposed by two key chairmen, Long and Ullman. But if the administration did not propose a major overhaul of the welfare system, it would be attacked vociferously from the left, even though the liberal groups did not have the political power to drive a comprehensive plan to pas-

mittee, was far less likely to be supportive of major increases in coverage and benefit levels, despite his Georgian roots, although ironically he was not opposed to a cash-out of food stamps (it would create a more efficient welfare system). Like Long, he had been an unwavering foe of comprehensive welfare reform (he also sat on the Finance Committee).

sage. Widespread recognition of problems—everyone agreed that something was wrong with the welfare system—had generated only philosophical divisions about solutions and not a unified, energetic coalition intent on working change.

In *health insurance,* the administration also faced complex jurisdictional divisions within the Congress. In the Senate, the conservative Finance Committee had basic responsibility over medicare and medicaid and over any new requirements for employers that would be enforced through the tax code.* A major question on the Senate side was whether a health insurance bill reported out of the Finance Committee would be referred to the Senate Human Resources Committee, and then to Senator Kennedy's Health Subcommittee.† In the House, jurisdiction was also split—most of medicare was in the Ways and Means Committee, with a bit of medicare and all of medicaid in Interstate and Foreign Commerce.‡

*Chairman Long and Health Subcommittee Chairman Talmadge had also been outspoken foes of universal comprehensive health insurance and long-time supporters of a much more narrow catastrophic approach that would only provide protection against the increasingly high costs of major illness. Earlier in the decade, however, Long had also joined Senator Ribicoff in proposing a more generous bill that included a catastrophic element but also proposed significant expansion of basic health coverage for the poor and near poor and the federalization of medicaid to deal with the administrative failures of that state-run program. The Long-Ribicoff bill did not, however, include any significant cost containment provisions. It was reintroduced in 1979.
†Kennedy, of course, was the most vocal champion of a national health insurance that would be universal (apply to *all* citizens) and comprehensive (provide coverage for basic services, not just catastrophic expenses). He would demand such a referral because a national health bill would affect the smaller, discretionary health programs over which his subcommittee had jurisdiction. A major health insurance proposal was perhaps *the* dominant issue with which Kennedy was identified. Kennedy had bested Long in the 1969 vote for senate whip (a job Kennedy subsequently lost to Robert Byrd), and their differences on a range of issues definitely carried over to the decade-long debate on national health insurance. Indeed, despite his ardor for health insurance, Kennedy had never taken a bill out of his Health Subcommittee to the full Human Resources Committee, let alone to the Senate floor. One important reason: the votes in Senate Finance or on the floor were never there, in part because of Long's adamant opposition.
‡Neither Ways and Means Health Subcommittee Chairman Dan Rostenkowski of Illinois nor Chairman Ullman were advocates of a universal, comprehensive plan. Although Wilbur Mills had joined Kennedy, early in the seventies, to propose a universal, comprehensive bill, Ullman, as in so many other ways, did not emulate his predecessor's congressional example. And on the eve of the new administration, both he and Rostenkowski were wary of major new spending initiatives.
    Commerce Health Subcommittee Chairman Paul Rogers of Florida was a moderate. Neither he nor Commerce Chairman Harley Staggers would be out in front pushing for a universal, comprehensive bill. But they could be expected to support a president of the same party.

The congressional complexities were reflected in byzantine interest group politics.

—Organized labor was an ardent supporter of a universal, comprehensive plan; indeed, labor had been seeking national health insurance legislation for nearly sixty years, and the AFL-CIO had urged adoption of a national health insurance bill since its formation in 1955.

—The major health-care providers—the medical and hospital associations—had initially opposed medicare and medicaid, but had learned to profit from such programs, and so did not oppose expansion of benefits. But with their tremendous lobbying power, they violently opposed the mandatory cost controls or restraints that in our more austere age would have to be an essential initial part of any universal, comprehensive national health insurance proposal.

—The insurance companies, which would also have great impact on Capitol Hill on this issue, were especially wary of national health insurance, since it could completely alter their basic methods of doing business. (For example, payroll tax financing would dramatically vitiate underwriting—their central risk-assessment, premium-setting function.) The companies would also be concerned about any nationalizing of regulatory provisions: decades of experience with state insurance commissions had led the industry to the conclusion that it could exert greater influence on a state-by-state basis to bend governmental provisions to its perceived needs.

—Business, especially small business, was also very wary of a plan that might impose substantial new financial burdens. And either premium or payroll financing was likely to add to the cost of doing business for companies with a hundred or fewer employees. Although businesses with more than a hundred employees were already likely to provide their employees with the type of mandated private coverage that a national health plan might require, businesses with less than a hundred workers employed about 50 percent of the 73 million full-time equivalent workers.*

*Of businesses with two to nine employees, 50 percent did not have group health insurance in 1980; and of businesses with ten to ninety-nine employees, 15 percent did not have such health coverage.

—Despite the glaring inadequacies of medicaid, advocates for the poor were even less organized on the health insurance issue as the Carter administration assumed office than they were on welfare reform.

—Increasingly, lower- and middle-income citizens were being covered through private health insurance arrangements, often provided by the employer.

—As with welfare reform, state and local governments would generally be expected to support a major national health insurance proposal. But they would be willing to trade off a measure of control over medicaid only for substantial fiscal relief.

**4. Welfare Reform: The End at the Beginning.** Substantial welfare reform and national health insurance, of the type President Carter ultimately proposed, involved, at bottom, dramatic new public expenditures for poor people—on the order of $15 to $20 billion in 1982 dollars (the earliest year either program would have begun to take effect) for *each* proposal. Enactment of either major social program would thus have required an enormously sophisticated and sustained administration effort.

Yet that is not how even the most charitable observer would characterize the Carter administration's effort to pass major welfare reform legislation. Indeed, in retrospect, it is now apparent that critical decisions were made at the beginning of the administration with inadequate appreciation of their implications —decisions that contributed significantly to the failure of a legislative effort that would have been a difficult uphill battle under the best of circumstances. In fact the end came at the beginning in three related decisions—decisions that underscore the importance of proceeding with care during the first six months of an administration and the need to plot out the next four years with as much precision and sophistication as possible.

*First*, a critical decision regarding the *scope* of the welfare reform proposal was made in the twilight period between the election and the inauguration by the President-elect. Jimmy Carter concluded that he had promised a complete overhaul of the welfare system and that his administration would submit such a comprehensive bill, rather than a more incremental welfare reform proposal, to the Congress. In essence, a major over-haul would include the following basic elements outlined in Carter campaign speeches to the governors and mayors:

—The major federal needs-tested income transfer programs (AFDC, food stamps and SSI) would be consolidated and sim-plified.
—A nationally uniform minimum benefit for families with chil-dren would be established.
—Benefits for able-bodied single individuals and childless cou-ples would be simplified, improved and, most important, fully funded by the federal government (replacing the patchwork of food stamps and general assistance benefits for this contro-versial group).
—Two-parent families with an unemployed principal earner would be eligible for cash assistance in all states.
—Jobs could be provided for those on welfare who could work.

With these changes (which included substantial fiscal relief to the states and localities), the implication should have been clear: comprehensive welfare reform could not be done on the cheap. It would, as noted, also not be done with the cooperation of the two key committee chairmen, Al Ullman and Russell Long.

This decision was apparently made with some finality by the President during the course of a transition group briefing in December. Members of the transition team on income security policy laid out for the President-elect the costs of comprehensive reform and the problems in the Congress that had derailed wel-fare reform efforts during the first half of the decade. But the presentation came at the end of a long meeting on a variety of income security matters, and according to those present at the meeting, the President-elect somewhat testily concluded that he would have nothing of incrementalism: the system needed a complete overhaul, and he would propose one.

Key Cabinet members were not closely consulted at the time —they either had not been selected by the President-elect or were preoccupied with the problems of staffing their depart-ments. Thus the secretaries-designate of Labor, HEW and Trea-sury and the director-designate of the Office of Management and Budget—all of whom had a major stake in the decision—were not really part of an important threshold choice in the battle for welfare reform. And at this point the President had not held in-depth discussions with the most influential members of the Congress on how to proceed in key areas like welfare.

The issue was never really reopened in the chaotic first months of the administration. As formal briefings on the welfare system were presented to the President after the inauguration, there was no serious challenge to the assumption that the proposal would be comprehensive, in roughly the sense mentioned above, despite repeated reports that such a bill would have trouble in the Congress. With the threshold question apparently decided during the transition, the presidential meetings focused on the various options for a comprehensive plan. The President was confident that the system was so flawed—and the American people knew it was so flawed—that there would be support for a major overhaul of the much-criticized system.

Others in the administration who had doubts about the political viability of a comprehensive approach did not object as strenuously as they might have—and probably should have—at this time. The liberals in the administration—HEW Secretary Califano, Labor Secretary Marshall, Domestic Affairs Advisor Eizenstat, Vice President Mondale (a veteran of the Finance Committee) and, on this issue, CEA Chairman Schultze—had a substantive preference for a comprehensive approach. All had strong ties to the liberal wing of the Democratic Party, and in the early days of the Democrats' return to executive power, were not inclined to incur the wrath of activist liberals within the party. Further, some of them assumed that as *a,* perhaps *the,* major presidential social policy initiative for the first half of the first term, the administration would fight hard for welfare reform—and a big plan was a good going-in position even though an orderly retreat might have to be made toward a smaller, incremental plan with the onset of the congressional wars. Moreover, in the opening months of the administration, none of the senior advisors were willing to disagree pointedly with the new President, whatever their doubts—especially with a president who clearly seemed to have made up his mind. Thus, the question of whether an incremental bill was preferable was never discussed seriously within an administration committed ineluctably to a comprehensive approach.

The basic thrust behind the quick and unequivocal decision to go with a comprehensive proposal was the President's inherent sense of the manifest problems with the welfare system based on his experience as governor. But of equal importance was the attitude, held firmly at the beginning of the administration, that the President was going to keep all of his campaign promises. Initially the President and his close advisors felt that the best way to maintain the President's reputation for integrity —the personal characteristic that had been one of his key campaign themes—was to be a unique modern president and take campaign promises very seriously. This instinct—it could hardly be called an approach, much less a strategy—was based on broad public relations themes and not on the realities of Washington and the politics of governing. That approach, more than almost anything, led to a host of flawed decisions on the administration's legislative proposals.

A *second* critical decision made early in the welfare reform process was the President's paradoxical insistence that his advisors prepare a "no-additional-cost" proposal by a May 1 target date, an injunction delivered by the President at his first briefing on the issue in March. That injunction reflected the President's very contradictory impulses. Although he wanted a plan broad enough in scope to rationalize the hodgepodge of present programs, he was not anxious to propose a big spending program. He thus stated that he wanted to achieve his comprehensive goals with the same amount of money currently being spent in the needs-tested assistance and jobs programs that were to be affected by the reform—that is to say, about $25 billion in fiscal 1978 (as estimated in the spring of 1977).*

The no-additional-cost stricture could have worked as an effective form of internal discipline on the policy development process to highlight the costs of various elements of a proposal. But this mode of proceeding subsequently caused all sorts of distortions. In early May, unable to decide on the shape of the final plan under the tremendous pressure of an artificial deadline, the administration publicly announced general principles

---

*The relevant programs were: AFDC, food stamps, SSI, the earned income tax credit (EITC), CETA programs for the low-income worker and the work incentive now (WIN) tax credit for private employers.

that would guide welfare reform. And the internal technique became an external commitment when the President insisted that one of those principles be a no-additional-cost constraint.*

The problem, of course, was that it was simply impossible to have comprehensive welfare reform at no higher additional cost. Given the prior decision to propose a systematic overhaul, the no-additional cost mandate was never realistic. The constraint, in the simplest terms, meant that the same amount of money would be spread among more people, reducing dramatically the benefits to existing recipients—an untenable position for a newly elected Democratic President, as President Carter was warned repeatedly. The President hoped that simplification and consolidation of the welfare system would lead to cost savings, and although estimates existed that welfare expenditures could be reduced by a national computerized cash assistance program,[13] these savings could not remotely offset the new costs associated with increased benefits: a new jobs program; expanded tax credits for the working poor; fiscal relief; and a commitment not to harm existing recipients.

To reconcile the two inconsistent desires embodied in the impossible concept of comprehensive welfare reform at no additional cost, the program subsequently announced in August 1977 had to present an elaborate explanation of the net costs. As announced, the bill entailed only $2.8 billion in additional outlays. Problems soon surfaced. The cost of the program was given in 1978 dollars, although the program would not begin to take effect until 1982. A number of offsets were counted against new expenditures to calculate program costs, but some of these were based on assumptions subject to dispute.[14] Although each of these assumptions was stated explicitly in administration briefing papers, the Congressional Budget Office, a few weeks later, estimated the cost of the plan at more than $14 billion above the administration figure. The CBO used different assumptions (1982, not 1978, dollars, and no credit for some of the offsets).

In the end, the administration and CBO agreed that the net

*Principle number one in the President's statement of May 2, 1977, included at the President's insistence, was: "No higher initial cost than the present systems." But the President remained committed to comprehensive reform: " . . . the present welfare system would be scrapped and a totally new system implemented."

cost of the administration's comprehensive proposal would be about $19 billion in 1982 dollars, without the disputed offsets. In an attempt to meet the President's inconsistent desire for a major reform bill that would not entail major costs, the administration made a mistake. The inconsistency stemmed in turn from the contradictions in the policy and politics of welfare reform. In fact, the President's policy inconsistencies had a certain strained political logic to them. He knew that liberals in the party would demand a major reform effort, yet after two years of campaigning, he also sensed the conservative mood of the country. Indeed, it must be remembered that in the spring of 1977 the President was being hectored by liberals in his own party for not moving swiftly or boldly enough on the social policy agenda. In a sense, then, the President's contradictory substantive impulses were understandable: he did need a generous bill to satisfy those to his left, but he needed a less expensive bill to hold the center. The problem was that he could not follow both political impulses in his actual policies, and the contortions surrounding the cost issue reflected an unsuccessful attempt to do just that.

The emerging dispute over program costs obscured what the administration had hoped would be the major selling points of the proposal, which the President personally named the Program for Better Jobs and Income (PBJI) to avoid a FAP-like acronym. For the first time, a major jobs component was integrated with a consolidated cash assistance structure. That consolidated structure was then simplified, which made possible a more efficient system. At the same time, two-parent families, single individuals and childless couples would all receive a minimum national payment if they were unable to work. And there was substantial fiscal relief. It was, the administration hoped, a package that creatively blended liberal and conservative themes, resolving welfare reform's vexing dilemmas in a way that could attract broad-based support. Senator Moynihan termed the plan "magnificently crafted." And indeed, the initial reaction to the plan was generally favorable,* the most immediate and vocal

---

*A Harris poll of September 15, 1977, found 70 percent answering affirmatively, 13 percent answering negatively and 17 percent not sure of their position on the question: "Do you favor or oppose Carter's new program of jobs and income support?"

plaudits coming from the New Coalition, which quickly endorsed the proposal.[15]

The growing cost issue, and the confusion engendered by a no- or low-cost comprehensive plan, would have caused problems and made retreat to a more incremental plan somewhat tricky. But a *third* key decision made early in the administration doomed welfare reform.

As part of the early and unrealistic strategy to carry out campaign promises, the President insisted that a number of major proposals steam forward toward Capitol Hill during the first twelve months of his administration. Thus Carter proposed: an economic stimulus package (introduced in January 1977); a hospital cost containment bill (introduced in April 1977); an innovative and controversial bill to restore financial integrity to the strained social security system (introduced in May 1977); a major set of energy proposals (introduced in April 1977); comprehensive welfare reform (introduced in August 1977); and a comprehensive set of tax reforms (introduced in January 1978).* Every one of the proposals had to be routed, in whole or in part, through Senate Finance and House Ways and Means.

This was clearly legislative overload of the first order. The tax-writing committees could not handle all these complex and controversial bills in a single Congress. There was simply not enough time, and the administration simply could not develop the requisite political muscle to push that many proposals through committees that in many respects were in fundamental disagreement with major elements of each proposal. The problem was foreseen in the spring of 1977 when the tax reform package began to take shape within the administration, but the President then wanted to press ahead with both welfare and tax reform (even though social security finance, hospital cost containment and energy were not exactly sailing through congressional shoals unimpeded). Despite the enormous attention paid to welfare reform as one of the President's top priorities in 1977, it was in fact never considered seriously either by the full Senate

*Moreover, the jobs portion of the welfare bill would have to await what turned out to be a controversial reauthorization of the Comprehensive Employment and Training Act (CETA).

Finance or full House Ways and Means committees in 1978.*

The possibility of a compromise proposal—with a net annual cost in the $10 to $14 billion range (in 1982 dollars)—was floated by the New Coalition in May and June of 1978 with the active help and support of the administration. And it appeared that such a compromise had a chance of moving through Ways and Means if only Chairman Ullman would agree. But then Proposition 13 passed; confusion over spending spread through the Congress; and with only a limited number of legislative days left in the session, welfare reform was quietly put to rest in the House. Meanwhile, the administration bill never had even that much consideration in the Senate.[16] In 1977, the administration had anticipated a showdown over the issue in the Senate in the waning days of the 95th Congress, but that of course never happened. In short, the issues were never joined. There just wasn't time.

Moreover, other action early in 1978 not only sealed the fate of welfare reform but left the unfortunate impression of an administration not sure what it was doing in either welfare or congressional relations, thus undercutting the administration's future credibility on the issue. Faced with an energy program in tatters and the President's popularity sinking in the aftermath of the Lance affair, the White House decided that welfare reform would no longer be carried at the top of the domestic agenda despite enormous presidential hoopla in 1977. The first inkling of the White House decision was a leak from top presidential aides in January 1978, prominently displayed on the front page of the *Washington Post*, which asserted that the administration did not expect welfare reform to pass. This was a misguided attempt to lower expectations. And it infuriated the

*In order to expedite the legislative process, the administration prevailed on House Speaker O'Neill to establish a special ad hoc welfare reform subcommittee drawn from the three relevant House legislative committees (Ways and Means, Education and Labor, and Agriculture). But unlike the ad hoc energy committee, this special entity, which was chaired by Jim Corman of Ways and Means, did not have the power to report out a bill for consideration on the House floor. Any proposal that emerged from the special committee would have to be referred back to the parent committees for full consideration (otherwise Al Ullman would not agree to the unusual procedure). The special welfare reform subcommittee labored mightily during the fall of 1977 and in the first weeks of 1978. By February 1978 it had reported out a bill that was even more expensive than the administration proposal. But the parent committees never took that bill up. The press of other legislative business was simply too great, and the opposition of Al Ullman to a bill of that magnitude was too strong.

members of the special House welfare reform subcommittee who had been laboring during the congressional recess to produce a bill on a timetable that would allow serious consideration by both houses of the Congress before the end of the session. Although the President quickly dispatched a personal note to the Hill urging the special committee to continue, the impression of an administration that did not know what it was doing and that had very uncertain resolve about welfare reform was indelibly established.

The leaks were put out at about the same time that the President, against the advice of most of his substantive and political advisors, made final decisions about a major tax reform package and determined it should have precedence in Ways and Means and Finance over welfare reform. The tax program was subsequently decimated after months of fruitless debate. And welfare reform was thus demoted in importance (it wasn't even mentioned in the delivered text of the State of the Union Address), delayed in key committees and ultimately destroyed without ceremony. Without any coherent strategy of how to relate welfare reform to the whole administration program in the Congress, the bill never had a chance.

In the 96th Congress, the administration adopted a different approach. It sought a more modest bill.[17] It consulted in depth on Capitol Hill before it was introduced, putting a premium on a proposal that was "doable" without major surgery in the Congress. It worked carefully with Members and Hill staffers to produce a crucial alliance between Ways and Means Chairman Ullman and Ways and Means Public Assistance Subcommittee Chairman Corman before the bill was announced. It sought bipartisan support and was in fact able to secure expressions of agreement from an impressive array of senators, including Republicans Howard Baker, Henry Bellmon and John Danforth. And it did not make the issue a major item on the presidential agenda, choosing a lower profile to avoid as much controversy as possible on what is always a potentially controversial and, in the end, an unpopular subject.

The cash portion of the bill—which, when scaled back, cost $3 billion rather than PBJI's $11.2 billion—cleared the full Ways and Means Committee *and* the House floor in late 1979. But the bill never got out of Senate Finance, the committee once again encumbered by another round of legislative overload (the second Carter energy plan—primarily the windfall profits tax— and national health insurance took up most of the committee's legislative days in late 1979 and the beginning of 1980). And then, when gloomy inflation figures appeared during the first half of 1980, a resurgence of concern about government spending made consideration of the initiative out of the question. And the jobs portion—also scaled back from PBJI's 1.2 million new CETA jobs at a net cost of $8.1 billion to about half that number (including private sector and retargeted CETA jobs) at a net cost of $2.7 billion—never made it out of committee in either house.

There might have been a welfare reform bill in the Carter first term, although it was, under any circumstances, a long shot. But passage would have required strategic skill and a much more single-minded commitment to the issue than the administration was able to muster. If the administration had sought a medium-sized bill (that is to say, net cost in the $10 billion range) it could have introduced the large, comprehensive proposal, moved the debate in that direction, and then tried to compromise back toward the center along the lines proposed by the New Coalition. But such a strategy would have required that welfare reform be one of the top two or three domestic program issues;* that the President devote substantial time to the effort personally; and that the White House be prepared to hold other issues back until welfare reform was resolved. Even then, given the controversial nature of the subject and the conservatism of the time, securing passage of a medium-sized bill would have been chancy. As it was done, it was not chancy: it was impossible.

Alternatively, the administration could have determined that the key domestic priorities to be considered by the 95th Congress were to be energy, social security financing, and hospital cost containment, and then adopted a lower-key two-Congress strategy aimed at moving the more modest, incremental welfare bill through the 95th Congress and securing passage in the first

*In our terminology, welfare would have had to be a presidential-level issue.

(nonelection) year of the 96th Congress.* But that would have meant proposing a smaller (and lower profile) bill in 1977, letting the legislative process grind away at it in 1977–78, and probably not sending a national health insurance bill to the Congress in 1979 (the year that would have been targeted for passage of welfare reform, and that would have required action by Senate Finance and House Ways and Means).[18] It would also have meant some sharp words for the President from liberals in his party, and perhaps a break on the issue.†

**5. Health Insurance: The Politics of Ambivalence.** If welfare reform was doomed because of decisions made outside of a strategic context at the beginning of the administration, enactment of national health insurance never really had a chance because of decisions postponed and fuzzed over due to a lack of strategic direction. Like welfare reform, national health insurance was a subject so potentially controversial that a coherent and concerted four-year effort, under the best of conditions, was probably necessary to get it through in some form. But the one thing that the administration effort lacked was coherence.‡ The administration's uncertain approach toward health insurance stemmed from a profound ambivalence among many key actors about the issue on a variety of levels—an ambivalence that the President did not resolve until it was too late.

---

*Under this plan, welfare reform would have been a mixed presidential/secretarial issue that involved behind-the-scenes presidential decision-making but less public presidential involvement than Carter gave welfare in 1977. In the Carter administration, welfare did get demoted, but it was done under the press of events and, as indicated, with little sense of its place in the strategic firmament.

†It is an open question, for example, whether Jim Corman would have initially accepted a more modest bill. His willingness to cosponsor the administration's second, incremental bill was born in part of the problems encountered by its first, comprehensive proposal.

‡The decision to go forward with welfare reform rather than health insurance during the 95th Congress was also made by the President, with almost no consultation, during the transition period. Whether that was the right decision is not the point here. But it certainly had a major impact on health insurance. As welfare slowed down, health insurance was held up behind it, and as we indicate below, the issue never really got placed in a congressional time frame that would have allowed serious consideration. But there seems to have been very little systematic discussion of how difficult either issue would be; how these issues would relate to other major domestic initiatives; what the politics of either issue would be; and how those politics would help or hurt the President.

• *Size and Cost.* Although Carter had promised universal, comprehensive health insurance during the campaign, the costs involved were significant. In 1978, HEW estimated that at a minimum such a bill would have a net cost of between $40 to $50 billion in 1980 dollars—about 75 percent of that coming from federal outlays and the rest from newly mandated private expenditures. The administration had always said that expenditures for national health insurance would not begin until fiscal 1982 or 1983, and had always expected that the bill would be phased in. Nevertheless, the expense seemed strikingly out of line when the public wanted the budget balanced and spending restrained.

For the first two years of the administration, the President was ambivalent about whether he could support the full national health insurance proposal with its extraordinary price tag. He publicly paid lip service to his campaign promise of a universal, comprehensive bill and told the advocates of such a bill—the AFL-CIO, the UAW and Senator Kennedy—that he would honor his commitment. Yet he became increasingly concerned privately about the economic and budgetary implications of such a significant federal undertaking.

The ambivalence was mirrored in a wonderfully vague section of the principles for national health insurance that the President announced in July 1978, eighteen months after the inauguration. The principles were an attempt to show progress on the issue, although in fact there was nearly complete indecision within the administration on how to proceed. Principle 6 stated:

> The plan will involve no additional federal spending until FY 1983, because of tight fiscal constraints and the need for careful planning and implementation. Thereafter, the plan should be phased in gradually. As the plan moves from phase to phase, *consideration should be given to such factors as economic and administrative experience under prior phases.* The experience of other governmental programs, in which expenditures far exceed initial projections, must not be repeated. [Emphasis supplied.]

This was clearly drafted to give the administration an out. It could in effect propose only a first phase of a universal, compre-

hensive national health plan, and then give "consideration
. . . to such factors as economic and administrative experience
under prior phases." And it hardly satisfied Senator Kennedy,
who lambasted the phasing approach as an unacceptable retreat
from a universal, comprehensive national health plan.

- *Timing.* The ambivalence about size and cost came out in
parallel ambivalence about timing—whether to push for legislation in any meaningful way at all. With the recognition in 1978
that the administration had sprayed major initiatives on the
Hill, and was losing on many fronts, the administration was
afraid to propose a national health insurance bill that would
come to the same end in the Congress—especially with a major
welfare bill in trouble. But when HEW Secretary Califano suggested early in 1978 that health insurance might not be sent to
the Congress until 1979, the White House, fearing that such a
signal could antagonize Senator Kennedy, immediately said that
the secretary was not speaking for the President.

Indeed, only pressure from Senator Kennedy and organized
labor kept the administration publicly active on health insurance in 1978 at all, forcing announcement of the national health
plan principles in July. Carter's political advisors came to realize
that they did not want to risk a break with Kennedy on the issue
before the Democratic midterm convention in Memphis in December 1978. And unable to decide on the outlines of a bill, they
pushed a decision on the actual shape of the proposal off into the
next year.

The problems of timing were compounded because the administration's hospital cost containment legislation had not
passed the Congress in 1978 and was going to be redrafted and
resubmitted in early 1979. Cost containment was an important
budget cutter (the federal savings were estimated at a total of
over $20 billion for the first five years), but it was also seen as
an important predicate for the national health plan. Yet given
how controversial cost containment had been and given how
controversial the national health plan would be, the administration did not want to link them because that would delay consideration of cost containment until 1980.*

---

*Lengthy hearings in both the House and the Senate would be required on a national
health bill.

The timing problems meant that it was May 1979 before the administration announced its actual proposal. It then proposed only a Phase I bill (albeit a quite generous one under the circumstances: $18 billion in new federal spending and $6 billion in newly mandated private costs). It also outlined the full universal, comprehensive bill and explained the relation between it and Phase I. But the administration did not prepare legislative language or cost estimates for the larger bill.

Ironically, the decision to go forward at all was driven as much by Russell Long as by Ted Kennedy. In early 1979, Long began serious consideration of health insurance in the Finance Committee. Sensing the weakness of Kennedy's position (a universal, comprehensive bill had little chance in the 96th Congress) and seeing the possibility of an alliance with Carter, Long, who was anxious to do something by way of social policy for his constituents before his 1980 election campaign, started to move. And the administration had to hurry to catch up. After reiterating its commitment to health insurance, it could not let the Finance Committee develop legislation without an administration proposal on the table. It was especially worried that Long might move a "catastrophic only" bill through the committee that would have no cost containment provisions and no expanded coverage for the poor and near poor.

But May 1979 was too late. Senate Finance proceeded fitfully, and in the summer of 1980, it finally shelved a health insurance bill that had begun to look somewhat like the administration's Phase I proposal—which in turn bore some resemblance to the plan proposed by Senator Long and Senator Ribicoff earlier in the decade. Obviously no health insurance bill ever reached the Senate floor (Kennedy was far too busy campaigning to work on one of his key domestic issues in the Congress) nor did a bill emerge from either of the House committees with jurisdiction (Ways and Means or Commerce).

• *The Politics of Governing vs. the Politics of Renomination.* Behind the administration's ambivalence about the size and timing of its health insurance proposal was a basic confusion: did it want to move to the center and legislate, or did it want to protect its flanks with the activist, liberal wing of the Democratic Party, especially with the AFL-CIO and the United Auto Workers?

Universal comprehensive health insurance had long been an

article of faith for the unions, and as noted, Carter had told the UAW that he would support such a proposal if elected. Any deviation from this position risked a break with the UAW, and a shift by the union to Edward Kennedy for the Democratic nomination in 1980. The AFL-CIO also had strongly held views on national health insurance. Despite repeated administration overtures, neither the AFL-CIO nor the UAW was ever willing to consider seriously compromising traditional and deeply felt commitment to a universal, comprehensive national health plan.*

But in the judgment of most congressional observers, there was absolutely no chance that a universal, comprehensive bill was going to be enacted during either the 95th or the 96th Congress: in part because of legislative preoccupation with a host of other issues; in part because of the more conservative mood on the Hill; in part because of opposition from key leaders like Long and Ullman; in part because, labor aside, there was no strong outside pressure for a major bill (and major counterpressure against a proposal with the requisite cost controls). Indeed, absent a willingness on the part of the unions or Kennedy to strike a compromise on a more moderate, less ambitious bill with some chance of legislative success, the administration began to focus on a bill that could be enacted—that not only would provide protection against catastrophic expenses but also would include significant cost controls, other system reforms and expansion of comprehensive benefits for the poor and near poor. If a vehicle emerged from Senate Finance and appeared to have a chance in the Senate as a whole, the administration would have to press the two health subcommittees in the House to begin consideration of its proposals.

To follow this path, however, would lead to a break with labor —and possibly with Ted Kennedy.

• *Carter vs. Kennedy.* The ambivalence about whether to play the politics of renomination or the politics of governing was exacerbated by the growing threat of Senator Kennedy. He used his position as a powerful liberal senator and spokesman for a

*A generous, mandated national health plan would remove an expensive item from collective bargaining agreements, increasing the possibilities for higher wages.

wing of the Democratic Party to prod the administration constantly on issues of concern to him—most saliently, national health insurance. Despite protestations, Kennedy took great delight in being considered as a possible alternative to Carter for the 1980 Democratic presidential nomination. Many inside the administration could not understand why Kennedy was unwilling to work on a compromise proposal that was smaller than the universal, comprehensive ideal but that nonetheless involved substantial federal expenditures (in the $15 to $20 billion range annually), one that would help literally millions of poor and near poor (*15* million additional poor in the administration's Phase I bill)—unless Kennedy was interested only in the 1980 nomination.

The White House was uncertain about how to meet the Kennedy threat. Initially, most close advisors to the President argued for conciliation. If Kennedy had no reason to be angry with the administration, he couldn't or wouldn't run against it. This was the dominant view of the White House political advisors during 1977–78. Thus during that period the President sought to be conciliatory, to state that he would propose a universal, comprehensive plan and to avoid a split even in the face of extreme provocation.[19] But after the midterm convention in Memphis, when Kennedy attacked the administration on health and budgetary issues, there was a greater willingness to risk a split and to shift position: propose a narrower bill and then let Kennedy challenge the President on health insurance in the face of worsening economic conditions. Many in the administration came to believe a more modest, but still quite expensive approach that laid the foundation for a larger plan would, when it was examined closely, be seen as superior to a full-blown universal, comprehensive plan, both in the Congress and in the nation. Even so, there was great concern that going to the brink with Kennedy was not worth it—there was not enough time to force the issue in the Congress, and the damage within the party outweighed the slim chance of a legislative victory.

There was another source of ambivalence toward Kennedy on health matters. He was the strongest congressional champion of hospital cost containment. Like the administration, he recognized that it was simply irresponsible to propose additional health coverage and an expansion of health costs unless one could change the health-care system and ensure an end to the unceasing and intolerable increases in health inflation. After three bitter years of controversy, hospital cost containment failed, but it was not for lack of Kennedy's effort. Both in the 95th and 96th Congress, his health subcommittee and the Senate's Human Resources Committee reported out bills that were very, very close to the administration's proposals.* He was thus an important ally on this and on other important administration initiatives.

In the end, events forced Carter's hand on Kennedy. Because of inflation and the dollar's weakness, the administration concluded in the winter of 1978–79 that it had to propose a restrained budget (for fiscal 1980). Politically, many in the administration found it hard to reconcile the administration's economic and budgetary policies with a universal, comprehensive plan. The break came in March, when the administration announced it would send only a Phase I bill to the Congress later in the spring.

But the ambivalence about Kennedy not only contributed to the delay that made it impossible to legislate but may also have produced just what the Carterites wanted to forestall. It may have been interpreted by Kennedy as weakness, not as an attempt at conciliation, and this perceived weakness may have been one of the factors that lured Kennedy into the presidential race.

• *The White House Against Itself.* Beyond confusion created by the Kennedy threat was a disappointing performance by the White House on the issue. The political advisors did not consider it their business to master the substance of health insurance policy; thus, they never thought strategically about how to handle it and never spent much time talking to the top policy and congressional personnel in the departments and the White House who did have some understanding of the choices facing the President. For example, Stu Eizenstat was given the responsibility to coordinate development of health insurance within

---

*In both congresses, Senator Long's Finance Committee, which shared jurisdiction over the issue, narrowly defeated the administration's proposal—although in the 96th Congress, Long lent his personal support to the administration bill.

the EOP, but he had great difficulty getting the political people
to participate in a way that would have educated them, allowed
them to make informed decisions and, most importantly, presented the President with clear options.

The policy process always proceeded in something of a political vacuum, a clearly fatal flaw on an issue that involved intricate political decisions. Top administration officials, both in the
departments and the EOP, were never clear about the views of
the President and his top political operatives on the key questions—the relation to the unions, to Long and Kennedy, and to
the politics of governing and the politics of renomination. There
were important, deeply held differences about the proper course
of action at various points during the first half of the administration's first term:

—stay with Kennedy and the unions and propose a universal,
   comprehensive bill, albeit one with phasing; then not push
   very hard, since the legislative process could not accommodate another major social policy proposal, leaving the issue to
   wither away.
—work with Long, and with House liberals like Jim Corman
   and Charles Rangel who split with Kennedy on the issue, to
   legislate, calling Kennedy's bluff.
—retain a general commitment to a universal, comprehensive
   plan, but if at all possible, explicitly defer serious consideration of the issue to the second term, when the economy would
   (it was hoped) be stronger and the legislative calendar less
   crowded.

Yet hardly any meetings were held to discuss options in the
context of the administration's overall congressional and political strategy. At some point the President had to choose. But he
waited until it was too late and too much damage had been done
on all fronts.

The separation of the political aides from the White House
policy staffers and from key department personnel led to an
inability to make firm decisions and send out clear signals. At
times HEW officials were told to stand up to labor and explain
the President's problems on health insurance, but when the
labor representatives went to the White House and complained,

they were told that the President would not abandon them. At the center was a president who had begun to be buffeted severely by events; who was, as expected, being pulled more and more into foreign affairs; and who was, given the inability among the top White House aides to give him clear options that combined policy and politics, incapable of giving strong direction and unambiguous internal leadership within the administration on the issue.

The ambivalence within the administration, the lack of clear decision-making, the inability to relate health insurance to other matters flowing through the Congress, all contributed to the general confusion and delay that surrounded the issue. In the end the President chose to break with Kennedy on health insurance, to work with Long and to push for legislation. But given an inability to consider the issue as part of a four-year strategy, this belated decision in the spring of 1979 had little impact on events. As with welfare, this was not a proposal that was hotly contested into the session's waning days and became the focus of a bitter legislative battle with national reverberations. Despite the enormous publicity that surrounded the aspects of the issue clearly related to presidential politics, and despite the issue's role in contributing to Kennedy's challenge to Carter, the issue was not put in a meaningful legislative posture soon enough by the administration to give it a chance of enactment. And given the confusion in dealing with the Congress that went back to the administration's opening days, it *could not have been* placed in a real legislative context by the time the President made his final decision.

**6. Lessons.** Cynics might argue that the Carter administration craftily got what it wanted with both welfare reform and national health insurance. It obtained some credit with moderate liberal groups for making the proposals, even though neither was enacted. And it did not get much blame. As the election approached, the political climate had turned so conservative— was so dominated by the issues of budgetary restraint and problems in the economy—that the legislative failures could not be used against the administration by its political adversaries at either end of the political spectrum. And as an added bonus, the break with Kennedy on health insurance may have been one of the key factors, or at least a key pretext, for the entry of the Massachusetts senator into the race, thus giving the President an opportunity to come from behind and beat a powerful rival for the Democratic nomination.

But if these were the results, they were most assuredly not what the administration intended. An enormous amount of effort—albeit inconsistent and not always effective effort—from the President on down was devoted to both issues. The administration did want to legislate in both areas, recognizing that very profound problems still existed in health and welfare. And it desperately sought to keep Senator Kennedy out of the race for the nomination, failing, as did nearly all other sensate political beings, to realize that he would not be as strong a candidate as appeared to be the case during the first three years of the administration.

That it failed legislatively on these two controversial issues is hardly surprising, given the powerful policy and political conflicts that lurk beneath their surfaces and given the worsening economic circumstances that bedeviled the administration over the course of the term. The reasons why welfare reform and national health insurance bills, after a decade of debate, are not law encompasses many more factors than the problems of the Carter administration. But the inability of the Carterites to act strategically with a Congress of the same party unquestionably doomed what would have been high-risk efforts, and therein lie some lessons for the future.

—Quick decisions were made in the first six months on the whole approach toward the Congress and the legislative agenda that were to burden the administration for the remainder of the first term.

—The White House failed to see the difficulty and complexity of working major reforms through the Congress in a four-year period or to understand how to orchestrate those efforts and not to overload key committees.

—It did not appreciate the constraints—in the economy, the budget, the Congress and the interest groups—that would make an attempt at major changes in social policy so difficult.

—It did not understand how few issues the President could be intimately and personally identified with, and did not appreciate the differing implications of styling issues presidential or mixed presidential/secretarial.

—It did not clearly see the choices implied by the different, sometimes contradictory levels of politics. On welfare reform, the broad contradictions of general election promises that had different political appeal to different groups became explosive dilemmas that could not be reconciled in policy or in the politics of governing (a complete *but* no-cost overhaul of the welfare system). On health insurance, the administration oscillated between the politics of nomination and the politics of governing. And in the end it got the worst of both worlds: a break with Kennedy and the UAW and no incremental reform enacted into law.

—It did not clearly delegate responsibility within the administration for the various proposals, and instead created substantial confusion on both issues—both internally and in the posture it presented to the Congress and the public at large.

—It was incapable of joining politics and policy, in part because the political aides simply did not fully appreciate the substance of the issues or their implications and thus the nature of the political *and* policy choices facing the President. This was an especially serious problem given the difficulties —for *anyone*—of fusing the politics with the policies of these issues.

—Ultimately it failed to blend these two issues into a systematic and coherent strategy of governing and, as in so many other areas in domestic affairs, it thus was unable to realize any part of the lofty objectives in health and welfare that it had brought to the White House in the bright, innocent days of 1977.

**7. Postscript.** We must reiterate: the reasons that the Carter administration's efforts at welfare reform and national health insurance failed extend far beyond a lack of strategy at the center of the administration. The external constraints were substantial; the policy trade-offs painful; the congressional politics and jurisdictional thickets entangling; the group politics contradictory and confusing; and the dominant public attitude of the time inhibiting. Perhaps a newly elected Democratic President had no choice but to send forward these cherished initiatives of his party, knowing that his chances of success were slim at best but also knowing that he could not demonstrate as much to the liberal wing of his party unless he tried.

Yet these issues are, in a broader sense, paradigmatic. They are like many high-risk, complex and confusing issues that you may have to confront—that may, either by your own choosing or by the force of events, present themselves as presidential or mixed presidential/secretarial issues. You may lose on them. But without understanding their own unique problems of policy and politics, without sorting out the politics of governing, nomination and general election, without relating those problems to the other large concerns that the administration faces over the course of four years—in short, without putting them in a strategic context—you won't be able to understand the choices in policy, in politics, and *between* policy and politics that you will have to make. And your chances of reaching the political and policy goals that you do choose, either consciously or (if you can't think strategically) semiconsciously, will be significantly reduced—perhaps, as in the case of health and welfare, to virtually nothing.

# VI·
# POLICY CHOICES: THE NEXT FOUR YEARS

## A. Introduction

**T**HE basic policy problem confronting you in domestic affairs is choice among conflicting priorities. Problems press in from all sides crying out for solution: inflation and unemployment, low productivity growth and high tax burdens, the weakness of the dollar and our dependence on overseas energy sources, the diverse claims on the federal budget of tax cuts, defense spending and outlays for existing or future domestic programs. Yet severe competition, even conflict, exists here between and among the national objectives. In the near term, over *your* term, the steps taken to achieve one important objective are likely to conflict with measures designed to reach another.

Indeed, if constraints limit the actions and undercut the effectiveness of the presidency as an institution, so contradictions in national policy pose the basic threshold problem you must face in domestic affairs. In ways that are not yet fully understood, but that clearly have to do with a malfunctioning economy, we are entering a painful era of intense competition for relatively limited resources. And you will be faced with decisions that are painful because one policy may have to be sacrificed on the altar of another one. Whether a period of this sort will be short-lived (half a decade) or prolonged (the rest of the century) cannot be predicted by anyone.

Our purpose in Chapter 6 is to lay out many of the broad choices in economic policy and domestic programs that you will face. Our task is not to prescribe which goals you should adopt, but to describe the implications of choosing particular goals, indicating, in broad strokes, the trade-offs between them. It is obvious: you cannot achieve them all. And you must decide whether you will starkly commit yourself to a few goals, at whatever the cost in terms of the other objectives, or whether you will try to have a little of everything. To put it another way, we do not propose here a strategy of governing. But it is the stuff —on the policy side—from which a strategy in domestic affairs will be formed.

*First,* we describe the choices in economic policy. We set out prototype courses that illustrate the implications of choosing as your primary goal to lower unemployment, to reduce inflation, to increase productivity or to follow a middle-of-the-road path. And we indicate the problems and the uncertainties that will attend each of the prototypes. With diminished economic performance come the contradictions: the painful choices between worthy values; the possibility that these choices may exacerbate conflict in the society.

*Second,* we analyze the problems of budget priorities. The budget of course will be the battleground for the contesting economic, defense and domestic claimants. It is from the budget that you must cut taxes to stimulate growth, balance outlays and revenues to release savings for private investment, or finance increased defense spending or domestic programs. You will *not* be able to reduce taxes, cut budget deficits, and increase defense or domestic spending simultaneously.

*Third,* we lay out some of the major claims on the federal budget that may arise from worthy items on the expansionist agenda in domestic affairs. We also outline items pending on the managerial agenda. While the latter are important, they are not likely to provide enough savings, either through outright budget cuts or increased efficiency, to finance new domestic programs—or to finance tax cuts and increased defense spending.

We continually underscore the importance of trying to think in a four-year time frame, which is hazardous thanks to the manifest uncertainties inherent in economic and budget forecasting. But that exercise has real benefit, forcing your administration to concentrate on the broad choices available within a realistic time horizon. Our actual predictions lay no claim to precision—they can and should be supplanted by the much more sophisticated, though hardly certain, projections of your experts. But they do illustrate a way of thinking about the business of executive government that should be useful to you and your top appointees.

Your capacity to lead will be sorely tested by your choices in domestic affairs. But if no easy answers are to be had, it becomes terribly important that you draw connections between the choices that you do make, while also acknowledging the importance of the goals that you *cannot* seek to advance at this time. You will make a serious mistake if you imply that your short-term choices mean abandoning other goals for the longer term. It is essential that you help the nation focus not on just a particular program or policy, but on the broader context in which you will make any choice that you do. This concluding section begins that process.

## B. Economic Policy: Conflicting Goals and Uncertain Methods

Economic policymaking is subject to a supreme caveat: The economy does not perform obediently to presidential dictates, nor does it recognize a four-year span as the logical period in which to demonstrate fundamental changes of course. The U.S. economy is uniquely vast and diverse; its driving forces are complex, deeply entrenched and imperfectly understood, to say the least; the policy tools available to influence the economy are blunt, slow and clumsy—and controlled more by the Congress and the Federal Reserve Board than by you.

What all this means is that you cannot hope to steer the economy in any precise sense. The most you can do over four years is influence its course and structure in a very general way. To accomplish even this much will require that you carefully choose a manageably small and mutually reinforcing set of general economic objectives and pursue them with relentless consistency, keeping your policies and the political forces at your command clearly in focus over your whole term. If, instead, you become bogged down in detail, or you become diverted by an excessive number of conflicting goals, or you decide to change strategic course in midterm, you will forfeit any prospect of affecting what the economy will look like four years hence.

From a presidential perspective, economic policy has two major elements. There is, first, *macroeconomic strategy*—goals and policies with regard to such economy-wide variables as real GNP growth, unemployment, inflation, productivity growth and the like. Second, there are discrete issues of abnormal importance to *the economy's basic structure.*

We sketch below, for illustrative purposes, the kinds of choices you will confront in both of these areas—macroeconomics and major structural issues. The choices presented here are oversimplified. Your economic advisors can add the subtleties and variations. Our purpose is to alert you to the basic fact of choice—something which economic advisors have in the past been known to obscure—and to give a broad sense of implications.

## 1. Macroeconomic Policy.
**(a) The problems reprised.** The economy you inherit has serious macroeconomic problems in five interrelated dimensions. While the 1980 recession altered the aspect of each of these problem areas somewhat, the basic dilemmas predated that downturn and will vex you throughout your term.

• *Inflation:* Barring a new shock from oil or food prices, the 1981 inflation rate will run in the 9 to 11 percent range, depending on the index used. There is no plausible way to reduce this inflation rate significantly without tolerating a large amount of slack in all markets for a long time (perhaps all four of your years). Inflation will very likely stop falling or start rising as soon as unemployment falls below the pivot point—somewhere about 6.5 percent. Also, it is very possible that inflation will increase, quite apart from general market conditions, if real GNP growth exceeds the growth rate of potential GNP—about 2.5 percent annually—by a significant amount for a sustained period.*

---

*Actual GNP growth can exceed the growth of GNP potential so long as idle resources, created by recession, remain at large in the economy. But the faster this gap between actual and potential GNP is closed, the greater inflationary pressures will be.

- *Unemployment:* The unemployment rate is likely to float in the 8 percent range throughout much of 1981. Actual employment will be rising, but the labor force will be rising just about as swiftly. During your term, you would have to run the economy at a reasonably fast pace—at least 3 percent real GNP growth—to make a dent in the unemployment rate. For every 1 percent of real growth beyond about 2.5 percent, the unemployment rate will fall by about 0.5 percent a year.

- *Productivity growth:* The economy's productive potential—its resource base for generating increases in real income—is stagnant. Labor productivity (real output per man-hour) is growing on a trend path of no more than 1.5 percent a year; it may indeed be in the 0 to 1 percent range.* The only sure policy for accelerating the trend is to increase significantly the growth rate of capital per worker—i.e., to stimulate investment. But this method takes time. To increase productivity growth by about 0.5 percent by the end of your term, you would have to increase investment by about 10 percent annually, beginning almost immediately.

- *Energy:* Real oil prices will be rising over most of your term. Most projections put this increase at 2 to 4 percent annually, even in the absence of another oil shock. These real price increases will greatly complicate your inflation problem, and will spell trouble for you in the international sector. They will also entail steady increases in the dollar amount of the nation's oil import bill—which is already almost $90 billion annually. To moderate the oil import bill you would have to cut oil import volumes. Over a four-year period, the reduction could only be effected with massive conservation efforts, requiring, for instance, a major new gasoline tax. Otherwise, declining U.S. oil production will probably roughly offset conservation gains and shifts to non-oil energy sources, leaving import volumes relatively unchanged.

---

*In the 1950s and 60s, the rate was about 3.0 percent. Labor productivity growth is total productivity growth (i.e., growth in potential GNP) divided by the growth in the labor force.

• *Dollar and trade:* The U.S. current account should be roughly in balance through much of 1981, with the dollar relatively stable. But the foreign accounts and the dollar will be highly sensitive over the rest of your term to the general macroeconomic strategy you adopt. The dollar will almost surely weaken significantly if U.S. inflation remains considerably higher than that abroad, or if high GNP growth here drives our current account into deficits proportionately larger than those of other major currency countries. To hold up the dollar under such circumstances, you would have to keep U.S. real interest rates very high (to draw in foreign capital), thus braking domestic economic expansion.

**(b) The policy instruments available.** For these macroeconomic problems, the federal government has at its disposal four main instruments of policy. Unhappily, the instruments are not solely yours to manipulate.

• *Fiscal policy:* Subject to the offsetting effects of monetary policy, manipulations of the federal budget deficit can affect the economy's overall rate of activity. Generally, the larger the deficit, the greater the prospect that real GNP growth will increase, unemployment fall, inflation stop falling or start rising, oil imports increase, and the dollar weaken. How large these effects will be for any given increase in the deficit is difficult to predict; the impact depends on the posture of the private economy and of the other policy instruments; also, changes in the deficit have psychological impacts on consumers, investors and dollar speculators which are very difficult to assess.

Your deficit policy also will affect productivity growth, but here the effect is even more conjectural and indirect: the larger the deficit, the more private capital the Treasury must borrow to finance the resultant federal debt, and thus the more expensive capital will be to businesses that need it to make productivity-enhancing investments. Therefore, other things being equal, the smaller the deficit, the better the prospects for investment and productivity growth.

• *Monetary policy:* By controlling the growth rate of the money supply, the Fed can strongly influence the long-term growth rate of dollar GNP. The faster the money supply grows, the higher GNP will be. At first, the increase in GNP would manifest itself as real growth—more goods, services and jobs—but after a lag of a year or so, much of this growth would end up as pure inflation. Because faster money growth generally entails higher inflation, encourages capital to move abroad, and fuels import-stimulating growth, expansive monetary policy by the Fed almost invariably causes the dollar to fall.

• *Tax policy:* Tax policy is of course a part of fiscal policy: lower tax revenues entail bigger deficits and thus expand aggregate demand pressures on the economy. However, tax policy also exerts an important influence on the supply of productive resources in the economy. This is because marginal tax rates (the tax rates on the taxpayer's marginal dollar of income or consumption) influence basic economic behavior. In very general terms, the lower the marginal rate on wages, the greater the incentive to join the labor force or to work harder; the lower the marginal rate on savings income and investment, the greater savings and investment (and thus ultimately, productivity growth) will be; the higher the marginal rate on consumption (either generally or on some specified product), the smaller consumption of the taxed items will be. Accordingly, any particular flow of tax revenues to the government can have markedly different long-term effects on the composition of economic activity—labor versus capital, consumption versus investment—depending on the structure of the tax system that raises that revenue.

In the extreme case, one can conceive of a tax system so burdensome at the margin that a rate reduction would actually increase total revenues—because it would cause a huge increase in productive resources (labor and investment) and thus in taxable income. This is the so-called Laffer curve effect. But few economists believe that the tax structure is sufficiently burdensome at the margin to create such an effect: marginal tax rate cuts *will* increase productive resources, but not enough to offset anything like the initial revenue loss, and the partial offset will take several years to develop. Accordingly, tax cuts in our system will inevitably enlarge the deficit—the demand-side pressures—as well as stimulate productive potential. Thus in setting tax policy, you must be concerned about revenue effects as well as the impact on long-term productive potential.

• *Wage-price policy:* Finally, you can attempt—through legislation or moral suasion—to constrain wage and/or price inflation
to prescribed limits or guidelines. General agreement exists
among economists that price guidelines are very difficult to
administer—there being far too many prices in the economy to
monitor or control—and that attempts to apply price guidelines
would quickly cause enormous distortions and inefficiencies,
which would eventually slow the growth of productive potential. Wage guidelines are more practical, but could have an influence only if supported by fiscal and monetary policies consistent
with the guidelines. A wage guideline works merely by speeding the adjustment of wages to underlying macroeconomic conditions. However, it is in practice extremely difficult to translate
a macroeconomic posture into a precisely consistent guideline,
and the political difficulties of applying restraints on wages but
not on prices would probably prove insuperable.

Legislation to enforce guidelines could be of the usual controls variety—subjecting violators to a criminal fine—or could
invoke the tax code, giving complying parties a special tax break
or subjecting violators to a special tax surcharge. Using the tax
system does not solve the major technical or political problems
inherent in guidelines, but some politicians and economists find
tax inducements less offensive than criminal fines as an enforcement tool.

**2. Five Alternative Strategies.** The object of any macroeconomic strategy is to arrange the available policy instruments
in a pattern to bring about improvement in the five major problem areas: inflation, unemployment, stagnating productivity,
energy dependence, and dollar instability. Unfortunately no
strategy can bring maximum relief simultaneously on all fronts.
Over the relatively brief span of four years, some of the objectives are in clear conflict. You have no choice in one respect: you
must make painful choices among them.

There are many conceivable permutations of macroeconomic
strategy. For purposes of illustration, we present five stylized
alternatives, each stressing a different set of objectives and putting reliance on a different configuration of policy instruments.
Explaining which choice you make to the American people may

be as important as the actual path you try to follow. Our alternatives are oversimplified and hardly exhaust the possibilities, but they may help you find your way toward a sound decision.

## Option I. Stimulus Strategy: Rapid Near Term Growth.*

You could place your emphasis on generating a high rate of real GNP growth over the next several years so as to reduce unemployment to, for example, the 5 percent range by the last half of your term. This strategy would aim to burn away the idle resources and market slack created by the 1980 recession as quickly as possible, through a general stimulation of aggregate demand for goods, services and labor. Reaching 5 percent unemployment would entail average annual real GNP growth rates of more than 4 percent for the next four years.

To accomplish this, you would need sizable consumption-oriented tax cuts or large budget spending increases—that is to say, very substantial deficits—accompanied by a Federal Reserve Board policy of accommodating the high GNP growth path through a commensurate expansion in the money supply.

The high GNP growth would eventually generate increased tax revenues, and the high employment levels would reduce budget outlays for unemployment-related programs. The budget deficit would thus narrow again as you approached your low unemployment goal. Thus you could portray the strategy as aiming for budget balance when the economy reaches high employment. Speeding up of economic growth would cause a follow-on increase in business investment as firms sought to keep up with mushrooming consumer demand. Thus the strategy might lead to some increase in productivity growth in subsequent years.

However, the strategy would pose very substantial risks.

- If you were unable to persuade the Fed to a liberal monetary policy, your large budget deficits and the initial burst of GNP growth would swiftly run into sharp constraints in the financial markets. Real interest rates would rise very dramatically, choking off business investment and drying up credit for mortgages and consumer loans. The fiscal boom would in

*This strategy very roughly accords with the initial plans of the Carter administration when it took office in 1977.

effect be strangled by tight financial conditions. You would face a new recession within a year or two of your inauguration.

• If the Fed went along with your expansionist plans, inflationary expectations would revive swiftly throughout the economy. The inflation rate itself might be held in check for a year or so by wage-price guidelines or controls, but any such system would crack and shatter as soon as the boom began to create tight markets for particular products or categories of labor. Within eighteen months or so, the inflation rate would be rising again, heading up dangerously from the high double-digit base you inherited.

• The boom could almost certainly cause the dollar to fall on the exchange markets within a year or so. This would add to inflation. The declines might well be drastic, creating financial panic and a serious loss of general confidence in your leadership throughout the world.

• The boom would lead to substantial increases in oil imports, thus tightening the world oil market and exposing the U.S. economy to the certainty of rising real oil prices and to a substantial risk of another major oil shock on the order of 1973 or 1979.

• Rising inflation, a falling dollar and a tightening world oil market would almost inevitably bring economic expansion to a disorderly recessionary conclusion before the end of your term. At that point, real GNP growth would become negative and unemployment would once more rise swiftly back toward 8 to 9 percent. You would have completed a circle—except that you would have pushed the basic inflation rate up several more percentage points.

## Option II. Foundation-Building Strategy: Disinflation and Investment*

You could place your emphasis for four years on building a foundation for *future* GNP and employment growth by significantly reducing the basic inflation rate and pursuing policies to increase substantially the rate of investment and thus the rate of productivity growth and of *potential* GNP growth.

*This strategy very roughly accords with the economic policies advocated by Representative John Anderson in the 1980 campaign.

To move significantly toward price stability in four years—for example, to reduce inflation to the 5 to 6 percent range by 1985—this strategy would require that both fiscal and monetary policies strongly emphasize demand restraint. For fiscal policy, you might for instance seek annual budgets that *would* balance under disinflationary economic circumstances—that is, along a path of annually declining inflation rates. This fiscal posture would swing the budget into de facto surplus as soon as inflation stopped declining, which would tend to brake economic activity and encourage the desired deceleration of inflation.

At the same time, the Fed would have to reduce the rate of money supply growth each year, in concert with the desired path of declining inflation.

A strategy of restrained aggregate demand would keep the dollar strong and imports (including oil imports) relatively low. The international sector of the economy would thus also be contributing to the fall in inflation.

To boost investment, the strategy would seek a major shift of national resources from consumption to investment. Tax cuts would be heavily concentrated in the industrial sector—for example, accelerated depreciation, increased investment tax credits and corporate income tax cuts. The strategy would aim to curb the heavy flow of capital into housing and consumer durables, redirecting it to industrial investment. The fiscal restraint required for disinflation would preclude large net tax reductions for individuals, except insofar as expenditure growth could be squeezed to accommodate them. The strategy might engage in substantial tax switching: cutting marginal income tax rates, particularly on income from savings, but, at the same time, offsetting the revenue losses by increasing taxes on consumption—for example, a large increase in gasoline excise taxes (which would also help reduce oil imports and keep world oil prices from rising too swiftly). Budget expenditure cuts would be directed at income transfer programs, which affect total consumption. By contrast, federal investment programs—for example, to expand the transportation infrastructure or energy supply capacity, would not be cut.

This strategy would build a far more secure and potent base for rapid GNP and employment growth in the late 1980s and 90s and would avoid the risk of precipitating another big recession in your term through reigniting inflationary acceleration or precipitating financial instability. But the strategy also poses major risks:

- It involves minimal reduction in the high unemployment rate you inherited. Unemployment would probably decline only to about 7.5 percent near the end of your term. Minority and youth unemployment rates would remain very high throughout the period.
- The drive for more investment would face two obstacles. First, the slow growth of general demand might lead to sluggish investment by businesses, even with major tax incentives in place. Second, Congress and the public might balk at tax and spending policies that shift resources massively from consumption to investment (and thus from the relatively poor to the relatively rich) in a period of sluggish growth and high unemployment.
- If other major nations also followed a policy of restrained demand, the interaction could produce a major world recession. This would deprive the less-developed countries of the export markets they need to buy oil. The world trade and financial structure might well face great strains.
- The strategy is not *guaranteed* to bring about significant disinflation. Workers might resist decelerating their rates of wage increase for several years, even in the face of restrained aggregate demand. Also, a world oil price shock, generated by political events in the Middle East, could destroy your disinflationary progress overnight. For both reasons, the strategy's success might in practice require supplementation by wage guidelines or controls. However, labor unions would be loath to cooperate with any such program in the face of policies that tolerate high unemployment and favor a regressive tax structure.

## Option III. The New Right Strategy: Big Marginal Tax Rate Cuts and Tight Money*

This strategy would seek to stimulate the growth of productive potential—to generate more labor effort and investment—by

*This strategy accords very roughly with the program advocated by Governor Reagan during the early phases of the 1980 campaign. He subsequently scaled back his program to resemble Option IV.

cutting marginal tax rates on labor and capital income very deeply,* and then to contain the inflationary demand pressures that would be generated by the resultant budget deficits through strict control of money supply growth by the Federal Reserve Board. The theory is that the economy's productive potential would rise swiftly over your four years, allowing ever-higher real GNP growth rates (and employment gains) consistent with a steady, or even declining, rate of inflation.

Proponents of this strategy believe that the normal rate of real GNP growth might rise from 2.5 to 3 percent today to the 4 to 5 percent range by the mid-1980s, creating a situation where low unemployment (5 percent or so) might coexist with stable or falling inflation. Eventually, the proponents claim, potential GNP would rise sufficiently to generate enough revenues to offset the budget deficits initially created by the big tax cuts.

This is an untested theory. As a keystone of national policy, experimenting with the theory would raise large risks:

- It is questionable, at best, whether the Fed could—as either a technical or political matter—hold the line on money supply growth in the face of huge budget deficits and rapidly rising GNP growth rates. If the monetary dike broke, the strategy would generate the same kind of inflationary boom threatened by strategy 1.
- It is not clear that tight money is enough to contain inflationary pressures generated by large fiscal demands. The interaction of fiscal and monetary policies in influencing the inflationary process remains an area of considerable mystery and controversy to professional economists.
- If the Fed did in fact hold the line on money growth, real interest rates would soar in the face of huge budget deficits. This would radically alter the composition of economic activity—for example, sharply repressing housing and consumer durables spending, which are very sensitive to interest rates, and putting corporations dependent on debt financing into a severe credit squeeze. Unpredictable structural shifts of major

*The Kemp-Roth plan would shave income tax rates across the board by 30 percent in three years. Some versions also provide a large pro-investment tax cut for business through liberalizing depreciation allowances.

dimensions would occur throughout the economy. Also, the high interest rates would greatly strengthen the dollar by sucking foreign short-term capital into U.S. banks and bonds. This could cause unforeseeable gyrations in the international financial system.

• Most importantly, it is far from clear that even the sizable marginal tax rate cuts envisioned by the strategy would greatly increase the growth of productive resources throughout the economy. The Kemp-Roth tax cuts would mean that tax rates for the average American in 1985 would still be higher than during most of the 1950s and 1960s. This period saw considerable growth in real GNP potential—about 3 to 4 percent a year—but not the 4 to 5 plus percent rates sought by Kemp-Roth advocates. It is therefore probable that the Kemp-Roth tax cuts would generate very large deficits for many years.

## Option IV. Middle-of-the-Road Strategy: Moderate Growth*

You might try to ply a course midway between the high growth and high employment aspirations of a stimulus or Kemp-Roth strategy and the stern goals of disinflation and capital formation characterizing strategy 2. Between these decisive extremes, there is broad room for muddling through.

A middle-of-the-road strategy might aim to reduce unemployment gradually to the 6 to 6.5 percent range in the mid-1980s by running the economy in the interim at a moderate pace—for example, at an average rate of about 3 to 3.5 percent for real GNP. This moderate path of recovery might permit a modest decline in the inflation rate over your term—perhaps as much as two percentage points—if oil and food prices and the dollar behaved themselves. More likely, however, the inflation rate would drift and wander about, ending your term just about where it began, uncomfortably close to double digits.

The strategy here would involve setting both fiscal and monetary policy on an even-keel course. Budget deficits in the

---

*By the end of the 1980 campaign, the economic programs of both President Carter and Governor Reagan fell into this broad category.

$40 to $50 billion range would be acceptable in FY 1981, in the immediate wake of the recession, but should narrow to balance by about 1984, when unemployment would be reaching the 6.5 percent pivot-point range which typically signals reaccelerating inflation. Over the whole period, monetary policy would keep the rate of money supply growth roughly constant, refusing to accommodate surges of inflation or excessive growth but making no significant attempt to squeeze out the high ongoing inflation rate (as this would depress real GNP and employment growth).

The strategy's fiscal posture would probably provide some room for tax cuts, but absent an extremely tight lid on expenditure growth, the available tax cuts would probably result in average tax rates in excess of the (very high) levels they attained in late 1979 and 1980—that is to say, tax revenues running between 21 and 22 percent of GNP. For the sake of productivity growth, the strategy might direct one-third of the tax cuts toward pro-investment incentives for business, which would mean that average tax rates for individuals would drift significantly upward over your term.

This strategy avoids large risks. But it equally forfeits doing much about the economy's fundamental problems.

- Inflation would remain very high, leading the American people to conclude (correctly) that their government had decided to accept near-double-digit inflation as virtually a permanent affliction. This in turn would accelerate efforts throughout the economy to index all forms of income, payments, taxation and the like to inflation.
- If our major trading partners chose more disinflationary strategies for their own economies, which is likely, the dollar would weaken over your term.
- Employment and productivity gains would appear modest and slow in coming to most people, and the high tax burdens would be a constant source of complaint.
- You would be criticized for allowing the economy to drift along an unexciting and unsatisfactory course, with no hope in sight of a breakthrough to a higher real growth rate or a markedly lower inflation rate.

## Option V. Shock Strategy: Disinflation Now*

You might seek to purge the economy of high inflation in a single bold strike, and then attempt to nurse the economy back to reasonable growth at a very low level of inflation.

This strategy would involve coordinating monetary, fiscal, and wage-price policy to produce a giant quantum drop in the inflation rate over your first twenty-four months in office. For instance, the Fed would suddenly reduce the growth rate of the money supply to a level consistent with only negligible—e.g., 3 percent—inflation; you and the Congress would throw the budget sharply into surplus, through tax increases or very deep budget cuts; and you would—assuming Congress gave you the authority—impose wage and price controls amounting to a virtual freeze for twelve to eighteen months. Thereafter, you would lift the controls but maintain monetary and fiscal policies in the restrained posture required to hold inflation to negligible levels.

If successful, this strategy would obviate the long, painful process of disinflation inherent in more gradual approaches to the wage-price spiral and would also avoid any permanent addiction to wage-price controls. By the last half of your term, you might be able to operate the economy at the pivot-point unemployment rate—that is to say, about 6.5 percent per year—and enjoy the simultaneous benefits of moderate economic growth and price stability.

But this bold course also involves serious risks:

- It would be exceptionally difficult to secure the necessary cooperation of the Fed (monetary restraint) and the Congress (fiscal restraint and wage-price controls authority) to the steps needed for a sudden disinflationary shock. During the process of discussing the plan with the Fed and Congress, the private economy would be thrown into great uncertainty.
- The temporary wage-price controls would have to apply to *existing* labor contracts—a course usually avoided in wage-price programs—for otherwise the plan would introduce

---

*This strategy includes some of the suggestions made by Senator Kennedy and some economists and bankers during 1980.

huge and unsustainable wage differentials among similar workers, firms and unions. It is unlikely that Congress would give you authority to tear up existing union contracts.

• A sharp fall in the inflation rate would create immense financial strains in the economic system. In particular, borrowers on long-term instruments (for example, homeowners with mortgages and many small businesses) would suddenly confront a much increased *real* cost in paying off their debts. This would likely generate a wave of bankruptcies unless you obtained legislation permitting the renegotiation of most long-term financial contracts.

• When wage-price controls were lifted, workers and firms would likely attempt to resume their inflationary ways. These attempts would collide against tight macroeconomic policies and generate at least a moderate recession. It is only *after* that recession that the system would likely settle down to a path of low inflation and reasonable growth. This is far less costly than the *multiple* recessions needed to reduce inflation to 2 to 3 percent under the other scenarios—but the costs might coincide inconveniently with the last half of your term.

*Summary:* Each of these strategies involves major uncertainties. Exactly what the economy would look like four years hence under any of the strategies cannot be predicted with any confidence. However, to bring out the differences of approach, we display on pages 319 through 323 a plausible (although obviously speculative) course for the key variables in each scenario.

You should keep in mind that choosing a strategy is only half the battle. The other half is explaining to Congress, the Fed, and the nation generally why you chose as you did and what can reasonably be expected by way of benefits and costs. You must build a political coalition behind your choice—an exercise requiring compelling rhetoric—but you must at the same time limit potential political costs by guarding against excessive promises of optimism—an exercise requiring brutal candor. In macroeconomics, political success involves simultaneously rallying your troops and dampening their expectations.

**3. Structural Issues.** In the long perspective of history, the economic legacy of your administration will not be a series of

## Stimulus Strategy

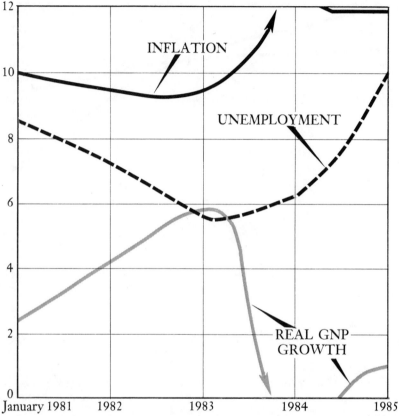

Annual Growth Rates, in percent

The story here is one of strong growth leading to an inflationary binge and a consequent cyclical setback. Somewhere in the middle of your term, prices could begin to move sharply higher, the dollar could collapse, and financial markets could panic the economic system into a large recession. Your economy and budget deficit could end up in significantly worse shape than they were on Inauguration Day.

## Foundation – Building Strategy

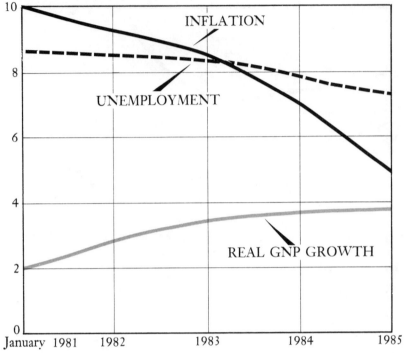

Annual Growth Rates, in percent

The story is one of declining inflation and very slowly falling unemployment. With productivity growth and the dollar rising strongly, and the budget deficit vanishing, the economy could have built a strong base for growth in the latter half of the 1980s.

# New Right Strategy

Annual Growth Rates, in percent

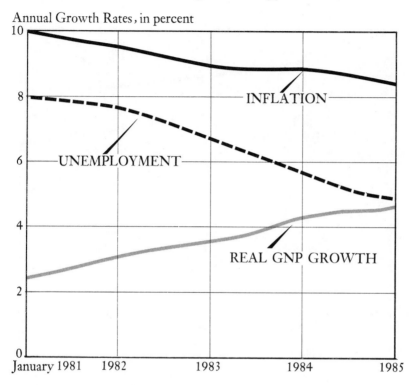

The story here presumes that the Fed successfully contains inflation through tight money, while the big cuts in marginal tax rates allow large gains on the employment front after several years. Productivity rises strongly. But the budget deficit remains large. The dollar rises because of high interest rates. *However*, the story assumes that Fed policy alone can contain inflation. If that assumption is unfounded—as it well might be—the chart could resemble closely the disastrous chart for the stimulus strategy.

## Middle-of-the-Road Strategy

Annual Growth Rates, in percent

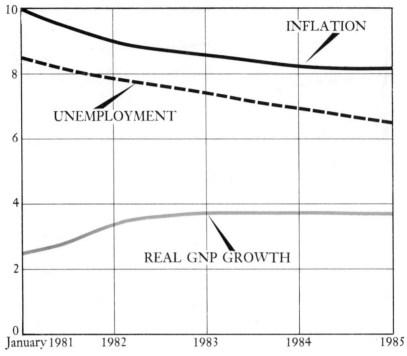

The story here is one of steady, slow improvement on the unemployment front, with inflation moving down almost imperceptibly. The deficit could be shrunk to near zero by the end of your term. There would likely be undramatic productivity gains; the status of the dollar would be unpredictable, though either large declines or rises are unlikely.

# Shock Strategy

Annual Growth Rates, in percent

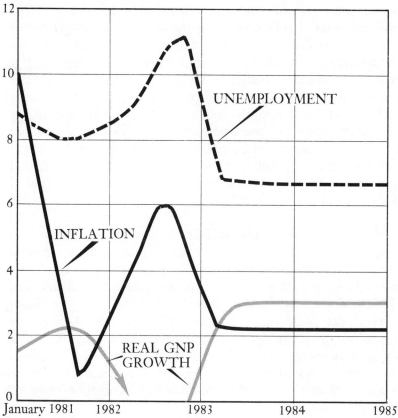

The story here is of a dramatic fall in inflation, followed by a final inflationary recession, culminating at last in stable, low inflationary growth. Should the strategy succeed, the dollar would strengthen noticeably.

transient unemployment and inflation statistics but the impact of your policies on the way the economy works, on its basic structure. This legacy may be built less by federal macroeconomic policies—monetary or fiscal—than by decisions you make, or fail to make, on certain major issues bearing upon the economy's major structural problems. Economists, business people, union officials and others naturally have their own list of major structural problems. An important part of conducting a strategic presidency is choosing a manageably small set of problems and attacking them in a coherent and persuasive manner. In this section, we briefly note the structural problems which in our judgment deserve your closest attention over the next four years. In each case we merely indicate the broad questions that will arise, leaving detailed analysis and recommendations to your economic advisors.

(a) **The future of the dollar.** From the late 1940s to the early 1970s, the U.S. dollar—pegged to gold—was the main anchor of the world monetary system. In 1971, however, the dollar's link with gold was severed by President Nixon, and since 1973 the dollar has been permitted to float on foreign exchange markets, its value relative to foreign currencies being determined by the daily forces of demand and supply. While the dollar remains the world currency used most often to finance world trade and to back up the creditworthiness of other nations, the dollar's central status is under long-term challenge from three sources.

First, as Germany and Japan extend their economic power and their shares of world trade, the deutsche mark and the yen are becoming increasingly attractive alternatives to the dollar, both as media of trade and stores of value. Second, as inflationary forces erode the real value of all paper currencies, many world investors are parking their wealth in noncurrency moneys, such as gold. Third, during the dollar's long history as the world's central currency, foreigners acquired hundreds of billions of dollars worth of securities, bonds and bank accounts denominated in dollars—which may now be ripe for diversification into other currencies or into noncurrency moneys.

Acting together, these three forces generate a long-term downward pressure on the dollar's value relative to other forms of money. This is of serious concern, because dollar stability is important for controlling inflation, as well as for the general perception of U.S. political leadership and prestige.

Your administration will be expected to address the dollar's future in the world financial system in a comprehensive way. Through restrained fiscal and monetary policies, and occasional intervention in the foreign exchange markets, you can probably keep the dollar reasonably strong and stable for the foreseeable future. But you need to address the broad options for long-term institutional reform, which, in very simplified form, are as follows:

• Should we move back toward a system that pegs the dollar to the price of gold for official international currency transactions? This would end the experiment with floating exchange rates. It would introduce tremendous rigidity into monetary policies, both domestic and international, but some analysts argue that such rigidity is essential to reinstill anti-inflationary discipline into those policies.

• Should we press toward development of a new international currency to replace the dollar as the central medium of world finance, gradually converting the International Monetary Fund into a true world central bank? Past U.S. administrations have made tentative moves in this direction by pushing IMF issuance of so-called special drawing rights (SDR's) and by exploring creation of a so-called substitution account in the IMF, which would buy dollars in exchange for SDR's. Moving in this direction would eventually require ever closer international coordination of national economic policies, under the direction of the IMF.

• Should we encourage evolution of the DM and the yen (and perhaps the re-evolution of the British pound) into true reserve currencies, to supplant the dollar's central role in Europe and Asia? This strategy would lead toward a multipolar system of world finance, with different currencies holding sway in different geographic areas. The attempt to create or rely on a single world reserve currency—be it gold, the dollar or the SDR—would be given up as unrealistic.

**(b) Energy.** The energy crisis—high oil imports and a high import bill—will continue throughout your term. The Carter administration broke major historic deadlocks of U.S. energy policy by beginning the price decontrol of oil and new natural gas and by launching a multi-billion-dollar effort to promote development of synthetic fuels from coal and oil shale. But you will find several big chunks of unfinished business on your agenda.

• *Recycling of OPEC surpluses:* The OPEC nations ran a trade surplus of more than $110 billion in 1980, which translates into an equal deficit for the oil-importing nations. This huge international disequilibrium is likely to grow throughout your term, placing enormous financial strains on the poorer oil-importing nations. In the 1970s, the much smaller OPEC surpluses were recycled relatively efficiently to the oil-importing countries through the borrowing and lending activities of big U.S. and European private banks. But the banks seem unwilling to go much further into this risky business. If you do not take the lead in fashioning better public mechanisms to recycle the OPEC surpluses, through the IMF and/or the World Bank, some third world nations may repudiate their international debts—that is to say, declare a form of national bankruptcy—which could have serious consequences for the whole international financial system.

• *Natural gas decontrol:* The 1978 legislation to phase out price controls on new natural gas by 1985 was badly structured and will in fact leave gas prices well below world market levels in 1985. Early legislative surgery is needed to achieve orderly decontrol in the 1980s, but there are few more controversial issues in the whole energy field than natural gas pricing. You must decide fairly quickly whether to take on this important battle. To do so would place a major lien on your political capital. Failing to do so would mean tolerating major inefficiencies in the use and production of natural gas.

• *Strategic petroleum reserve:* The Carter administration aimed to build a strategic petroleum reserve of 1 billion barrels, enough to replace all U.S. oil imports for about twenty weeks in the event of a major interruption of OPEC supplies. But the reserve now contains only about 100 million barrels, enough for about two weeks. If you move aggressively to fill the reserve, the

Saudi Arabian government may retaliate by cutting back on its own oil production, thus precipitating a sharp rise in world oil prices. In addition, filling the reserve will cost your budget perhaps $2 billion per year and put some upward pressure on world oil prices in the process. But failure to fill the reserve would leave the nation vulnerable to oil blackmail for years to come. The reserve is the only emergency measure likely to enhance U.S. oil security over the 1980s. Your policy on filling the reserve will therefore be among the most important economic and foreign policy decisions you will make over your term.

• *Energy conservation:* Increased production options—synthetic fuels, renewable sources such as solar and biomass, and even increased coal production—will not significantly affect the U.S. energy picture until the 1990s. More efficient use of existing energy resources represents the only realistic way to ease the energy crunch in the 1980s. But making more productive use of existing energy resources will not be easy. Energy use in the nation's buildings can be cut in the next decade 25 to 30 percent below what it would be based on today's pattern of use. To achieve these reductions, however, will require investments in existing buildings of more than $50 billion. This investment would be highly cost-effective (in simplest terms, an investment of about $12 in conservation would be the equivalent in energy use of one barrel of oil or about $30, according to some estimates). Undoubtedly the increased cost of energy will stimulate some of this investment. But how the federal government could appropriately accelerate this investment by millions of individual building owners remains far from clear. Similar reductions in energy use can theoretically be achieved in the commercial, industrial and transportation sectors. Whether or not you choose to pursue conservation strategies aggressively, you will find yourself under constant pressure from those in and out of the Congress who support an increased federal role to accelerate the nation's energy productivity.

• *Environmental trade-offs:* The meteoric rise of world oil prices, coupled with the subsidies available from the new Synfuel Corporation, have made it economic for private firms to develop the nation's massive coal, oil shale, and offshore oil resources. This raises the possibility of considerable relief for our oil needs by the *mid- to late 1990s.* But a formidable battery of environmental regulations and prohibitions stand in the way. Unless a means is found to break through the regulatory barrier —some workable national consensus on the environmental costs we are and are not willing to pay for energy development over the 1980s—the drive for more domestic energy production will bog down throughout your term in endless bureaucratic and judicial battles. You will confront the issue almost immediately: the Clean Air Act comes up for renewal in 1981, and the conflict between clean air and more coal-burning is direct and dramatic. But the environmental obstacles in fact exist on dozens of fronts. You must structure a fair and sensible national debate on the issue.

(c) **Regulatory reform.** The 1970s witnessed an explosion of new federal regulatory statutes governing air pollution, water pollution, workplace health and safety, consumer product safety, strip-mining and so forth. Economists estimate that roughly 10 percent of total business investment is now typically devoted to complying with federal regulatory mandates. Such figures are at best very approximate, but they are sobering, and the regulatory burdens seem likely to increase sharply in the 1980s. In the late 1970s, arguments were developed in Congress and the business community against the growth of regulations. A plausible case was made that excessive regulatory burdens were aggravating the nation's productivity and inflation problems. However, no consensus has developed on how to minimize regulatory burdens without reneging on environmental, health and safety objectives that enjoy widespread support throughout the country.

From your perspective, the problem is as much institutional as political. Most of the controversial regulations emanate from executive branch agencies, and are thus blamed on you, but in fact you have virtually no control over the regulatory process. Indeed, no one does. Each agency, governed by its own statutory mandate, formulates regulations more or less on its own, in esoteric dialogue with interest groups and the courts. Unlike federal spending, which is subject to central annual budget review in the Executive Office and in the budget and appropriation committees of the Congress, the private spending mandated by federal regulations is subject to virtually no coordinated analysis or review.

The issue you must face is whether you wish to develop central review procedures for regulations. The Carter administration experimented in this area, creating a regulatory council to foster coordination among regulatory agencies and giving to CEA the lead in reviewing the economic merits of a small number of major new proposed regulations each year. You will be under pressure to go much further—to establish a genuine budget process in the EOP that can exercise control over regulatory activities throughout the executive branch. This may be the only effective way to fight overregulation, but there are enormous dangers involved: politically powerful environmental, consumer and labor groups will fight any centralized review of regulations, and the legal authority of the President or his advisors to overrule the decisions of the regulators is ambiguous and controversial. Furthermore, this would be a major addition to the EOP's routine work load at a time when your personal effectiveness is best served by streamlining as much as possible the routine chores of the institutional presidency. And by centralizing the issue, you may bring numerous no-win issues into your backyard—and perhaps onto your lap.

**(d) Structural unemployment.** Whatever your general macroeconomic policies may do to the overall national rate of unemployment, they will leave relatively unaffected the very high rates of unemployment likely to obtain among minorities in the old urban centers and among workers in the old industrial heartland of the country, stretching from Philadelphia to St. Louis.

Ghetto unemployment has run at two to four times the national rate for many years—very likely for many decades. Efforts to deal with the problem through public jobs programs have done some good, but only so long as the public jobs were available: there has been little shift from public employment to permanent private sector jobs, while retraining and transition efforts either have been underfunded or have proved disappointing. Similarly, federal programs to rebuild the old urban centers have occasionally and selectively succeeded in a bricks-and-mortar sense, but with little impact on minority unemployment. The federal dollars—whether subsidies or tax incentives—have never been (and perhaps could never be) sufficient to overcome the many impediments to a massive flow of private job opportunities back to the old urban centers. You thus inherit a chronic and serious problem to which no one has ready answers, and for which any politically plausible response is likely to be extremely expensive in budgetary terms.

The structural unemployment problems in the industrial heartland are of more recent vintage. World industrial and trade patterns have shifted decisively against the industries that once formed the core of the American economy: steel, autos, rubber, glass, etc. While these industries will obviously not disappear, they are shrinking in size and economic importance as the nation's natural advantages in world trade shift forward to new high-technology industries (based on computers, microprocessing, biological engineering, etc.) and backward to coal, oil shale, synthetic fuels and other energy resources. Also, increased automation in the old-line manufacturing industries means that employment will fall even faster than production. The result will be, throughout the 1980s, a difficult problem of social adjustment throughout the former industrial heartland. The problem will be aggravated by a sharp shift in wealth toward the energy-rich sun belt, as oil prices continue to climb.

The government has no real strategy to deal with this historic adjustment problem. Any solution would have to involve a sizable public transfer of income and wealth to the areas of industrial decline. You would find that a tricky task at best: the sun-belt areas would resist politically, and any transfer that results in propping up the declining industries or subsidizing the real wage levels prevailing in the old industrial areas would blunt the nation's overall productivity growth and international competitiveness. However, without some government lubrication of the adjustment process, social and political conflict may well become a semi-permanent feature of the area.

## C. The Budget: Of Deficits and Spending Priorities

The budget lies at the crossroads of all your fiscal, tax and spending policies. The decisions you make here will largely define the priorities of the domestic presidency. To conduct the office strategically, you need to grasp the budgetary problems as a unified whole, over a four-year period. In this section we attempt to present such a perspective, albeit in brief and skeletal fashion. Our chief purpose is to convey a rather bleak but supremely important message: you are in a tight budgetary bind.

To avoid large budget deficits near the end of your term, when economic recovery may bring unemployment down to the 6 to 7 percent range, the pivot point for inflation, you will have to exercise great restraint on *both* expenditure growth *and* tax reductions over the next four years. If you instead insist upon sizable expenditure increases (for example, for defense) *or* upon large tax cuts, the prospect of rough budgetary balance by mid-decade will vanish—and with it may well disappear hope of containing inflationary forces over the remainder of the decade.

**1. The Value and Mischief of Long-term Budget Projections.** The only way to grasp the budgetary problems facing you is to project budget outlays and tax revenues over a multi-year path, assuming a particular underlying course for the economy. A long-term perspective is necessary because the economy, which materially affects outlays and revenues, will alter significantly over your term and because major program and tax changes cannot be accomplished in a single year and will produce economic effects only with a considerable lag. Multi-year budget-planning is vital to conducting a strategic presidency. You should therefore insist that all important money and economic issues be presented to you in the context of a multi-year budgetary projection. OMB, working with CEA and Treasury, should update these long-term projections at least four times a year, and you should set aside a day or so at each update to explore the lessons and implications with your economic advisors.

But you should understand as well the weaknesses inherent in multi-year budget projections. Over the last fifteen years, such exercises have often led presidents into a false sense that the future would yield big budget surpluses; presidents concluded that tens of billions of dollars of long-term budget room were available for sizable tax cuts and new spending programs. Invariably, expected budget surpluses have failed to materialize; the federal budget has shown a surplus exactly once in the last twenty years. After the fact, the big deficits were rationalized as economically appropriate or inevitable. In fact, however, they were usually unplanned, and eventuated in large measure because presidents, confidently anticipating a mythical fiscal dividend, proposed and secured spending increases and tax cuts beyond the nation's fiscal means.

To avoid a similar surprise, you must understand the common pitfalls of multi-year budgetary fortune-telling.

- *Economic optimism:* Budget projections typically assume that the economy will describe a pleasant four-year course of robust real growth, shrinking unemployment and moderating inflation. The projections never incorporate the nasty turns that have in fact dominated the U.S. economy for fifteen years: recessions, oil price shocks, dollar crises, escalating inflation. Economic mishap can swiftly destroy any projected budget surplus. Budget outlays soar with inflation, because so many programs are indexed; they rise with unemployment, because many programs are designed to supply income to the unemployed. Tax revenues, by contrast, swell with inflation but are sharply reduced by any falloff in the real growth of private sector incomes. To get a grasp on all these effects, you should insist that your advisors regularly run alternative budget projections on worst-case economic assumptions.

- *Outlay optimism:* Budget projections typically incorporate only currently enacted programs. It is easy, but very misleading, to forget that you and the Congress will inevitably add new programs to the budget over a four-year period. If you do not do so, you will break a two-hundred-year historical pattern. Equally important, the budget projections typically underestimate the growth of existing programs. Programs legally indexed to inflation are shown growing apace with the price level, but nonindexed programs are often shown with straight-line funding—a zero increase even in dollar terms. In fact, most discretionary programs typically grow even in real (inflation-indexed) terms. Federal outlays as a whole have averaged 3–4 percent real growth per year since 1960. Multi-year budget projections will usually show a much lower outlay growth path than that. Do not believe it: take outlay projections for what they are—a lowest possible case.

- *Tax revenue optimism:* Over a four-year period, tax revenues under current law will invariably show enormous growth, generating big budget surpluses in the outyears. This is because inflation and real income growth will drive taxpayers into ever-higher income tax rate brackets. You should not be fooled by this phenomenon. Congress will not allow average tax rates to rise in this fashion; pressure for tax cuts—some mitigation of the current law rise in average tax rates—will prove irresistible. Furthermore, without *some* tax cuts, the economic forecast underlying the revenue projection would prove unattainable. Large budget surpluses, especially those generated by ever-rising tax burdens, are not consistent with continued economic growth. The economic forecasts therefore invariably assume a certain pattern of tax cuts (and/or spending increases) and resultant budget surpluses or deficits.

**2. Your Budgetary Dilemma in Brief.** With these warnings in mind, we now subject you to your term's first multi-year budget review. It will be skeletal and rough. But the basic news, mostly bad, should be clear enough.

Because we wish to prove to you that your budget flexibility is very limited, we shall violate our advice above and shall use rather optimistic economic assumptions. If we can convince you that the picture is bleak even on such rosy assumptions, you will easily appreciate how much more difficult things would become if the economy turned (typically) sour.

You inherit a budgetary and economic situation very far out of any desirable equilibrium. The economic problems have been canvassed earlier:\* high unemployment, high inflation and low real GNP growth in both potential and actual terms. As for the budget, federal outlays ran at about $580 billion† in FY 1980, or 23 percent of GNP. Tax revenues ran at about $520 billion or 21 percent of GNP, leaving a budget deficit of about $60 billion.

What you would of course like to do by the end of your term (FY 1985) is balance the budget at reasonable tax rates in an economic context of both low unemployment and low inflation. The difficulties involved in getting the economy to low unemployment and low inflation by 1985 have been discussed earlier. The question now before us is whether—even assuming rela-

---

\*See pp. 305–323 above.
†This excludes $24 billion of off-budget expenditures and direct loans and $72.4 billion of new off-budget loan guarantees in FY 1980. For simplicity's sake, the discussion here excludes off-budget items.

tively favorable economic developments—you can attain rough budget balance at reasonable tax rates. This will in fact be extremely tough to do.

There is of course no scientific definition of reasonable tax rates. Average tax rates have drifted upward over the past twenty years. Federal tax revenues were 18.6 percent of GNP in 1960, 20.2 percent in 1970, and about 21 percent in 1980. There is today a general consensus that federal taxes are too high in an economic sense: marginal income and payroll tax rates are almost certainly placing a drag on employment levels, work effort, willingness to enter the labor force, and savings activity; high corporate tax rates on investment income are holding back capital formation and productivity growth. For this reason, you should not *aim* for yet another rise in the tax/GNP ratio over the next five years.

For the sake of analysis, let us assume that your goal is to keep the tax burden in 1985 about where it is now, at 21 percent of GNP. This will strike most everyone as a very timid goal. But if you also want ultimate budget balance, it is in fact an ambitious one.

To balance the budget by the end of your term, you will of course also have to get outlays to 21 percent of GNP, down from the 23 percent ratio that obtained in FY 1980, which is where the difficulties arise.

To reduce the outlay/GNP ratio requires that GNP grow faster than budget outlays over the next four years.

History teaches that this will be a difficult task. The outlay/GNP ratio has never fallen for more than three consecutive years in the post–World War II era, and has never come down by as much as two full percentage points.

To assess your chances of overcoming historical trends, we must examine more closely the two sides of the outlay/GNP ratio—GNP growth and outlay growth—over the next four years.

**3. GNP Growth.** The easiest way to make GNP grow is to increase the inflation rate. But this is undesirable in itself, and is also a partially self-defeating way to chase budget balance. Many budget programs are automatically indexed to inflation and will thus *not* grow more slowly than GNP when the latter is expanding solely or mainly through inflation. What you need instead is higher *real* GNP growth—more goods, services and jobs, not more inflation.

Just how much real GNP growth is attainable over your term, no one can say with precision. The potential rate of GNP growth—the rate sustainable over a long period—is now only about 2.5 percent per year, and no measures you might take in 1981 or 1982 will have a substantial impact on GNP potential until very late in your term (if then). Accordingly, real GNP growth beyond 2.5 percent will have to be fueled largely by the idle resources left after the 1980 recession.

On balance, average real GNP growth of about 4 percent per year is certainly the very most you can expect. Let us also very optimistically assume that inflation on the CPI declines to about 7 percent in 1985, and that the unemployment rate descends smoothly to about 6 percent in 1985. These assumptions roughly mirror the *very best results* possible under the middle-of-the-road strategy discussed above, pp. 315–316.*

We emphasize again that this is an extremely rosy projection. The odds are stacked heavily against it. Cyclical setbacks are likely to keep real GNP growth from averaging 4 percent annually and oil price shocks or general market pressures are likely to keep inflation higher than projected. Putting together high GNP growth and declining inflation will prove a particularly difficult trick. Accordingly, we repeat, you should regard these economic circumstances as the outer boundary of feasibility. In all probability, things will go worse and make your budget problems even more intractable.

In this best case, the GNP in dollar terms would rise from $2.5 trillion in FY 1980 to $4.4 trillion in FY 1985. To attain the desired 21 percent outlay/GNP ratio by FY 1985, budget outlays would have to rise no higher than about $900 billion by

*The economic assumptions and the projections of outlays and revenues used in this section are drawn largely from the draft working paper "Update to Five-Year Budget Projections: Fiscal Years 1981–85" issued in August 1980 by the Congressional Budget Office. The key economic assumptions are as follows: Real GNP grows (fourth quarter to fourth quarter) by 3.5 percent in calendar 1981, and 4.0 percent in 1982, 1983, 1984 and 1985. The unemployment rate reaches 9 percent in 1981 and then falls smoothly to 6 percent in 1985. The CPI inflation rate (fourth quarter to fourth quarter) falls from 9.1 percent in 1981 to 7.1 percent in 1985.

1985. Can you accomplish this? And what policy decisions would be necessary to do so?

**4. Outlay Growth.** It turns out that you can reach your target for outlays in FY 1985—21 percent of GNP—*if* (a) you add no new programs to the budget, *and* (b) you restrict the growth of all existing programs to the rate of inflation—that is to say, if you exactly maintain the *real* value of *existing* programs, but add nothing on top of that.* On our economic assumptions, this would boost outlays to a level of about $900 billion in FY 1985 (versus $580 billion in FY 1980), or 20.9 percent of GNP.

But this outlay path will probably not suit your policy purposes. As we point out later in this chapter, you will face enormous pressures to increase many spending programs in real terms over the next four years. Our message is that you cannot do so without either producing an FY 1985 deficit or tolerating a rise in taxes above 21 percent of GNP.

One area where you may wish or have to increase outlays in real terms is defense. The Carter administration's commitment to 3 percent real growth annually in defense is regarded in the Congress as a minimal benchmark. You could of course attempt to cut real outlays elsewhere in the budget to make room for real defense increases. However, this is much easier said than done. Defense constitutes about one-fourth of the budget. If the other three-fourths of the budget were available for real cuts, to offset defense increases, the task would be relatively simple: to offset each 3 percent annual rise in real defense spending, you would have to cut nondefense spending by only 1 percent in real terms —a significant but not murderous reduction. However, most of the nondefense budget is *not* available for real cuts. Only about 10 percent of the nondefense budget is decided year by year through fully discretionary appropriations actions: the rest of nondefense spending is taken up paying legal claims, complying with prior-year contracts, meeting interest payments on the

*The assumption does make room for all statutorily required outlay increases in all permanent programs—for example, social security and federal interest payments— which may in some cases produce real outlay growth. All other programs are kept at their real level in FY 1981—i.e., are protected against erosion by inflation.

national debt, or funding entitlement payments prescribed by multi-year income transfer programs (such as social security, civil service pensions, food stamps, revenue sharing, and the like). Making cuts in many of these areas is simply illegal; in the other areas, cuts would involve changing organic authorizing statutes that have the fierce support of large and vociferous constituencies of beneficiaries. On balance, your chances of making real cuts in these nondiscretionary areas range from slim to nonexistent.

But if you focus instead on the very small discretionary part of the nondefense budget for your offsetting cuts, you will find yourself stymied by common sense. To offset annual 3 percent real growth in defense would require an annual cut of about *7.5 percent* in the real value of discretionary nondefense programs. By 1985, you would have cut these programs by more than 30 percent in real terms from their levels in 1981. These programs include most of the federal government's commitment to basic research, environmental regulation, energy development, mass transit, law enforcement, job training, and economic development. Not even the most avid scourges of federal spending have suggested paring these programs back by 30 percent in real terms.

Realistically, therefore, you must face a sobering conclusion. To squeeze outlays down to 21 percent of GNP by FY 1985 you must

—have excellent and unbroken luck with the economy.
—avoid *all* new programs.
—make no real increase in the overall program level existing in FY 1980.
—accept that you have very little latitude to combine real increases in one area (for example, defense) with real reductions in other areas.

Assuming you either cannot or do not wish to abide by such conditions, you must accept that *either* the tax revenue/GNP ratio will rise over 21 percent in FY 1985, *or* your budget will run substantial deficits right through FY 1985, at the risk of generating higher inflation than you inherited. And if you adopt a different economic strategy, the news could be worse.*

**5. Implications for Taxes.** We began with the assumption that you should aim at rough budget balance in FY 1985, with both taxes and outlays at about 21 percent of GNP. This both does and does not give you room for tax cuts. It *does* give you room for sizable pieces of tax-cut *legislation:* without such tax-cut bills, federal taxes would rise under current law even faster than national income, pushing the ratio of tax revenue to GNP in 1985 to 25 percent. These increases would come from higher payroll tax rates (already scheduled in current law), from rising revenues out of the windfall profits tax and the corporation tax, and from the tendency of inflation and real economic growth to drive taxpayers into ever higher income tax brackets. If you allowed all these pre-legislated or automatic tax increases to pile up, the budget (assuming the spending restraint outlined above) would start swinging into surplus in FY 1982, and these surpluses would—if our economic forecast held up—amount to about $180 billion by FY 1985. Very likely, however, such large surpluses—and the rise in tax rates—would drag down economic performance and prevent our rosy forecast from being realized. That is why we assume you will instead aim only for budget balance in FY 1985—and will cut taxes by about $180 billion in the interim.

But of course these will not be genuine tax cuts. In the end, the $180 billion in legislated tax cuts will leave the overall rate of tax—the ratio of federal tax revenues to total national income —right where it was in late 1980: at 21 percent of GNP.

Your major choice is how to distribute the tax cuts as among diverse tax sources and different groups of taxpayers. We expect that you in fact will enjoy very little latitude in this choice. Congress has traditionally and wisely sought every few years to offset at least roughly the bracket-creep effect of inflation on income tax rates. If this tradition holds, income tax cuts for this purpose will consume about $90 billion of revenue between now

---

*For instance, a strategy that requires budget balance well before 1985 would certainly require tax/spending ratios to GNP of more than 21 percent. Similarly, a strategy entailing a recession during your term would boost these ratios dramatically.

and 1985, reducing the revenue-to-GNP ratio from 25 percent to 23 percent, and leaving you with only about $90 billion to distribute in further tax cuts. Of this, Congress will almost certainly wish to use about $25 billion to liberalize the tax treatment of depreciation, an efficient way to spur capital investment. This leaves you with only $65 billion.

We strongly advise you to keep *that* in the bank—i.e., avoid committing it for any purpose at this early stage of budgetary planning. Your economy may play recessionary tricks on you, making the $65 billion vanish overnight. Or you may find that a sizable budget *surplus* would make economic sense late in your term. Or you may find—almost certainly will find—that cutting spending down to 21 percent of GNP by FY 1985 is simply impossible.

On the other hand, if you do limit tax cuts to offsetting inflation-caused bracket creep and liberalizing depreciation, other taxes will be going up sharply. For instance, bracket creep caused by *real* income growth will be proceeding apace, creating higher effective income tax rates for most families, and payroll tax rates will also be climbing. In short, even with a healthy economy and stringent spending restraint, you will find it very difficult to plan prudently for a future other than one of rising federal tax rates for most American families.

**6. Conclusion.** You have a serious budgetary dilemma. Even on reasonably *optimistic* economic assumptions, you cannot bring spending and tax revenues into rough balance by 1985 without exercising uncommon restraint *both* on outlay growth *and* on tax-cutting. In effect, you can afford virtually no real growth in budget spending, and even then must limit your tax reductions to an inflation offset for individual income taxes and a moderate tax incentive for investment, and perhaps a small cut elsewhere in the tax system. If you wish to attain budget balance *before* FY 1985, or to run the economy more slowly for purposes of disinflation, the squeeze on outlays and tax cuts will be even more severe. Substantial real defense increases will require a degree of stringency elsewhere in the budget that appears politically unrealistic, or a relaxation of the goals of budget balance or maintenance of the current ratio of tax revenues to GNP.

Our outlook is sufficiently bleak to justify considering radical measures. But even here your options are limited and risky.

- You could forget budget balance as even an ultimate goal and trust that a strict monetary policy would successfully hold the line on inflation. If you lose this bet, however, the resultant inflationary reacceleration would likely destroy your presidency.
- You could seek to conduct major legislative surgery on some of the giant uncontrollable programs in the budget so as to shift down the curve of outlay growth in a major way. But making a defensible case will be difficult and your chances of success in Congress would be very slim.
- You could seek a new tax source that would not have the same adverse effects on economic incentives caused by high marginal income and payroll tax rates. The prime candidates are taxes on consumption, and the best of the lot would probably be a large increase in the federal gasoline excise tax (now 4 cents per gallon). For instance, a 50 percent ad valorem tax on gasoline would raise about $50 billion in new revenue in FY 1985 and would simultaneously reduce oil consumption by about 700,000 barrels a day, saving about $10 billion annually in oil imports. Every other industrial nation (except Canada) has high gasoline taxes. But the congressional appetite for new taxes—and especially for a gasoline tax—is meager, and, unless combined with a tax cut elsewhere skewed to the poor and near poor, this proposal would be regressive.

At the very least, it is obvious that you must tread cautiously before accepting any real *increases* in budget spending. Your problem, on optimistic assumptions, is illustrated by the table on page 341.

## D. Domestic Programs: Blending the Expansionist and Managerial Agendas

The constant tension in domestic programs will be how to reconcile the expansionist agenda that had its roots in the New Deal but emerged with great force in the 1960s with the managerial agenda that was its growing counterpoint in the 1970s. The impetus for *both* agendas will continue to be strong

*The Budget Dilemma in FY 1985 on the Optimistic Path**

|  |  | *Billions of Dollars* | *Percent of GNP* |
|---|---|---|---|
| 1. | Outlays, constant real level (no real increases) 1980–1985 | 900 | 21 |
| 2. | Revenues | 1,080 | 25 |
| 3. | Income tax cut to offset bracket creep due to inflation | −90 | |
| 4. | Revenues net of tax cut (line 2 minus line 3) | 990 | 23 |
| 5. | Budget room or surplus (line 4 minus line 1) | 90 | |
| 6. | Some claims on $90 billion of budget room | | |
|  | • Pro-investment tax cut in 1981 | 25–50 | |
|  | • 3 percent annual real increase in defense | 25–30 | |
|  | • Representative domestic program expansions | 50–125 | |

* See note on p. 335, above.

during the 1980s. But both must be understood in the larger economic and budgetary context sketched in above.

Our focus here is solely on domestic programs with important government spending dimensions.* We want to identify major expansionist claims on the federal budget during the next five years in order to show you how important a role these programs will continue to play in federal governance. We also want to identify various initiatives on the managerial agenda in domestic programs—aimed primarily at spending reductions, reor-

*We do not discuss extraordinarily important quality-of-life or fairness issues if they do not have a major spending component. For example, we do not discuss legal enforcement of civil rights laws, a critical domestic function of the federal government, although we do discuss spending programs aimed at eradicating the legacy of discrimination and poverty.

ganization and increased effectiveness—to provide you a sense
of their potential and their limits.

### The Expansionist Agenda

An understanding of domestic programs must take place
against the backdrop of a historic shift that has occurred away
from defense and toward nondefense spending in the federal
budget over the past fifteen years. In 1965, defense expenditures were $50 billion, or 42 percent of the federal budget and
7.3 percent of GNP. Although total defense spending had
risen to $131 billion by 1980, it had dropped to 23 percent of
the federal budget and 5.1 percent of GNP. In 1965, nondefense, nonspace and nonforeign federal expenditures totaled
$59 billion, or about 50 percent of the federal budget and 8.5
percent of GNP. And by 1980 these expenditures had grown
to $417 billion, or 74 percent of the federal budget and 16.2
percent of the GNP.

At the core of the growth in nondefense federal expenditures
were outlays associated with domestic programs.

—*First,* there are the *benefit payments for individuals.* Old age,
disability, lack of employment opportunities, racism or prolonged poverty can deprive millions of our citizens of a decent
standard of living. During the last forty years, and especially
during the past fifteen, the federal government has sought to
cushion the blows from such circumstances and to provide
individuals with either cash or in-kind assistance (food, housing, medical care), often when earned income or private savings have not been able to meet the basic needs of certain
groups of our citizens. *Payments for individuals have grown from
about one-quarter to one-half of the federal budget from 1965 to 1980*
($31 billion in 1965 to $268 billion in 1980).

—*Second,* there are *expenditures to state and local governments,*
not just for their share of programs providing payments for
individuals, but also for such basic governmental functions as
sanitation, law enforcement and transportation. These federal expenditures have grown from $7 billion to $54 billion
(from 6 percent of the federal budget to 10 percent of the
budget) in the period 1965–80.

**1. Domestic Program Claims on the Federal Budget—
A Five-Year Overview.** To give you a sense of how great are
the future demands of domestic programs on the federal budget,
we present here an overview of spending projections for the five
years 1981–85. For existing programs, we make certain general
economic assumptions and we also assume that most continue
to provide current services—that is, are adjusted upward each
year so that inflation does not erode the level of services provided in the base year (fiscal 1980).* For new programs we make
the admittedly unrealistic assumption that they are fully operational in fiscal 1983, the first budget of your term, and then
remain in place for the 1983–85 period (with costs increasing
due to inflation and population growth).

Our overview is not intended to be—and cannot be—very
precise. Changes in economic assumptions will change program
costs. All present domestic programs are not required by law to
contain an annual inflation adjustment; political reality here,
however, is that many do get an annual funding increase so that
they operate at current services. Our list of new programs is
representative but not exhaustive, and costs for new programs
are obviously rough estimates at best. *The overview is intended,
however, to give you a feel for the orders of magnitude*—for the continuing dramatic claims that existing domestic programs will
make on the budget in the future and for the potential additional
costs of new items on the expansionist agenda. It is also intended
to underscore the importance of looking five years into the
future and combining economic, budgetary and programmatic
decisions as you develop a strategy in domestic affairs.

*In essence,* this exercise, coupled with our general analysis of
the budget in the preceding section, shows that under midcourse economic assumptions used by the Congressional Budget

---

*The individual projections included in this section are based in general on the Congres-
sional Budget Office's February 1980 estimates and use the economic assumptions then
prevalent. These assumptions are slightly different than the assumptions used in the
general discussion of the budget and elsewhere in this section, but the differences have
relatively small effects in the 1983–85 period. It was necessary to use the February
assumptions because CBO does not reestimate the costs of individual programs at
midyear. In any event, as we have emphasized, this exercise is intended to illustrate a
broad line of reasoning and does not pretend to the relative sophistication that your
advisors will be able to provide on a quarterly or twice-yearly basis.

Office in the summer of 1980, *existing* domestic programs, if adjusted for inflation and other factors (such as population growth), will drop slightly from 16.2 percent to 15.4 percent of GNP in 1983 and to 14.3 percent of GNP in 1985. But this assumes an optimistic rate of real growth in GNP of 4 percent. If this real growth is in fact closer to zero on average than to 4 percent, then existing programs will of course hardly change as a percent of GNP over the five-year period. Moreover, if half the total cost of our representative sample of new items on the expansionist agenda was added to these existing domestic program costs, the percentages would, on a 4 percent growth assumption, be 16.5 percent of GNP in 1983 and 15.7 percent of GNP in 1985. Again, if this optimistic real growth of GNP is wrong, domestic programs would be an even higher percentage of GNP on our half-of-new-initiatives assumption.

As we have indicated above, if you also want to increase defense as a percent of GNP, your total federal budget as a percent of GNP could rise to historic heights *just* maintaining existing domestic programs. Accordingly, the average tax burden will also climb to historic levels unless you plan to run historic deficits. Obviously, if you seek to enact additional items on the expansionist agenda, the problem is only exacerbated. *Yet many of these new programs address serious national problems and great human needs.*

(a) **Domestic programs: Entitlements.** Nearly 80 percent of the federal budget is now uncontrollable. In other words, it cannot be altered in the coming budget year. Some of these uncontrollable expenditures involve contractual commitments from earlier years and interest on the national debt. But more than 40 percent of the total federal budget entails domestic program expenditures that are relatively uncontrollable in one of the following senses. The program is funded automatically through a trust fund. The program is funded automatically out of general revenues and is not affected by the appropriations process (that is to say, the basic statute must be amended before there can be a change in funding). The program is funded out of general revenues in a virtually automatic fashion. For example, the Congress may have placed a cap on the entitlement, as with the food stamp program, but when program costs are estimated to exceed the cap, the cap is overridden and the necessary funds appropriated. Moreover, of these domestic program entitlements, many are also automatically indexed to inflation— approximately 27 percent of the total budget—and many of the remaining entitlements may be effectively indexed. For example, reimbursement of health-care providers under medicare and medicaid is adjusted to take into account the rising cost of medical care.

The table on pages 346–347 indicates projected expenditures for the major domestic entitlement programs over the next five years.

**(b) Domestic programs: Discretionary.** Discretionary domestic programs are those that are considered relatively more controllable by the annual appropriations process. They totaled about 23 percent of the whole federal budget in 1980. For most of the discretionary programs, the levels of spending authorized by law (budget authority) are higher than actual expenditures (outlays). Similarly, certain other discretionary programs have statutorily set full-funding levels that suggest appropriate per-person outlays for all eligible beneficiaries.* It goes without saying that interest groups exert continual pressure to drive discretionary programs up to full authorization or full-funding levels; they also make cutbacks in these noncontrollable programs difficult.

The table on page 348 shows projected expenditures for the ten largest discretionary domestic programs over the next five years. We have assumed that they are funded at a current-services level—that is to say, program costs are increased so that inflation does not reduce the level of services provided in the previous year.†

---

*For example, the bilingual education program serves approximately 400,000 children annually, but there are those who estimate the number of children eligible for the program to be nearly ten times that number. Similarly, in the Education for All Handicapped Children Act of 1975, the Congress authorized expenditures to meet the *additional* cost of educating a handicapped child, but in fiscal 1980 the average federal expenditure was less than 15 percent of these additional costs.

†The slight decrease in discretionary programs as a percentage of both the federal budget and GNP is due, among other things, to the following: projections that loan agencies such as the Federal Home Loan Mortgage Association and the Agricultural Commodity Credit Corporation will sell more loans than they buy; decreases in discretionary public works funds; and decreases in price support outlays.

*Projected Costs of*
*Major Domestic Entitlement Programs\**
*(outlays in billions per fiscal year)*

| | 1965 | 1980 | 1981 | 1982 | 1983 | 1984 | 1985 |
|---|---|---|---|---|---|---|---|
| *Formally indexed by law* | | | | | | | |
| Old age, survivor and disability insurance | 17.5 | 117.9 | 137.3 | 156.6 | 176.8 | 196.3 | 216.4 |
| Civil service retirement | 1.4 | 14.6 | 16.9 | 19.3 | 21.9 | 24.5 | 27.3 |
| Food stamps | + | 8.7 | 10.1 | 11.2 | 12.0 | 12.5 | 13.5 |
| Supplemental security income | 1.8 | 6.4 | 7.1 | 7.8 | 8.5 | 9.1 | 9.8 |
| Railroad retirement | 1.2 | 4.7 | 5.1 | 5.5 | 6.0 | 6.5 | 6.9 |
| Black lung | 0 | 2.0 | 1.9 | 1.8 | 1.9 | 2.0 | 2.1 |
| *Total formally indexed* | 21.9 | 154.3 | 178.4 | 202.2 | 227.1 | 250.9 | 276.0 |
| *Not formally indexed by law* (but assumed to grow with inflation except as indicated) | | | | | | | |
| Medicare | 0 | 33.5 | 39.1 | 45.5 | 52.5 | 60.6 | 69.8 |
| Unemployment insurance | 3.1 | 15.6 | 22.0 | 23.2 | 21.3 | 21.3 | 21.5 |
| Medicaid | .3 | 14.2 | 15.9 | 18.1 | 20.3 | 22.7 | 25.1 |
| Veterans pensions, compensation, and life insurance | 4.8 | 12.2 | 13.4 | 15.3 | 17.2 | 19.1 | 21.0 |
| Veterans education | + | 2.2 | 1.8 | 1.7 | 1.5 | 1.4 | 1.3 |
| Veterans health and medical | 1.3 | 6.4 | 6.6 | 6.9 | 7.1 | 7.2 | 7.3 |
| AFDC (no inflation factor) | 1.1 | 7.1 | 8.1 | 9.0 | 9.8 | 10.4 | 11.0 |
| Earned income tax credit (no inflation factor) | 0 | 1.7 | 1.6 | 1.5 | 1.4 | 1.3 | 1.3 |
| *Total not formally indexed* | 10.6 | 92.9 | 108.5 | 121.2 | 131.1 | 144.0 | 158.3 |

| Total domestic entitlements‡ | 32.5 | 247.2 | 286.9 | 323.4 | 358.2 | 394.9 | 434.3 |
|---|---|---|---|---|---|---|---|
| Total domestic entitlements as percent of GNP | 4.7 | 9.6 | 10.1 | 10.1 | 9.9 | 9.8 | 9.6 |
| Total domestic entitlements as percent of federal budget* | 27.4 | 43.9 | 46.3 | 47.1 | 48.0 | 48.9 | 49.6 |

* The 1965 and 1980 figures are taken from the President's budgets for FY 1967 and FY 1981. The 1981–1985 projections are based on CBO estimates and assume a real defense growth of 3 percent. See footnote on page 335.
† Did not exceed $50 million in 1965.
‡ Does not include interest on the federal debt and undistributed offsetting receipts.

*Projected Costs of*
*Discretionary Domestic Programs*
*(in billions per fiscal year)*

| | 1965 | 1980 | 1981 | 1982 | 1983 | 1984 | 1985 |
|---|---|---|---|---|---|---|---|
| General health and medicine* | 1.9 | 8.8 | 10.0 | 10.8 | 11.9 | 12.8 | 14.1 |
| Elementary and secondary education† | .4 | 7.3 | 8.0 | 8.8 | 9.8 | 10.7 | 11.7 |
| CETA | 0 | 6.7 | 8.0 | 8.6 | 9.4 | 10.2 | 11.1 |
| Higher education† | .4 | 5.5 | 5.5 | 6.2 | 6.4 | 6.5 | 6.8 |
| Housing assistance | .2 | 5.3 | 5.8 | 6.6 | 7.7 | 8.7 | 9.9 |
| Child nutrition and WIC | .3 | 4.7 | 5.0 | 5.5 | 6.0 | 6.6 | 7.3 |
| Other manpower | .6 | 4.3 | 4.2 | 4.5 | 4.9 | 5.3 | 5.7 |
| Social services (including child day care) | 0 | 3.1 | 2.6 | 2.7 | 2.7 | 2.7 | 2.7 |
| Low-income energy assistance | 0 | 1.7 | 1.6 | 1.6 | 1.6 | 1.6 | 1.6 |
| Vocational rehabilitation | .1 | 1.1 | 1.3 | 1.4 | 1.5 | 1.6 | 1.7 |
| Total | 3.9 | 48.5 | 52.0 | 56.7 | 61.9 | 66.7 | 72.6 |
| Other discretionary domestic programs (agriculture, transportation, development, etc.) | 15.1 | 80.1 | 78.7 | 86.2 | 91.7 | 95.2 | 99.8 |
| Total discretionary domestic programs§ | 19.0 | 128.6 | 130.7 | 142.9 | 153.6 | 161.9 | 172.4 |
| Total discretionary programs as percent of GNP | 2.8 | 5.0 | 4.8 | 4.5 | 4.3 | 4.0 | 3.8 |
| Total discretionary programs as percent of federal budget | 16.0 | 22.8 | 22.2 | 20.8 | 20.6 | 20.1 | 19.7 |

NOTE: The 1965 and 1980 figures are taken from President's budgets for FY 1967 and FY 1981. The 1981–1985 projections are based on CBO estimates.
* Includes such discrete programs as research and training activities at the National Institutes of Health, health resources training, alcohol and drug abuse.
† Includes such discrete programs as aid to local education agencies, Indian education programs, federal impact aid, and child development.
‡ Includes such discrete programs as basic educational opportunity grants and fellowships.
§ Does not include interest on the federal debt and undistributed offsetting receipts.

**(c) Existing domestic programs: In sum.** The table below summarizes projected domestic program expenditures during the next five years, broken down according to payments for individuals and payments to state and local governments.

*Projected Domestic*
*Program Expenditures*
*(in billions per fiscal year)*

|  | 1980 | 1981 | 1982 | 1983 | 1984 | 1985 |
|---|---|---|---|---|---|---|
| Benefit payments for individuals | 268.2 | 303.9 | 333.4 | 376.5 | 408.3 | 448.0 |
| Other grants to state/local governments* | 54.7 | 58.8 | 63.1 | 64.2 | 65.4 | 67.4 |
| Total† | 322.9 | 362.7 | 396.5 | 440.7 | 473.7 | 515.4 |
| Total as percent of federal budget‡ | 57.3 | 58.6 | 57.8 | 59.0 | 58.7 | 58.9 |
| Total as percent of GNP‡ | 12.5 | 12.7 | 12.4 | 12.2 | 11.7 | 11.4 |

* Expenditures in this category are for such programs as community development, transportation and revenue sharing.
† Does not include interest on the federal debt and undistributed offsetting receipts.
‡ It must be emphasized that these are gross projections made in the second half of 1980. A change in the economic assumptions could have important, even dramatic, effects.[1] The 1965 and 1980 figures are taken from the President's budgets for 1967 and 1981. The 1981–1985 projections are based on CBO estimates.

Assuming no reductions, expenditures for existing domestic programs over the next five years are certain to rise in absolute terms, could well rise as a percentage of the federal budget (depending on the rate of increase in defense), and could stay about the same as a percentage of GNP (if, as may be likely, our assumption about real GNP growth is optimistic).*

**(d) New programs.** Despite the dramatic growth in spending for domestic programs over the past fifteen years, and the potential continued growth in those programs during the next

*It must be emphasized that these are gross projections made in the second half of 1980. A change in the economic assumptions could have important, even dramatic, effects.[1] The 1965 and 1980 figures are taken from the President's budgets for 1967 and 1981. The 1981–1985 projections are based on CBO estimates.

*Rough Estimates of Costs*
*For Representative New Domestic Programs**
*(outlays in billions per fiscal year)*

| | 1982 | 1983 | 1984 | 1985 |
|---|---|---|---|---|
| I. *Social security* | | | | |
| (a) Additional financing for old age and survivors program | 1–3 | 13–17 | 25–35 | 40–60 |
| (b) Women's equity | 0 | 18 | 20 | 22 |
| II. *Needs-Based Income Maintenance* | | | | |
| (a) Incremental welfare changes | 3.1 | 3.4 | 3.5 | 3.5 |
| *or* | | | | |
| (b) Minimalist welfare changes | 1.9 | 2.0 | 2.1 | 2.1 |
| (c) Energy assistance to low-income population | .7 | .8 | 1.0 | 1.3 |
| III. *Health Care Expansions* | | | | |
| (a) Elderly | 6.7 | 7.2 | 8.0 | 8.9 |
| (b) Poor (nonelderly) | 12.2 | 13.2 | 14.6 | 16.2 |
| (c) Employed† | 3.0 | 3.2 | 3.5 | 3.9 |
| (d) Other | 1.2 | 1.3 | 1.4 | 1.6 |
| IV. *Long-term care* | | | | |
| (a) Medium-sized expansion: Existing programs | 1.8–2.3 | 1.8–3.9 | 2.8–8.1 | 3.2–11.1 |
| *or* | | | | |
| (b) Medium-sized expansion: New program | 2.2 | 2.4 | 2.8 | 3.2 |
| *or* | | | | |

| | 18.2–27.0 | 17.2–29.2 | 20.2–38.4 | 28.3–50.3 |
|---|---|---|---|---|
| (c) Major expansion: New program | | | | |
| *V. Manpower, training and education* | | | | |
| (a) Jobs for hard-to-employ primary earner in poor families | 2.7 | 2.9 | 3.2 | 3.4 |
| (b) Youth employment | 3.3 | 3.6 | 3.8 | 4.2 |
| (c) Higher education | 2.7 | 3.0 | 3.2 | 3.5 |
| *VI. Housing, transportation and urban affairs* | | | | |
| (a) Low-income housing | 3.0 | 4.0 | 4.5 | 5.0 |
| (b) Middle-income housing | 1.0 | 1.0 | 1.0 | 1.0 |
| (c) Mass transit | 1.2 | 1.7 | 1.8 | 2.0 |
| (d) Municipal finance | ? | ? | ? | ? |
| (e) Auto industry | ? | ? | ? | ? |
| (f) Basic transportation system | ? | ? | ? | ? |
| *Totals* | | | | |
| (i) All new programs [including II(a) and IV(b)] | 44.3 | 79.9 | 101.3 | 128.4 |
| (ii) All new programs as percent of GNP | 1.4 | 2.2 | 2.5 | 2.8 |
| (iii) One-half of new programs | 22.2 | 40.0 | 50.7 | 64.2 |
| (iv) One-half of new programs as percent of GNP | .7 | 1.1 | 1.3 | 1.4 |

\* Assumes program is fully operational in 1983 and subsequently funded at current services level, except as otherwise indicated.
† Does not include mandated costs paid by private employers to private insurers of $9.8 billion in 1983; $10.9 in 1984; $12.1 in 1985.

five, there are other major unfinished items of business on the expansionist agenda. Some are long-standing and controversial issues—like national health insurance and welfare reform—that in the main provide needed benefits for the poor and near poor. Other items, however, will gain their impetus from the increasingly powerful elderly population of the nation—for example, refinancing the social security system or providing a new program to help defray the costs of long-term care. Other big-dollar items may attract very broad-based constituencies: women from all shades of the political spectrum may push for greater equity in the social security system; and state and local governments may seek new funds to help rebuild the basic infrastructure—roads, sewers, ports—of their cities.

The table on pages 350–351 summarizes the projected costs of some of the big-ticket items that you may have to confront—or may want to enact. Although hardly exhaustive, our list surely covers many of the major expansionist domestic programs likely to be debated during your term.* But it will be difficult, if not impossible, to finance new proposals during the next five years unless you are able (or willing) to cut existing domestic programs or slow the expected rate of increase in defense.

In the following sections, we provide only thumbnail sketches of these representative items on the expansionist agenda. Each issue bristles with complexity and, if you are interested, deserves a detailed briefing. But it is also important to lay them end to end to illustrate some striking domestic needs.

**2. Social Security.** The social security system will require some major changes in the coming decades.[2] The biggest and most successful federal social program annually sends checks to more than 30 million Americans; its trust funds receive payroll tax revenues from 110 million more; it expends (in 1980) about $120 billion annually in the old age, survivors and disability programs (plus an additional $34 billion in medicare); it constitutes more than one-fifth of the federal budget; and it covers 90 percent of the workers in America.

*Where the estimates are based on existing proposals that have been scrutinized by the executive and the Congress, they are drawn from administration or congressional analyses. In other areas, we just offer crude guesstimates.

Yet in the longer term some powerful forces will put tremendous strains on social security financing. The payments from present workers pay for the benefits of present recipients. Yet due to lower fertility rates and other factors, there will in the future be more retirees and fewer workers. This is the demographic trend now popularly recognized as the aging of the population. A companion trend is the aging of the aging: the basic fact that the life expectancy of a person reaching sixty-five is increasing significantly.* Moreover, the demographic trend of more retirees relative to workers is accentuated by trends in labor force participation: a longer period of education before entering the work force and then early retirement.

This means that the ratio of workers to beneficiaries is estimated to decline from 3.3 in 1980 to 2.2 by the year 2030, which in turn means that to maintain benefits at existing levels, the cost of social security—as a percent of taxable payroll—will start to climb dramatically around the turn of the century. In stark terms, the following table illustrates the projected changes:

|  | Social security payments as percent of GNP | Social security beneficiaries as percent of population |
|---|---|---|
| 1980 | 4.5 | 15 |
| 1990 | 4.7 | 16 |
| 2020 | 5.3 | 22 |

Dealing with the necessary cost increases will constitute a basic challenge to federal social policy. Planning must begin now for the reforms required—and this planning should take place in the context of a larger analysis of federal income security policy that we suggest below.

*Yet there are some very important near-term problems that you will have to face during the coming four years, that involve additional expenditures for the social security system and that deserve or will demand high priority on the expansionist agenda.*

(a) **Short-term financing.** In 1977, Congress enacted a series of amendments to shore up the financially strapped social

---

*Seventy-five percent of the population will reach age sixty-five, and the average life expectancy at sixty-five is more than fifteen years.

security system. Two key changes are scheduled to take effect in 1981.* With these amendments and with other tax increases scheduled for 1985 and 1990, the Congress and the administration hoped that the social security system would remain financially sound until the end of the century.

Shortly after the 1977 amendments were enacted, serious concern emerged about the inflationary effects of the 1981 payroll tax increase. Although the issue is not without controversy, general agreement exists that financing a given increase in social security expenditures by the payroll tax is more inflationary than financing it by the progressive income tax (i.e., through general revenues). Thus in 1979 and 1980, policymakers began serious discussions about finding alternative methods of financing the additional revenues required that would otherwise be generated by the payroll tax increase scheduled for 1981.

But with a dramatic worsening of economic conditions in 1980, the issue shifted: would additional revenues, over and above those generated by the 1981 payroll tax increase, be necessary for the old age, survivors and disability funds?†

Thus as a result of the 1980 recession, you will have to decide, first, whether to leave the scheduled 1981 payroll tax increase in place and, second, whether to augment the social security trust funds for old age, survivors and disability insurance with *additional* revenues. The two questions should be separated. Less

*Before the amendments, 85 percent of the total earnings of all workers was subject to the payroll tax; effective in 1981, 95 percent will be taxed. In 1981, the tax rate for both employer and employee for old age, survivors and disability insurance (but not for medicare) will rise from 5.08 percent to 5.35 percent of the taxable earnings (if medicare is included, the tax rate will rise from 6.13 to 6.65 percent).

†The reason for such an increase is directly related to two factors: current-cost financing and the effects of a recession.

—Current-cost financing is a basic principle of social security that has been honored since at least the early 1950s. All payroll taxes collected are paid into trust funds, one for old age and survivors, another for disability. And current-cost financing means that current revenues are almost immediately paid out to current beneficiaries. Yet to protect against increases in benefits or reductions in revenues, the trust funds must keep certain reserve levels, usually expressed as the amount in the trust fund at the beginning of the year as a percentage of the total expenditures projected for that year.

—A recession, however, causes a sharp dip in revenues. Although benefits must continue to be paid to retirees, dependents and the disabled, the number of workers being taxed during a recession obviously declines as unemployment increases. And then the trust-fund reserves may drop below appropriate reserve levels. The 1980 recession led to such a drop in revenues.

inflationary alternatives to the scheduled increase in the payroll taxes may exist, and at the end of 1980 policymakers were discussing a tax credit that would offset social security taxes and in effect indirectly provide general revenue financing. But *even if* other revenue equivalents are found and even if there is maximum borrowing (up to adequate reserve levels) from *both* the disability and health insurance funds, there will *still* need to be *additional* revenues for the old age and survivors trust fund to keep it solvent if economic conditions are worse than our assumptions. In the second half of 1980, it appeared that the *rough* range of that need would be substantial (as indicated in the following table) and the numbers will be even worse if the Congress does not allow borrowing from the health insurance trust fund, or if the recession is more prolonged than expected.

| | *1982* | *1983* | *1984* | *1985* |
|---|---|---|---|---|
| Additional funds needed to keep social security trust funds at adequate reserve levels (in billions per fiscal year) | 1–3 | 13–17 | 25–35 | 40–60 |

Whether the needed funds should come from more payroll taxes or from general revenues will constitute a vexing question. But you will have to find additional revenues if the social security system needs them. You have no choice.

(b) **Women's equity.** One of the most pressing problems facing the social security system over the next decade is the issue of making the system more equitable for women. Yet changes to meet the legitimate demands from women will be complicated and costly. And work on those reforms will begin in the Congress during your coming term if the executive branch tries to ignore the issue.

The number of working women and the number of divorced women have grown dramatically since the 1930s when social security was enacted.* These changes have led to an understand-

*More women are working today. Nearly 50 percent of married women will work in 1980, compared with about 17 percent in 1940. In 1940 about 25 percent of the adult

ing that in at least two major, though not consistent, respects, the present social security benefit structure is unfair. *First,* the program does not sufficiently recognize the contribution of the working wife. Although a two-earner family may contribute much more in payroll taxes, it may get back about the same amount in benefits as a single-earner family. *Second,* the protection afforded a homemaker with little or no work record, who is subsequently divorced, is not strong enough.

One proposal to remedy these defects is called earnings sharing,* which is based on the premise that marriage is an economic partnership. Couples should therefore pool their earnings, and each partner should receive credit for half the total earnings for purposes of calculating ultimate social security benefits. A husband or wife, or divorced partners, would each be entitled to retirement or disability benefits based on half the couple's total earnings for the years they were together and 100 percent of any earnings each had before the marriage or after the split-up.

A number of technical problems have to be worked out with earnings sharing or with other approaches to women's equity in social security. *But a major problem with any solution is that switching immediately to a different benefit structure will injure some present and future beneficiaries;* it will advantage some but disadvantage others who benefited under the old system. Protecting those present recipients, who justifiably expect to receive the benefits according to the present system, means that achieving equitable treatment of women will entail significant additional costs to the system in the coming years. If a rough earnings sharing plan were to go into effect in fiscal 1983, with the condition that no present or future beneficiaries would suffer as a result, the additional cost to the federal government would be as much as $18 billion in that year with the following range of potential expen-

---

female population was in the labor force; in 1978 about 50 percent was in the labor force.

Divorces are more common. In 1940, one out of seven marriages ended in divorce; today the rate is about one in three.

There is a growing understanding that marriage is an interdependent partnership, and that the homemaker role has very real economic value.

*A major task force established by the Congress within the Department of Health and Human Services has been studying alternatives that would deal with these and other inequities. Moreover, the 1979 Social Security Advisory Council has also begun to address the set of questions.

ditures in subsequent years: up to $20 billion in 1984 and up to
$22 billion in 1985.

Obviously an immediate switch to earnings sharing is not
possible or desirable, and a transitional program will have to be
developed. But women's equity in social security is an idea
whose time has come—or is going to come soon. And it may
have to be seen as simply the most glaring of the inequities in
the social security system. Because it is an issue that affects two
broad groups in the population, retirees and women, your administration will have to handle it with great skill and sensitivity.

**3. Needs-Based Income Maintenance Programs.** After
a decade of debate and only limited successes (the enactment of
the supplemental security income program in 1972 and the enactment and expansion of the earned income tax credit in 1975
and 1979), welfare reform (at least by that specific name) is less
likely to be an issue in the 1980s. A real reduction in the number
of Americans in poverty has occurred during the past fifteen
years,[3] but substantial reform goals have still not been achieved.

Millions of Americans still live in poverty, a disproportionate
number of them black and southern and in families headed by
a single parent. Millions of poor Americans are dependent on
needs-tested public program transfers because they cannot find
employment that would give them earned income, even though
they are able to work. The adequacy of welfare benefits has been
constantly eroded by inflation over the past five years—especially in AFDC—and still varies widely from state to state for
reasons beyond cost-of-living differentials. States and localities
bear disproportionate financing burdens in supporting the very
poor, and greater financial equity between states has not been
achieved (or clearly defined). Administrative confusion and
complexity still hinder the system, partly due to variations between states and partly due to overlapping programs with different requirements.

If goals are unattained, it is in part because the dilemmas
remain: how to reconcile adequate benefits with popular desire
to hold down costs; how to strike the balance between work and
welfare; how to provide state and local fiscal relief while keeping
federal costs down; how to strike the proper balance between

state and federal roles in administration; how to make the programs simpler and less error-prone when major consolidation of programs does not seem politically possible.

Welfare reform could be shunted once again to the back burner, given the nation's immediate fiscal problems and welfare's long-standing political difficulties. Yet the House did pass the cash assistance portion of the Carter administration's incremental welfare reform plan by nearly a hundred votes in the fall of 1979, and possibly welfare reform will remain a visible issue, perhaps more from the initiative of strong congressional actors than from those in the executive branch. If it does remain an issue, the debate in the near term is likely to be between two relatively modest alternatives.

(a) **Incremental reform.** One possibility will be a renewed effort to enact a bill like the Carter incremental assistance cash plan (the jobs element of that bill is discussed below). The essential elements of such a proposal are: a national minimum benefit for families with children, mandatory cash assistance coverage for two-parent families, a modest expansion of the earned income tax credit, a measure of fiscal relief for the states and a variety of administrative simplifications.

The cost of this incremental reform on the cash assistance side alone would be: $3.4 billion in fiscal 1983; $3.5 billion in fiscal 1984; and $3.5 billion in fiscal 1985.

(b) **Minimalist reform.** An alternative to the incremental reform would be what might be termed minimalist reform, although both conservatives (who would object to minimalist) and liberals (who would object to reform) would not use that phrase. Such a plan would include: a small block grant to low-benefit states; a small grant to all states to offset the effects of inflation; an expansion of the earned income tax credit similar to the expansion in the incremental bill; and even more modest fiscal relief. Like the incremental bill, the minimalist reform would seek to introduce a number of administrative simplifications.

The approximate cost of such a minimalist reform would be in the range of: $2 billion in fiscal 1983; $2.1 billion in fiscal 1984; and $2.1 billion in fiscal 1985.

(c) **Low-income energy assistance.** The decontrol of oil prices has led to dramatically increased energy costs for all Americans. But these costs have imposed a special burden on the poor. Average energy costs per household (largely from heating and gasoline costs) are expected to increase from $1,678 in 1978 to $2,688 by the middle of 1980. The percentage of disposable income expended on energy is estimated to increase from 25 percent for the poor in 1978 to 35 percent in 1980.

To meet the initial impact of decontrol, Congress and the administration agreed on a low-income energy assistance plan for the winter of 1979–80 that would cost $1.6 billion. And another one-year plan—for fiscal 1981—was included in the Crude Oil Windfall Profits Tax Act of 1980. Again, there is a broad consensus within the Congress that this type of special needs-based program is necessary as a matter of fundamental equity if energy conservation and reduced dependence on overseas oil is to be effected in part through increases in the price of energy.

But the Congress did not make provision for an ongoing program of low-income energy assistance. And such a program is sorely needed, with energy costs projected to rise in the coming years at a much higher rate than the average income of those who are poor.

Accordingly, an initiative that your administration will very soon face is to establish a more permanent program of energy assistance to the low-income population. Although several available mechanisms do exist, the program is likely to have two basic elements: a discretionary emergency assistance component that allows state and local government to provide aid to those with special problems (such as complete heat loss in the home); and a more uniform payment to all eligible citizens (weighted, to a degree, on regional differences in energy cost increases). The actual distribution of funds to the states will, however, be an issue of some controversy, since northern states believe that the money should go for home heating, while the sun-belt states maintain that they should receive funds for the poor who must pay higher costs for cooling.

The program in 1979–80 cost $1.6 billion and is estimated to cost $1.6 billion in 1981. A minimum projected cost for fiscal

1982–85 would be approximately $2.4 to $2.9 billion per year, or between $800,000 and $1.3 million more than the program approved in fiscal 1981.

**4. Health Care.** As noted in Chapter 5, the health-care system is now the nation's third largest industry, and is growing at an extraordinary rate, with total health costs projected to rise from $244 billion in 1980 (9.5 percent of GNP) to $438 billion in 1985 (or 9.7 percent of GNP). Addressing the vast array of problems in the health-care sector will occupy the attention of health planners and policymakers for the next twenty years. Indeed, *given its huge claim on our national resources, the health-care system will be one of the major domestic policy issues for the rest of the century.*

The expansion of health benefits will continue to have a prominent place on the expansionist agenda. But expanded coverage is unlikely unless it is only one component of a three-part approach: the other two must be to hold down costs and to institute other reforms in the health system that will enhance competition, increase access, emphasize prevention and improve the management of public programs. Enacting benefit expansions will be very difficult unless they are accompanied by significant reforms in the health-care reimbursement system that will yield substantial savings. Yet the Congress is so divided on the appropriate methods of health cost containment that legislating the necessary cost-saving foundation will not be easy.

To understand possible benefit expansions it is useful to divide the total U.S. population of 231 million (1980 estimate) into four groups: the aged, the poor, the employed and all others. The benefit expansions outlined below are drawn from the Carter administration's Phase I national health plan proposal. As noted, that proposal attempted to find a middle way between a full-scale universal, comprehensive plan and a pure catastrophic plan that did not provide meaningful benefits for the poor and near poor. Obviously, single elements for one of the population groups could be selected, or each element could be altered to provide a larger or smaller plan (and to increase or decrease cost). While there are other ways to provide benefits to the four groups, the Phase I plan gives a sense of the kinds of costs involved for representative program expansions.

(a) **The aged and disabled.** At present, 24 of the 29 million aged and disabled are eligible for health insurance under medicare. But even though medicare has vastly improved coverage for the elderly and the disabled, it still does not provide complete protection against the costs of a catastrophic illness or medical problem. Present cost-sharing arrangements expose medicare beneficiaries to striking costs in the event of major illness.*

An important benefit expansion would be to limit the out-of-pocket exposure for the elderly and disabled to a manageable amount during each year. For example, setting a ceiling of $1,250 per person for the elderly and disabled would cost $4.5 billion in 1983; $5.0 billion in 1984; and $5.6 billion in 1985. If the legislated limit on out-of-pocket expenses were to increase per person (to $1,500 or $2,000), the cost of this benefit expansion decreases.

In addition to the 24 million elderly and disabled covered by medicare, 4 million poor elderly and disabled presently are covered by medicaid. Unlike medicare, medicaid provides *comprehensive* protection—that is to say, no cost-sharing by the patient. A second benefit expansion for the elderly would therefore be to extend the comprehensive coverage of medicaid to the 1 million poor elderly and disabled without such coverage. The cost would be: $2.7 billion in 1983; $3.0 billion in 1984; and $3.3 billion in 1985.

(b) **Low income (nonaged).** At present, almost 16 million poor receive fully subsidized care under medicaid. These 16 million are categorically eligible for medicaid: that is, they are covered by medicaid only because they are eligible for either AFDC or the supplemental security income program. But despite medicaid's coverage, millions of the poor and near poor still receive *no* subsidies for health care and thus either receive no health care, wholly inadequate health care or health care in very inappropriate settings (such as the emergency rooms of hospitals—often financially strapped public hospitals).

---

*Most saliently, today the number of hospital days that medicare will fully subsidize is limited, and all medicare recipients must pay for at least 20 percent of physician services.

Benefit expansions for the low-income population could be implemented in the following manner. First, 10.5 million additional poor who had family income at or below 55 percent of the poverty level and who were not categorically eligible for medicaid would receive fully subsidized health care. This expansion would cost $9.4 billion in 1983; $10.4 billion in 1984; and $11.5 billion in 1985. As the eligibility threshold rises (from 55 percent to 65 or 75 or 85 percent of the poverty level), the costs also rise. Second, the 11 million poor and near poor who have incomes within $3,000 of 55 percent of the poverty level and who are not categorically eligible would become eligible for a year of fully subsidized care if their net income, after the past year's medical expenses are deducted, is less than 55 percent of poverty. Under this so-called spend-down provision, approximately 4 of the 11 million poor and near poor would annually become eligible for a year of fully subsidized care. The cost of this expansion would be $3.8 billion in 1983; $4.2 billion in 1984; and $4.7 billion in 1985.

(c) **Employed.** There are at present 156 million full-time workers (25 hours per week, 10 weeks per year) and their families. Of these, 56 million do not have protection against the costs of major illness, and tens of millions of additional workers and their spouses/dependents do not have adequate basic health plans. Rather than providing public health care for this group, employers would be required by law to provide a basic health plan that would have a $2,500 limit on out-of-pocket expenses a worker and family would have to pay in any year.

This so-called employer mandate would cost employers a net of more than $9.8 billion in 1983; $10.9 billion in 1984; and $12.1 billion in 1985. Many of these employers would be relatively small businesses with fewer than forty employees, since most large businesses already have coverage that exceeds the minimal federally mandated plan. The costs to the employer would be for premium payments to private insurance companies meeting federal standards. To the extent that the limit on patient cost-sharing for covered services decreased (from $2,500 to $1,500 or $1,000), the cost of the premium and thus the expense to the nation's employers would increase, and to the extent the limit increased, the net cost would decrease.

The employer mandate would be a private, not a federal, cost. But there would be some federal costs associated with the employer mandate. Subsidies would be necessary for the working poor because they would be required, like all workers, to pay up to 25 percent of the premium costs (as opposed to the out-of-pocket limit on payments for services). And small businesses which at present do not provide any coverage for their workers would require transitional subsidies because of dramatic short-term increases in payroll costs. Together these two subsidies could, depending on design, cost the federal government in the range of $3.0 to $3.5 billion in 1983, with slight increases thereafter.

**(d) All others.** The three basic expansions outlined above account for 222 million of the nation's 231 million total population in 1980. Of the remaining 9 million, approximately 7.5 million already self-insure. The remaining 1.5 million—many of whom are part-time workers, divorcees, or the partially disabled with incomes in the $8,000–$13,000 range—should at the least be able to buy a reasonably priced catastrophic plan. To make such a plan reasonably priced will require a governmental subsidy of premium payments in the range of $1.3 to $1.6 billion for the period 1981–85.

As this brief discussion demonstrates, the cost of improving health coverage for millions of Americans is not cheap. The expansions we have outlined—which many would consider minimal—would have a net federal cost of $25 billion in 1983; $27.5 billion in 1984; and $30.6 billion in 1985.

**5. Long-Term Care.** The subsection on health outlined benefit expansions relating to the provision of services for acute health care problems. There are, we indicated, still dramatic gaps in our nation's acute care coverage, and it will be expensive to eliminate them. But another health-related problem—with the potential for enormous expenditures—looms on the horizon: long-term care. Indeed, it is likely to become *the* major issue in aging policy for the rest or this century.

Long-term care refers to health and social services provided to the *chronically* disabled, usually the elderly. More specifically, long-term care is provided to individuals who suffer from functional impairments due to a variety of health-related conditions. It can be provided in a number of settings: from heavily medical environments, like hospitals and nursing homes, to more personal environments like foster homes, congregate housing arrangements and the individual's own home. It entails a variety of services: from a doctor's continual monitoring and continuous skilled nursing to rehabilitative services performed by nonmedical personnel to homemaker and other chore services performed by nonlicensed, nonmedical personnel. The distinguishing characteristic that separates a long-term care recipient from the pure health-care recipient (although the line is fuzzy) is the difference between care for acute illness and care for chronic impairments.

The effort necessary to meet the need for long-term care over the next decade is significant. Our purpose here is merely to give you a sense of the order of magnitude and to underscore that even in a period of limited resources this is a major national problem that will not go away.

- *Need: Present and Future.* At present there are an estimated 5 to 6.5 million individuals with functional impairments who need long-term care. By 1985 these numbers will have grown from 5.5 million to 7.2 million. Of those in need, approximately 88 percent are elderly.[4]

- *Problems.* There has yet to be a systematic and comprehensive analysis of the long-term care problem, but some of the more salient difficulties are: individual burden;* overinstitutionalization;† gaps in coverage;‡ fragmentation of responsibility;§ and cost to government.‖

*The average yearly stay in a nursing home costs over $20,000. But a high percentage of the chronically disabled, and especially the elderly disabled, have total annual incomes well below that figure.

†Most of the incentives in public financing programs are toward care in hospitals or nursing homes, even though it would be both less expensive and better for the patient in many instances if care was provided in less restrictive settings like foster homes, congregate housing arrangements or personal homes.

‡The need for the less restrictive types of home health care—intermediate nursing facilities, personal care homes, congregate housing and home health care—presently is estimated to exceed the supply. And the gap is estimated to rise over the coming decade unless action is taken.

§A variety of governmental programs have overlapping responsibility for long-term care: medicare, medicaid, Title XX, veterans' programs and the Older Americans Act.
‖At present, approximately $32–36 billion is spent on long-term care by private ($15–18 billion) and public ($17–18 billion) sources. Of the public cost, $8.9–9.3 billion is federal and $8.4–8.9 billion is state and local. And of the federal cost, approximately $1.1–1.4 is spent by medicare; $5.8–5.9 billion by medicaid; and $1.6 to $2.4 billion by veterans' programs.

Under existing federal programs, increased utilization and inflation will combine to increase existing federal long-term care program costs from $9 billion today to $15 to $17 billion by 1985. But the following schematic options, based on a recent Congressional Budget Office study, indicate the range of *additional* federal costs that could result from dealing with the long-term care problem:[5]

*Additional federal costs*
*(in billions per fiscal year)*

|  | 1983 | 1985 |
|---|---|---|
| —Modification of existing programs to encourage noninstitutional long-term care | +1.8–3.9 | +3.2–11.1 |
| —Creation of a unified grant program that would be controlled through the appropriations process | +2.4 | +3.2 |
| —Creation of a national entitlement program that would replace much private spending with public spending | +17.23 | +28.50 |

These are nothing more than very rough estimates. But they give you a sense of how large this major problem is—and could become.

## 6. Manpower, Training and Education.

**(a) Jobs for the hard-to-employ poor.** Despite the oft-heard criticism that the poor do not want to work, the reality is quite different. The priority problem is to develop jobs for the hard-to-employ poor who head welfare families. Building on existing employment and training programs, the Carter administration sought to provide job and training opportunities for wage earners in welfare-eligible families as part of both its comprehensive and incremental welfare proposals. A proposal to provide jobs for some of the population could include the following elements. (1) The preference would be for private sector jobs, and a combination of new job search and tax credit initiatives would seek to improve private sector placement. (2) If, however, an eight-week job search did not turn up a private sector job, the primary earner in a family receiving welfare would be placed in a job or training position under the CETA system, which position would last for no longer than fifty-two weeks. (3) The recipient would then have to begin another eight-week search for a private sector job, and if a job were proffered and not taken, welfare benefits would be cut off.

To create approximately 620,000 jobs (including tax credits for private sector placement) would have a net cost in 1983 of $2.9 billion; in 1984 of $3.2 billion; and in 1985 of $3.4 billion. If successful, the results of this program for the very poor would be to lift 350,000 families comprised of 1.5 million individuals over the poverty line. Although a program of this type has not been tried on a large scale, field demonstrations run by both Labor and HHS indicated that it has a reasonable chance of success. Certainly for those who believe in the principle of jobs for those who can work and assistance for those who cannot work, especially for heads of families, it is an undertaking worth the risk—if the funds are available.

(b) **Youth employment.** The problem of youth unemployment is well-known. The unemployment rate among those sixteen to nineteen has averaged nearly 18 percent during the last five years, while the average rate nationally has been 7 percent. And the unemployment rate for that age group among minority youths has been a striking 36 percent on average. Given the resulting problems—crime, drug abuse, long-term unemployability, reliance on transfer programs—this is obviously a high-priority problem.

At present, about $4 billion is spent on programs targeted at youth unemployment. These programs reach about 1 million of the approximately 1.4 million unemployed youths between the ages of fourteen and twenty-one. But additional steps are needed, both in our nation's secondary schools and in workplace environments for youths who have left school. In 1980 the Congress considered youth employment legislation. In essence the legislation sought to streamline the existing youth employment programs administered by the Labor Department through the CETA prime sponsors at the state and local levels. It also sought to channel funds directly to local school districts in very poor areas in order to provide basic skills education to secondary school students and to provide vocational skills in areas that lacked vocational training.

The cost of these proposals would be $2 billion in 1983; $2.2 billion in 1984; and $2.3 billion in 1985. Whether the precise specifications of the 1980 proposal are advanced in coming years, youth unemployment will be a major national problem for which additional federal funds are sought.

(c) **Higher education.** The authorizing legislation for student aid in the higher education program expired at the end of FY 1980. In 1979, the House passed a bill raising the maximum grants from $1,800 per year to $2,520 per year and allowing 75 percent of a student's expenses to be covered by such grants rather than 50 percent. CBO estimated the cost of such increases at $2.5 billion in 1981 dollars. In 1980, the Senate passed its own version of the higher education authorization bill which was touted as a budget-saving measure. However, the Senate version actually changed the maximum grants and reimbursed expenditures to figures almost equivalent to those in the House version but phased them in between 1981 and 1985. The conference accepted much of the House version, but in early September, the full Senate rejected the conference report. Nevertheless, the argument appears to be over phasing, not substance, and it seems likely that Congress will pass a bill which adds several billion dollars to federal higher education outlays by 1985.

The cost of these proposals could be $2.7 billion in 1982; $3 billion in 1983; $3.2 billion in 1984; and $3.5 billion in 1985.


Although the basic laws aimed at improving access and equal educational opportunity have been enacted in both elementary and secondary and higher education, pressure will still exist for full funding in these education programs. There may also be requests for additional programs and new funding from the federal level in three major areas: equalization of elementary and secondary school finance (a major federal study will be completed in 1982–83); institutional, as opposed to student, aid for failing private colleges as declining enrollments and escalating costs begin to exact their toll; and requests from the major research universities for funds to rebuild their basic research plants. We do not specify a set of potential costs that might be associated with these items, but the issues may emerge during your term.

## 7. Housing, Transportation and Urban Affairs.

(a) **Low-income housing.** New federal subsidies for low-income housing (which in fiscal 1980 totaled $5.3 billion) do not appear likely. But a shift could take place within existing HUD programs toward an emphasis on *rental* subsidies and moderate rehabilitation, resulting in additional outlays of about $200 million per year from fiscal 1983–85. Also possible, but less likely, is elimination of the rent ceiling, which establishes limits on the rental rates that landlords may charge the poor. If this ceiling was to be lifted, more poor people could participate in the basic (Section 8) housing assistance program, since more housing would be available for program participants. If this was to happen, and if the Congress was to appropriate only 50 percent of the needed funds, the costs would be: $3 billion in 1982; $4 billion in 1983; $4.5 billion in 1984; and $5 billion in 1985.[6]

(b) **Middle-income housing.** During the 96th Congress, both the House and Senate considered new provisions that would subsidize production of rental housing for middle-income Americans. In the summer of 1980 the House, for example, approved a provision allowing low-income housing subsidies to families with annual incomes of up to $30,000. The cost of providing such subsidies to all families in this income range could run into the tens of billions of dollars annually. The House provision limited expenditures to $60 million, which was to be retargeted from existing appropriations. While the House provision was struck in conference with the Senate, future congressional attempts to provide housing subsidies to middle-income families are likely to be of a limited nature, with annual caps of less than $1 billion.

Moreover, a tremendous demand for housing looms in the 1980s, with estimated need for new units ranging between 23 and 27 million units (compared to about 18 million built during the 1980s). Whether the federal government will have an increased direct or indirect role in financing construction and home ownership, given the magnitude of the need, is uncertain, but it is a problem that will receive substantial attention.

**(c) Mass transit and energy conservation.** The Congress also appears likely to enact a mass transit bill in 1980 that would have net costs of $1 billion per year during the period 1981–85. If you add to these costs modest grants to local governments for auto traffic reduction programs and subsidies to railroads other than Conrail, then increases in mass transit spending would be in the range of $1.2 billion in 1982; $1.7 billion in 1983; $1.8 billion in 1984; and $2 billion in 1985.

**(d) Municipal finance.** It is no secret that many cities will be facing major fiscal stress in the coming decade. Part of the problem is brought on by the recession and a dip in revenues. But another part of the problem is due to longer-term economic decline, an eroded tax base and increased costs for services. Moreover, the basic infrastructure of many cities—sewers, water systems, roads, other capital items—has been ignored as capital funds have been diverted to meet rising operating costs. The trend of federal aid to cities to help meet these capital needs and other basic municipal services through revenue sharing or more targeted programs has been slightly downward.* Whether the trend can be sustained in the face of urban fiscal difficulties is an important question for the future.

**(e) The auto industry.** Whether the federal government will be required to spend significant sums to prop up the automobile industry is also an open question.

*Between 1978 and 1980, federal aid to local governments for public works declined from $3.1 billion to $0.4 billion.

It is simply not possible to hazard a guess about potential federal outlays for municipal finance and the auto industry. This issue should, however, be on any list of possible problems in domestic affairs requiring a programmatic response, and is one with important budgetary implications.

(f) **The basic transportation system.** Recent studies have estimated that the nation's basic transportation system—its airways, highways, waterways and railways—will require an investment of $1.2 *trillion* over the next twenty years. The degree to which that staggering amount comes from public, and federal, funds will of course be a subject of significant debate—as will the question of which mode of transportation is to be improved in what place at what time. It is clear, however, that there will be some significant claims on federal funds—to take a simple example, the FAA needs a new traffic control computer system, and present estimates put the cost of such a system at $1.5 billion.

**8. The Limits of Phasing.** In a period of budgetary restraint, various expedients can be used to avoid overt spending in the immediate future. One is to use tax expenditures (various credits, deductions or deferrals) that reduce revenues but don't involve an increase in outlays. A second is to utilize off-budget techniques by providing benefits through loans or loan guarantees. A third is to approve a major spending program but to phase it in over time. Increasingly, the third technique is being proposed to avoid confronting major outlays in the near term while ensuring that appropriate administrative structures can be put in place during the early stages of a program.

There is nothing wrong with the third technique, but to postpone costs in the near term limits flexibility in the longer term. A new program that is phased in becomes an uncontrollable when it is scheduled to take effect, since the Congress would have to enact a new piece of legislation to further defer an effective date required by statute.

### The Managerial Agenda

It is beyond partisanship that government should work better: like programs should be consolidated; spending should be cut when programs aren't working; and effectiveness in the delivery of governmental services should be increased. Yet it is also beyond doubt that such goals are extraordinarily hard to achieve—even in an austere time. Concern about management must confront a basic paradox: much, much more attention is paid to the creation of public programs than to their implementation. In a way that's not surprising: management is detailed and technical—in a word, dull.

Yet the managerial agenda is likely to receive much more than lip service during the coming years as officials seek to prevent unruly growth of new initiatives, prune away some of the more ragged growth from the past or increase the productivity of government efforts. Our purpose here is to discuss briefly the three major thrusts of the managerial agenda—reorganizing, controlling spending and increasing effectiveness. While important and worthy of sustained attention, none of the items on the managerial agenda are going to work truly dramatic change. It will be a slow, undramatic process. In essence:

—Major reorganization, while desirable, is not worth a substantial presidential commitment.

—Control of spending, while popular in general, will be very difficult in the particulars. You will have to be very selective, very strategic, very organized *and* very dogged. Even then, you will only be able to slow only the *rate of increase* of domestic spending.

—Increasing effectiveness, while necessary, involves a long twilight struggle, often with the middlemen—in the private sector and in state and local governments—who actually perform the functions of the federal government. Clear goals ought to be set so that you can demonstrate that government —and governmental officials—can accomplish what they set out to do.

**1. Reorganization.** Reorganization ought to be clearly broken down into two types. The first—creation of new superdepartments that bring together similar functions or activities now strewn about executive government—is a false hope, as we have indicated. One of the Carter administration's mistakes in management was to emphasize reorganization of this type rather than increased effectiveness. People want government to work better. They care very little about the shape of the executive organization chart unless it clearly furthers effectiveness.

This is not to say that major departmental consolidations within the present executive structure are not desirable: they are. But the problem is less a conceptual one for your analysts and more a political problem for your friends and supporters in the Congress. Any movement on this front ought to start with a joint executive-congressional effort to assess the *closely related* problems of executive branch organization and congressional committee jurisdiction. In the past, they have never been reviewed together, and major executive proposals have foundered on the rocks of incompatible committee interests. An obvious person to head such a comprehensive effort, a man with experience at both ends of Pennsylvania Avenue, is Gerald Ford. Perhaps a Ford Commission, like the Hoover Commission of the late forties, could develop some momentum for a major realignment in executive *and* congressional organization.[7]

But the past decade has seen major unsuccessful efforts at committee realignment and departmental reorganization—although not joint efforts—in both the House and Senate and in the executive branch. To repeat: let someone else try to generate movement. Unless there is political momentum, until the ideas can come down off the shelves of good government and into the halls of Congress, it is not worth your time, or the time of your high officials.

A second type of reorganization—consolidating existing functions according to a reorganization plan below the departmental level—is worth pursuing selectively. The first-term Carterites in the President's reorganization project (the M of OMB) generated a slew of ideas. You can't implement them all, but you can probably use some of them or others that may surface in the next four years. This relatively low-visibility effort is surely worth taking on when you are given the power by the Congress to effect subdepartmental reorganizations that do not require affirmative congressional action and will take effect upon your initiative unless the Congress vetoes the proposal. During the first Carter term, sensible groupings were effected; for example, civil rights enforcement activities were consolidated and the relationship between Treasury and Labor on the administration of the Employee Retirement Income Security Act (ERISA) was clarified.

**2. Spending Control.** As we have noted, the federal budget has been taking up an increasing share of GNP, and so-called domestic program uncontrollables have been taking up an ever-greater share of the budget. These trends are likely to continue or at least level off unless a concerted effort is made to slow the rate of increase in spending or to cut programs.

**(a) Problems.** But even a concerted effort will run into some basic problems.

*First,* you can accomplish very little in the next two or three years. Programs are in place; people are employed; contracts are let. The fiscal 1982 budget which you will propose early in 1981 and which will take effect on October 1, 1981, Congress willing (which it won't be), is, as noted, nearly 80 percent uncontrollable. The prospects for your next budget—which will involve spending through September 1983, the eve of the next presidential election campaign—aren't much better. And even if you were able to make changes in the entitlement programs that provide payments to individuals, those changes would almost certainly be prospective in effect, with existing recipients grandfathered in. Thus any savings would not be likely to occur until late in your term, if then.

*Second,* powerful substantive pressures drive domestic spending. Demographic trends affecting the elderly—the aging of the population, early retirement, real benefit increases in social security based on higher earnings—push up program costs. Inflation also drives up costs—automatically in the indexed programs, but inexorably in other domestic programs as well (since failure to adjust for inflation is in effect a cut in the level of services). A recession dramatically reduces revenues and increases outlays—and as we have seen, causes significant problems in the social security system. Most substantive pressures increase the costs of the very programs that are the most uncontrollable: payments for individuals where eligibility is automatic; benefit levels that are determined by formula; benefits that are adjusted automatically by inflation; and those areas where the necessary budget authority is automatically approved by the Congress, without meaningful discretion in either the executive branch or the Congress (other than seeking a change in law).

*Third*, obvious political pressures accompany the substantive pressures. More than half the population—more than 115 million Americans—benefit directly from federal spending, either because they are employed by government, are employed by private parties whose wage bills are paid by government, or receive government benefits. And millions more are indirectly affected. The elderly, now an especially powerful group, will become even more powerful, and currently receive in direct form about 25 percent of the federal budget. Members of the Congress, meanwhile, guard the programs under their jurisdictions from spending cuts. State and local officials rely on federal expenditures for a substantial part of their resources, and have planned for the next five years under certain assumptions about federal support. Finally, the middlemen in federal programs have become increasingly ardent advocates of sustained spending.

*Fourth*, there are complex philosophical questions about what programs, if any, should be cut, and the mere cry of fiscal austerity won't answer such questions. Justifications for specific cuts must be sound. What program is clearly worthless? What is equitable? A typical problem here is illustrated by the social insurance programs, whose financing is based on earmarked contributions from employees and employers. The truth is that to date only a fraction of the ultimate benefit received has been attributable to the personal contribution. Many argue, nonetheless, that these are earned rights. To reduce those benefits is therefore to break an implied contractual relationship between the worker and the government. Flaws exist in the social contract reasoning, but it is a popular and politically appealing notion.

Moreover, it is very difficult—and we believe wrong—to argue that the needs-tested programs that help the poor should somehow be reduced, especially since inflation has been eroding AFDC. In any event, the social insurance programs are far bigger and have been growing faster than the needs-based programs.* Although not generally realized, entitlements have the

*For example, while social security payments as percent of GNP have risen from 3 percent in 1965 to 4.5 percent in 1980, cash payments in the income-tested programs have risen from 0.8 percent of GNP in 1965 to 0.9 percent in 1980.

advantage of fairness, since they remove substantial areas of bureaucratic discretion. To the extent that attempts are made to remove some of the automatic features of entitlements, a correspondingly larger bureaucracy is required to carry out discretionary tasks.

A final point. Controlling spending may be analogous to fighting inflation: a slow, multifaceted process that is hard to dramatize and that while receiving popular assent does not command popular attention. This adds to your difficulties.

**(b) Techniques.** To have any chance of making a serious dent in present spending patterns, you must at the very least do the following.

—Consistently think of the budget in four- or five-year—not one-year—cycles, and develop information and projections in those terms. Although the projections will always be susceptible to (sometimes dramatic) change, as economic assumptions shift to and fro, the exercise remains absolutely essential.

—Develop a special congressional operation, under your chief of congressional relations, who does nothing but worry about the politics of the budget.

—Work closely with the Congress to develop methods that support the congressional budget process and create greater uniformity between the executive budget-making cycle and the congressional cycle. A common definition of terms is a start (until 1980 the Congress and the executive defined current services for existing programs differently). Common economic assumptions and multi-year forecasts would also help.

—In this connection, keep constantly in mind something that your recent predecessors have tended to forget—that everyone on Capitol Hill forced by his or her role to see the government whole and to integrate policies and programs is your potential ally, regardless of party and regardless of having an office at the other end of Pennsylvania Avenue. This is true of the majority and minority leadership and the members of the Budget and Appropriations committees. To the extent that the politics of governing is the politics of integrating, you will need these allies (although they may not want you to embrace them too openly).*

—Target carefully. Across-the-board approaches—support of proposals to limit spending to a percentage of GNP or to balance the budget under certain conditions—will cause enormous political battles, and if successful (which is doubtful), will then lead to meat-ax cuts that hit desirable as well as undesirable items. At the other extreme, going to the Hill each year with hundreds of little cuts will mean that you may have to fight hundreds of little skirmishes. Better to target on some major issues selectively, make the case on those issues, and try to drive them through. They are likely to result in bigger long-term savings, anyway.

—Practice the politics of governing. You have to marshal political support if you are going to make major changes. Presidents since Eisenhower have, for example, ritualistically tried to eliminate or trim back the so-called impact aid program of assistance to school districts—with uniform lack of success. The opposing array of interests (4,000 of the nation's 16,000 school districts receive some of the funds) has stymied the effort, rendering it a good piece of policy with no political life (although in recent years there has been some movement in reducing the program).

—Explain the budget to the American people—there is massive disinterest in and confusion about the budget's structure. If you choose to make a stand on spending a presidential issue, you should at least take the time and trouble to simplify and dramatize the issue for the electorate.

(c) **Outlays: Types and targets.** In the winter of 1980, responding to a request from influential members of the House Budget Committee, the Congressional Budget Office issued a report called *Reducing the Federal Budget: Strategies and Examples.*[8] The report identified five broad types of spending reductions as a way to organize thinking about the subject. These were:

*And if you choose to make spending reductions an issue and work with the opposing party and the Budget and Appropriations committees, you risk incurring the wrath of other potential friends, on other matters, on the authorizing committees. Thus you may not want to embrace the opposing party's leaders or the Budget and authorizing committees too openly.

—achieving management efficiencies: ending duplication, reducing fraud and abuse, improving program administration.
—targeting more effectively: aiming benefit payments and subsidies at those most in need.
—shifting responsibility to state and local governments: transferring federal activities and greater financial responsibility to other levels of government.
—shifting responsibility to the private sector: reducing or ending some of the subsidies to private parties, for example, by requiring user fees for waterways or airports.
—revising judgments about what we can afford: reversing past policy decisions because they have proved too costly in light of changing priorities and circumstances.

The report then listed fifty-six ideas for spending reductions—some of them useful, some of them politically impossible. This is the kind of list that your staff will have to draw up and then choose from.

Two major targets of opportunity cited by the CBO report will illustrate both the potential and the problems of reducing spending.

*First,* the two closely related items that could produce the greatest savings over the five-year period 1981–85 involve the income security programs. One proposal was simply to cap the indexed increase in social security benefits at 85 percent of the CPI—which, according to CBO estimates at the time, would have saved nearly $40 billion over the five-year period. A second was to use an index other than the CPI because that measure exaggerates the actual increases in the cost of living for the aged.* If such was done and was applied to social security, railroad retirement, SSI, veterans' pensions and military and civil service retirement, CBO estimated that the cumulative five-year savings would amount to about $30 billion.

But substantial theoretical and philosophical problems surround both ways of saving money. Retirees stand in a special place in our society and the point of indexing is to provide them

---

*The distortion occurs, some argue, because the CPI includes an inappropriate measure of home ownership costs.

with roughly the same standard of living as when they ceased work. Why, then, should there be a 85 percent cap on the additional indexed payments they receive? Also, if the present CPI does not accurately reflect the consumption patterns of the retired population, what is a more accurate measure? These issues and a host of related ones are likely to be debated at the start of your term. The arcane subject of indexing is likely to be center stage because of its significant fiscal implications. But the political difficulties of effecting a change are obvious, given the importance of the elderly.

The political problem is illustrated by the flurry of activity surrounding the first budget resolution of the fiscal 1981 budget. This resolution was passed before the effects of the recession were clear and while there was tremendous national interest in the congressional attempt to produce the first balanced budget in twelve years. Congress made a number of potential cuts in the outlay budget that President Carter had submitted in January. But the original Carter 1981 budget estimated $220.1 billion for income security. The first congressional resolution included virtually *no* cuts, and approved outlays of $219.6 billion for the income security programs.

*Second,* the next largest item on CBO's list of outlay reductions was the hospital cost containment legislation proposed by the Carter administration in the 96th Congress. CBO estimated that this proposal, if enacted, would have saved the federal government nearly $17 billion over the five-year period (*and* would have saved all payers, public and private, a total of nearly $40 billion, resulting in a CPI that would have been lower by 0.6 percentage points in 1985). With private insurance and government programs paying the bills, little incentive exists for hospital administrators, doctors or patients to be cost-conscious. As a result, substantial waste occurs in the hospital industry— waste that adds to inflation and drains away public funds at a time when the nation can least afford it. The Carter administration sought a short-term regulatory approach that would have revised reimbursement for all payers and limited the rate of increase of hospital revenues.

The legislation was of course hotly contested for most of the administration's first three years—and in the fall of 1979 was ultimately defeated on the House floor by a substantial 234 to

166 vote.* Opponents argued that waste in the industry was overstated; that the legislation did not distinguish precisely enough between efficient and inefficient hospitals; and that it would increase federal regulation. More importantly, the doctors and hospitals mounted one of the most intense lobbying campaigns against the bill seen on Capitol Hill during the 1970s. A bill that would have led to substantial budget savings and possessed an anti-inflationary effect to boot was defeated. When the CBO report on spending reductions was issued in February 1980, Representative Richard Gephardt (D-Mo), one of the members who had requested the study, observed that "we suffer from a national schizophrenia" because everyone wants to reduce the federal budget but no one wants to give up his share of federal aid.[9] In the fall of 1979, it was a Gephardt substitute that placed sole reliance on the hospital industry's voluntary cost reduction effort (spawned in response to much tougher legislation), gutted the administration bill and killed the chances that additional savings would come from rapidly escalating federal expenditures for hospitals. (Without mandatory cost containment and with voluntary efforts, estimates in the summer of 1980 were for an increase in federal spending for hospitalization from $46.5 billion in 1981 to $79.1 billion in 1985.)

Like the retirement programs, federal health care will be a tempting target for those who wish to reduce federal expenditures, given the size of health-care spending and its rapid rate of increase. Yet as with retirement benefits, difficult conceptual problems are still with us. Is there, for example, a meaningful alternative to the regulatory approach rejected in 1979?† Moreover, difficult, perhaps insurmountable, political problems will once again present themselves, given the strengths of the lobbies

*A compromise hospital cost containment bill narrowly passed the Senate in the fall of 1978 at the end of the 95th Congress, but there was not enough time for House consideration before the session ended.

†There are three broad alternatives for the future. *First*, with the development of more detailed information, there can be a more sophisticated version of the federal regulatory approach that builds on the case mix for various types of hospitals and is thus more sensitive to efficiency/inefficiency in hospitals of the same type. A *second* approach is to change the tax laws to ensure greater competition. But there are substantial questions about this type of proposal: Will the Congress enact it? Will it have any significant effect on costs? How long will it take before there is any effect, let alone a significant one? A *third* approach is to rely on state health cost commissions. They have been effective in states with mandatory programs—but only about a quarter of the states have such effective programs. These state programs are primarily regulatory in approach.

likely to oppose any reduction in the billions of dollars paid to their members each year.

A third target of opportunity worth noting is the technique of straight-lining, which applies to the discretionary programs and simply means providing the same amount of funds in a subsequent year as in a base year. Although such is not nominally a cut, it is in fact a reduction. Inflation makes $100 in 1980 worth much less in 1982, and the services that can be provided in 1982 are thus reduced. The interest groups who care about the discretionary programs will not be fooled. But your budgeteers are more likely to try straight-lining in the discretionary programs than outright reductions in absolute amounts appropriated.

**(d) Tax expenditures and off-budget items.** In addition to outlays, two other types of governmental activity—tax expenditures and off-budget items, primarily governmental credit programs—should be carefully scrutinized as part of the managerial agenda's overall concern about the effect of federal programs and legislation on the economy and the shape of the federal budget.

*Tax expenditures* are defined as revenue losses attributable to provisions of the federal tax code which allow a special exclusion, exemption or deduction from gross income or which provide a special credit, a preferential rate of tax or a deferral of tax liability. Tax expenditures are entitlements, for like automatic spending programs they are automatically in effect unless Congress enacts a specific law amending or repealing them. The 1974 Budget Act requires a yearly listing of all tax expenditures. In fiscal 1981, the tax expenditure budget is estimated to be more than $200 billion,[10] and assuming no further changes in the tax laws, it is estimated to rise to $332 billion by 1985, an average annual increase of 13 percent.

These provisions of the tax law are considered expenditures because they are equivalent to direct payments by the federal government to the affected taxpayers. They are of increasing importance for a variety of reasons, including the following:

—With restraints on spending, legislators may seek to provide federal benefits through the tax system rather than through direct outlays.

—Tax expenditures and direct spending programs should be coordinated because they are often related. For example, certain federal transfer payments are exempted from taxation, such as social security benefits, and as those payments increase, so does the corresponding amount of tax expenditure.

—The tens of billions of foregone revenues associated with tax expenditures could, if the relevant laws were changed, provide new revenues that could in turn either finance new spending programs (defense or nondefense) or offset other tax reductions (i.e., tax cuts for the general population or productivity tax cuts).

Nonetheless, as with other entitlements, substantial opposition often exists to any change in the preferential treatment afforded individuals or groups by the tax code. Efforts here must be just as selective and politically grounded as efforts to cut spending.

*Off-budget* items also entail substantial commitment of federal resources. These occur most often in federal credit programs, which are of three broad types: direct loans from the federal government; federal guarantees of private lending; and lending by privately owned government-sponsored entities (such as the Federal National Mortgage Association). Like federal purchases, tax expenditures and transfer payments, credit programs are used to alter resource allocation and income distribution. They also clearly involve a commitment of governmental funds either in the form of direct on-budget subsidies (as in the case of direct loans, where the interest rate is subsidized) or indirect availability of funds (as in the case of guaranteed loans).

The Carter administration began a systematic accounting and evaluation of federal credit activities. In 1979, for example, OMB estimated that of $410 billion advanced in the nation's credit markets, $73 billion was advanced under federal auspices. The purposes of the credit control system were to ensure that credit programs were efficiently meeting goals; to lead to a more systematic understanding of how federal credit was distributed among sectors of the economy; and to assess the impact of the credit activity on the economy as a whole.

This is an important initiative, one that could lead to potential spending reductions and to more effective federal management of a basic activity. It should be continued.

**3. Increased Effectiveness.** This is the least glamorous but perhaps most important area of the managerial agenda. As with possible spending reductions, it will be important for your advisors to generate a list of possible initiatives to advance efficiency and effectiveness. They can then pare it down and present to you a list of potential priority efforts. And from that list, as part of the strategy of governing, you can develop an agenda in the area on which you want to build a record for the administration. As part of the process, put in place an early warning system between the White House and the departments so that you or top EOP aides are aware of major scandals or other embarrassing problems as soon as possible, and can swiftly take corrective action.

Perhaps the most important step you could take to promote greater efficiency within executive government is to orient the management component of OMB's effort toward real concern about management issues and strategies, and away from the preoccupation with reorganization that existed during the Carter years. OMB's management arm should be a major source of creative thinking, and the point where useful initiatives taken in the departments can be analyzed for possible use elsewhere in executive government.

Although important savings can be made from initiatives designed to increase efficiency, what can be accomplished without legislation is less than you might think (although still significant).[11] Such legislation is obviously closely related to legislation enacted to reduce spending, and can engender the same congressional and interest group opposition, even though it will appear to involve only minor technical changes in the law.

There are myriad possibilities if you wish to emphasize increased effectiveness. We will simply suggest some organizing themes—simplification, consolidation, evaluation, performance standards, personnel management and accountability—and give examples. Part of the problem in showing results in this broad area of management stems from diverse requirements developed by the executive and imposed on others, but another part of the problem lies with the Congress, which has created the host of overlapping, confusing and at times burdensome requirements that the executive is obliged to carry out.

(a) **Simplification.** The host of federal regulations constitute an enormous and often confusing corpus of law. As a general matter, the number of paperwork requirements imposed by the federal government can be reduced, leading to fewer man-hours per year that various recipients of federal funds must devote to compliance. In some cases, regulations can simply be eliminated; others can be written in shorter, simpler form.

Simplification not only reduces the governmental load but is clearly essential to achieving other management goals. A major area for potential improvement can be found in the income maintenance area. The nation's cash and in-kind income tested programs (including medicaid) expended approximately $61 billion in 1980. Yet as we have seen, these programs have confusing and inconsistent administrative elements. Major simplifications could improve access for those who are eligible, reduce the opportunity for error and promote more cost-effective administrative systems. These include:

—Common eligibility standards for the needs-tested programs could be developed, and then, with only minor changes in the law, implemented. The Carter administration had a major task force working on this problem during its first term.

—Common accounting procedures could also be implemented, such as monthly reporting of income and other efficiencies in calculating benefits. CBO estimates that such simplifications, if applied to all the federal needs-tested programs, could save nearly $2 billion in the five-year period 1981–85.[12]

—Another common source of error in welfare programs is the complexity surrounding deductions of itemized work expenses from income in calculating what benefit is due. Simplifying this work expense disregard would also promote efficiency and reduce error.

(b) **Consolidation.** As noted, organizational consolidations of existing governmental functions that can be effected without new legislation can have significant utility in the shorter term. But another, similar type of consolidation exists—namely, making more uniform the basic functions that are required of federal grantees but that are today often imposed in disparate ways by different executive branch units. Some obvious targets:

—Planning requirements must often be met by states and localities before they can receive federal grants-in-aid. But these requirements often in turn require similar information but in different forms. Consolidating planning requirements —and devising shorter ones—would be a welcome reform, both for those who have to complete the forms and those who have to read them.

—A similar reform could be instituted with respect to the financial and auditing requirements imposed on those who receive federal funds. Such requirements could at the least be simplified, and where possible, consolidated.

(c) **Evaluation.** Unfortunately, when your political appointees assume their positions in the departments and agencies, they may not have a detailed understanding about how a particular program is working, given its congressional objectives. Moreover, the permanent civil servants sometimes have great difficulty providing a satisfactory answer to basic questions, because the program has not been adequately evaluated.

But improved evaluation techniques are important for reasons beyond the elementary need for program operators to communicate to their superiors.

—Evaluation is necessary at an operational level to help define objectives, and once objectives are chosen, to ensure that they are being carried out. As we have noted, the Congress often leaves the question of a program's precise objectives fuzzy. Accordingly, evaluation techniques can help provide greater definition when, as is often the case, there is significant flexibility or ambiguity in definition. Evaluators must work with operators to carry out the interactive process of definition and measurement.

—Evaluation is also necessary at a more theoretical level— to determine whether the particular theories that underlie a particular piece of legislation are valid or are producing unintended side effects. Evaluation in an operational sense would help set goals that those managing the programs could try to meet: a certain number of cases per caseworker; a certain number of procedures, on average, performed by a public health service doctor. But evaluation in the more theoretical sense would assess whether the theory of change upon which the legislation was founded is in fact valid.

Given the uncertainties and problems of evaluation in the theoretical sense, substantial resources should be devoted to evaluation in the operational sense so that a real attempt is made to define objectives and seek to carry them out.

**(d) Performance standards.** Closely related to the first sense of evaluation is the establishment of performance standards for judging the effectiveness of federal employees and of the public and private recipients of federal funds. Setting performance standards involves painful, detailed discussions with program managers about appropriate standards for assessing performance—including, though not limited to, program objectives—but it is a task, like evaluation, that is often not carried out rigorously by the permanent government and is often not adequately supported by your political appointees.

**(e) Personnel management.** Under the Civil Service Reform Act of 1978, federal executives now have been given much greater authority, flexibility and incentive to motivate and manage the federal work force. Yours will be the first term under the new civil service system, and it will be important that you provide a concrete demonstration that the changes have made a difference in the performance of high-level federal civil servants.

**(f) Accountability.** Ensuring careful handling of federal money is naturally a basic element of the accountability theme. A dramatic innovation in recent years has been the creation of inspectors general in the major departments to make sure that fraud, abuse and waste are kept to a bare minimum. The publicized tip of the iceberg is outright fraud. But this is literally a tiny percentage of the rough estimates of total waste in federal programs. For example, fraud (willful misrepresentation) and waste (inappropriate services and other program violations) have been estimated at less than 1 percent of the then Department of Health, Education and Welfare's $210 billion in expenditures for 1980.

Of much greater importance is the development of financial management systems for controlling the vast flows of money from the federal government to others in our society. Such systems are the responsibility of either the departments' inspectors general (who can identify problem areas) or the assistant secretaries for management and budget (who can lead efforts to change basic practices to resolve problems). Devising and then putting in place more adequate financial management systems is highly technical work, often involving sophisticated knowledge of computer systems; it nonetheless constitutes a priority item on the managerial agenda. Ensuring that all the departments have satisfactory up-to-date systems should be a major initiative of your coming term.* Effective systems will integrate the simplification and consolidation reforms described above.

Of particular concern in recent years has been the proliferation of private contractors and consultants. Introducing basic financial management techniques for an ever-growing sector, which increasingly is charged with performing federal functions, will be another major challenge of financial accountability. Competitive bidding and the ending of sole-source procurement are examples of techniques that ought to be systematically considered and then systematically implemented as basic federal practice. Greater accountability and responsiveness could of course be accomplished by having functions carried out by federal employees, but that could run into the commonplace (though often misplaced) political promise of presidential candidates to reduce the federal work force.

Finally, you will encounter the thorny and complex set of questions surrounding the accountability of state and local governments to federal purposes. Obviously, most of the management initiatives discussed above apply to the relationship between the federal government and state and local governments. But there is the larger question of whether federal funding

---

*Financial management systems involve such issues as: accounting systems, internal controls (to reduce fraud, abuse and waste), cash management (e.g. paying the government's bills on time so that no interest costs are incurred), audit follow-up (to resolve issues expeditiously), outlay estimating and debt collection.

should be through categorical grants (narrowly targeted special-purpose programs), block grants (broader programs giving state and local governments substantial discretion within a broad function—for example, the nearly $3 billion distributed to the states for social service spending under Title XX of the Social Security Act) or revenue sharing (giving states and localities maximum discretion over the use of federal funds). And more fundamental questions of course involve not just administrative relationships but the appropriateness of existing fiscal roles and responsibilities.

Since federal grants now constitute about 25 percent of the revenue expended by state and local governments, it is hard to imagine that significant reduction could occur without causing substantial pain and suffering, either because state and local governments had to make up lost revenue or because they had to curtail services. But each of the funding mechanisms has problems—categoricals lead to substantial administrative costs at all levels of government and divided accountability, while revenue sharing dilutes federal purposes. And the pressures created by an increased regionalization of our politics only add to the complications.

Answers to questions will not emerge overnight, nor will you be able to jam dramatic change down the throat of the Congress, or the state and local governments, who will have a powerful voice within the Congress on the matter. Taking a longer view of intergovernmental fiscal relations, of the related issues of administration and accountability, may be necessary in what is clearly an unsettled area. Part of this review should perhaps be included in an overall analysis of executive government's income security programs.

**4. Long-Term Analysis: The Income Security System.** As we have indicated, vast national resources are expended through a complex array of programs as payments for individuals. These programs—social insurance, needs-tested cash and in-kind transfers, public service employment, social service efforts and various types of tax expenditures—now constitute the largest single federal function and, depending on the method of measuring, constitute approximately half of the federal budget.

A long-term effort is needed to make sense out of the welter of programs here. As a matter of moral leadership, you should work with the Congress now to start such a broad-gauged review—not because it will help you much during the coming term or even thereafter, but because it needs doing in the coming decade. An important dimension of the analysis should be a comparison of the experience in Western Europe and Japan, where the growth of payments for individuals, as a percentage of GNP and government spending, is also dramatic, causing severe fiscal problems and a rethinking of the structure of public and private programs.*

Most of the programs providing benefits to individuals have grown in an incremental fashion since 1935. Although they have individually or in some combinations been the subject of numerous studies by congressional and executive panels and commissions,[13] an overview is needed.

—The interrelationships between the programs are not well understood, although many citizens benefit from a number of them. Thus changes in a particular program are often not considered with the effects on other programs clearly in view, in part because good information is not available.

—The cost of the programs has been rising rapidly, and the system must be seen as a whole to understand the significant cost implications for the future—and how these costs relate to the general growth of the economy and to our national economic health.

—The adequacy of the programs for various groups within our society is also questionable—for example, the working poor may not qualify for important income-tested programs like medicaid—and the gaps in coverage must be closed.

—There are substantial work disincentives within the total income security system, due in part to the overlap between the programs.

—The programs suffer from sharply divided jurisdictional responsibilities in the Congress, diffuse management respon-

---

*Western European countries devote a higher percentage of their national product to government than the United States does, nearly 45 percent of GNP as opposed to nearly 35 percent (federal, state and local) in this country.

sibilities between a host of agencies and departments in the federal government, and confusing differentiation of roles between federal, state and local governments that varies, often without good reason, between programs. For example, one recent study found that more than a hundred congressional committees, ten of the thirteen Cabinet departments and at least seven independent agencies have responsibility for income security programs.

—Variation among program features—eligibility, benefits, administrative procedures—confuses the public and contributes to waste and error in program implementation.

—There are fundamental questions about such basic conceptual building blocks for the income security programs as poverty, disability and unemployment, and increasingly, old age and retirement.

Not only does the federal income security program go to the heart of what we, as a civilized society, provide for our poor and elderly, our disabled and the survivors of those who have died, but it also has an increasingly important impact on major economic problems: the use of the payroll tax to finance social security payments affects the rate of inflation; the relationship between private and public pension systems affects the critical question of national savings patterns; and this in turn affects the amount of capital available for new investment and increased productivity.

We recommend that early in your term you work with the Congress to constitute a permanent national advisory council on income security policy. It should be charged with: developing a systematic definition of income security policy; developing the alternatives for such policy; developing methods for simplifying, evaluating and more effectively managing the system; developing a detailed understanding of the relationship of the system to the private sector income security activities and to the economy as a whole; and evaluating the future of the income security system in the context of the future growth of the federal budget.

The primary role of the advisory council should not be to make recommendations. Rather it should seek to define issues and demonstrate interrelationships; to identify areas where additional studies are necessary; to pull together the host of studies that already exist; and to set out the basic choices and their implications. Anomalous as it may seem, the respective roles of the social security system and other pension and retirement plans in providing adequate retirement income in the next quarter century have not been clearly articulated. Such an advisory council is necessary because no single entity in the federal structure has responsibilities broad enough to encompass all the programs and policies that should be considered.

Running parallel to the work of the independent advisory group should be an interdepartmental work group—of at least an assistant secretary level—to begin to consider the results of the council's efforts in a more broadly political context for executive government.

# VII·
# THE STRATEGIC
# PRESIDENCY

Thisis memorandum has attempted to set forth a practical ideal for your conduct of the domestic presidency.

It is practical, we believe, because a strategic approach systematically addresses the intricate set of questions you must try to answer during your term in office. It is an ideal because you will never be able fully to attain in practice what we suggest in theory.

To conduct a strategic presidency will require an extraordinary act of presidential will. The pressures of the moment will be immense; the difficulties in thinking ahead profound; and the complications of policy and politics, structure and process labyrinthian.

Your office is a place of action, but if you cannot think carefully, you cannot act purposefully. If you cannot be a fox, you may not survive politically to become a lion. Even so, the conflicts and contradictions of contemporary policy and politics may mock your strategic efforts. But you must try.

The concept of a strategic presidency is neither optimistic nor pessimistic, neither liberal nor conservative, neither active nor passive. It is, we hope, realistic—an idea with explanatory power for the many who will observe the Presidency and with practical value for the very few who must give coherence to executive government as the President.

# NOTES

## CHAPTER I

1. Fred I. Greenstein, "Change and Continuity in the Modern Presidency," in *Classics of the Modern Presidency* (Harry A. Bailey, Jr., ed., 1980), p. 413. See also Richard Rose, "Government Against Sub-Governments," in *Presidents and Prime Ministers* (Richard Rose, ed., 1980), p. 297.
2. Thomas E. Cronin, *The State of the Presidency* (1980), pp. 148–150.
3. See, for example, Amitai Etzioni, "The Lack of Leadership: We Found It—In Us," *National Journal* (February 22, 1980), p. 334.
4. The transition papers tended to cover discrete subjects relating to executive government. See, for example, a memorandum from Jack Watson to Jimmy Carter, "Some Thoughts on Organizing the Executive Office of the President," November 3, 1976. The relationships between the various papers were not explored in an overarching summary memorandum. Nor was a document ever prepared that remotely approaches our concept of a "strategy of governing."

    During the last two years of President Carter's first term, when he was de facto and then de jure chief of staff, Jordan was deeply preoccupied with campaign strategy, but not, apparently, with the strategy of governing. See Martin Schram's articles in the *Washington Post* (June 9–11, 1980) detailing Jordan's role as chief campaign strategist during his tenure as chief of staff.
5. After the first year of the Carter presidency, the Vice President was charged with drawing up an agenda for the administration. This agenda was at least a start toward ensuring that administration initiatives did not crash into each other. And it did try to give some sense of the relative importance of the various pieces of administration business. But it did not represent an attempt to synthesize policy and politics; it did not relate the different levels of importance to different methods of conducting the administration's business; it was not an organic document that was monitored and updated; it was not discussed widely within the top levels of the administration when it was being formulated; and in short, it had very little operative effect. It was, however, a clear step in the right direction. But the effort fell far short of what would be contained in our strategy of governing or how such a strategy would be used.
6. James M. Burns, *Roosevelt: The Lion and the Fox* (1956), pp. 403–404.

## CHAPTER II

1. Anthony King, "The American Polity in the Late 1970s: Building Coalitions in the Sand," in *The New American Political System* (Anthony King, ed., 1978).
2. Three speeches during the Carter administration began to develop with some clarity the ways in which the presidential environment had been altered: Remarks of HEW Secretary Joseph A. Califano, Jr., before the National Press Club, November 28, 1978; remarks of Domestic Affairs Advisor Stuart E. Eizenstat before the Women's National Democratic Club, January 4, 1979; and remarks of President Jimmy Carter at the John F. Kennedy Library Dedication Ceremony, October 20, 1979.
3. Charles L. Schultze, *The Public Use of Private Interest* (1977), p. 9. See also Advisory Commission on Intergovernmental Relations, *The Federal Role in the Federal System* (1980).
4. Hugh Heclo, *A Government of Strangers* (1977), p. 18.
5. Richard M. Pious, *The American Presidency* (1979), p. 238.
6. *National Journal* (June 28, 1980), p. 1072.
7. Office of Management and Budget, *Managing Federal Assistance in the 1980s: A Report to the Congress of the United States Pursuant to the Federal Grant and Cooperative Agreement Act of 1977* (1980), p. 7.
8. Hugh Heclo, "Issue Networks and the Executive Establishment," in King, note 1 above, pp. 89–94.
9. Ibid., p. 93.
10. See Sar A. Levitan and Gregory Wurzburg, *Evaluating Federal Social Programs* (1979); Richard Rose, *Managing Presidential Objectives* (1976); Alice Rivlin, *Systematic Thinking for Social Action* (1971).
11. James L. Sundquist, "The Crisis of Competence in Government," in *Setting National Priorities: Agenda for the Eighties* (Joseph A. Pechman, ed., 1980), p. 543.
12. Herbert E. Alexander, *Financing Politics: Money, Elections and Political Reform* (2d ed., 1980); Common Cause, *How Money Talks: The Impact of Money on Congressional Decision-Making* (1979).
13. Heclo, note 4 above, p. 59.
14. A House Select Committee on Committees was established in 1973 under the chairmanship of Richard Bolling (D-Mo). Its proposal to thoroughly restructure the House committee system was not accepted, however.
    A Senate Select Committee to Study the Senate Committee System was established in 1976 under the chairmanship of Adlai Stevenson III (D-Ill). Its sweeping reforms were also rejected, although the Senate did create the Committee on Energy and Natural Resources out of the Interior and Insular Affairs Committee.
15. Richard E. Cohen, "If the Chairman's Word Isn't Law, Can This Be the Finance Committee?" *National Journal* (April 12, 1980), p. 600.
16. National Opinion Research Center, General Social Survey, 1978; Louis Harris News Release on NORC General Social Survey, October 25, 1977.
17. National Opinion Research Center, General Social Survey, 1978; Louis Harris News Release on NORC General Social Survey, October 25, 1977.
18. Center for Political Studies, Institute for Social Research, University of Michigan.
19. Statistical Abstract of the United States, 1979.
20. Everett Carll Ladd, Jr., and Seymour Martin Lipset, "Public Opinion and Public Policy," in *The United States in the 1980s* (Peter Duignan and Alvin Rabushka, eds., 1980), pp. 63, 67–68.
21. *Wall Street Journal,* December 10, 1979 (editorial page).
22. *New York Times*–CBS Poll, January 31, 1979.
23. *New York Times*–CBS Poll, August 3, 1977.
24. William Watts and Lloyd Free, *State of the Nation III* (1978), pp. 215–216.
25. Henry J. Aaron, *Politics and the Professors: The Great Society in Perspective* (1978), p.

159: "The political coalition that produced the outpouring of social and economic legislation in the mid-1960s has split. Social science research, a promising instrument for improving understanding of the social and economic problems, helped undercut the faiths that led to that legislation, and its internal laws guarantee that it will corrode any simple faiths around which coalitions are built."

## CHAPTER III

1. Thomas E. Cronin, *The State of the Presidency* (1980), pp. 250, 293.
2. Dom Bonafede, "Carter's White House, Heavy on Function, Light on Frills," *National Journal* (February 12, 1977), p. 234.
3. Harold Seidman, *Politics, Position and Power: The Dynamics of Federal Organization* (2d ed., 1975), p. 81.
4. See Stephen Hess, *Organizing the Presidency* (1976), pp. 8–9, 111–140; Richard Nathan, *The Plot That Failed: Nixon and the Administrative Presidency* (1975).
5. Hess's extremely valuable book (see note 4 above) makes a number of very penetrating points about the problems that affect departmental–White House relations. And it provides a very useful account of how previous administrations have been organized. But he puts more weight on collective deliberations by the whole Cabinet than that mechanism can bear.
6. In *The State of the Presidency*, Cronin summarizes this view (pp. 274–286).
7. See, for example, I. M. Destler, "A Job That Doesn't Work" and Peter Szanton, "Two Jobs, Not One," *Foreign Policy* (Spring 1980), pp. 80–91. See also Graham Allison and Peter Szanton, *Remaking Foreign Policy: The Organizational Connection* (1976).
8. In essence, the original Justice Department brief, which was to be filed *amicus curiae*, recommended a very burdensome test under which most affirmative action programs in education would have either been held invalid or been called into question through protracted litigation. The brief finally filed with the Supreme Court recommended a constitutional test that was much more hospitable to voluntary affirmative action programs in education.
9. *Congressional Record*, 1st Session, 92d Congress (June 3, 1971), p. 8140.
10. On "issue networks" see Hugh Heclo, "Issue Networks and the Executive Establishment," in *The New American Political System* (Anthony King, ed., 1978). Of high officials in the departments, John Ehrlichman said in 1972: "We only see them at the annual White House Christmas party; they go off and marry the natives" (Nathan, note 4 above, p. 40).
11. President Johnson's Task Force on Government Reorganization submitted a number of confidential reports during 1967. Its report on the "Future Organization of the Executive Branch" was transmitted to the President on September 15, 1967, and recommended consideration of the following consolidations: Social Services, National Resources and Development, Economic Affairs, Science and Environmental Preservation, Foreign Affairs and National Security Affairs.
12. President Nixon's Advisory Council on Executive Organization, headed by Roy Ash, went the Johnson task force one better and recommended the following domestic-affairs consolidations: Natural Resources, Community Development, Human Resources and Economic Affairs. This recommendation was accepted by Nixon and proposed to the Congress. See President's Message on Executive Reorganization, March 25, 1971, reprinted in full in Nathan, note 4 above, pp. 134–155.
13. Fred I. Greenstein, "Eisenhower as an Activist President," *Political Science Quarterly*, Vol. 94 (Winter 1978–80), p. 584. See also Aaron Wildavsky, "The Past and Future Presidency," *Public Interest* (Fall 1975).
14. Richard E. Neustadt and Harvey V. Fineberg, *The Swine Flu Affair: Decision-Making on a Slippery Disease* (1978).
15. George Reedy, *Twilight of the Presidency* (1970), p. 94.
16. "As requisites to successful departmental administration, the two most important

personal qualifications would seem to be administrative experience in a political environment and some acquaintance with the substantive policy problems of the department involved." Richard F. Fenno, Jr., *The President's Cabinet* (1959), p. 224.
17. See McGeorge Bundy, *The Strength of Government* (1968), p. 39.

## CHAPTER IV

1. The Executive Office of the President was established as a result of recommendations made to him by his Committee on Administrative Management, headed by Louis Brownlow, and approved by the Congress in 1939 pursuant to reorganization plan. In 1949 the commission, headed by former President Hoover, in effect endorsed the findings made a decade earlier by the Brownlow committee.
2. See Larry Berman, *The Office of Management and Budget and the Presidency, 1921–1979* (1979).
3. See generally Stephen Hess, *Organizing the Presidency* (1976), pp. 27–142, for a description of White House organization from Roosevelt to Nixon.
4. See draft paper by Lester M. Salamon, "The Presidency and Policy Formulation," prepared for the Presidential Management Panel of the National Academy of Public Administration (May 15, 1980), for an account of the development of the Domestic Policy Staff.
5. President Carter's first reorganization plan of his administration abolished the Domestic Council and substituted a Domestic Policy Staff in its place. The plan also made other minor changes in the EOP. Message from the President of the United States Transmitting Reorganization Plan No. 1 of 1977 (July 15, 1977).
6. Roger B. Porter, *Presidential Decision Making: The Economic Policy Board* (1980).
7. Ibid. The Economic Policy Board under President Ford was a large body—containing as regular members at all meetings virtually all of the economic actors in the EOP and the Cabinet. The White House coordinating staff accordingly played a crucial role in providing a central focus for the process. We recommend instead that the permanent economic committee be limited to Treasury, OMB and CEA, with the other actors brought in liberally to participate on issues of direct interest to them. Our smaller, permanent committee will provide a stable center of gravity for the economic channel—but a White House–based coordinating staff is still necessary to assure that nonpermanent members receive due process and to avoid the proliferation of ad hoc task forces and special committees to deal with major economic matters.

## CHAPTER V

1. See address by Jimmy Carter on urban policy to the United States Conference on Mayors, June 29, 1976; remarks by Jimmy Carter to the National Governors' Conference, July 6, 1976.
2. See Jimmy Carter speech before Student National Medical Association, April 16, 1976.
3. Report of the President's Commission on Income Maintenance Programs, *Poverty and Plenty: The American Paradox* (1969).
4. See Daniel P. Moynihan, *The Politics of a Guaranteed Income: The Nixon Administration and the Family Assistance Plan* (1973).
5. It is of course one of the ironies of timing in politics that by the end of the 1970s, when neither welfare reform nor national health insurance proposals had been approved by the Congress, many liberals who had opposed FAP and CHIP earlier in the decade as too spare would have been more than satisfied to see them enacted.
6. In fiscal 1966, the federal government implemented the medicaid program, predicting fiscal 1967 expenditures of about $550 million. Actual expenditures were $1.2 billion in 1967, and had reached $2.7 billion by fiscal 1970. Medicaid had not

received as much attention as medicare, and estimates on medicaid were not done with the care of the estimates for medicare. The medicaid example is still used to illustrate the problems in predicting actual costs. Similarly, the supplemental security income program was implemented in January 1974 (after passage in 1972). It substituted a national federally administered income support system for poor aged, blind and disabled adults for a state-administered program. Early administrative problems received substantial public attention, and led to concern about the pace at which major reforms could be effectively implemented.

7. See testimony of Lynn Cutler, vice chairperson, Advisory Commission on Intergovernmental Relations, Hearings Before the Subcommittee on Public Assistance of the Senate Committee on Finance (February 6 and 7, 1980), pp. 318–320.

8. A basic dilemma of welfare reform is the tension between the basic welfare benefit given to a person with no earned income and the level of earned income at which a person receives no welfare benefit whatsoever. If the basic benefit is reduced slowly as a person on welfare earns income, then the higher is the level of a person's earned income ($6,000? $7,000? etc.) when the welfare benefit becomes zero. And the higher the income level at which the cash assistance benefit becomes zero, the greater the number of people who will receive some benefit—that is to say, be on the welfare rolls.

   Yet if the basic benefit is reduced more quickly as a person gains earned income, thus in effect reducing the number of individuals receiving the welfare benefit, then there will be stronger work disincentives. The reason: if earned income substitutes substantially for the welfare benefit, then the net gain for working can be relatively small (for example, only 30 cents for every dollar earned).

   The difficult trade-offs between the amount of the basic cash assistance benefit, the speed with which the benefit is reduced as the recipient has earned income (the marginal tax rate) and the income level where there is no longer any welfare benefit (the break-even point) was illustrated by what the Carter welfare reformers called the Carey-Blumenthal triangle. Governor Carey, as chief executive of a state with a high cost of living, wanted a high basic benefit. But Treasury Secretary Blumenthal wanted a low break-even point so that welfare recipients were not also part of the positive tax system (which occurred at about $9,400 for a family of four). Yet a high basic benefit and a relatively low break-even point would mean high marginal tax rates and thus significant work disincentives. The ineluctable connections between these three variables—basic benefit, marginal tax rate and break-even point—are at the core of any welfare reform effort.

9. For example, one of the recurring causes of error in the AFDC program is the requirement that all work-related expenses be itemized (and then deducted in computing earned income). The Carter administration's 1979 welfare proposal standardized all work-related expenses at 20 percent of gross earnings. This figure represented the national average for such expenses, but about 4 percent of current AFDC recipients would have had reduced benefits because of the provision.

10. This was the administration's figure. See also Congressional Budget Office, *Profiles of Health Care Coverage: The Haves and Have-Nots* (1979).

11. Health cost containment through competition will involve changes in the deductions for medical care that may be just as difficult to enact politically as the Carter administration's regulatory approach to the problem of rising health costs. Moreover, even its strongest advocates would acknowledge that the effect of the competitive approach may not be felt immediately. Yet health costs continue to climb steeply.

12. The leadership conference of civil rights organizations issued statements on unemployment, support for the minimum wage, support for abortion funding and equal opportunity in higher education. The Urban League, at its annual conference in July 1977, emphasized urban schools, jobs, affirmative action programs and urban economic development. *New York Times*, April 2, July 25, July 28, August 16 and September 28, 1977.

13. These were estimated to be on the order of $500 million per year when the

consolidated cash assistance system was fully operational. This figure was only 1.5 percent of the total expenditures under the plan (in 1982 dollars).

14. The Congressional Budget Office raised five major objections to the administration's cost estimates: the exclusion of the costs of the EITC increases for nonwelfare recipients; the application of HEW projected fraud, abuse and waste savings to offset costs; the offset for CETA jobs that would supposedly not be needed; the application of wellhead tax revenues to net costs; and the savings from extended unemployment insurance benefits. The last three were dependent upon other legislation that never passed. The first two were based on administration decisions to count the nonwelfare dimensions of the expanded EITC as part of the costs of tax, not welfare, reform and to redirect anticipated savings to a specific source.

15. Liberal groups were a bit more grudging in their support. The Urban League's Vernon Jordan called the plan preshrunk but judged it acceptable if no further changes were made. Organized labor was not happy with the wage rates in the public service jobs component of the plan: it thought they were too low and would undercut other public sector jobs.

16. In June 1978, Senators Moynihan, Cranston and Long proposed a bill which would have replaced the current federal matching structure with a federal block grant (adjusted over time by prices, population growth and unemployment changes). The bill left current categorical and benefit provisions virtually intact and was primarily designed to provide fiscal relief to the states.

17.

|  | *1977 Bill* | *1979 Bill* |
|---|---|---|
| *Cash Proposal:* | Established universal cash coverage for all families with children, aged, blind and disabled and singles and childless couples. Consolidated AFDC, SSI and food stamps. Significantly expanded EITC. | Retained AFDC, SSI and food stamps. But created national minimum benefit in AFDC, required two-parent coverage, and cashed out food stamps for single SSI recipients not living in larger family units. Modest EITC expansion. |
|  | Net cost: $11.2 billion | Net cost: $3.0 billion |
| *Jobs Proposal:* | 1.2 million jobs to all family heads | 600,000 jobs to AFDC eligibles only |
|  | Net cost: $8.1 billion | Net cost: $2.7 billion |

18. Nick Kotz described the problem that Carter faced in the spring of 1977 this way: "Most members of Congress believe that welfare is a losing issue politically and wish that the matter would just fade quietly away.... President Carter must make some firm decisions. . . . Carter must gain a sufficient political grasp of this complex issue to proceed with a concrete plan that not only makes sense but can be passed by the Congress. Perhaps that approach is a grand new design . . . it is possible that ultimate presidential wisdom would dictate backing off from grand designs and working instead towards improving the present system. Progress can be achieved by taking small steps as well as large ones. And progress is what poor people and the nation as a whole need, not another decade of deadlocked debate over welfare reform." "The Politics of Welfare Reform," *New Republic* (May 14, 1977).

19. In the days just preceding President Carter's announcement of his principles for national health insurance in the summer of 1978, he and his top officials discussed the contents of those principles with Senator Kennedy and his staff. Yet despite the administration's willingness to discuss the document with Kennedy and to seek a compromise, Kennedy, in a rather unusual action toward a president of his

own party, held a press conference and attacked the principles—the day before the administration announced them.

## CHAPTER VI

1. As noted in Chapter 2, every percentage point increase in the unemployment rate leads to a $20 to $22 billion loss in revenue and a $5 to $7 billion increase in outlays, resulting in an increase in the deficit of $25 to $29 billion. Congressional Budget Office, "Projections for the Federal Budget: Fiscal 1981–85" (February 1980).
2. 1979 Advisory Council on Social Security, Reports on Financing and Benefits; Stanford G. Ross, *New Directions in Social Security: Considerations for the 1980's* (1979).
3. The Bureau of Census has reported (in its 1965 and 1978 "Current Population Report P-60") that there has been a dramatic decline in poverty between 1965 and 1978 even if only money income is counted:

|  | *1965* | *1978* |
|---|---|---|
| Total U.S. population (millions) | 191.5 | 215.7 |
| Total U.S. families (millions) | 48.3 | 57.8 |
| Persons in poverty (millions) | 31.9 | 24.5 |
|  | (16.7%) | (11.4%) |
| Families in poverty (millions) | 6.5 | 5.3 |
|  | (13.4%) | (9.1%) |

CBO has further estimated (for FY 1976) that if in-kind benefits such as food stamps, child nutrition and medicaid are included, the percentages drop even further:

|  | *Families in Poverty, FY 1976* | | *Persons in Poverty, FY 1976* | |
|---|---|---|---|---|
|  | *Number (millions)* | *Percent* | *Number (millions)* | *Percent* |
| Before transfers | 20.2 | 25.5 | 42.4 | 20.1 |
| After social insurance | 11.2 | 14.1 | 26.1 | 12.3 |
| After cash tranfers | 9.1 | 11.4 | 21.6 | 10.2 |
| After in-kind except medicare, medicaid | 7.4 | 9.3 | 16.8 | 7.9 |
| After in-kind including medicare, medicaid | 5.3 | 6.7 | 12.1 | 5.7 |

1976 U.S. Population = 217 million

4. See Chapter 5, pp. 266–301.
5. CBO Technical Analysis Paper, *Long-Term Care: Actuarial Cost Estimates* (August 1977).
6. James P. Zais, Jeanne E. Goedert and John Trutko, *Modifying Section 8: Implications From Experiments With Housing Allowances* (Urban Institute, 1979).
7. See Joseph A. Califano, Jr., *A Presidential Nation* (1974).
8. Congressional Budget Office, *Reducing the Federal Budget: Strategies and Examples* (February 1980).
9. *New York Times* (February 22, 1980), p. B16.
10. Budget of the United States Government for Fiscal 1981, *Special Analyses* (1980).

11. Office of the Inspector General, Department of Health, Education, and Welfare, *Annual Report* (1979), pp. 17–20.
12. Congressional Budget Office, note 8 above, p. 11.
13. Comptroller General's Report to the Congress, *United States Income Security System Needs Leadership, Policy and Effective Management* (1980).

# INDEX

ABOUT THE AUTHORS

BEN W. HEINEMAN, JR., served in the Carter administration as HEW assistant secretary for planning and evaluation and, before that post, as executive assistant to Hew Secretary Joseph Califano. A former Rhodes scholar, newspaper reporter, and Supreme Court law clerk, Heineman is now a partner in the law firm of Califano, Ross and Heineman. The author of a book on British race relations, he lives with his wife and son in Washington, D.C.

CURTIS A. HESSLER completed a tour of duty in the Carter administration as assistant secretary in the Treasury for economic policy, after serving as associate director of the Office of Management and Budget and executive assistant to Treasury Secretary W. Michael Blumenthal. A former Rhodes scholar and Supreme Court law clerk, Hessler practiced law in Los Angeles before joining the Carter administration. He also holds a graduate degree in economics. He, his wife, and son regard California as home.